Polar Projection Map

of Southern Hemisphere

PAULA McCRORY

All rights reserved
Made in Great Britain
by
The Aldine Press, Letchworth, Herts
with
Full-colour maps incorporated by arrangement
with John Bartholomew & Son Ltd
for
J. M. DENT & SONS (Canada) LTD
Toronto
Copyright 1936, 1958 by J. M. Dent & Sons (Canada) Limited
First edition 1936
Completely revised 1958
Further revised 1964
Further revised 1965
Further revised 1966
Further revised 1967
Further revised 1969
Further revised 1970
Further revised 1971
Further revised 1973

ISBN 0-460-90916-9

CONTENTS

THE SUPPLEMENT – IN 2 COLOURS

	Page
THE SOLAR SYSTEM	S4
SIZES AND DISTANCES OF THE PLANETS	S4
ECLIPSE OF THE SUN	S4
ECLIPSE OF THE MOON	S4
THE SEASONS	S4
GEOGRAPHIC TERMS AND SYMBOLS	S5
MAP PROJECTIONS	S6
WORLD TIME CHART	S7
WORLD ECONOMIC ACTIVITIES	S8
WORLD POPULATION	S9
WORLD DISTRIBUTION OF THE MAIN PRIMARY PRODUCTS	S10–S15
WHEAT, RYE, OATS	S10
BARLEY, CORN, RICE	S11
TEA, COFFEE, COCOA, TOBACCO, CANE SUGAR, BEET SUGAR	S12
PEANUTS, SOYBEANS, COTTON, FLAX, HEMP, JUTE	S13
RUBBER, SILK, PETROLEUM, COAL, NATURAL GAS, GOLD, SILVER, URANIUM	S14

	Page
IRON ORE, COPPER, LEAD, TIN, ZINC, BAUXITE	S15
WORLD POLITICAL AND MILITARY GROUPINGS IN DECEMBER 1968	S16–S17
WORLD EXPLORATION	S18–S19
CANADIAN EXPLORATIONS	S20–S21
ECONOMIC RESOURCES OF EASTERN CANADA	S22
ECONOMIC RESOURCES OF ONTARIO AND QUEBEC	S23
ECONOMIC RESOURCES OF WESTERN CANADA	S24
LAND USE IN SOUTHERN ONTARIO	S25
CANADIAN AIRWAYS	S26
THE ST. LAWRENCE SEAWAY	S27
HISTORICAL MAPS OF THE BRITISH ISLES	S28–S29
BEFORE 1066	S28
AFTER 1066	S29
POLITICAL BOUNDARIES OF EUROPE	S30
THE MIDDLE EAST—A STRATEGIC AREA	S31

NORTH AND SOUTH POLAR PROJECTIONS—*End-papers*

THE ATLAS – IN FULL COLOUR

	Page
NORTH AMERICA	1
WORLD—POLITICAL	2–3
WORLD—PHYSICAL	4–5
WORLD—TEMPERATURE	6
WORLD—RAINFALL AND WINDS	7
NORTH AMERICA—TEMPERATURE, PRECIPITATION, AND VEGETATION	8
CANADA—TEMPERATURE AND PRECIPITATION	9
CANADA—PHYSICAL	10–11
BRITISH COLUMBIA	12–13
PRAIRIE PROVINCES	14–15
SOUTHERN ONTARIO	16–17
NORTHERN ONTARIO	18
QUEBEC	19
SOUTHERN QUEBEC	20
NOVA SCOTIA	21
MARITIME PROVINCES AND NEWFOUNDLAND	22–23
UNITED STATES—PHYSICAL	24–25
UNITED STATES—POLITICAL	26–27
MEXICO, CENTRAL AMERICA, AND WEST INDIES	28–29
SOUTH AMERICA—PHYSICAL	30–31
SOUTH AMERICA—POLITICAL	32

	Page
SOUTH AMERICA—TEMPERATURE, PRECIPITATION, AND VEGETATION	33
EUROPE—TEMPERATURE, PRECIPITATION, AND VEGETATION	34
EUROPE, NORTH	35
BRITISH ISLES	36–37
EUROPE, CENTRAL AND SOUTHERN	38–39
INDIA, PAKISTAN, BURMA, BANGLADESH AND SRI LANKA	40
ASIA—TEMPERATURE, PRECIPITATION, AND VEGETATION	41
ASIA	42–43
THE FAR EAST	44
AFRICA—TEMPERATURE, PRECIPITATION, AND VEGETATION	45
AFRICA	46
SOUTH AFRICA	47
AUSTRALIA AND NEW ZEALAND—TEMPERATURE, PRECIPITATION, AND VEGETATION	48
AUSTRALIA	49
SOUTH-EAST AUSTRALIA	50
NEW ZEALAND	51
WORLD—CLIMATOLOGY	52

GENERAL INDEX 53–84

THE SOLAR SYSTEM

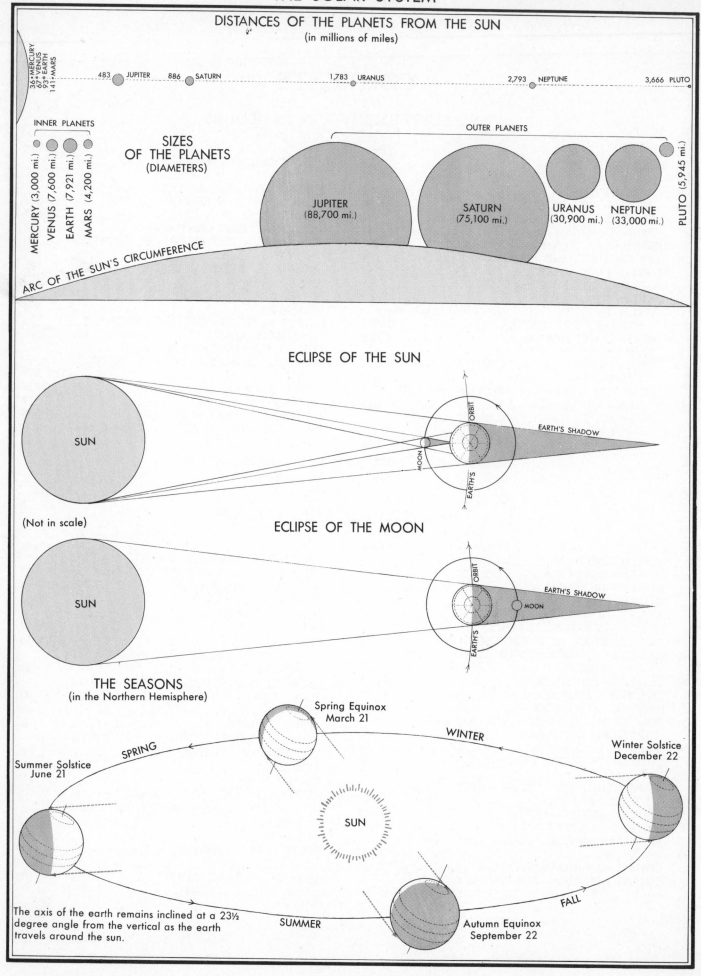

DISTANCES OF THE PLANETS FROM THE SUN
(in millions of miles)

36 · MERCURY
67 · VENUS
93 · EARTH
141 · MARS

483 JUPITER   886 SATURN   1,783 URANUS   2,793 NEPTUNE   3,666 PLUTO

SIZES OF THE PLANETS
(DIAMETERS)

INNER PLANETS

MERCURY (3,000 mi.)
VENUS (7,600 mi.)
EARTH (7,921 mi.)
MARS (4,200 mi.)

OUTER PLANETS

JUPITER (88,700 mi.)
SATURN (75,100 mi.)
URANUS (30,900 mi.)
NEPTUNE (33,000 mi.)
PLUTO (5,945 mi.)

ARC OF THE SUN'S CIRCUMFERENCE

ECLIPSE OF THE SUN

SUN

ORBIT
MOON
EARTH'S SHADOW
EARTH'S

(Not in scale)

ECLIPSE OF THE MOON

SUN

ORBIT
EARTH'S SHADOW
MOON
EARTH'S

THE SEASONS
(in the Northern Hemisphere)

Spring Equinox
March 21

WINTER

SPRING

Winter Solstice
December 22

Summer Solstice
June 21

SUN

SUMMER

FALL

Autumn Equinox
September 22

The axis of the earth remains inclined at a 23½ degree angle from the vertical as the earth travels around the sun.

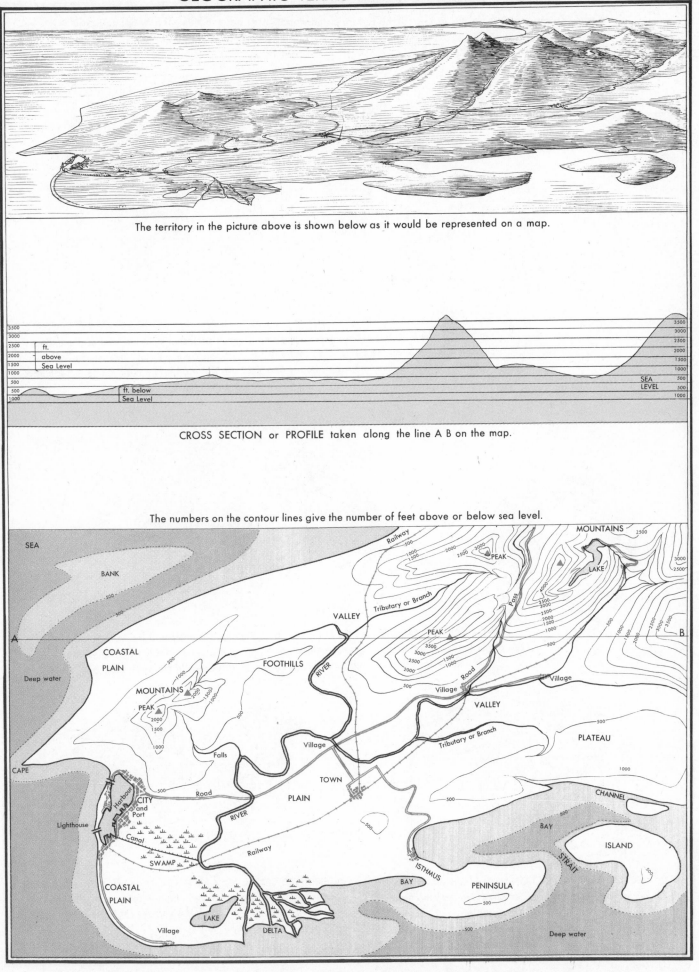

The territory in the picture above is shown below as it would be represented on a map.

CROSS SECTION or PROFILE taken along the line A B on the map.

The numbers on the contour lines give the number of feet above or below sea level.

MAP PROJECTIONS

A map is a representation of all, or part, of the surface of the world. These are examples of how flat maps are made from the globe. No map shows a part of the world as correctly as the globe itself.

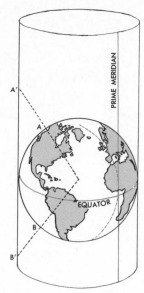

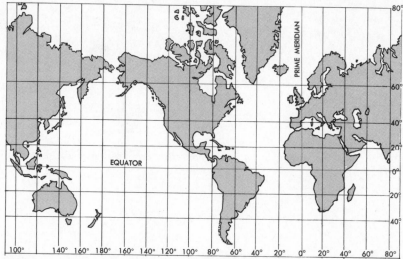

In MERCATOR'S PROJECTION the surface of the globe is projected onto the wall of a cylinder. Thus the line A B on the globe is represented by A' B' on the projection. Directions are shown accurately on the resulting map, but shapes and sizes are distorted in the north and south latitudes. The poles cannot be represented at all.

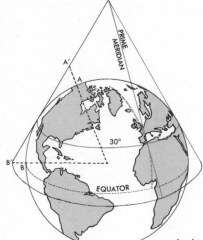

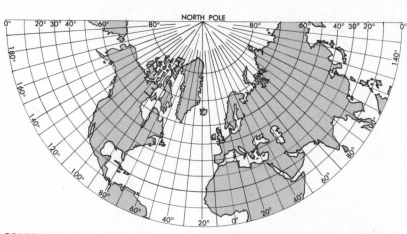

In this CONICAL PROJECTION the line A B on the globe is represented by A' B' on the cone. This projection is useful for showing one continent at a time and it gives a fairly true picture of the shape. It is suitable for areas reaching east and west but distorts areas in the north and south.

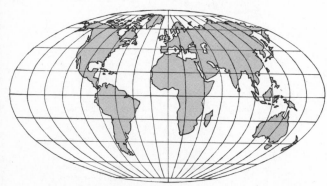

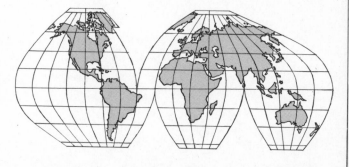

EQUAL AREA PROJECTION in oval form shows sizes accurately but tends to distort shapes in the n.e., n.w., s.e., and s.w. parts.

INTERRUPTED EQUAL AREA PROJECTION depicts shapes and areas accurately. Interruptions can be made in the oceans or over land masses depending on which the emphasis is to be placed.

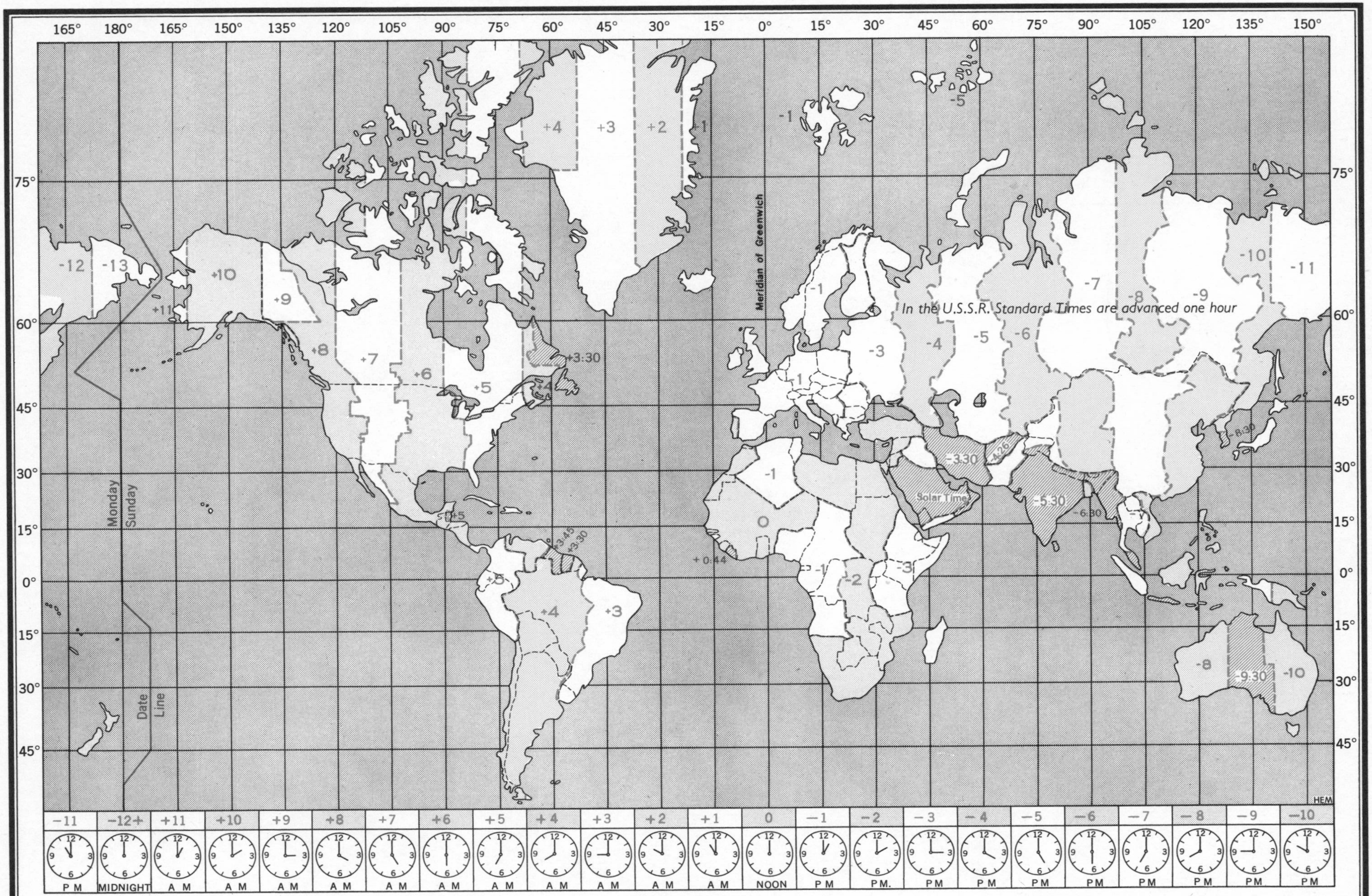

TIME ZONES

Time zones are outlined by alternating red and white strips. Areas for which time differences are less than one hour are distinguished by oblique lines.

The number of hours which needs to be subtracted from or added to local time to give Greenwich Time is indicated for each zone.

WORLD TIME CHART

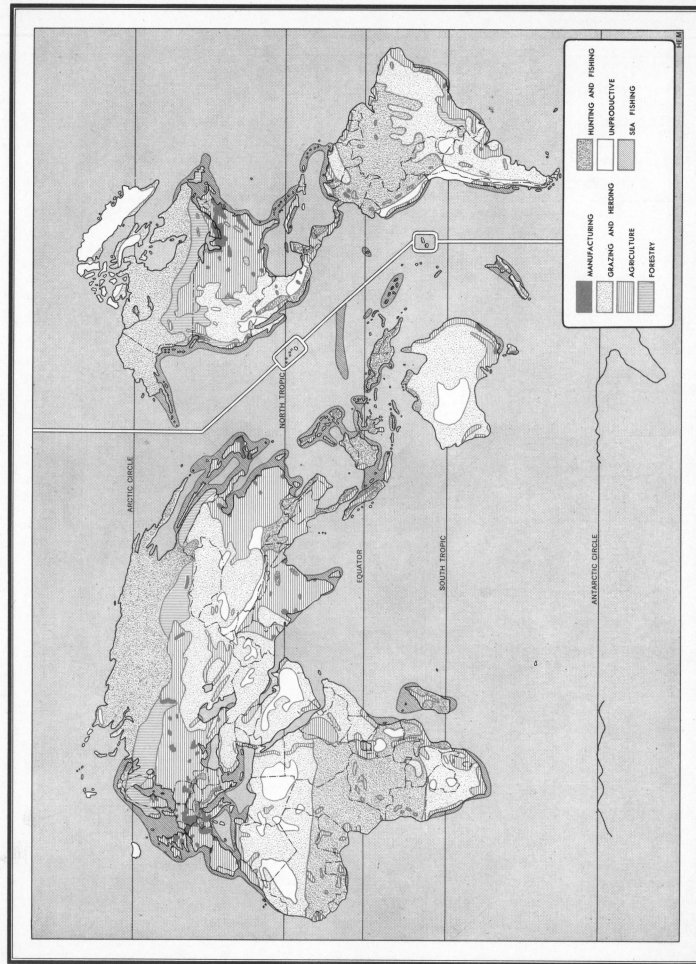

WORLD ECONOMIC ACTIVITIES

MANUFACTURING

GRAZING AND HERDING

AGRICULTURE

FORESTRY

HUNTING AND FISHING

UNPRODUCTIVE

SEA FISHING

ARCTIC CIRCLE

NORTH TROPIC

EQUATOR

SOUTH TROPIC

ANTARCTIC CIRCLE

HEM

WORLD POPULATION

INHABITANTS PER SQ. MILE

0 – 2

2 – 25

25 – 125

125 – 250

OVER 250

ARCTIC CIRCLE

NORTH TROPIC

EQUATOR

SOUTH TROPIC

ANTARCTIC CIRCLE

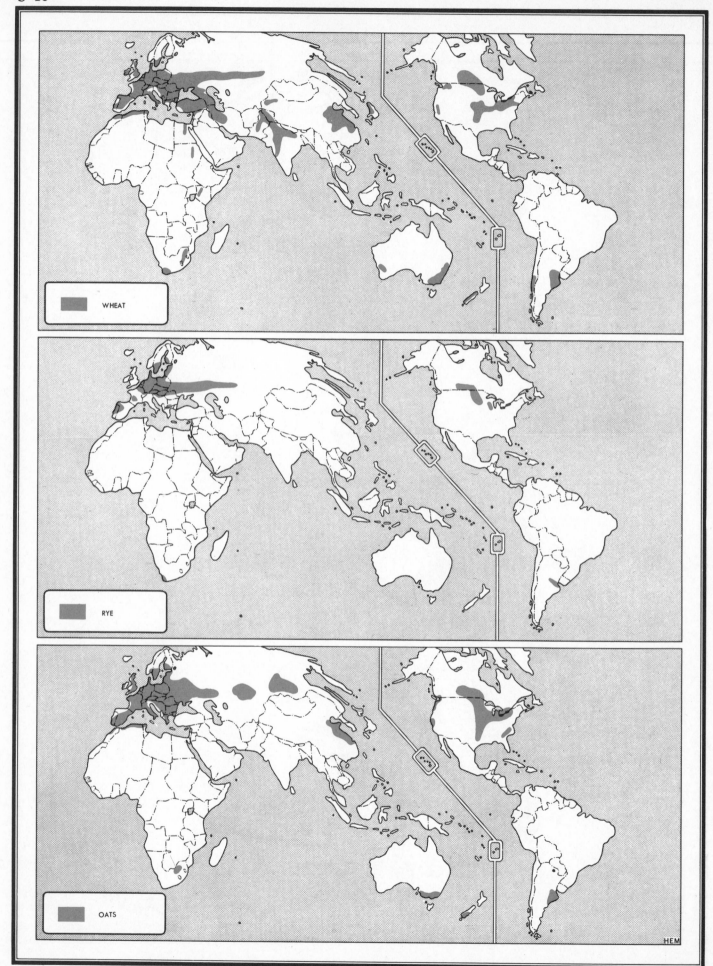

WORLD DISTRIBUTION OF MAIN PRIMARY PRODUCTS

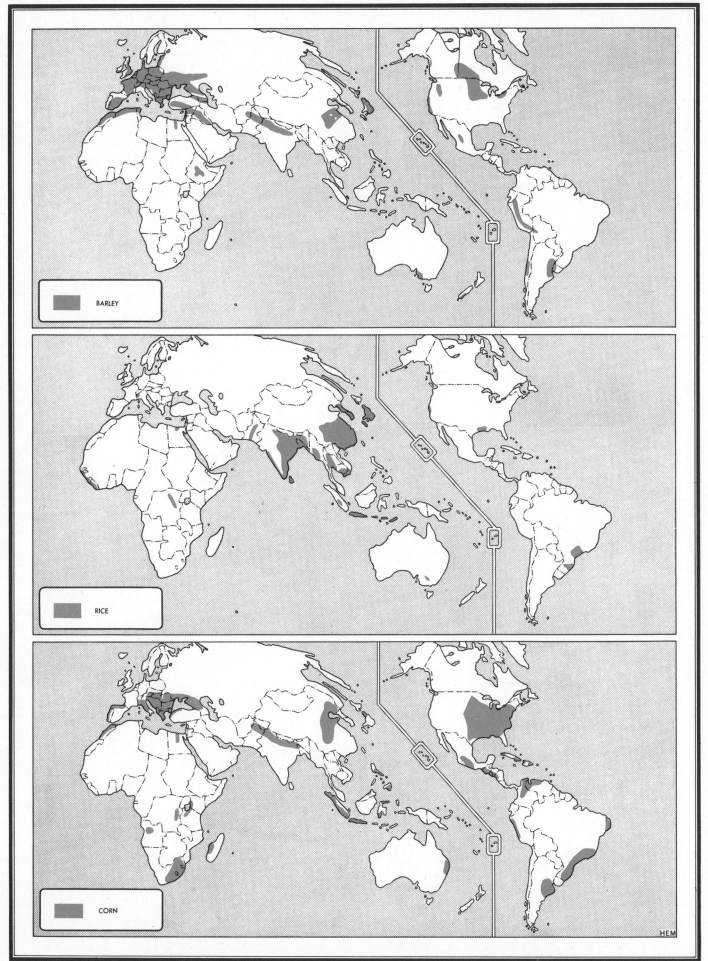

BARLEY

RICE

CORN

HEM

WORLD DISTRIBUTION OF MAIN PRIMARY PRODUCTS

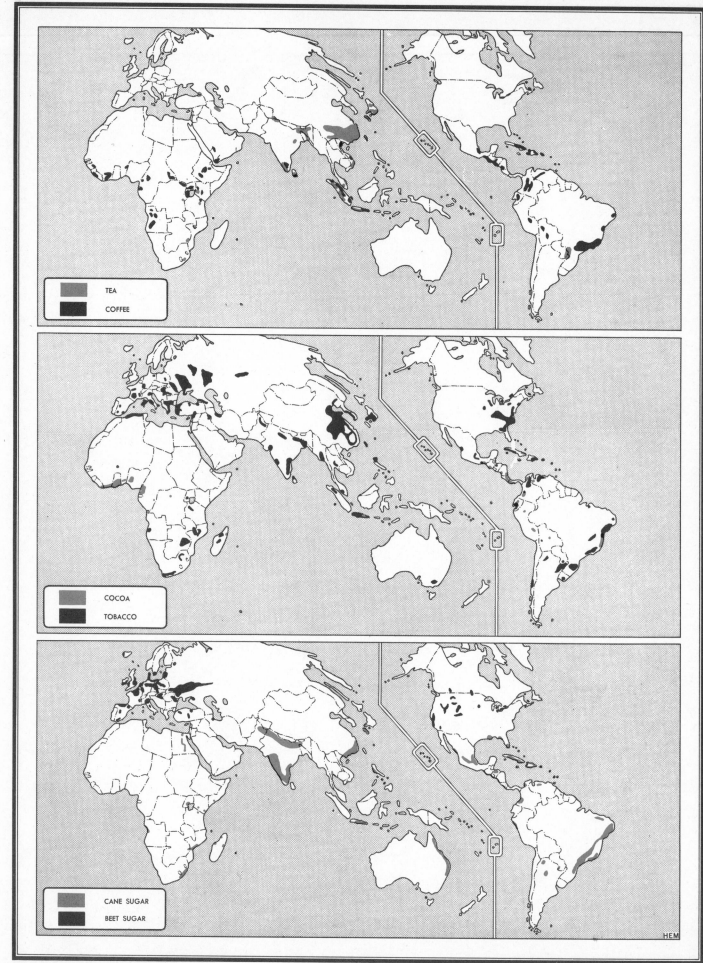

TEA

COFFEE

COCOA

TOBACCO

CANE SUGAR

BEET SUGAR

HEM

WORLD DISTRIBUTION OF MAIN PRIMARY PRODUCTS

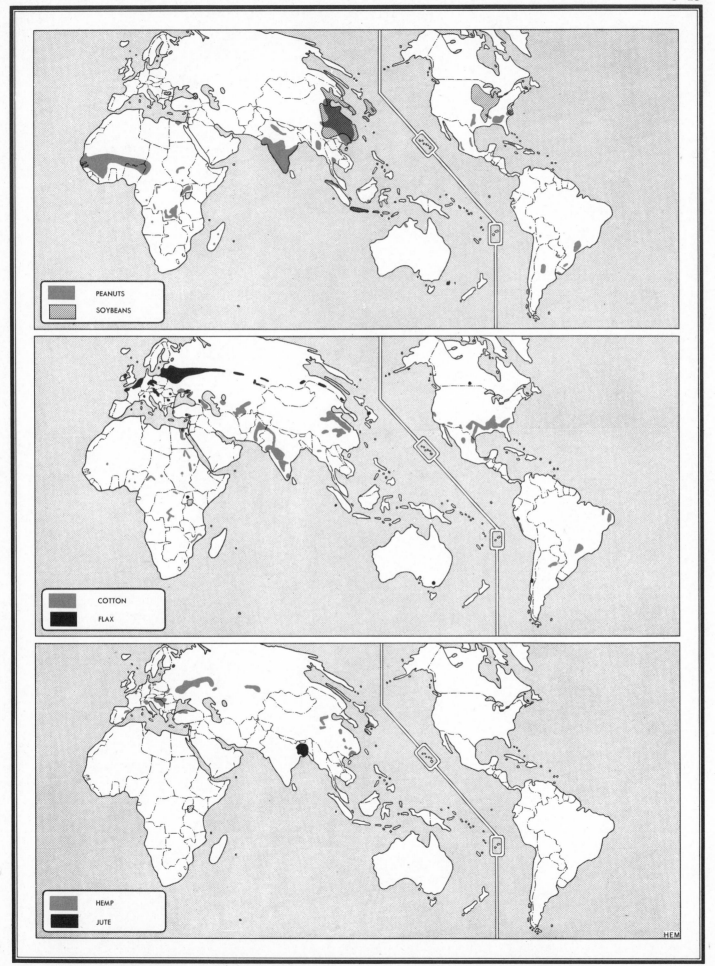

PEANUTS

SOYBEANS

COTTON

FLAX

HEMP

JUTE

HEM

WORLD DISTRIBUTION OF MAIN PRIMARY PRODUCTS

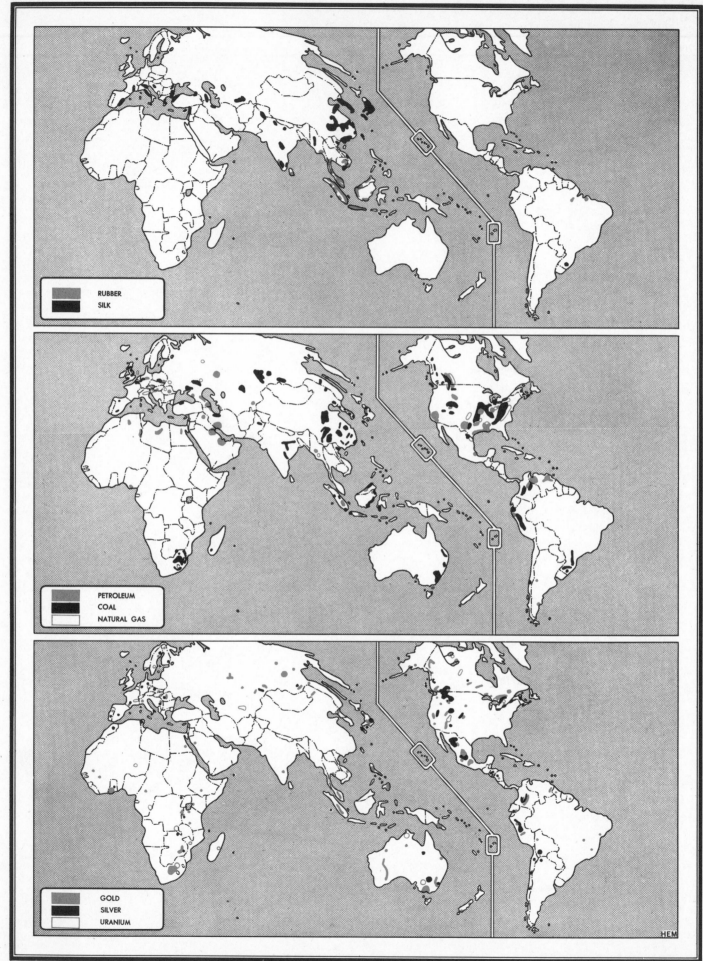

RUBBER
SILK

PETROLEUM
COAL
NATURAL GAS

GOLD
SILVER
URANIUM

HEM

WORLD DISTRIBUTION OF MAIN PRIMARY PRODUCTS

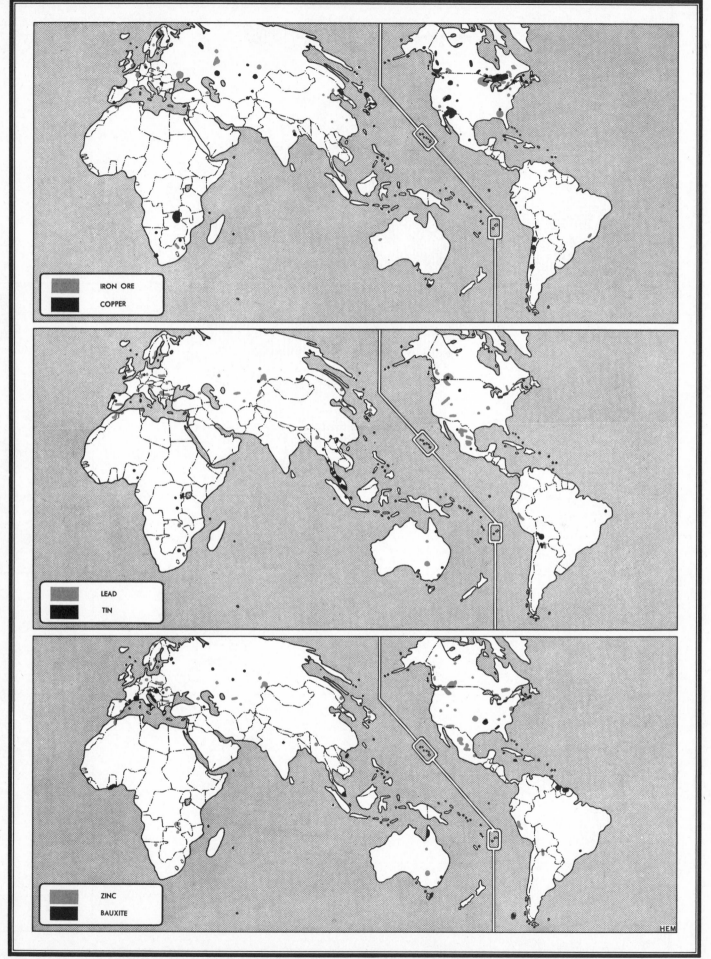

IRON ORE

COPPER

LEAD

TIN

ZINC

BAUXITE

HEM

WORLD DISTRIBUTION OF MAIN PRIMARY PRODUCTS

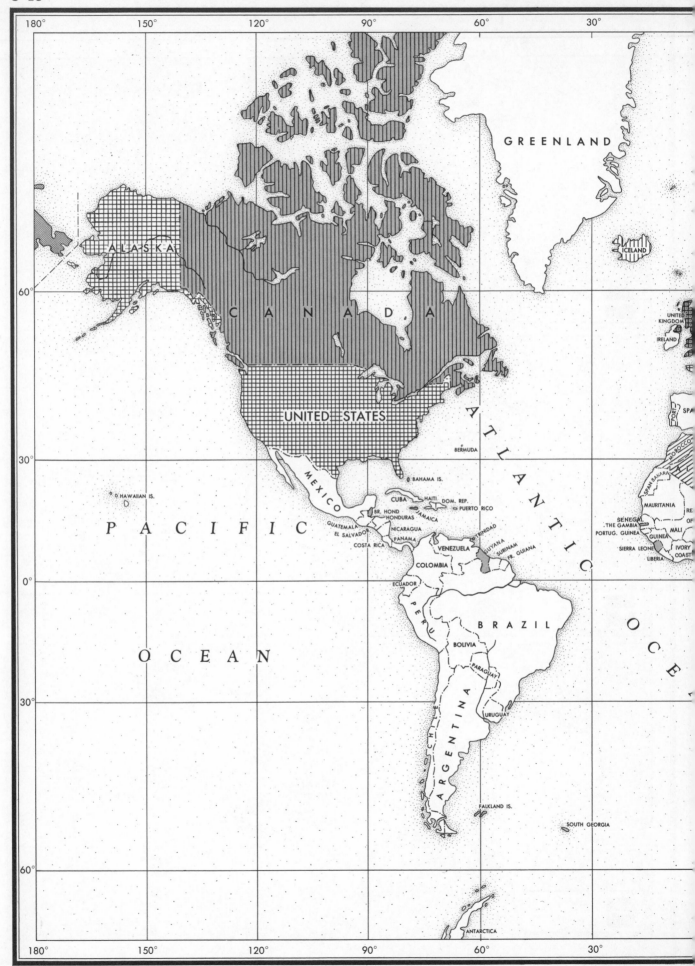

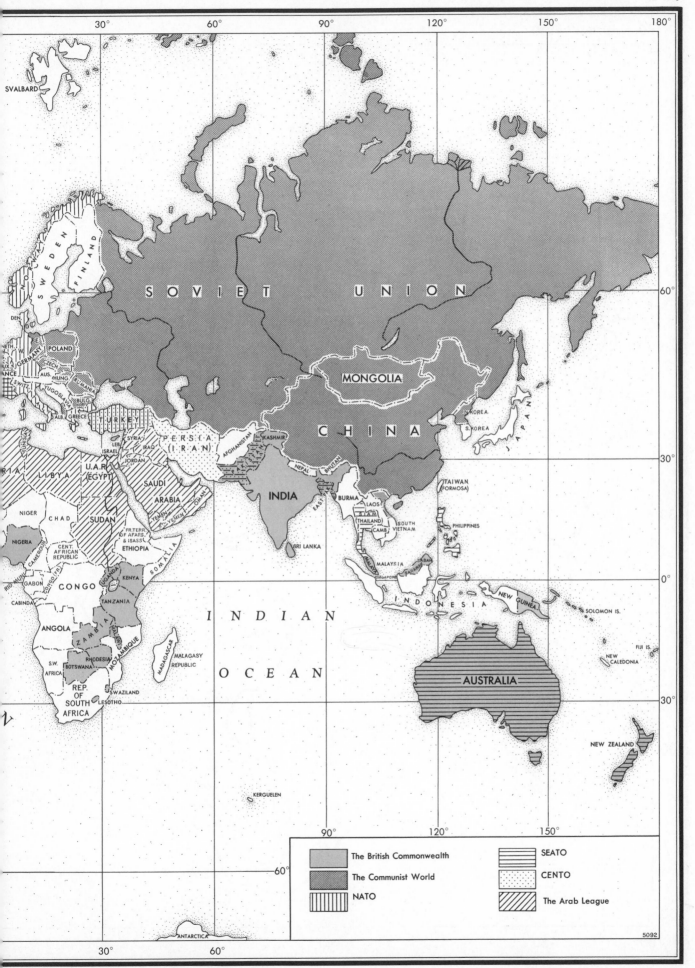

SVALBARD

NORWAY SWEDEN FINLAND

DEN.

S O V I E T   U N I O N   60°

NETH. POLAND
GERMANY
CZECH.
AUS. HUNG. RUMANIA
SWITZ.
YUGOSLAVIA
BULG.
ALB. GREECE
TURKEY
SYRIA
LEB. IRAQ
ISRAEL
JORDAN

PERSIA (IRAN)

MONGOLIA

AFGHANISTAN

KASHMIR

CHINA

N. KOREA
S. KOREA

J A P A N

TUNISIA
LIBYA
U.A.R. (EGYPT)
SAUDI ARABIA
YEMEN
S. YEMEN
OMAN

NIGER
CHAD
SUDAN
FR. TERR. OF AFARS & ISASS
ETHIOPIA
SOMALIA

NIGERIA
CAMEROUN
CENT. AFRICAN REPUBLIC
GABON
CONGO
UGANDA
KENYA
TANZANIA

NEPAL
BHUTAN
EAST PAK.
INDIA
BURMA
LAOS
SIAM
THAILAND
CAMB.
SOUTH VIETNAM
TAIWAN (FORMOSA)
PHILIPPINES

30°

SRI LANKA

MALAYSIA
SARAWAK
SINGAPORE

I N D O N E S I A
NEW GUINEA
SOLOMON IS.

0°

CABINDA
ANGOLA
ZAMBIA
RHODESIA
MOZAMBIQUE
S.W. AFRICA
BOTSWANA
SWAZILAND
LESOTHO
REP. OF SOUTH AFRICA

MALAGASY REPUBLIC
MADAGASCAR

I N D I A N

O C E A N

AUSTRALIA

FIJI IS.
NEW CALEDONIA

30°

NEW ZEALAND

KERGUELEN

60°

ANTARCTICA

	The British Commonwealth		SEATO
	The Communist World		CENTO
	NATO		The Arab League

5092

30° 60° 90° 120° 150° 180°

GROUPINGS IN DECEMBER 1968

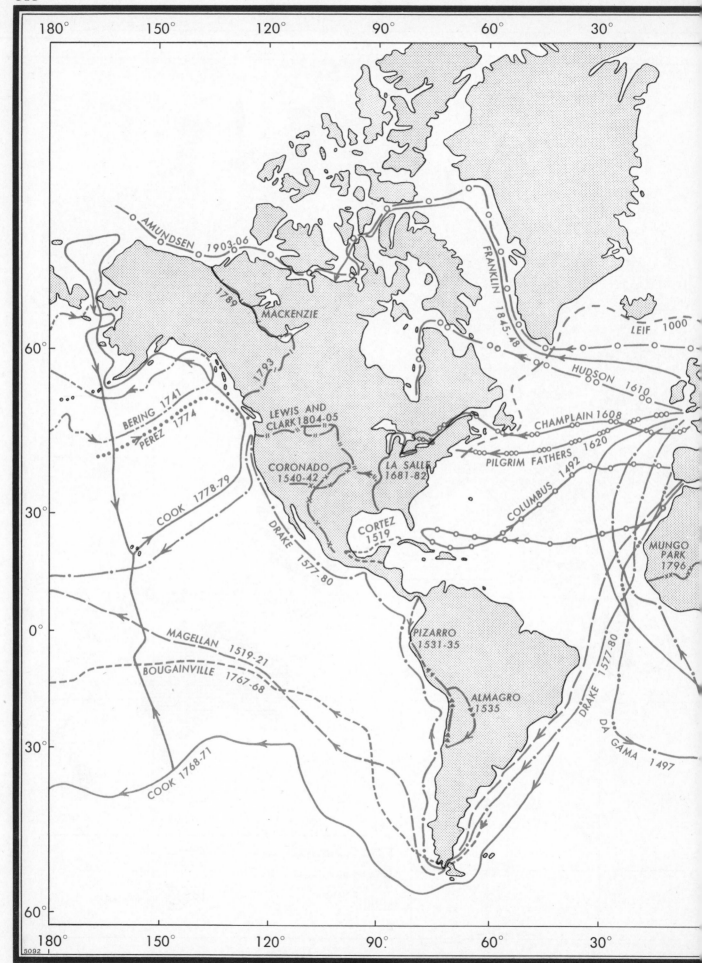

WORLD EXPLORATION

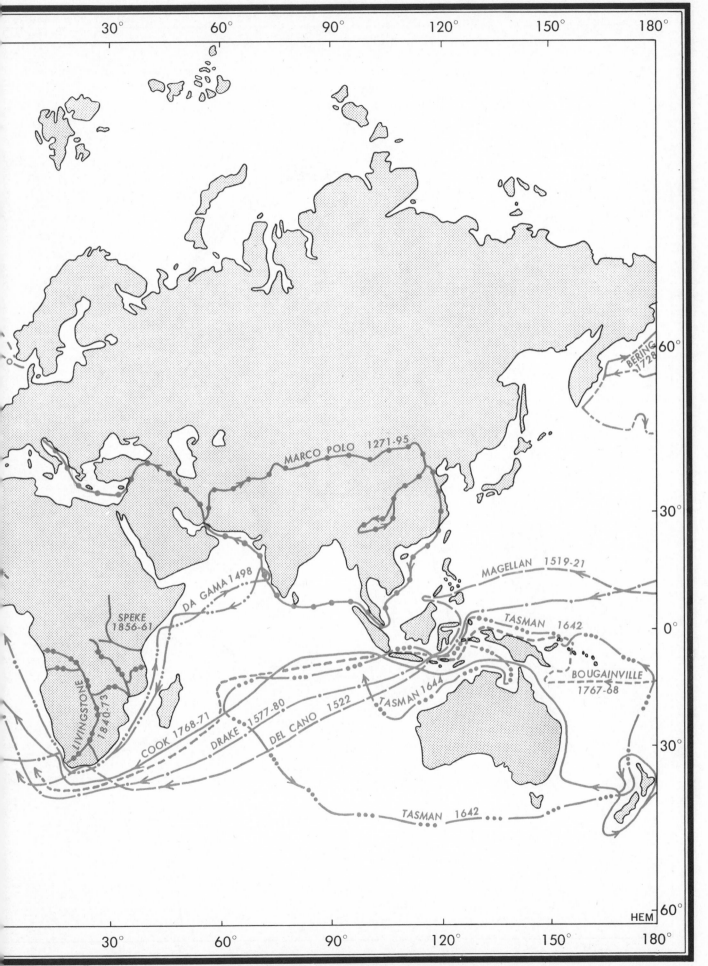

MARCO POLO 1271-95

BERING 1728

MAGELLAN 1519-21

TASMAN 1642

DA GAMA 1498

SPEKE 1856-61

BOUGAINVILLE 1767-68

TASMAN 1644

LIVINGSTONE 1840-73

COOK 1768-71

DRAKE 1577-80

DEL CANO 1522

TASMAN 1642

HEM

WORLD EXPLORATION

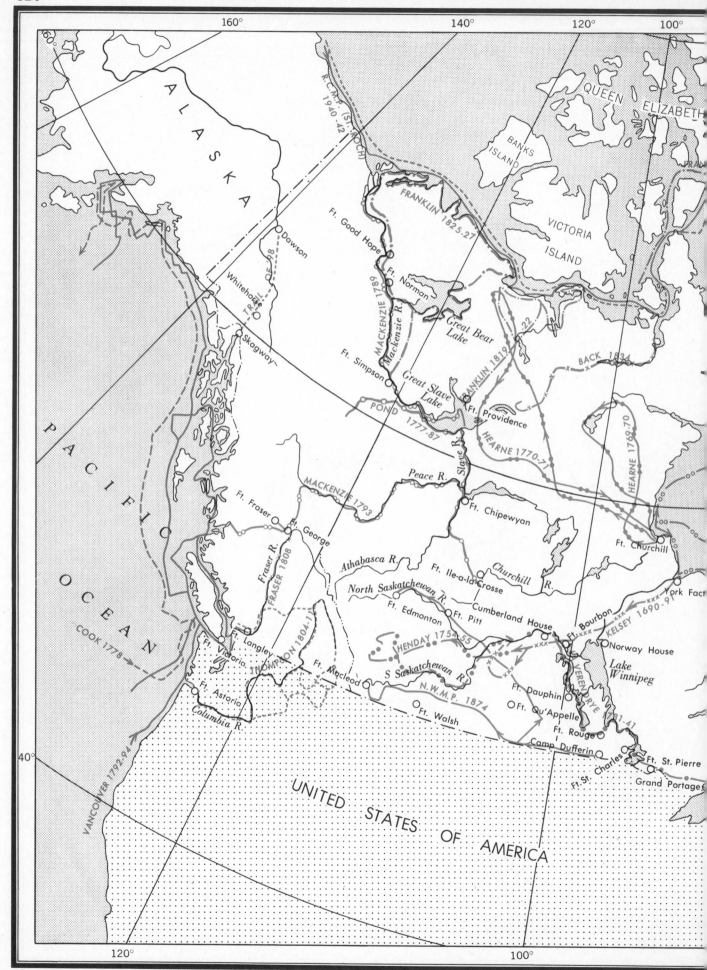

CANADIAN EXPLORATIONS

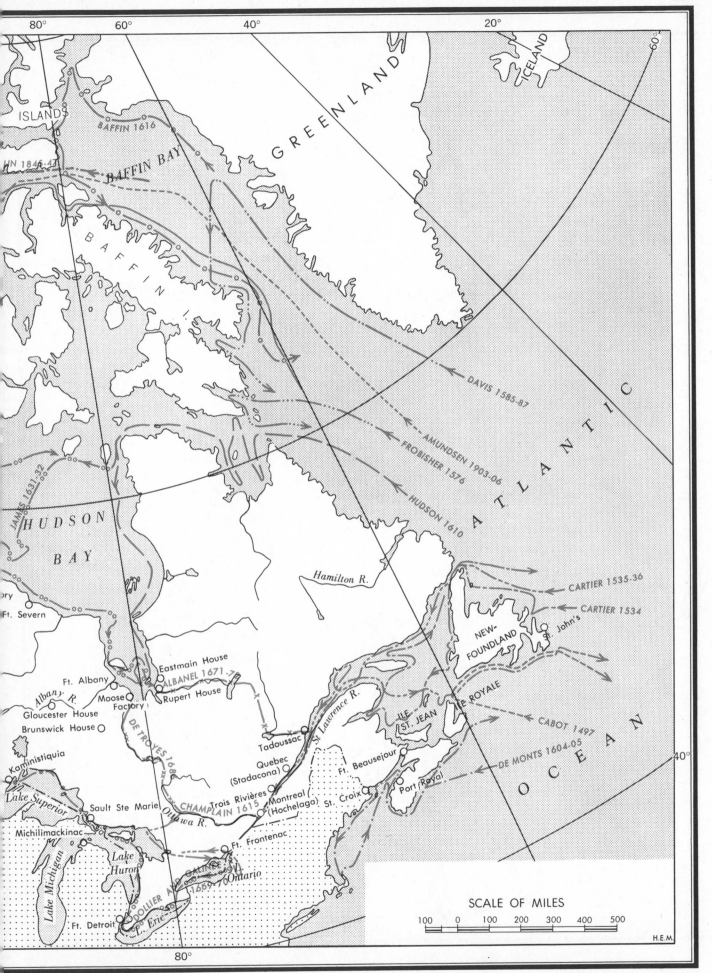

80°   60°   40°   20°   60°

ISLANDS

BAFFIN 1616

HN 1846-47

BAFFIN BAY

GREENLAND

ICELAND

BAFFIN I.

DAVIS 1585-87

AMUNDSEN 1903-06

FROBISHER 1576

HUDSON 1610

ATLANTIC

JAMES 1631-32

HUDSON BAY

Hamilton R.

CARTIER 1535-36

CARTIER 1534

Ft. Severn

St. John's

NEW-FOUNDLAND

Eastmain House

ALBANEL 1671-7

Ft. Albany

ILE ROYALE

Moose Factory

Rupert House

ILE ST. JEAN

Albany R.

CABOT 1497

Gloucester House

St. Lawrence R.

Brunswick House

DE TROYES 1686

Tadoussac

DE MONTS 1604-05

OCEAN

40°

Kaministiquia

Quebec (Stadacona)

Ft. Beausejour

Port Royal

Lake Superior

Sault Ste Marie

CHAMPLAIN 1615

Trois Rivières

Montreal (Hochelaga)

St. Croix

Michilimackinac

Ottawa R.

Ft. Frontenac

Lake Huron

Lake Michigan

Ontario

DOLLIER AND GALINEE

1669-70

Ft. Detroit

L. Erie

SCALE OF MILES

100   0   100   200   300   400   500

H.E.M.

80°

AND HISTORICAL ROUTES

MINERALS

Coal ———— C
Copper ——— Co
Iron ———— Ir
Lead ———— L
Zinc ———— Z
Asbestos ——— A
Gypsum ——— Gy
Salt ———— Sa
Petroleum
Natural Gas

PRINCIPAL FISH

Cod ——— C
Salmon ——— S
Halibut ——— Ha
Lobster ——— L
Herring ——— He
Mackerel ——— M
Hake ——— Hk
Smelts ——— Sm
Oysters ——— Oy
Haddock ——— H
Sardines ——— Sr
Tuna ——— Tu
Swordfish ——— Sw

Principal Industrial Areas
Developed Water Power Sites ——— WP
Farming Areas
Northern Limit of Commercial Timber Area

W.C. RUSSELL, Cartographer

ECONOMIC RESOURCES OF EASTERN CANADA

LABRADOR
QUEBEC
FURS
Pulpwood
Natashkwan R.
Moisie R.
Saguenay R.
Seven Islands
Mingan
Chicoutimi
Levis
QUEBEC
Thetford Mines
Maple Products
Riviere du Loup
Rimouski
GASPE PEN.
Lumber
Mixed
Chaleur Bay
Bathurst
NEW BRUNSWICK
Saint John R.
Fredericton
Saint John
Moncton
ANTICOSTI ISLAND
GULF OF ST. LAWRENCE
RIVER ST. LAWRENCE
Magdalen Is. (to Que.)
PRINCE EDWARD ISLAND
Charlottetown
Potatoes
Amherst
Truro
Apples
NOVA SCOTIA
Digby
Yarmouth
Halifax
BAY OF FUNDY
C. Sable
Sable I.
CAPE BRETON ISLAND
Sydney Mines
Mixed
ATLANTIC OCEAN
NEWFOUNDLAND
Pulpwood
Corner Brook
Gander
St. John's
Port aux Basques
Miquelon I. (to France)
C. Race
Placentia Bay
White Bay
Strait of Belle Isle
Belle Isle

0   50   100   150   200 MILES

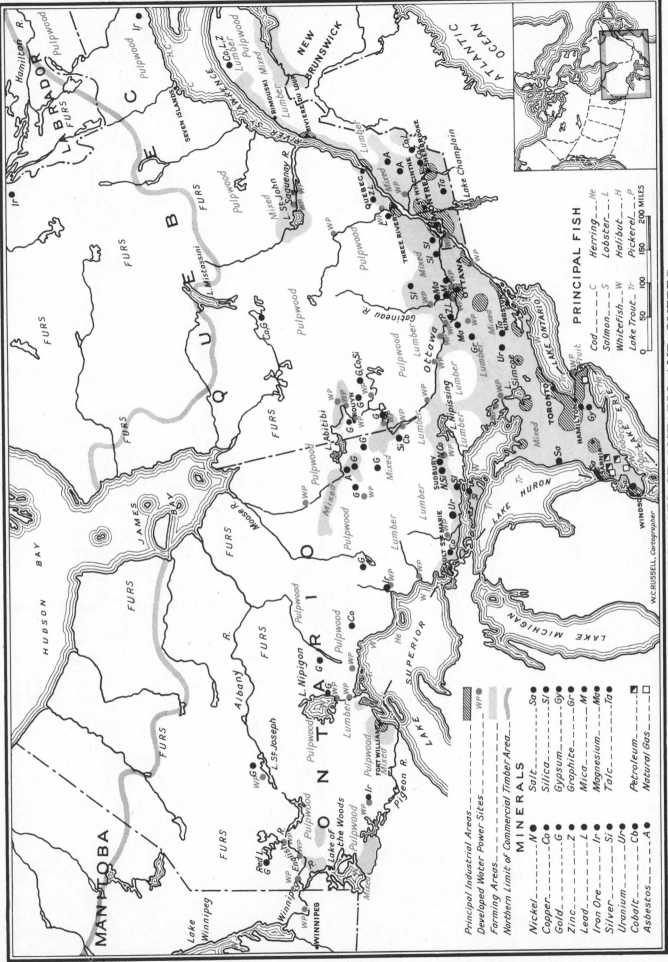

ECONOMIC RESOURCES OF ONTARIO AND QUEBEC

W.C. RUSSELL, Cartographer

PRINCIPAL FISH

Cod____C   Herring____He
Salmon____S   Lobster____L
Whitefish____W   Halibut____H
Lake Trout____Tr   Pickerel____P

0   50   100   150   200 MILES

Principal Industrial Areas____
Developed Water Power Sites____   WP
Farming Areas____
Northern Limit of Commercial Timber Area____

MINERALS

Nickel____N   Salt____Sa
Copper____Co   Silica____Si
Gold____G   Gypsum____Gy
Zinc____Z   Graphite____Gr
Lead____L   Mica____M
Iron Ore____Ir   Magnesium____Ma
Silver____Si   Talc____Ta
Uranium____Ur   Petroleum____
Cobalt____Cb   Natural Gas____
Asbestos____A

ECONOMIC RESOURCES OF WESTERN CANADA

W.C. RUSSELL, Cartographer

PRINCIPAL FISH

Salmon	S
Herring	He
Halibut	Ha
Whitefish	W
Lake Trout	Tr
Goldeye	G
Shrimp	Sh
Cod	C
Pickerel	P
Pike	Pk
Sole	So
Tuna	Tu
Clams	Cl
Smelts	Sm
Oysters	Oy

PRINCIPAL MINERALS

Gold	G	Uranium	Ur
Silver	S	Tungsten	Tu
Lead	L	Nickel	Ni
Zinc	Z	Iron	Ir
Copper	C	Coal	Co
		Sodium Sulphate	So
Salt	Sa		
Gypsum	Gy		
Asbestos	A		
Petroleum			
Natural Gas			

Principal Industrial Areas
Developed Water Power Sites
Principal Farming Areas
Northern Limit of Commercial Timber Area

Scale
0 100 200 300 400 MILES

HUDSON BAY
PACIFIC OCEAN

YUKON TERRITORY
NORTHWEST TERRITORIES
BRITISH COLUMBIA
ALBERTA
SASKATCHEWAN
MANITOBA
ONTARIO

Great Bear L.
Great Slave Lake
Dubawnt L.
Reindeer L.
Lake Winnipeg
Lake Winnipegosis
L. Manitoba

Mackenzie River
Liard R.
Thelon R.
Churchill R.
Nelson R.
Peace River
Athabaska R.
Saskatchewan R.
Assiniboine R.
Skeena R.
Fraser R.
Columbia R.
Yukon R.

WHITEHORSE
YELLOWKNIFE
SIMPSON
PRINCE RUPERT
TERRACE
PRINCE GEORGE
LILLOOET
VANCOUVER
VICTORIA
PENTICTON
NELSON
REVELSTOKE
EDMONTON
LLOYDMINSTER
CALGARY
LETHBRIDGE
PRINCE ALBERT
SASKATOON
MOOSE JAW
REGINA
THE PAS
DAUPHIN
BRANDON
WINNIPEG

QUEEN CHARLOTTE ISLANDS
VANCOUVER ISLAND
Hecate Str.
Juan de Fuca Str.

FURS · LUMBER · PULPWOOD · MIXED · WHEAT · LIVESTOCK · RANCHING · FRUIT

LAND USE IN SOUTHERN ONTARIO

W. C. RUSSELL, Cartographer

ONTARIO

SOUTHERN ONTARIO

REFERENCE

Cities ___ GUELPH
Other Principal Communities ___ Durham
Principal Highways
Principal Electric Generating Stations ___

AGRICULTURAL LAND USE

Special Crops
Dairy Specialties
Livestock
Livestock and Crops

Scale

0   25   50   75 Miles

QUEBEC

NEW YORK

OTTAWA RIVER

ST. LAWRENCE RIVER

Hawkesbury
Alexandria
CORNWALL
South Nation R.
OTTAWA
Carleton Place
Smiths Falls
Renfrew
Arnprior
Perth
Rideau
BROCKVILLE
Iroquois
Thousand Islands
KINGSTON
Rideau Lakes
Pembroke
Barrys Bay
Bancroft
Madawaska R.
Bognoechere
SHIELD
Madoc
Napanee
BELLEVILLE
Picton
Trenton
Bay
CONIFEROUS FOREST
THE PRE-CAMBRIAN
Haliburton
Kawartha Lakes
PETERBOROUGH
Rice Lake
Port Hope
Bowmanville
Madawaska R.
ALGONQUIN PROVINCIAL PARK
Bracebridge
Orillia
Beaverton
Port Perry
Millbrook
Scugog
Markham
Richmond Hill
OSHAWA
LAKE ONTARIO
Mattawa RIVER
Mattawa
NORTH BAY
Lake Nipissing
Sundridge
Huntsville
Muskoka Lakes
LAKE SIMCOE
Bradford
TOLERANT HARDWOODS
Vegetables
TORONTO
Hamilton
ST. CATHARINES
NIAGARA FALLS
Fort Erie
WELLAND
OTTAWA
French R.
Magnetewan
Parry Sound
BAY OF ISLANDS
Collingwood
Fruit
Stayner
NIAGARA
Orangeville
Georgetown
GUELPH
Hespeler
Brampton
NIAGARA ESCARPMENT
Grimsby
Oakville
Welland Ship Canal
Wanapitei L.
LIMIT
SOUTHERN
GEORGIAN BAY
OWEN SOUND
Durham
Mount Forest
Palmerston
WATERLOO
KITCHENER
STRATFORD
WOODSTOCK
Brantford
Simcoe
Tobacco
Vegetables
Delhi
SUDBURY
Elliot Lake
Blind River
Gore Bay
Little Current
MANITOULIN ISLAND
NORTH CHANNEL
Southampton
Walkerton
Wingham
NORTHERN LIMIT
Seaforth
St. Marys
LONDON
ST. THOMAS
Exeter
Goderich
Thames River
LAKE HURON
Sarnia
Strathroy
Petrolia
Bothwell
CHATHAM
Blenheim
Vegetables
Tilbury
Tobacco
Leamington
Pelee
WINDSOR
ESSEX
LAKE ST. CLAIR
MICHIGAN

MIXED DECIDUOUS

UNITED STATES

CANADA

NEW YORK

PENNSYLVANIA

LAKE ERIE

CANADIAN AIRWAYS

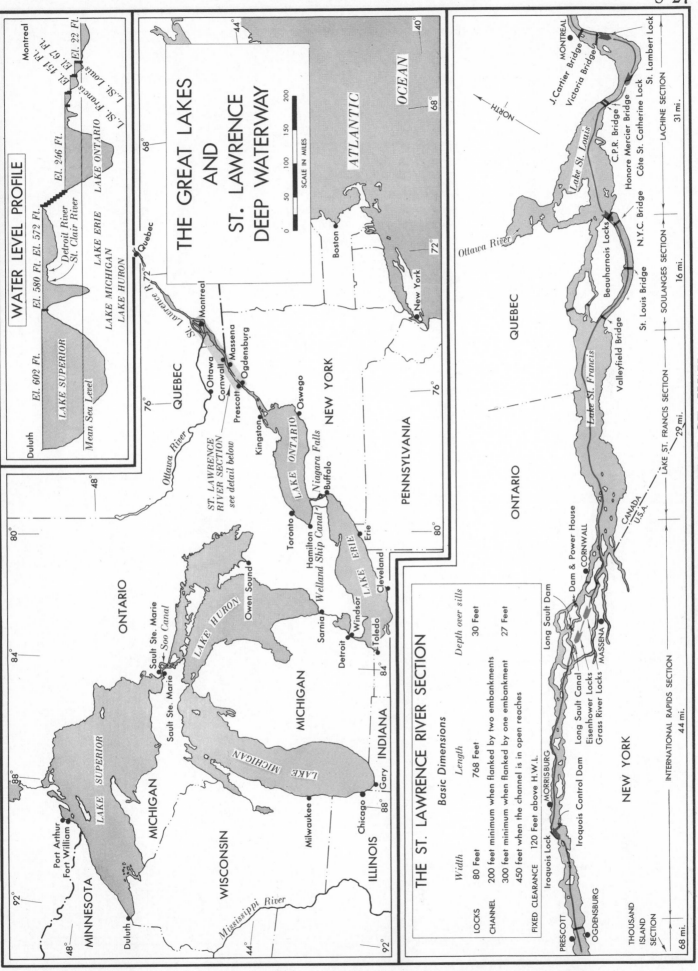

WATER LEVEL PROFILE

Montreal
El. 151 Ft.
L.St. Louis El. 67 Ft.
El. 22 Ft.
L.St. Francis
El. 246 Ft.

Duluth
El. 602 Ft.
El. 580 Ft. El. 572 Ft.

LAKE SUPERIOR
LAKE ERIE
LAKE ONTARIO
Detroit River
St. Clair River
LAKE MICHIGAN
LAKE HURON

Mean Sea Level

THE GREAT LAKES AND ST. LAWRENCE DEEP WATERWAY

SCALE IN MILES

0   50   100   150   200

ATLANTIC OCEAN

Boston
New York

Quebec
Montreal
Ottawa River
St. Lawrence R.
QUEBEC

ST. LAWRENCE RIVER SECTION
see detail below

Ottawa
Cornwall
Massena
Prescott Ogdensburg
Oswego

Kingston
LAKE ONTARIO
Niagara Falls
Buffalo

NEW YORK
PENNSYLVANIA

Toronto
Hamilton
Welland Ship Canal
LAKE ERIE
Erie
Cleveland

ONTARIO

Owen Sound
LAKE HURON

Sault Ste. Marie
Soo Canal
Sault Ste. Marie

Sarnia
Windsor
Detroit
Toledo

MICHIGAN
MICHIGAN

LAKE MICHIGAN

LAKE SUPERIOR

Port Arthur
Fort William

MINNESOTA
WISCONSIN
ILLINOIS
INDIANA

Duluth
Milwaukee
Chicago
Gary

Mississippi River

THE ST. LAWRENCE RIVER SECTION

Basic Dimensions

	Width	Length	Depth over sills
LOCKS	80 Feet	768 Feet	30 Feet
CHANNEL	200 feet minimum when flanked by two embankments		27 Feet
	300 feet minimum when flanked by one embankment		
	450 feet when the channel is in open reaches		

FIXED CLEARANCE   120 Feet above H.W.L.

PRESCOTT
OGDENSBURG
Iroquois Lock
Iroquois Control Dam
MORRISBURG
Long Sault Dam
Dam & Power House
CORNWALL
Long Sault Canal
Eisenhower Locks
Grass River Locks
MASSENA

NEW YORK
CANADA
U.S.A.

THOUSAND ISLAND SECTION
68 mi.

INTERNATIONAL RAPIDS SECTION
44 mi.

LAKE ST. FRANCIS SECTION
29 mi.

SOULANGES SECTION
16 mi.

LACHINE SECTION
31 mi.

Valleyfield Bridge
St. Louis Bridge
N.Y.C. Bridge
Beauharnois Locks
St. Lambert Lock
Côte St. Catherine Lock
Honore Mercier Bridge
C.P.R. Bridge
Victoria Bridge
J. Cartier Bridge
MONTREAL

Lake St. Francis
Lake St. Louis
Ottawa River

QUEBEC
ONTARIO

NORTH

THE ST. LAWRENCE SEAWAY

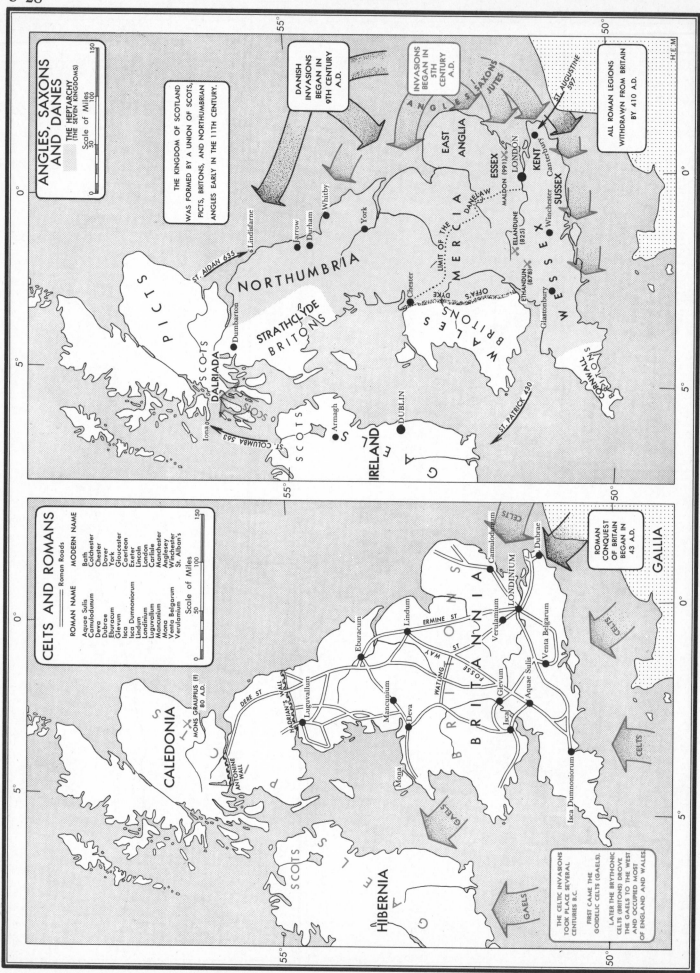

ANGLES, SAXONS AND DANES

THE HEPTARCHY
(THE SEVEN KINGDOMS)

Scale of Miles

DANISH INVASIONS BEGAN IN 9TH CENTURY A.D.

THE KINGDOM OF SCOTLAND WAS FORMED BY A UNION OF SCOTS, PICTS, BRITONS, AND NORTHUMBRIAN ANGLES EARLY IN THE 11TH CENTURY.

INVASIONS BEGAN IN 5TH CENTURY A.D.

ST. AUGUSTINE 597

ALL ROMAN LEGIONS WITHDRAWN FROM BRITAIN BY 410 A.D.

ANGLES
SAXONS
JUTES

EAST ANGLIA

ESSEX
LONDON
MALDON (991)
KENT
Canterbury
ELLANDUNE (825)
Winchester
SUSSEX
W E S S E X
ETHANDUN (878)
Glastonbury

PICTS
SCOTS
DALRIADA
Dumbarton
STRATHCLYDE BRITONS
ST. AIDAN 635
Lindisfarne
Jarrow
Durham
Whitby
York
NORTHUMBRIA
Chester
LIMIT OF THE
DANELAW
MERCIA
OFFA'S DYKE
W A L E S
BRITONS
CORNWALL
BRITONS

Iona
ST. COLUMBA 563
SCOTS
S
Armagh
DUBLIN
IRELAND
ST. PATRICK 430
G

CELTS AND ROMANS

Roman Roads

ROMAN NAME	MODERN NAME
Aquae Sulis	Bath
Camulodunum	Colchester
Deva	Chester
Dubrae	Dover
Eburacum	York
Glevum	Gloucester
Isca	Caerleon
Isca Dumnoniorum	Exeter
Lindum	Lincoln
Londinium	London
Luguvallum	Carlisle
Mancunium	Manchester
Mona	Anglesey
Venta Belgarum	Winchester
Verulamium	St. Alban's

Scale of Miles

ROMAN CONQUEST OF BRITAIN BEGAN IN 43 A.D.

CALEDONIA
MONS GRAUPIUS (?) 80 A.D.
DERE ST.
HADRIAN'S WALL
Luguvallum
ANTONINE WALL
Eburacum
Lindum
ERMINE ST.
Mancunium
WATLING ST.
FOSSE WAY
Deva
Mona
Isca
Glevum
Verulamium
LONDINIUM
Camulodunum
CELTS
Dubrae
Aquae Sulis
Venta Belgarum
B R I T A N N I A
Isca Dumnoniorum
GAELS
CELTS
GALLIA
CELTS

HIBERNIA
G
SCOTS
PICTS

THE CELTIC INVASIONS TOOK PLACE SEVERAL CENTURIES B.C.

FIRST CAME THE GOIDELIC CELTS (GAELS).

LATER THE BRYTHONIC CELTS (BRITONS) DROVE THE GAELS TO THE WEST AND OCCUPIED MOST OF ENGLAND AND WALES.

HISTORICAL MAPS OF THE BRITISH ISLES (BEFORE 1066)

Boundaries
Historic Towns
Towns with Battle Sites
Battle Sites
The Cinque ports are underlined

SCALE OF MILES
0   50   100   150

ATLANTIC

OCEAN

NORTH

SEA

OUTER HEBRIDES

OF SKYE

Moray Firth

Inverness × Culloden 1746

SCOTLAND

Glenfinnan
Fort William   Killiecrankie 1689
Glencoe 1692   Tay
Sheriffmuir 1715   Perth

Firth of Lorne

Firth of Forth

Stirling   Dunfermline   Dunbar 1296, 1650
Bannockburn 1314   Falkirk 1298, 1746   EDINBURGH   Prestonpans 1745
Halidon Hill 1333
Flodden 1513

Solway Moss 1542

55°   55°

Londonderry   Newcastle
Carlisle
Durham

Solway Firth

Belfast

ISLE OF MAN

Marston Moor 1644   Stamford Bridge 1066

R. Boyne 1690   Drogheda 1649   Preston 1648   York   Humber
IRISH SEA   1715   Towton 1461
Wakefield 1460

Shannon   Boyne

IRELAND   DUBLIN   E N G L A N D

Conway   Chester
Limerick   Caernarvon   Derby   Lincoln 1141
Barrow   Nottingham
Harlech   Shrewsbury 1403   Leicester
Bosworth 1485   Naseby 1645
Wexford 1649   Mortimer's Cross 1461   Coventry   Ely 1071
Waterford   Warwick   Northampton 1460
W A L E S   Worcester 1651   Stratford on Avon   Edge Hill 1642
Cork   Tewkesbury 1471   Evesham 1265
Pembroke   Gloucester   Barnet 1471
Monmouth   Oxford   St. Albans
Cardiff   Newbury 1643, 1644   Sheerness   Sluys 1340
Bristol   Windsor   LONDON   Canterbury
BRISTOL CHANNEL   Runnymede   Sandwich
Hastings 1066   Dover
Barnstaple   Winchester   Lewes 1264   Hythe   Dunkirk
Sedgemoor 1685   Portsmouth   Romney   Calais
Wareham   Agincourt 1415
Exeter   NORMAN INVASION 1066   Crécy 1346

Plymouth

50°   50°

ENGLISH CHANNEL

Dieppe 1942

CHANNEL ISLANDS

Harfleur   Rouen

NORMANDY

HEM

10°   5°   0°

5°

HISTORICAL MAP OF THE BRITISH ISLES (AFTER 1066)

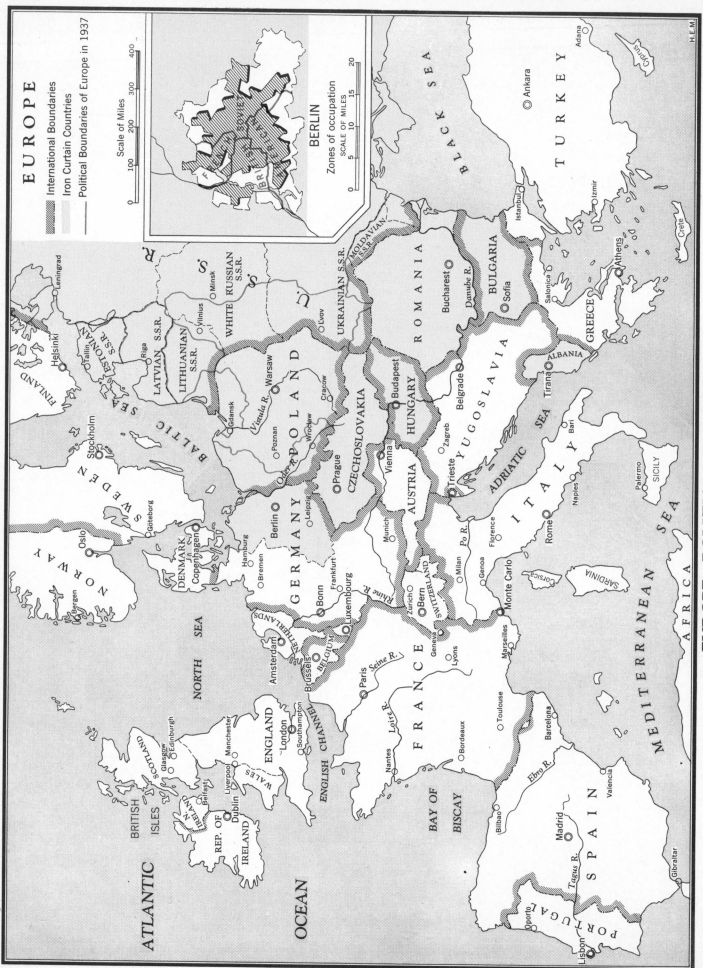

EUROPE—POLITICAL BOUNDARIES

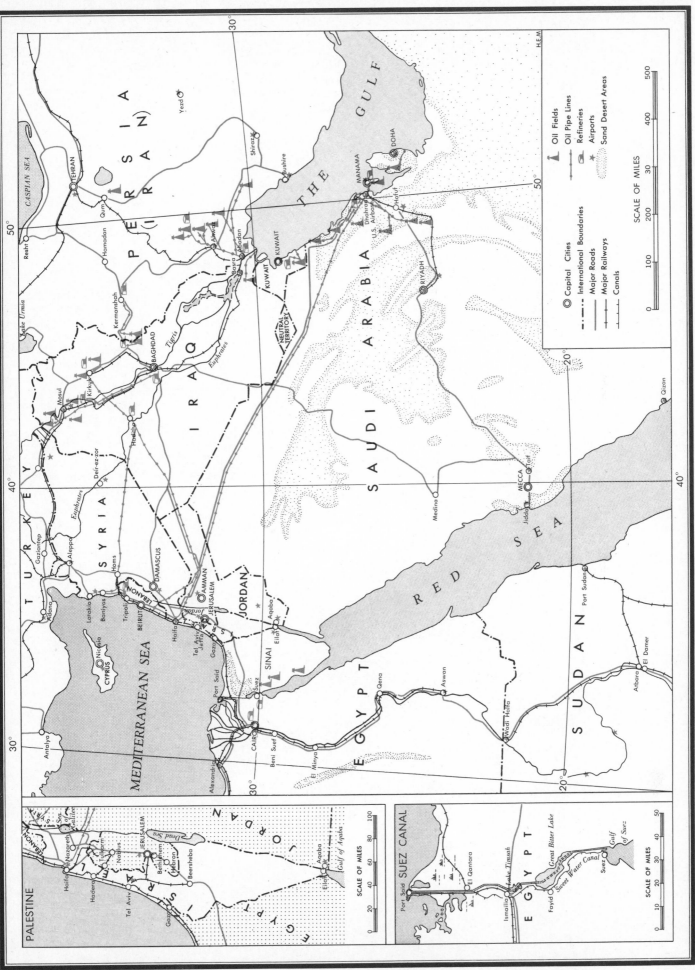

THE MIDDLE EAST—A STRATEGIC AREA

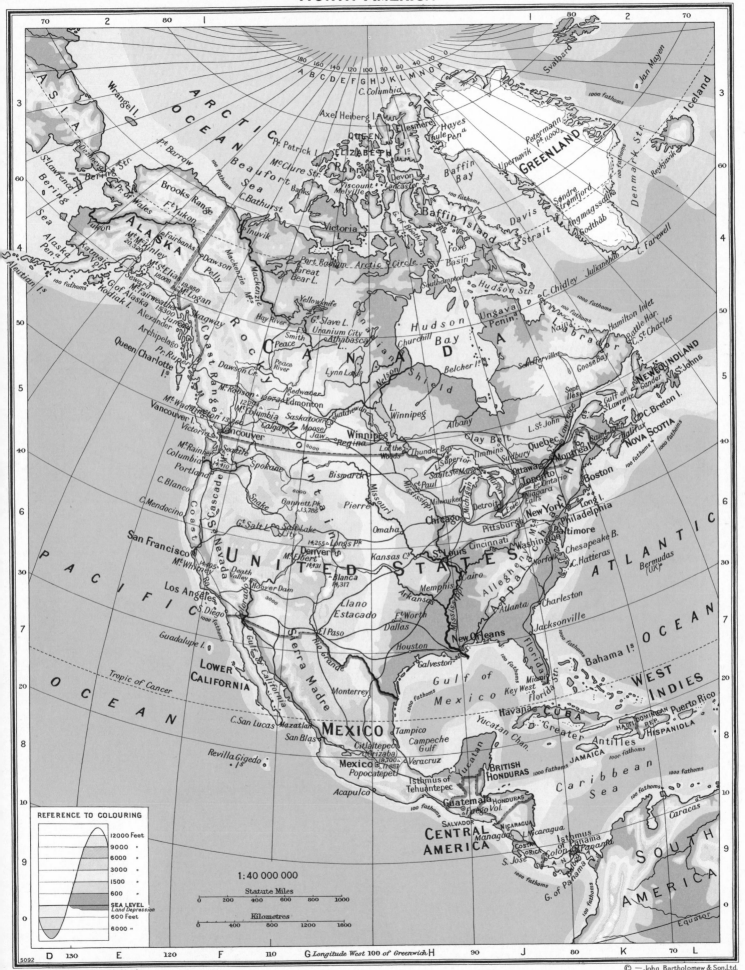

REFERENCE TO COLOURING

12000 Feet
9000 "
6000 "
3000 "
1500 "
600 "
SEA LEVEL Land Depression
600 Feet
6000 "

1:40 000 000

Statute Miles

0   200   400   600   800   1000

Kilometres

0   400   800   1200   1600

5092

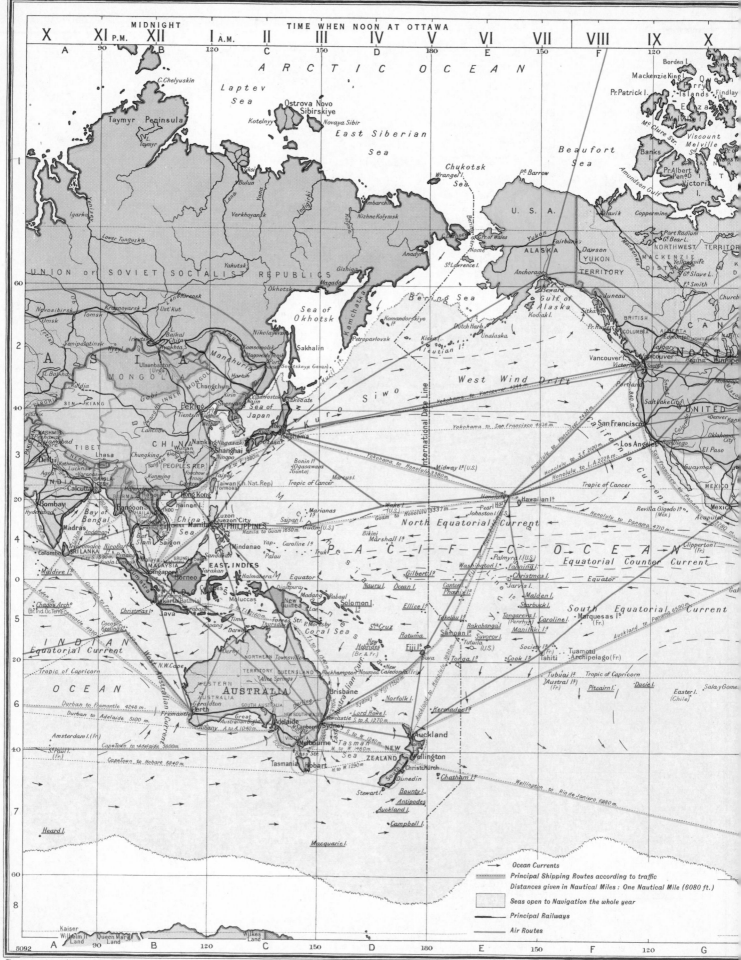

TIME WHEN NOON AT OTTAWA

| X | XI P.M. | MIDNIGHT XII | I A.M. | II | III | IV | V | VI | VII | VIII | IX | X |

A R C T I C   O C E A N

Laptev Sea

East Siberian Sea

Chukotsk Sea

Beaufort Sea

U. S. A.

ALASKA

NORTHWEST TERRITORIES

UNION of SOVIET SOCIALIST REPUBLICS

Sea of Okhotsk

Bering Sea

YUKON TERRITORY

BRITISH COLUMBIA

CANADA

A S I A

Manchuria

MONGOLIA

Sea of Japan

West Wind Drift

Vancouver

UNITED

CHINA

PEOPLES REP.

Sea of Japan

Kuro Siwo

Yokohama to Vancouver 4244 m.

San Francisco

Yokohama to San Francisco 4536 m.

TIBET

INDIA

Hong Kong

Tropic of Cancer

Bonin Is. (Ogasawara Gunto)

Marcus I.

Midway Is. (U.S.)

Yokohama to Honolulu 3380 m.

California Current

Los Angeles

Honolulu to S.F. 2100 m.

Honolulu to L.A. 2228 m.

Tropic of Cancer

MEXICO

Bay of Bengal

PHILIPPINES

Luzon

Manila to Guam 1650 m.

Marianas

Saipan I.

Guam (U.S.)

Wake I. (U.S.)

Honolulu 3337 m.

Pearl Hr.

Johnston I. (U.S.)

Hawaiian Is.

Honolulu

North Equatorial Current

Revilla Gigedo Is. (Mex.)

Acapulco

Honolulu to Panama 4710 m.

SRI LANKA

Colombo

Nicobar

MALAYSIA

Singapore

Borneo

Mindanao

Caroline Is.

Palau

Yap

Truk

Marshall Is.

Bikini

P A C I F I C   O C E A N

Palmyra I. (U.S.)

Washington I.

Fanning I.

Christmas I.

Equatorial Counter Current

Clipperton I. (Fr.)

Maldive Is.

EAST INDIES

Tarakan

Halmahera

Equator

Nauru I.

Ocean I.

Canton I.

Phoenix Is.

Jarvis I.

Malden I.

Starbuck I.

Equator

Chagos Arch. (Br. Ind. Oc. Terr.)

Cocos Keeling Is.

Christmas I.

Java

Celebes

Moluccas

New Guinea

Solomon Is.

Ellice Is.

Tokelau Is.

South Equatorial Current

Tongareva (Penrhyn)

Caroline I.

Marquesas Is. (Fr.)

I N D I A N

Equatorial Current

Batavia

Timor

Darwin

P. Moresby

Coral Sea

Sta. Cruz

Rotuma

Samoa I. (U.S.)

Tutuila

Rakahanga

Manihiki Is.

Suvorov I.

Society Is. (Fr.)

Tuamotu Archipelago (Fr.)

O C E A N

Tropic of Capricorn

N.W. Cape

NORTHERN TERRITORY

Townsville

QUEENSLAND

Rockhampton

New Hebrides (Br. & Fr.)

Fiji Is.

Suva

Tonga Is.

Cook Is.

Tahiti

Tubuai (Austral Is.) (Fr.)

Tropic of Capricorn

Durban to Fremantle 4248 m.

WESTERN AUSTRALIA

AUSTRALIA

SOUTH AUSTRALIA

Alice Springs

NEW SOUTH WALES

Brisbane

Noumea

New Caledonia (Fr.)

Sydney to Fiji 1760 m.

Norfolk I.

Kermadec Is.

Pitcairn I.

Ducie I.

Easter I. (Chile)

Sala y Gomez

Durban to Adelaide 5100 m.

Geraldton

Perth

Fremantle

Albany

Great Australian Bight

A. to A. 1040 m.

Adelaide

VICTORIA

Canberra

Sydney

Newcastle

Lord Howe I.

S. to A. 1270 m.

Amsterdam I. (Fr.)

Cape Town to Adelaide 5600 m.

West Australian Current

Melbourne

Tasman Sea

S. to W. 1240 m.

W. to W. 1290 m.

Auckland

NEW ZEALAND

Wellington

St. Paul I. (Fr.)

Cape Town to Hobart 5840 m.

Tasmania

Hobart

Bass Str.

T. 480 m.

Christchurch

Wellington to Rio de Janeiro 5980 m.

Heard I.

Dunedin

Stewart I.

Bounty Is.

Antipodes I.

Auckland I.

Chatham Is.

Macquarie I.

Campbell I.

Kaiser Wilhelm II Land

Queen Mary Land

Wilkes Land

| A | 90 | B | 120 | C | 150 | D | 180 | E | 150 | F | 120 | G |

Ocean Currents

Principal Shipping Routes according to traffic

Distances given in Nautical Miles : One Nautical Mile (6080 ft.)

Seas open to Navigation the whole year

Principal Railways

Air Routes

MERCATO

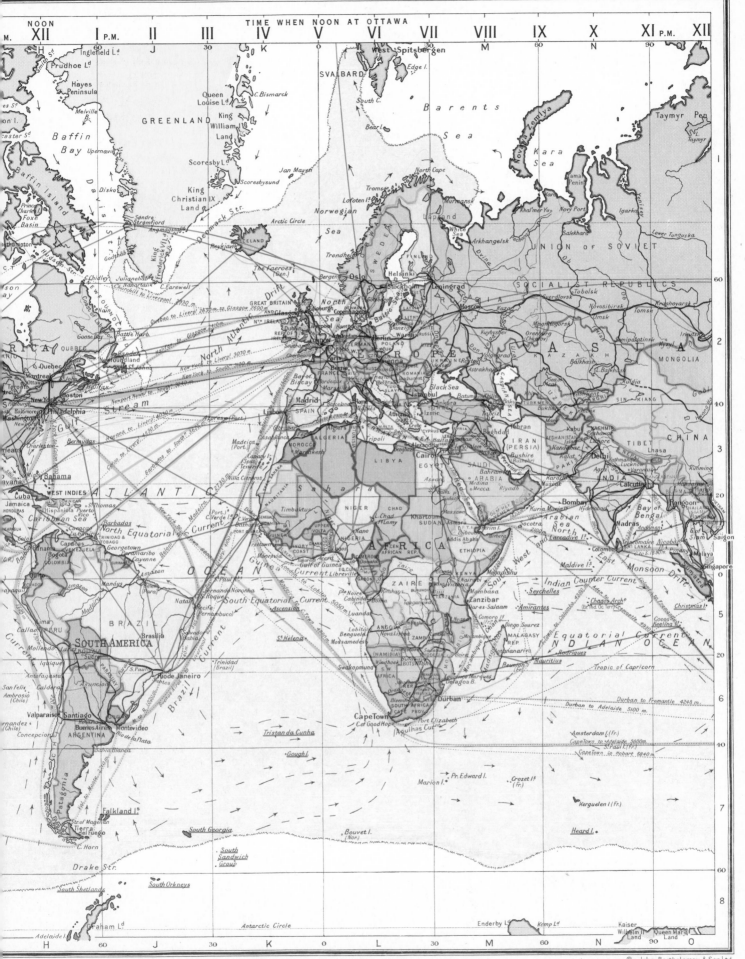

NOON
XII   I P.M.   II   III   IV   V   VI   VII   VIII   IX   X   XI P.M.   XII

JECTION

© – John Bartholomew & Son, Ltd.

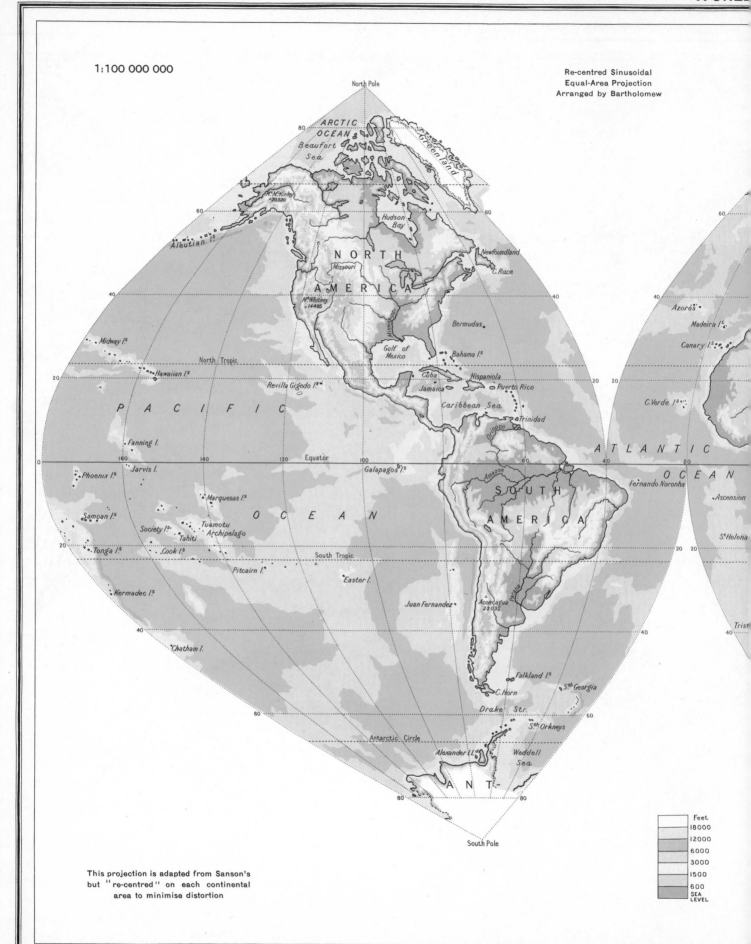

1:100 000 000

Re-centred Sinusoidal
Equal-Area Projection
Arranged by Bartholomew

North Pole

ARCTIC OCEAN

Beaufort Sea

Greenland

M^t McKinley 20.320

Hudson Bay

NORTH AMERICA

Aleutian I^s

Newfoundland

C. Race

Missouri

Mt Whitney 14.495

Mississippi

Bermudas

Midway I^s

North Tropic

Gulf of Mexico

Bahama I^s

Hawaiian I^s

Cuba

Hispaniola

Revilla Gigedo I^s

Jamaica

Puerto Rico

P A C I F I C

Caribbean Sea

Trinidad

Fanning I.

Orinoco

Galapagos I^s

Equator

Phoenix I^s

Jarvis I.

Amazon

SOUTH AMERICA

O C E A N

Marquesas I^s

Samoan I^s

Society I^s

Tahiti

Tuamotu Archipelago

Tonga I^s

Cook I^s

South Tropic

Pitcairn I.

Easter I.

Aconcagua 23.035

Paraná

Kermadec I^s

Juan Fernandez

Chatham I.

Falkland I^s

Sth Georgia

C. Horn

Drake Str.

Sth Orkneys

Antarctic Circle

Alexander I.L.

Weddell Sea

ANT-

South Pole

A T L A N T I C

Azores

Madeira I^s

Canary I^s

C. Verde I^s

O C E A N

Fernando Noronha

Ascension

St Helena

Trist

This projection is adapted from Sanson's
but "re-centred" on each continental
area to minimise distortion

Feet	
	18000
	12000
	6000
	3000
	1500
	600
	SEA LEVEL

5

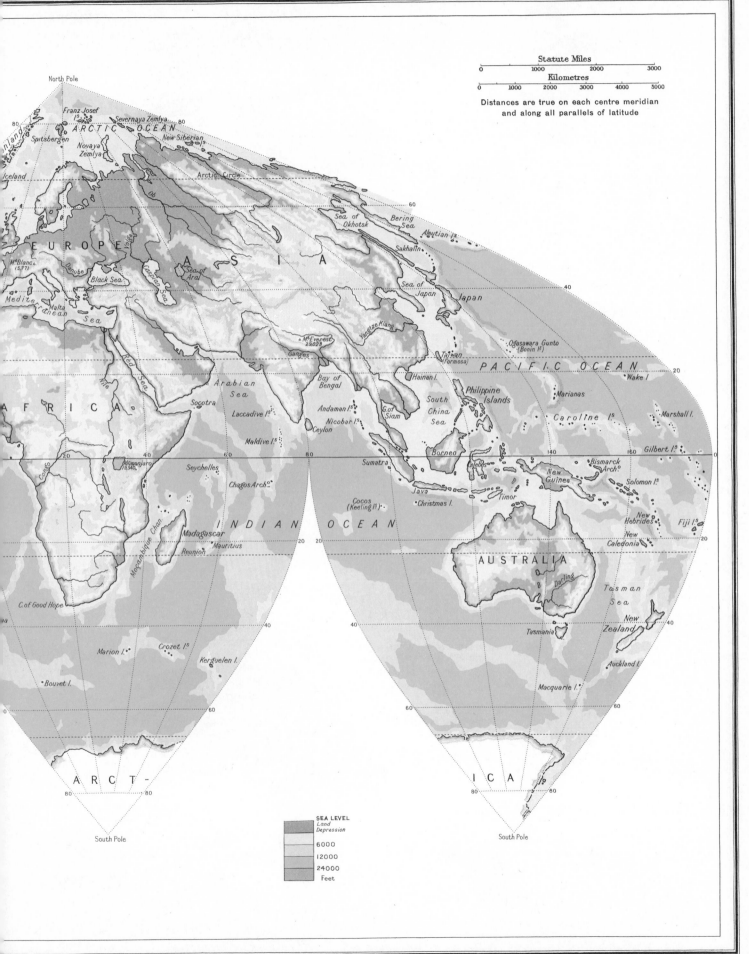

Statute Miles

| 0 | 1000 | 2000 | 3000 |

Kilometres

| 0 | 1000 | 2000 | 3000 | 4000 | 5000 |

Distances are true on each centre meridian
and along all parallels of latitude

North Pole

ARCTIC OCEAN

Franz Josef I^s

Severnaya Zemlya

Spitsbergen

New Siberian I^s

Novaya Zemlya

Iceland

Arctic Circle

Ob

EUROPE

ASIA

Sea of Okhotsk

Bering Sea

Aleutian I^s

Sakhalin

Mt Blanc
15,771

Black Sea

Sea of Aral

Caspian Sea

Volga

Danube

Sea of Japan

Japan

Mediterranean Sea

Malta

Red Sea

Mt Everest 29,028

Ganges

Yangtze Kiang

Ogasawara Gunto (Bonin I^s)

PACIFIC OCEAN

Taiwan (Formosa)

Nile

AFRICA

Arabian Sea

Bay of Bengal

Hainan I.

Wake I.

Socotra

Laccadive I^s

Andaman I^s

G. of Siam

South China Sea

Philippine Islands

Marianas

Caroline I^s

Marshall I.

Nicobar I^s

Ceylon

Maldive I^s

Borneo

Gilbert I^s

Kilimanjaro 19,340

Congo

Seychelles

Sumatra

Celebes

New Guinea

Bismarck Arch^o

Chagos Arch^o

Java

Timor

Solomon I^s

INDIAN OCEAN

Cocos (Keeling I^s)

Christmas I.

New Hebrides

Fiji I^s

Mocambique Chan.

Madagascar

Mauritius

New Caledonia

Reunion

AUSTRALIA

Darling

Tasman Sea

C. of Good Hope

Marion I.

Crozet I^s

Kerguelen I.

Tasmania

New Zealand

Auckland I.

Bouvet I.

Macquarie I.

ARCT-

ICA

South Pole

South Pole

SEA LEVEL
Land Depression

6000

12000

24000

Feet

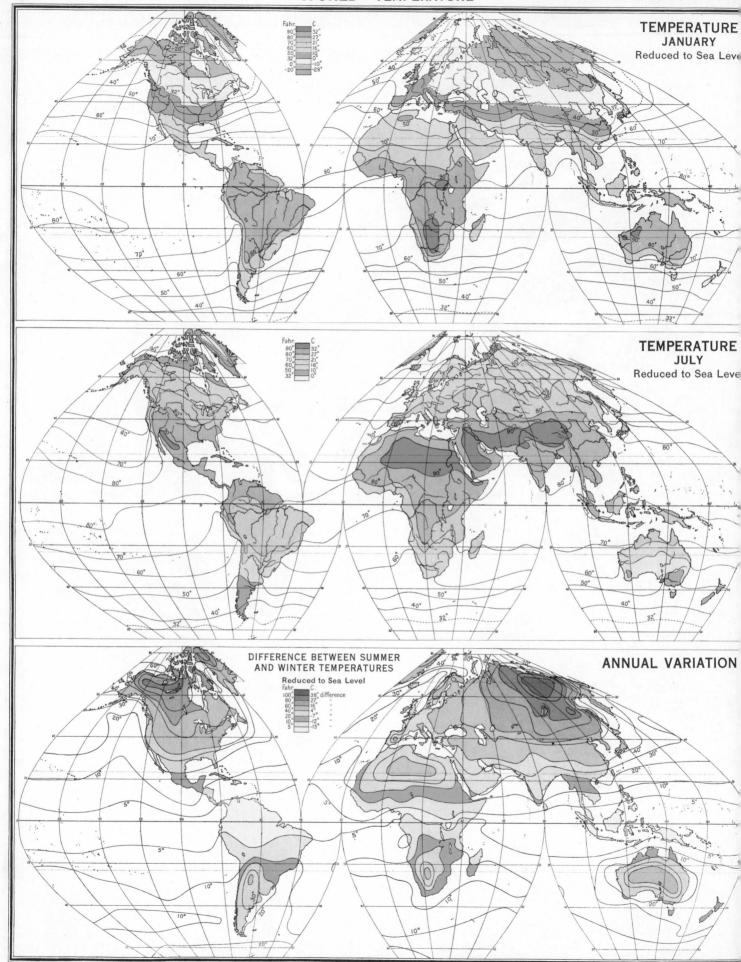

TEMPERATURE
JANUARY
Reduced to Sea Level

Fahr.	C
90°	32°
80°	27°
70°	21°
60°	16°
50°	10°
32°	0°
0°	-10°
-20°	-29°

TEMPERATURE
JULY
Reduced to Sea Level

Fahr.	C
90°	32°
80°	27°
70°	21°
60°	16°
50°	10°
32°	0°

ANNUAL VARIATION

DIFFERENCE BETWEEN SUMMER
AND WINTER TEMPERATURES
Reduced to Sea Level

Fahr.	C	
100°	38°	difference
80°	27°	
60°	16°	
40°	-7°	
20°	-12°	
10°	-15°	
5°		

The Edinburgh Geographical Institute

Interrupted Sinusoidal Equal Area Projection (Bartholomew)

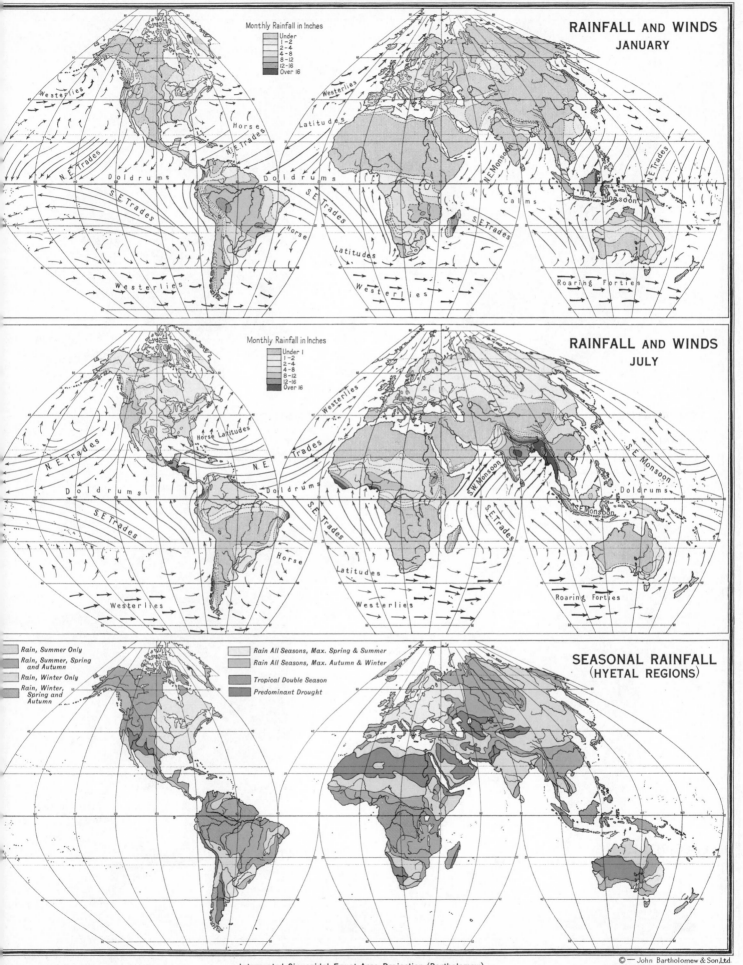

RAINFALL AND WINDS
JANUARY

Monthly Rainfall in Inches
Under 1
1-2
2-4
4-8
8-12
12-16
Over 16

RAINFALL AND WINDS
JULY

Monthly Rainfall in Inches
Under 1
1-2
2-4
4-8
8-12
12-16
Over 16

SEASONAL RAINFALL
(HYETAL REGIONS)

Rain, Summer Only
Rain, Summer, Spring and Autumn
Rain, Winter Only
Rain, Winter, Spring and Autumn

Rain All Seasons, Max. Spring & Summer
Rain All Seasons, Max. Autumn & Winter
Tropical Double Season
Predominant Drought

Interrupted Sinusoidal Equal Area Projection (Bartholomew)

© — John Bartholomew & Son, Ltd.

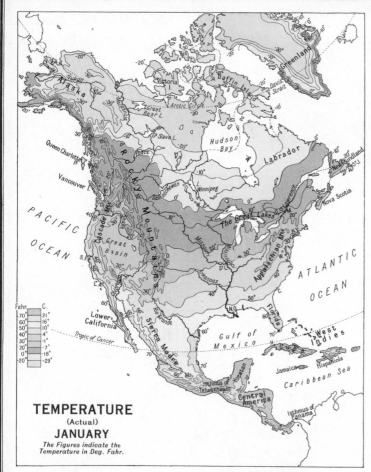

TEMPERATURE
(Actual)
JANUARY
*The Figures indicate the
Temperature in Deg. Fahr.*

Fahr.	C.
70°	21°
60°	16°
50°	10°
40°	4°
30°	-1°
20°	-7°
10°	-18°
-20°	-29°

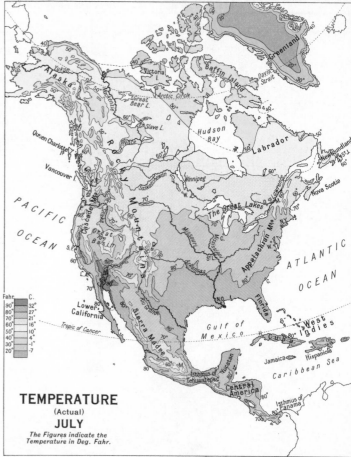

TEMPERATURE
(Actual)
JULY
*The Figures indicate the
Temperature in Deg. Fahr.*

Fahr.	C.
90°	32°
80°	27°
70°	21°
60°	16°
50°	10°
40°	4°
30°	-1°
20°	-7°

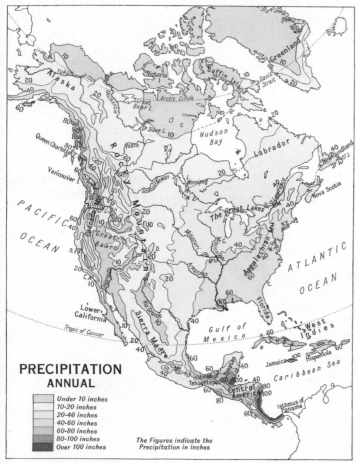

PRECIPITATION
ANNUAL

- Under 10 inches
- 10-20 inches
- 20-40 inches
- 40-60 inches
- 60-80 inches
- 80-100 inches
- Over 100 inches

*The Figures indicate the
Precipitation in inches*

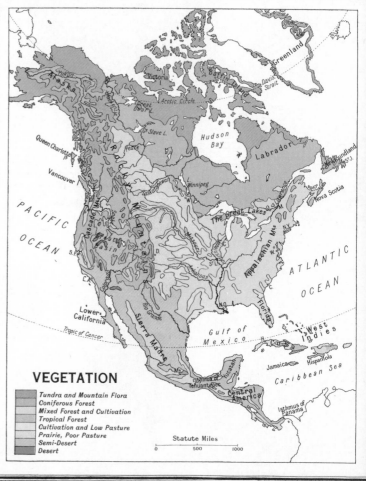

VEGETATION

- Tundra and Mountain Flora
- Coniferous Forest
- Mixed Forest and Cultivation
- Tropical Forest
- Cultivation and Low Pasture
- Prairie, Poor Pasture
- Semi-Desert
- Desert

Statute Miles
0   500   1000

The Geographical Institute, Edinburgh

1 : 75 000 000

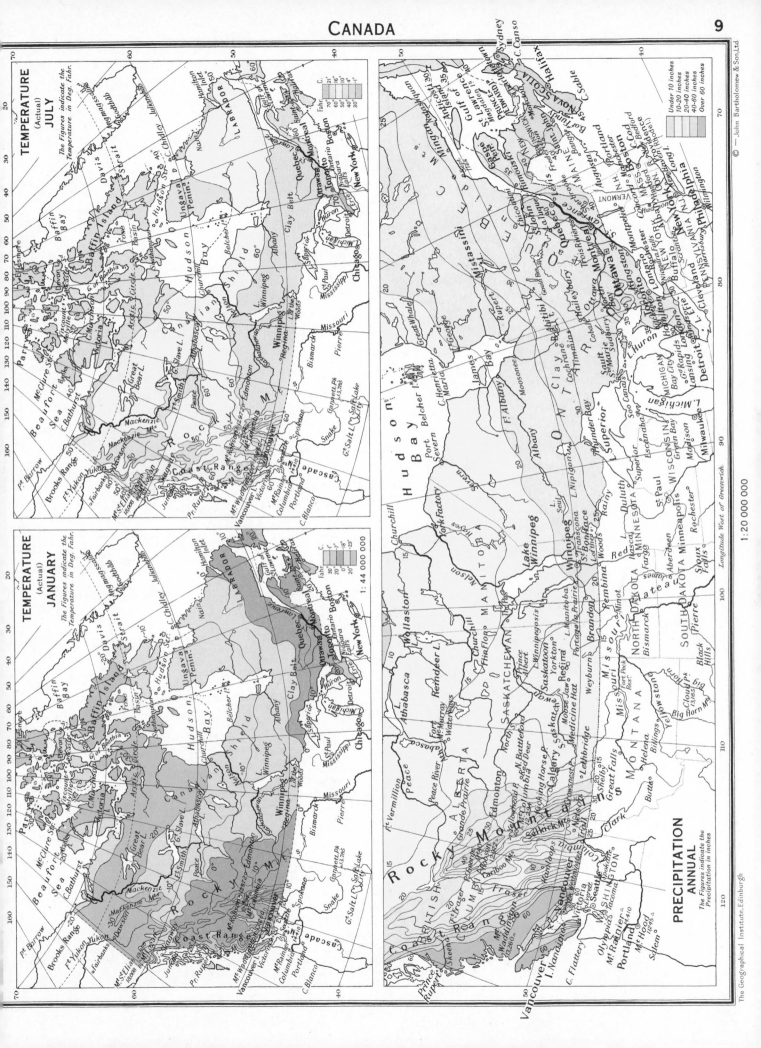

TEMPERATURE (Actual) JULY

The Figures indicate the Temperature in Deg. Fahr.

TEMPERATURE (Actual) JANUARY

The Figures indicate the Temperature in Deg. Fahr.

1:44 000 000

PRECIPITATION ANNUAL

The Figures indicate the Precipitation in inches

Under 10 inches
10–20 inches
20–40 inches
40–60 inches
Over 60 inches

1:20 000 000

Longitude West of Greenwich

© — John Bartholomew & Son,Ltd.

The Geographical Institute.Edinburgh

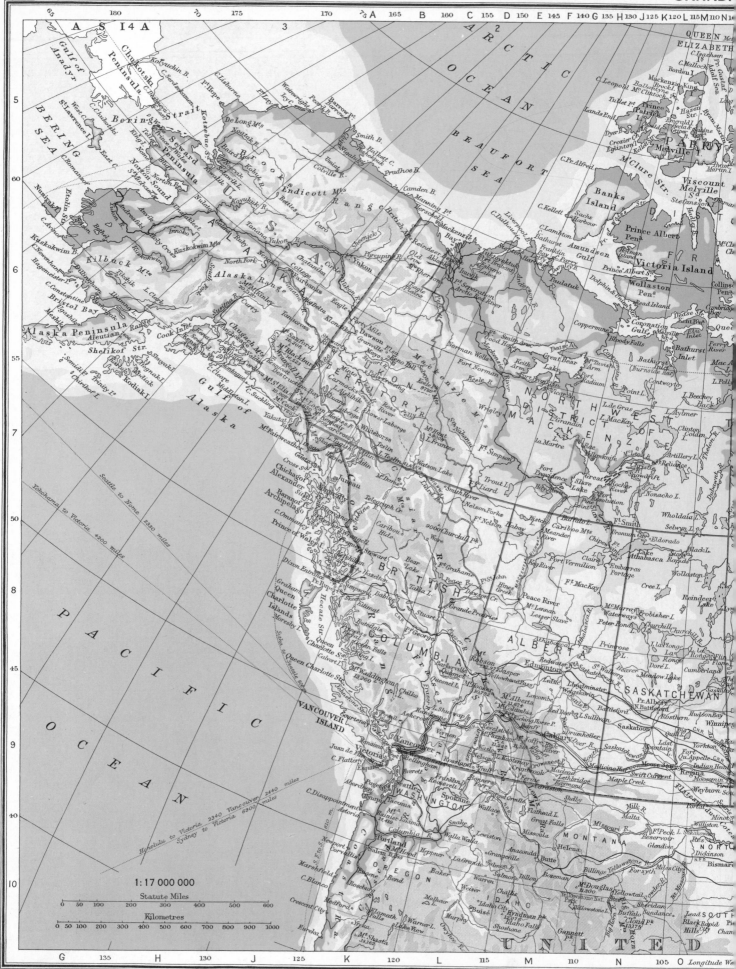

1:17 000 000

Statute Miles

Kilometres

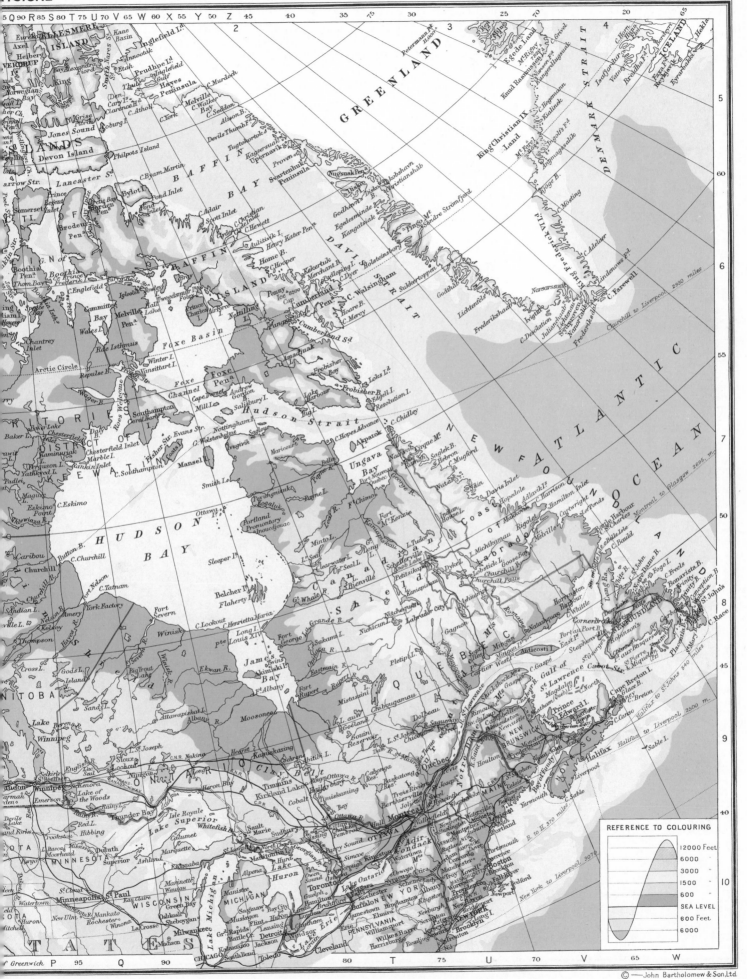

REFERENCE TO COLOURING

12000 Feet	
6000 "	
3000 "	
1500 "	
600 "	
SEA LEVEL	
600 Feet.	
6000 "	

© —John Bartholomew & Son,Ltd.

MACKENZIE

MACKENZIE DISTRICT

Great Slave Lake

Yellowknife

Wood Buffalo Nat. Park

Caribou Mountains

Clear Hills

MACKENZIE TERRITORY

Mackenzie River

Mackenzie Mts.

Fort Simpson

Fort Liard

Nelson Forks

Fort Nelson

Alaska Highway

ROCKY MOUNTAINS

Selwyn Mts.

YUKON TERRITORY

Pelly Mts.

Watson Lake

Liard River

Muncho Lake

Stone Mt. Park

Roosevelt

OMINECA Mts.

Whitehorse

Alaska Highway

Teslin

Atlin Lake

Carcross

Skagway

Cassiar Mts.

Stikine Ranges

Telegraph Creek

Stikine River

Dease Lake

COAST MOUNTAINS

JUNEAU

Lynn Canal

Stephens Pass.

Chatham Str.

SKEENA MOUNTAINS

Takla Lake

Babine Lake

CASSIAR MTS.

Peace River

Grande Prairie

Lesser Slave L.

Dixon Entrance

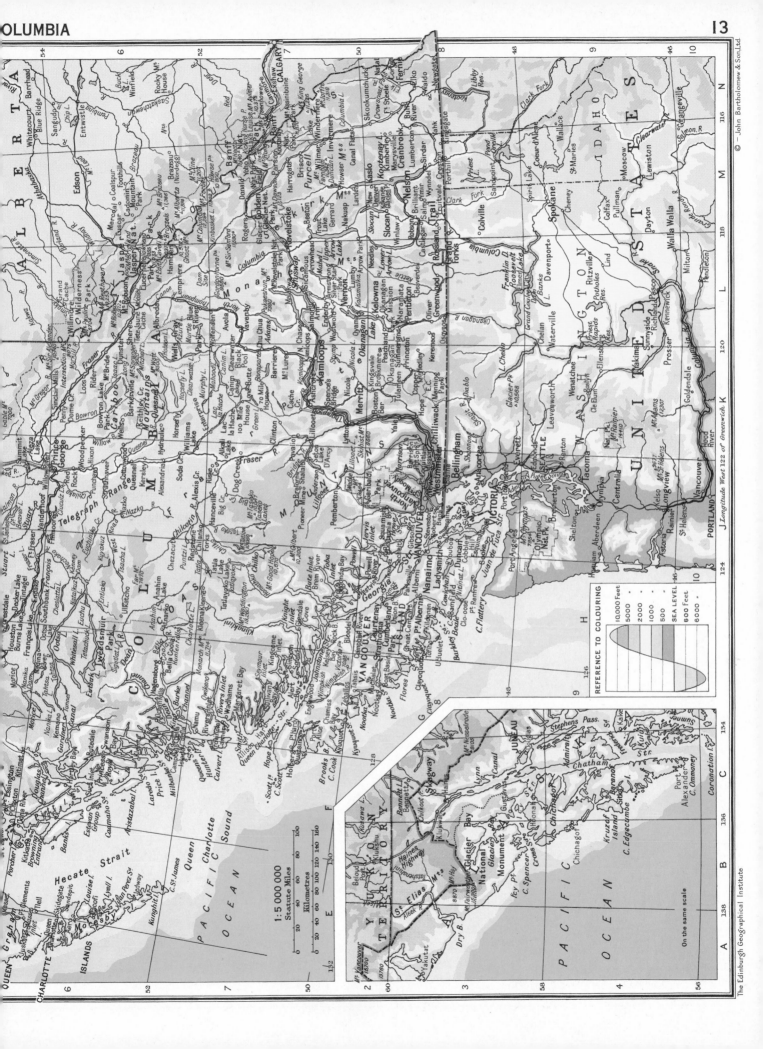

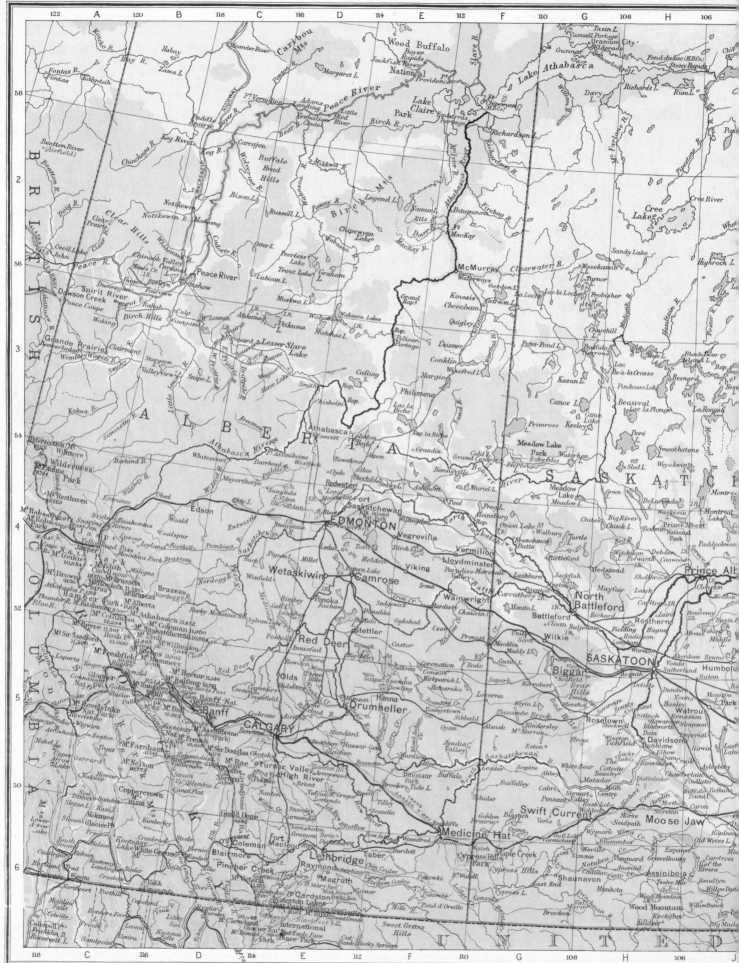

Note : The initials I.R.

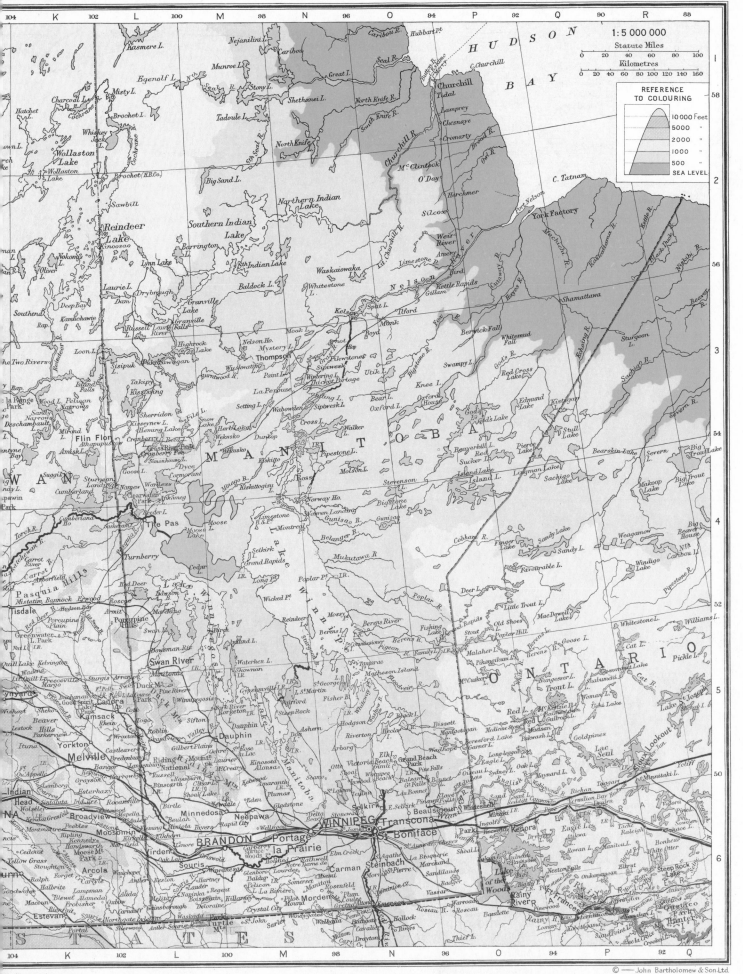

Indian Reservation.

Sault Ste. Marie
SOO CANALS
St. Mary's
Sault Ste. Marie
Dafter
Garden River
Echo Bay
St. George
Rydal Bank
Desbarats
Dunn Valley
Tunnel Dam
Matinenda L.
Quirke L.
Elliot L.
Elliot Lake
Nesterville
Iron Bridge
Spragge
Cutler
Webbwood
C.P.R.
Creighton Mine
Victoria Mine
Dam
Nairn
Whitefish
Espanola
Panache
Garson
Falconbridge
SUDBURY
Copper Cliff
Coniston
Markstay
Field
Verner
Crystal F.
Sturgeon
North
Lake Nipiss

Richards Ldg.
Bruce Mines
Thessalon
Hilton
St. Joseph I.
Tenby Bay
Blind River
Algoma
Spanish
Massey
Burwash
Wanup
Burwash (Estaire)
Alban
Noelville
Restoule
Commanda
Arnstein

ALGOMA
Hessel
Raber
Detour
Drummond I.
Cockburn I.
North Channel
Barrie I.
Little Current
Sheguiandah
Whitefish Falls
KILLARNEY PROV. PARK
Pickerel River
Killarney
Key Junction
Pickerel
Rutter
Bigwood
C.N.R.
C.P.R.
Ludgate
Key Harbour
Port Loring
PARRY SOU
Island L.
Sund

Mackinac I.
Johnswood
Cockburn Island
Meldrum Bay
Gore Bay
Kagawong
MANITOULIN
Manitou
Wikwemikong
Britt
Byng Inlet
Dunchurch
Magne

Bois Blanc I.
Cheboygan
W. Duck I.
Evansville
Manitoulin Island
Big Lake
Manitowaning
THIRTY
Ardbeg
Boakview
Waubamik
Magnetawan

Black L.
Onaway
Rogers City
Great Duck I.
CANADA
U.S.A.
Providence Bay
South Baymouth
South Bay
Lonely I.
Fitzwilliam I.
Pointe au Baril Sta.
GEORGIAN BAY
Shawanaga
Nobel
KILLBEAR POINT PR. PARK
Parry Sound
COASTLER PR. PARK
Spruc

Posen
Hillman
Alpena
LAKE
Main Channel
Cove I.
GEORGIAN BAY IS. NAT. PK.
Flowerpot I.
Tobermory
Cabot Head
Franklin I.
THOUSAND ISLANDS
Depot Harbour
Parry I. ISLANDS
Parry Sound
Otter Lake
Lake Joseph
MacTier
Lake Mu

Atlanta
Ossineke
North Pt.
Thunder Bay
Cape Hurd
Dyer Bay
Dyer Bay
Cape Chin
Isthmus Bay
Western Is.
Bala

Au Sable
Fairview
Mio
Barton City
Harrisville
HURON
Stokes Bay
Lions Head
Edenhurst
Cape Croker
Colboy B.
Christian I.
GEORGIAN BAY IS. NAT. PARK (BEAUSOLEIL I.)

581 feet above sea level

St. Helen
West Branch
Oscoda
Au Sable Pt.
Red Bay
Wiarton
Chiefs Pt.
Shallow Lake
Owen Sound
Nottawasaga Bay
Penetanguishene
Midland
Waubaushene

Alger
Omer
Tawas City
Hepworth
Allenford
Southampton
Port Elgin
Owen Sound
Thornbury
Meaford
Wasaga Beach
Collingwood
Elmvale
Stayner
Mid

Standish
Port Austin
Pt. Aux Barques
Clark Point
Amberley
Douglas Point
INVERHURON NAT. PARK
Kincardine
Tiverton
Cargill
BRUCE
Williamsford
Tara
Chatsworth
Holland Centre
Paisley
Chesley
Elmwood
GREY
Kimberley
Markdale
Flesherton
Duntroon
Creemore
SIMCOE
Angus
Cookstown
Honeywood
Hillsb

Bay Port
Bad Axe
Harbor Beach
Ripley
Walkerton
Teeswater
Mildmay
Hanover
Durham
Holstein
Dundalk
Corbetton
Shelburne
Alliston
DUFFERIN

Bay City
Unionville
Caro
Palms
Lucknow
Gorrie
Harriston
Clifford
Mount Forest
Laurel
Orangeville
Bolton
Tottenham
R

Freeland
Reese
Port Sanilac
Wingham
Palmerston
Arthur
Erin
Grand Valley
Woodbri
PEEL
Brampton

Saginaw
Vassar
Clifford
Sandusky
Port Albert
Dungannon
Blyth
Brussels
WELLINGTON
Hillsburgh
Fergus
Acton
Georgetown
Milton
HALTON
Palermo

MICHIGAN
Cass
Flint
Genesee
Lapeer
Lakeport
Port Sanilac
Grand Bend
Dashwood
PINERY PROV. PARK
IPPERWASH PROV. PARK
Goderich
Dunlop
Londesborough
Walton
Conestoga L.
Drayton
Flora
Elmira
Rockwood
Guelph
Waterdown
Bro

Owosso
Corunna
Genesee
Lapeer
Imlay City
Thedford
Centralia
Park Hill
Granton
St. Marys
Hickson
Drumbo
Lynden
Dundas
Han

Flint
Oxford
Romeo
Sandusky
Forest
Arkona
Ilderton
Thamesford
Paris
BRANT
Caledonia

Williamston
Fenton
Pontiac
Mt. Clemens
Wyoming
Watford
Strathroy
Lucan
MIDDLESEX
OXFORD
Woodstock
Ingersoll
Burford
Brantford
LINC

Port Huron
Point Edward
Sarnia
Petrolia
Mt. Brydges
London
Dorchester
Norwich
HALDIMAND
Hagersville
Cayuga

St. Clair
Courtright
LAMBTON
Brigden
Alvinston
Lambeth
Belmont
Springfield
Delhi
Simcoe
Jarvis
Selkirk

Oxford
Howell
Pontiac
Sombra
Oil Springs
Inwood
Shedden
St. Thomas
Aylmer
NORFOLK
Vittoria
Port Dover
Nanticoke
Mait

Detroit
Wallaceburg
Dresden
Bothwell
Glencoe
Dutton
Stanley
Port Bruce
Port Burwell
Long Point Bay
LONG POINT PROV. PARK
Long Point

Chelsea
Sth. Lyon
Livonia
Lake St. Clair
Chatham
Paincourt
Thamesville
Rodney
Wallacetown
Port Stanley
St. Williams
Port Rowan

Ann Arbor
Ypsilanti
Tecumseh
Riverside
Windsor
Tilbury
Comber
Kent Bridge
Ridgetown
Morpeth
Blenheim
RONDEAU PROV. PARK
LAKE ERIE
Westfield

La Salle
ESSEX
Amherstburg
Harrow
Kingsville
Leamington
Essex
Cedar Springs
Merlin
Erieau
Pt. aux Pins
572 feet above Sea Level

Wheatley
Pigeon Bay
PT. PELEE NAT. PARK
Pt. Pelee

SAGINAW BAY
Thames
West Lorne
Thames R.
LAKE HURON

Longitude West 80 of Greenwich

The Geographical Institute, Edinburgh

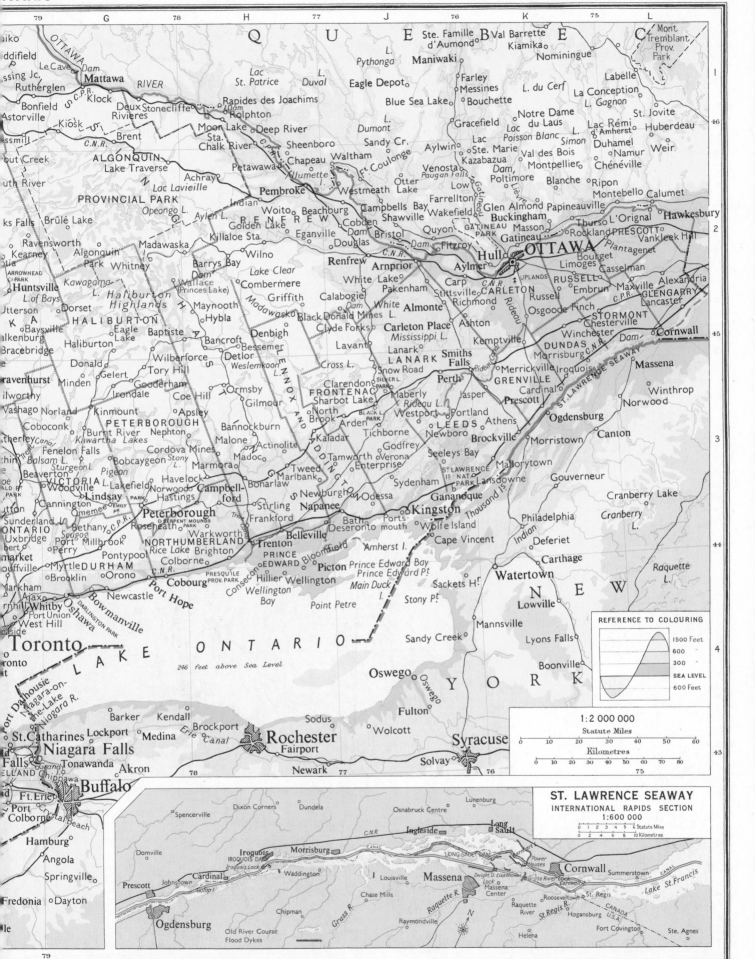

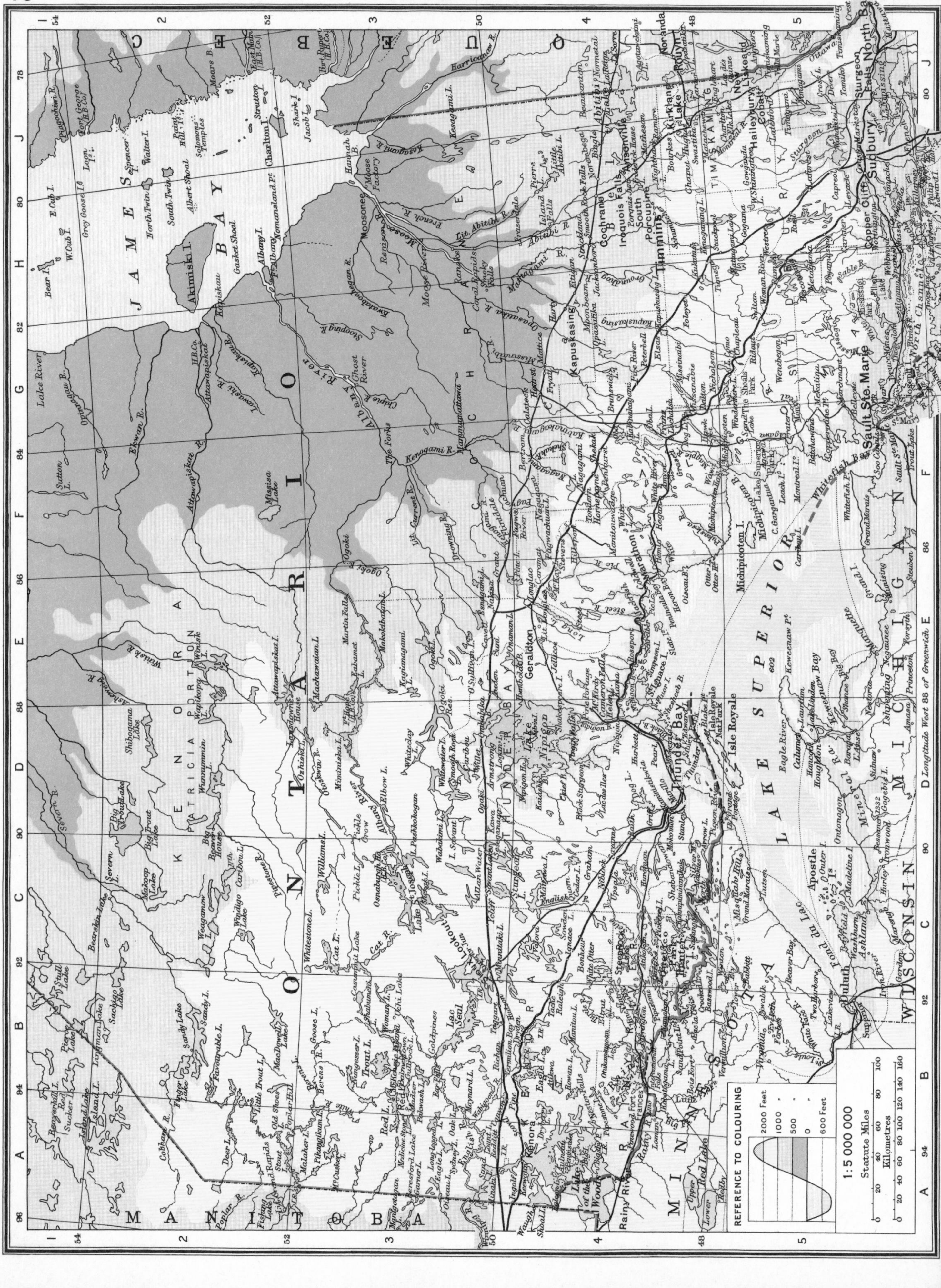

REFERENCE TO COLOURING
2000 Feet
1000
500
0
600 Feet
1:5 000 000
Statute Miles
Kilometres
D Longitude West 88 of Greenwich E
JAMES BAY
LAKE SUPERIOR
ONTARIO
MANITOBA
MINNESOTA
MICHIGAN
WISCONSIN
KENORA
PATRICIA PORTION
THUNDER BAY
COCHRANE
ALGOMA
SUDBURY
TIMISKAMING
Akimiski I.
Moosonee
Cochrane
Timmins
Kapuskasing
Hearst
Geraldton
Thunder Bay
Kenora
Sault Ste. Marie
Sudbury
North Bay
Rouyn
Noranda
Duluth
Isle Royale
Lake Nipigon
Lake of the Woods
Rainy River
Albany River
Attawapiskat R.
Michipicoten I.
Lake Superior

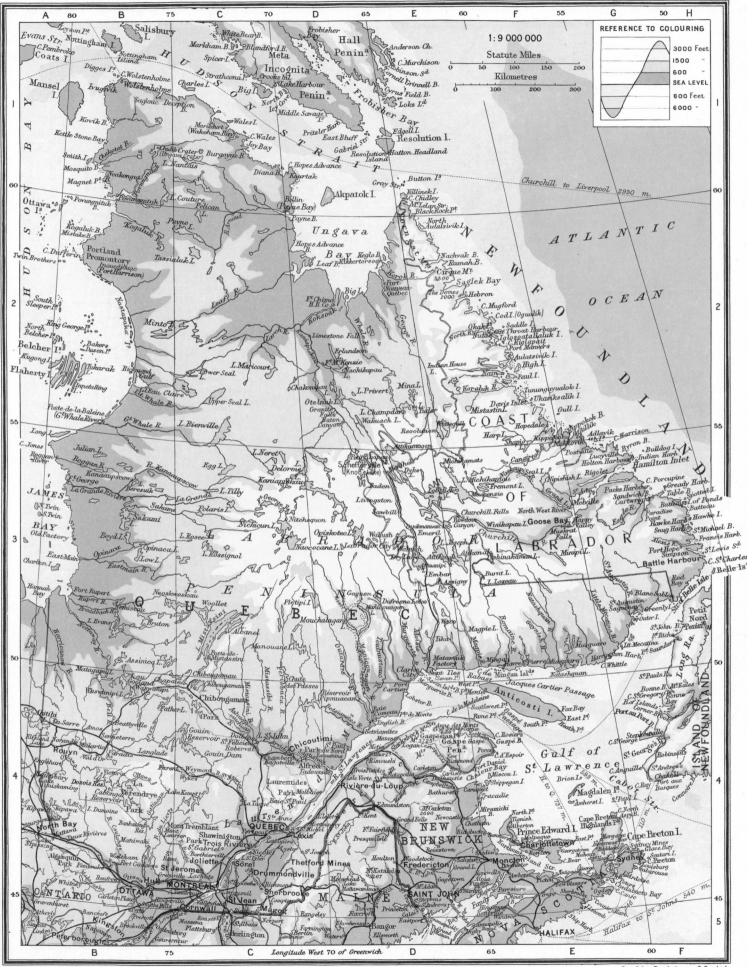

QUEBEC

REFERENCE TO COLOURING

3000 Feet
1500 "
600 "
SEA LEVEL
600 Feet
6000 "

1 : 9 000 000

Statute Miles

Kilometres

Longitude West 70 of Greenwich

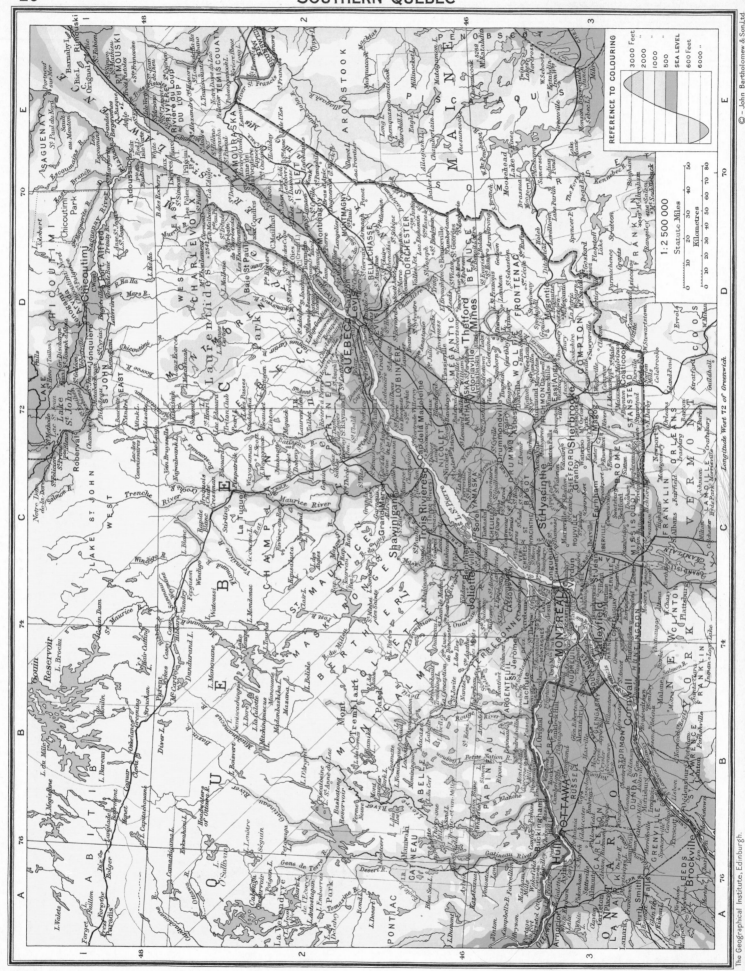

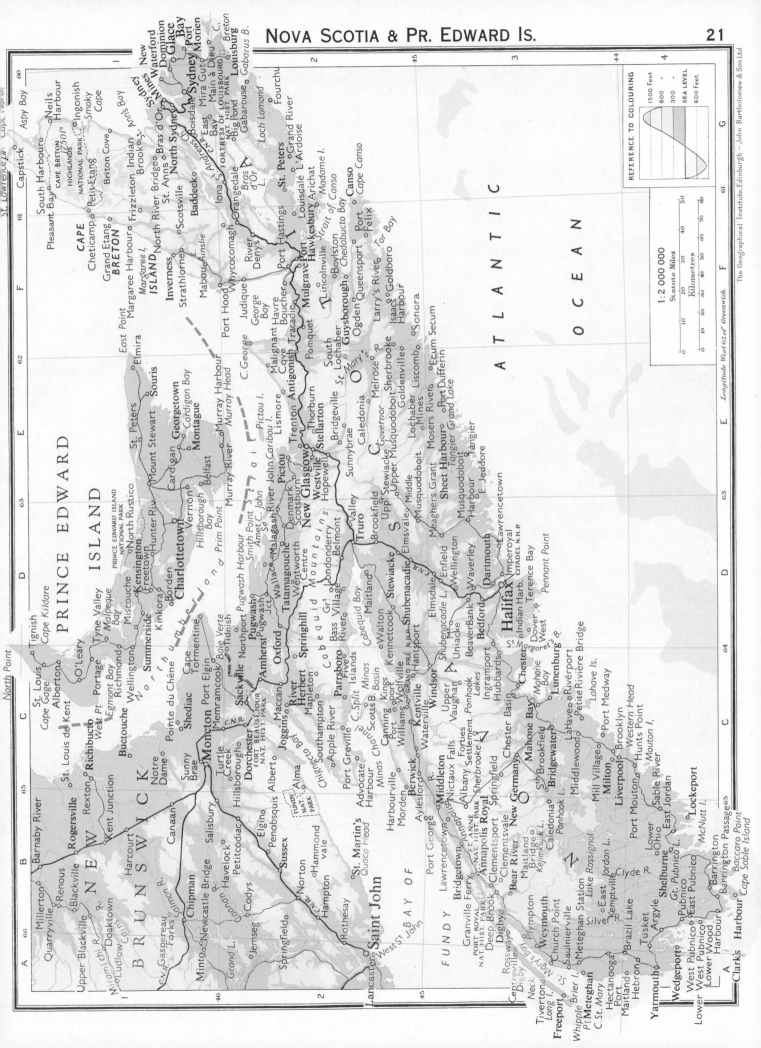

NOVA SCOTIA & PR. EDWARD IS.

REFERENCE TO COLOURING
1500 Feet · 600 · 300 · SEA LEVEL · 600 Feet

1:2 000 000
Statute Miles
Kilometres

The Geographical Institute, Edinburgh – John Bartholomew & Son Ltd.

Longitude West of Greenwich

ATLANTIC OCEAN

PRINCE EDWARD ISLAND

PRINCE EDWARD ISLAND NATIONAL PARK

CAPE BRETON ISLAND

CAPE BRETON HIGHLANDS NATIONAL PARK

NEW BRUNSWICK

BAY OF FUNDY

Saint John

Halifax

Dartmouth

Sydney

North Sydney

Sydney Mines

Glace Bay

Charlottetown

Summerside

Moncton

Truro

New Glasgow

Yarmouth

Canso

Strait of Canso

Northumberland Strait

Bras d'Or Lake

FUNDY NAT. PARK

FORT BEAUSÉJOUR NAT. HIST. PARK

FORT ANNE NAT. HIST. PARK

GRAND PRÉ N.H.P.

PORT ROYAL NAT. HIST. PARK

FORTRESS OF LOUISBOURG NAT. HIST. PARK

KEJIMKUJIK NAT. PARK

CITADEL N.H.P.

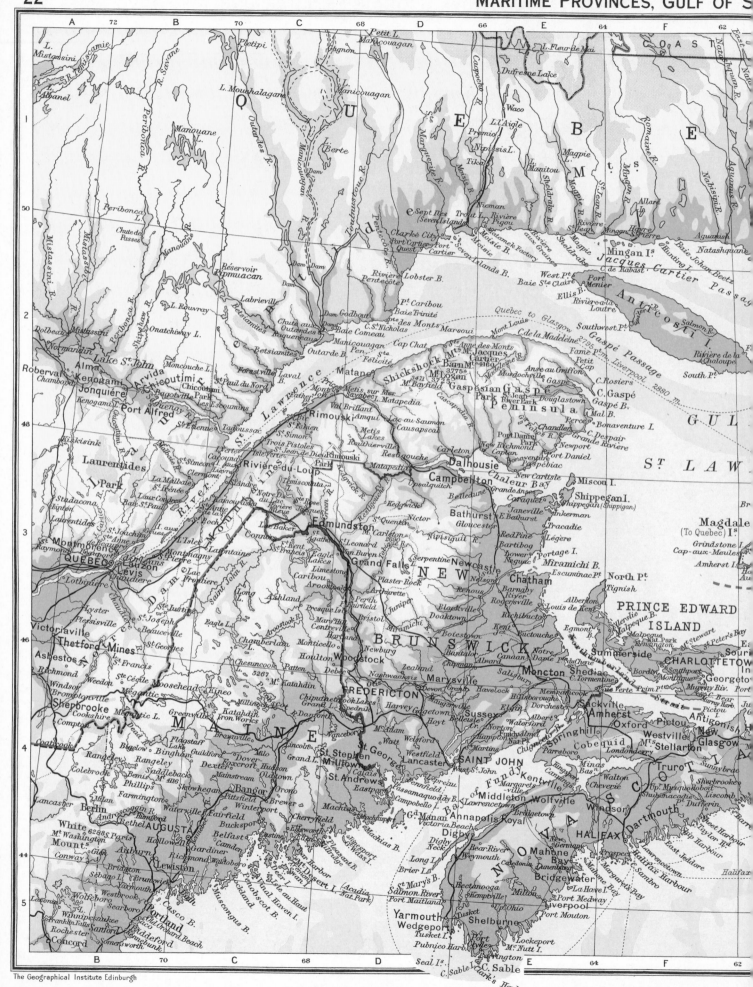

LABRADOR

ISLAND OF NEWFOUNDLAND

Newfoundland Peninsula
Long Range Mts.
White Bay
Notre Dame Bay
Bonavista Bay
Trinity Bay
Conception Bay
ST. JOHN'S
Avalon Pen.
Placentia Bay
Fortune Bay
St. Mary's Bay

ST-PIERRE & MIQUELON (F.R.)
Miquelon
St-Pierre
Langlade

Cabot Strait

Cape Breton I.
Cape Breton Highlands Nat. Pk.
Sydney Mines
New Waterford
Glace Bay
North Sydney
Sydney
Louisburg

Sable I.
(To Nova Scotia)

A T L A N T I C

O C E A N

Liverpool 2485, Glasgow 2410 m.

Halifax to St. Johns 540 m.

East Spit
West Pt.

Longitude West 60 of Greenwich

REFERENCE TO COLOURING
5000 Feet
2000 "
1000 "
500 "
SEA LEVEL
600 Feet

1:4 000 000
Statute Miles
0 20 40 60 80 100
Kilometres
0 20 40 60 80 100 120 140 160

© —John Bartholomew & Son, Ltd.

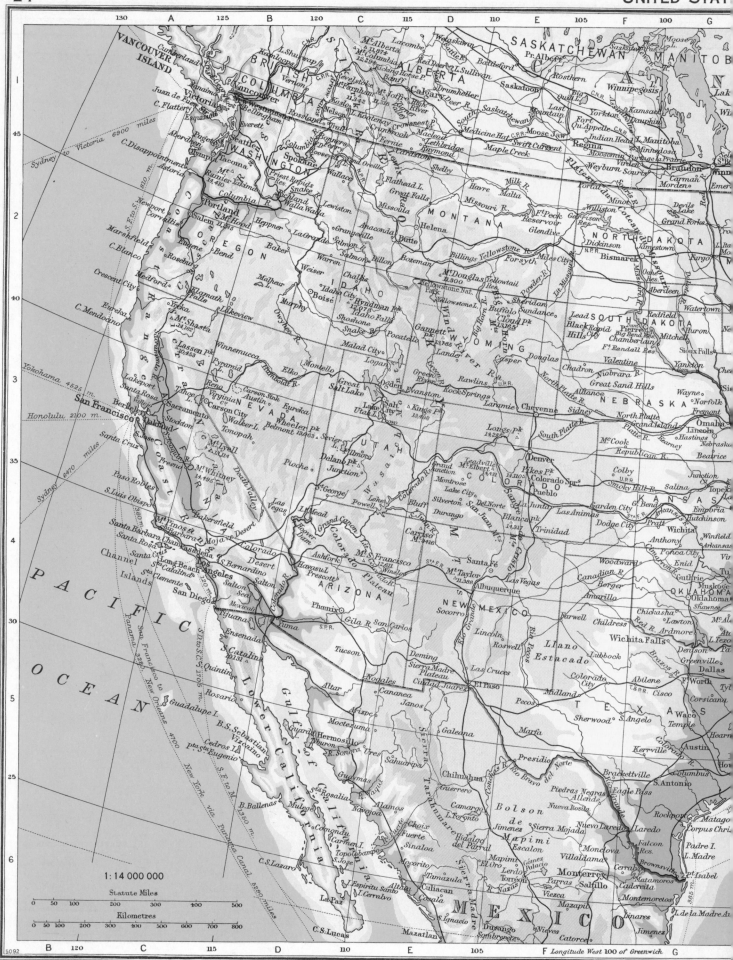

PACIFIC

OCEAN

1:14 000 000

Statute Miles

0 50 100   200   300   400   500

Kilometres

0 50 100 200   300   400   500   600   700   800

Longitude West 100 of Greenwich

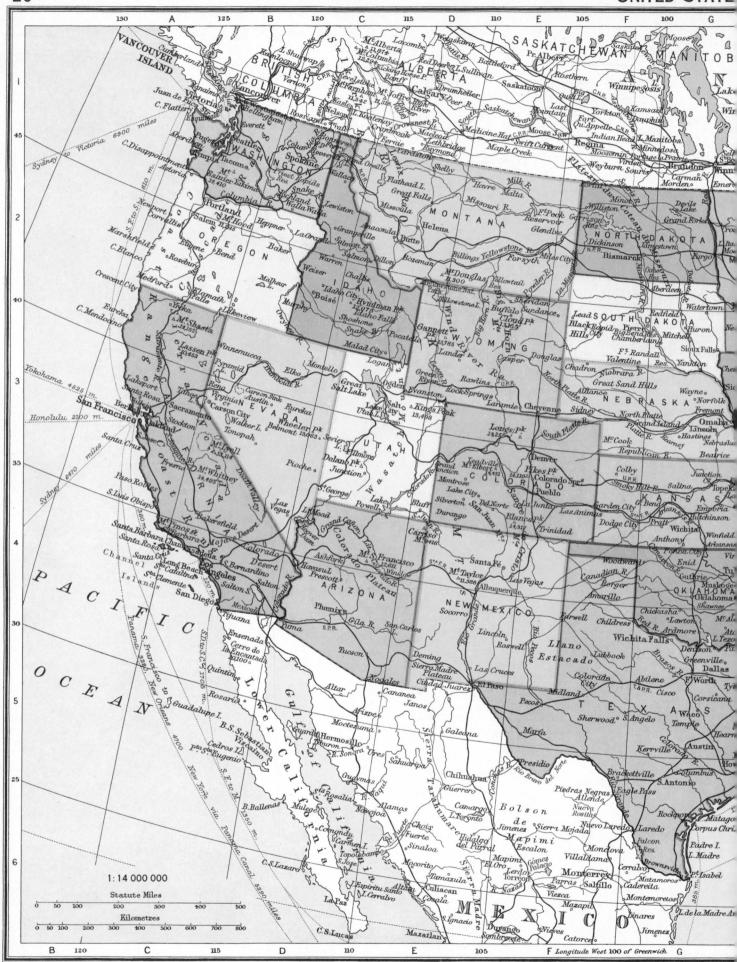

1:14 000 000

Statute Miles

Kilometres

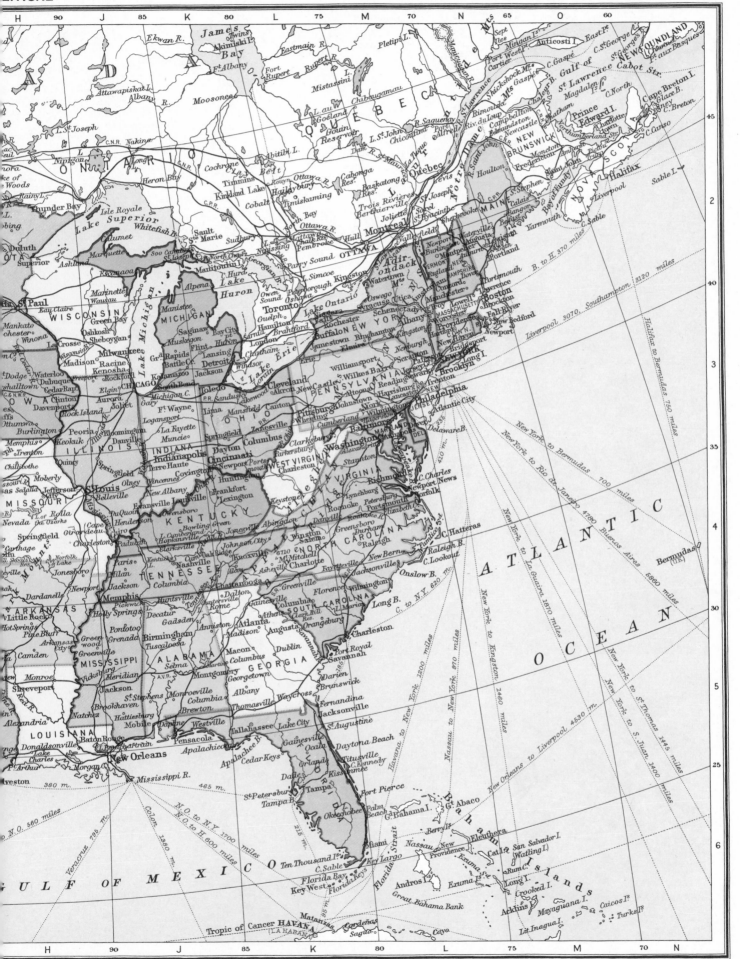

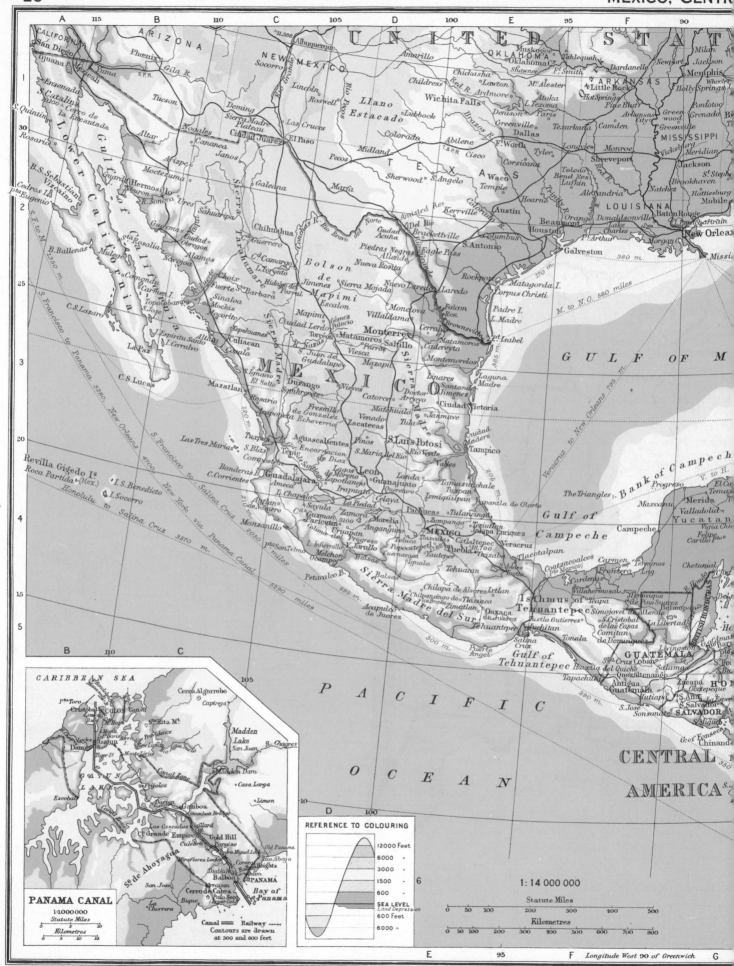

PANAMA CANAL

1:1,000,000

Statute Miles
0   5   10   15   20

Kilometres
0   5   10   15   20   25

Canal ═══ Railway ·····
Contours are drawn
at 300 and 600 feet

REFERENCE TO COLOURING

12000 Feet
6000 "
3000 "
1500 "
600 "
SEA LEVEL
Land Depression
600 Feet
6000 "

1 : 14 000 000

Statute Miles
0   50   100   200   300   400   500

Kilometres
0   50   100   200   300   400   500   600   700   800

Longitude West 90 of Greenwich

The Edinburgh Geographical Institute

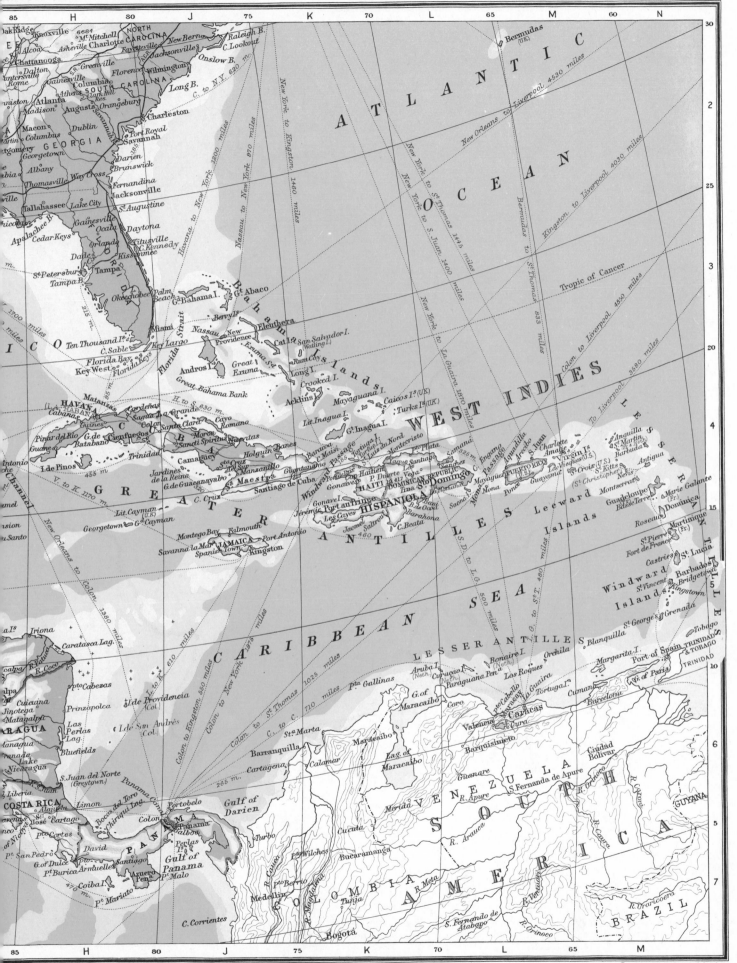

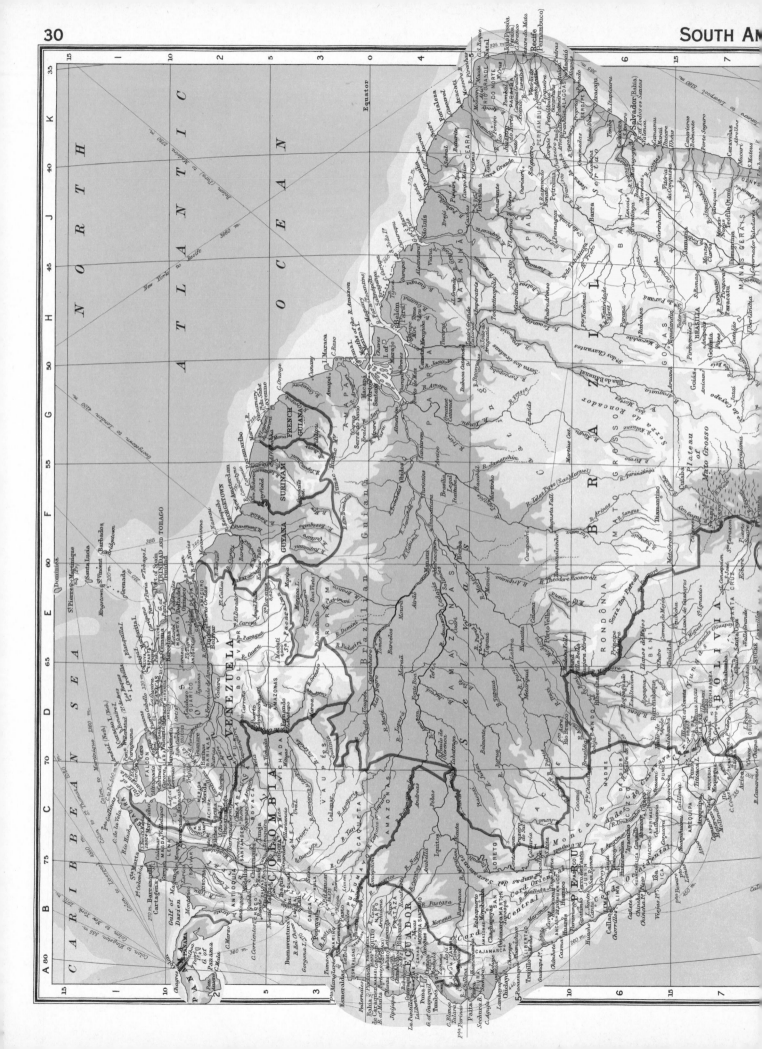

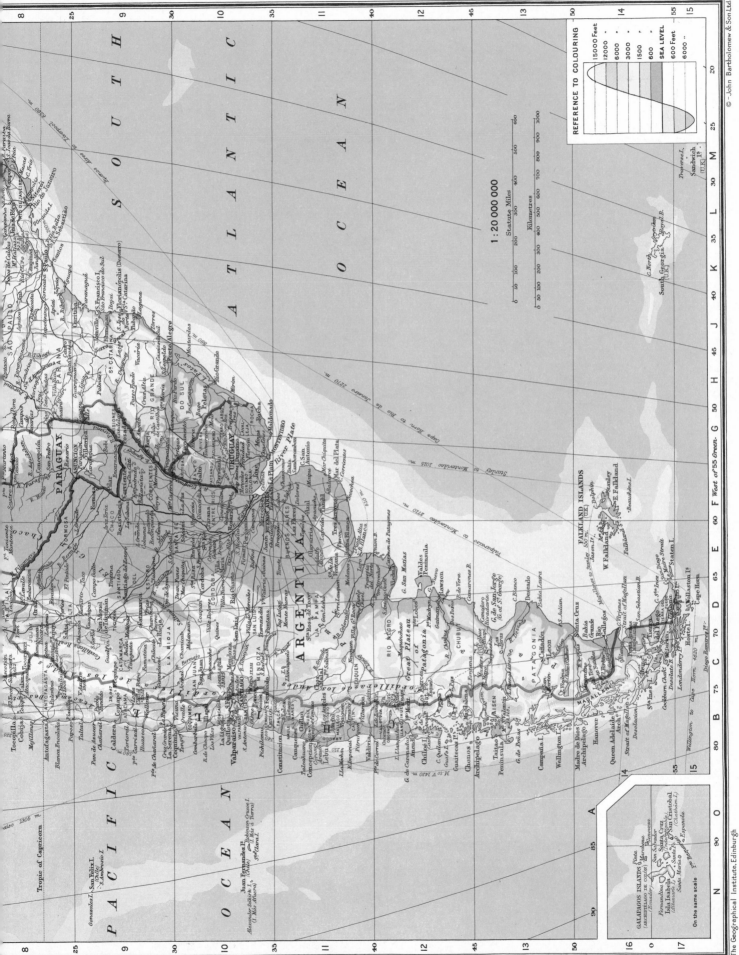

REFERENCE TO COLOURING

| 15000 Feet |
| 12000 " |
| 6000 " |
| 3000 " |
| 1500 " |
| 600 " |
| SEA LEVEL |
| 600 Feet |
| 600 " |

1 : 20 000 000

Statute Miles

Kilometres

SOUTH ATLANTIC OCEAN

PACIFIC OCEAN

PARAGUAY

ARGENTINA

URUGUAY

SÃO PAULO

RIO GRANDE DO SUL

RIO NEGRO

CHUBUT

PATAGONIA

Great Plateau of Patagonia

Cordillera de los Andes

FALKLAND ISLANDS

Tropic of Capricorn

Juan Fernandez I.ᵃ (Chile)

GALAPAGOS ISLANDS (ARCHIPIÉLAGO DE COLÓN) (Ecuador)

On the same scale

The Geographical Institute, Edinburgh

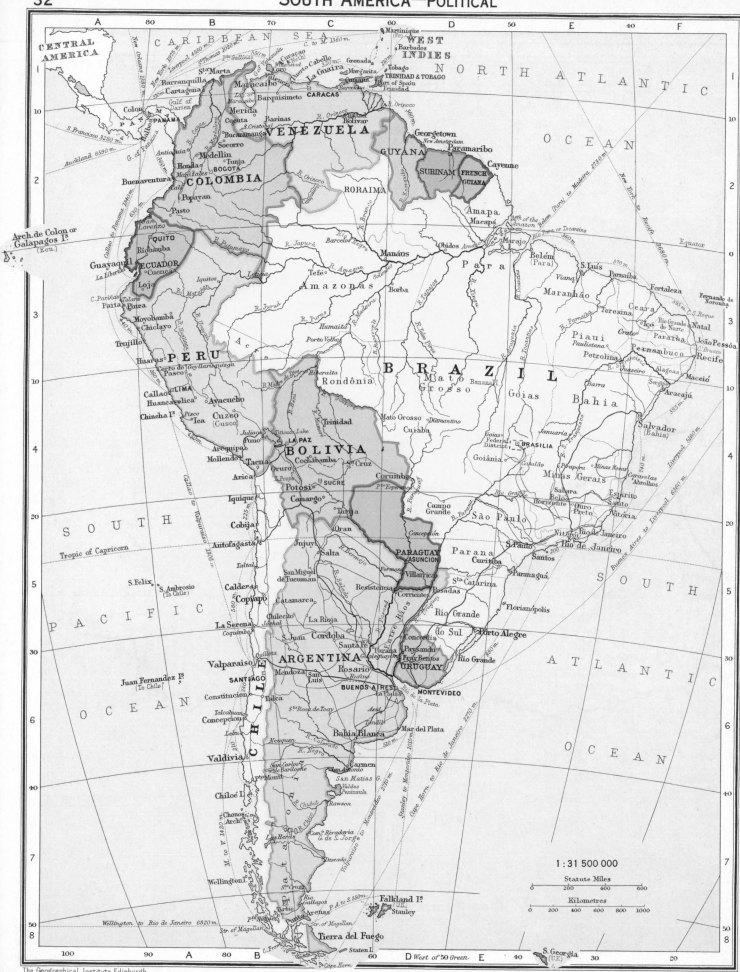

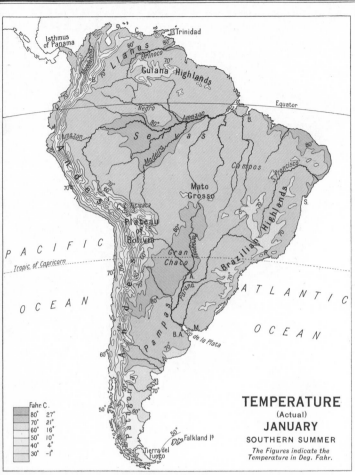

TEMPERATURE
(Actual)
JANUARY
SOUTHERN SUMMER
*The Figures indicate the
Temperature in Deg. Fahr.*

Fahr.	C.
80°	27°
70°	21°
60°	16°
50°	10°
40°	4°
30°	-1°

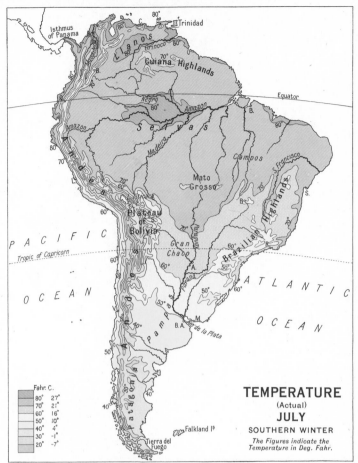

TEMPERATURE
(Actual)
JULY
SOUTHERN WINTER
*The Figures indicate the
Temperature in Deg. Fahr.*

Fahr.	C.
80°	27°
70°	21°
60°	16°
50°	10°
40°	4°
30°	-1°
20°	-7°

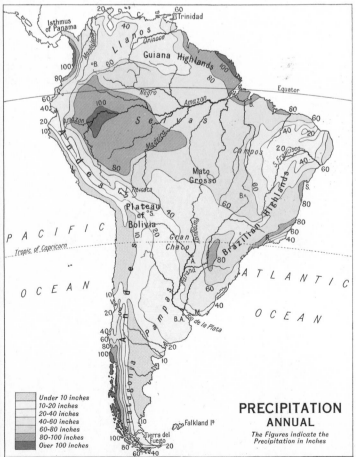

PRECIPITATION
ANNUAL
*The Figures indicate the
Precipitation in Inches*

- Under 10 inches
- 10-20 inches
- 20-40 inches
- 40-60 inches
- 60-80 inches
- 80-100 inches
- Over 100 inches

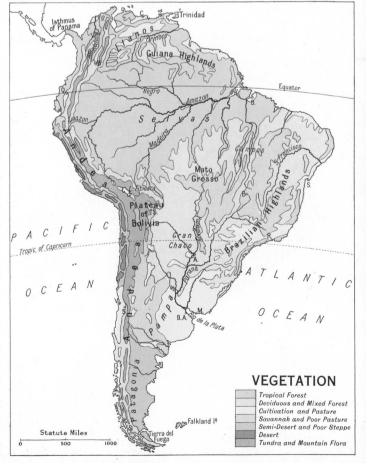

VEGETATION

- Tropical Forest
- Deciduous and Mixed Forest
- Cultivation and Pasture
- Savannah and Poor Pasture
- Semi-Desert and Poor Steppe
- Desert
- Tundra and Mountain Flora

Statute Miles
0   500   1000

e Geographical Institute, Edinburgh

© — John Bartholomew & Son, Ltd.

1 : 64 000 000

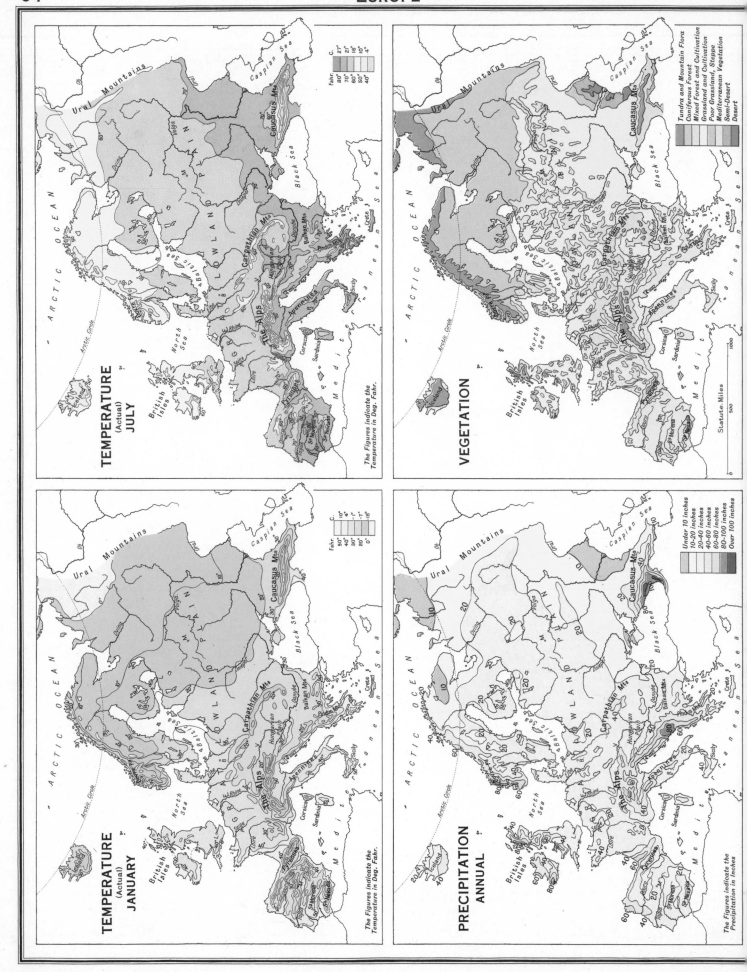

TEMPERATURE
(Actual)
JULY

The Figures indicate the
Temperature in Deg. Fahr.

Fahr.   C.
80°   27°
70°   21°
60°   16°
50°   10°
40°   4°

VEGETATION

Tundra and Mountain Flora
Coniferous Forest
Mixed Forest and Cultivation
Grassland and Cultivation
Poor Grassland, Steppe
Mediterranean Vegetation
Semi-Desert
Desert

Statute Miles
0   500   1000

TEMPERATURE
(Actual)
JANUARY

The Figures indicate the
Temperature in Deg. Fahr.

Fahr.   C.
50°   10°
40°   4°
30°   -1°
20°   -7°
0°   -18°

PRECIPITATION
ANNUAL

The Figures indicate the
Precipitation in Inches

Under 10 inches
10–20 inches
20–40 inches
40–60 inches
60–80 inches
80–100 inches
Over 100 inches

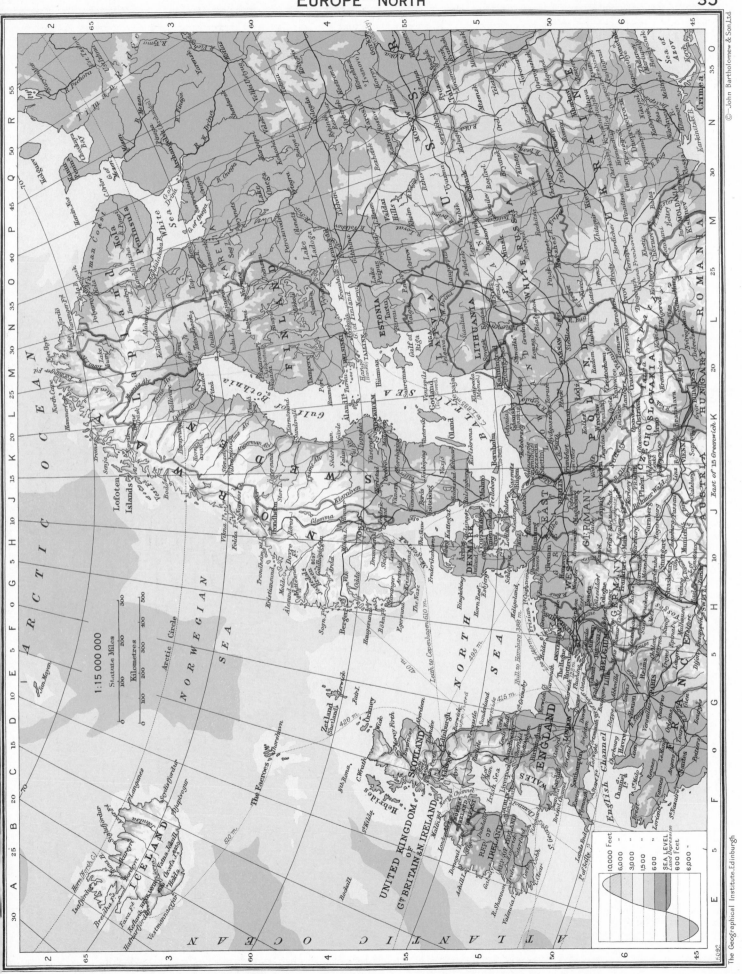

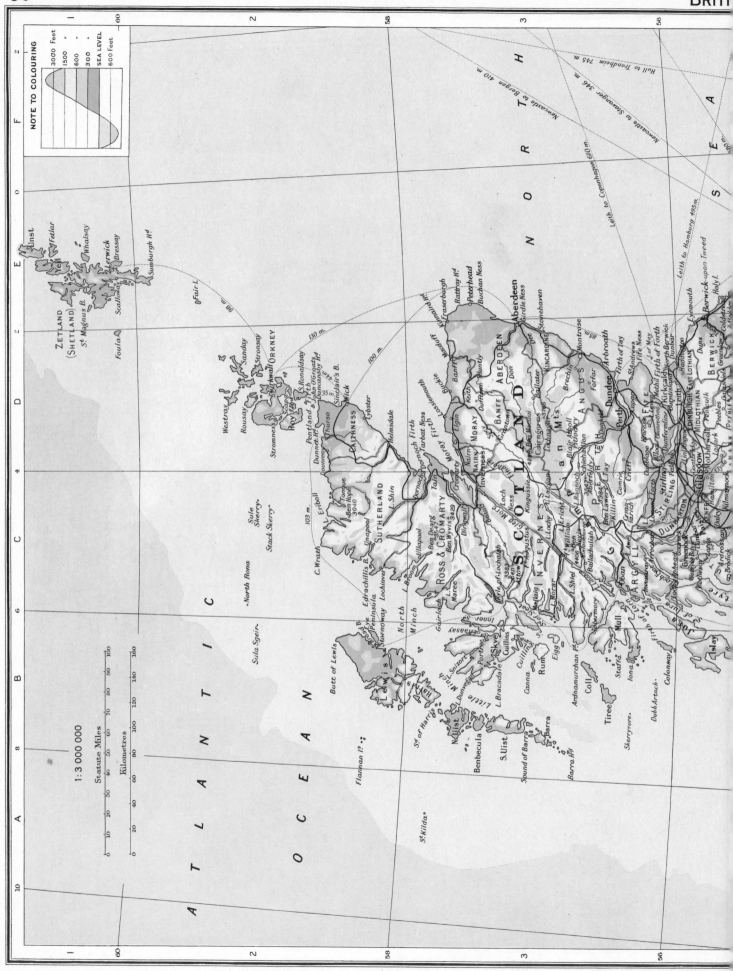

NOTE TO COLOURING

3000 Feet	
1500 "	
600 "	
300 "	
SEA LEVEL	
600 Feet	

1:3 000 000

Statute Miles

0 10 20 30 40 50 60 70 80 90 100

Kilometres

0 20 40 60 80 100 120 140 160

A T L A N T I C

O C E A N

N O R T H

S E A

ZETLAND
(SHETLAND)

Unst
Yell
Fetlar
Whalsay
Lerwick
Bressay
Scalloway
St. Magnus B.
Foula

Sumburgh Hd

Fair I.

ORKNEY
Westray
Rousay
Sanday
Stronsay
Stromness
Kirkwall
S. Ronaldshay
Pentland Firth
Duncansby Hd
John o'Groats
Hoy

North Rona
Sula Sgeir
Sule Skerry
Stack Skerry

C. Wrath
Durness
Edrachillis B.
Kylesku Peninsula
Unapool
L. Eriboll
Tongue
Ben Hope
3040
L. Shin
Stornoway
Lochinver
Ullapool
L. Broom

Flannan Is.
St. Kilda

Butt of Lewis
Lewis
Harris
S.d of Harris
N. Uist
Benbecula
S. Uist
Sound of Barra
Barra
Barra Hd

North Minch
Little Minch

Gairloch
L. Maree
Kyle of Lochalsh

CAITHNESS
Thurso
Dunnet Hd
Dounreay
Sinclair's B.
Wick
Lybster
Helmsdale

SUTHERLAND

ROSS & CROMARTY
Ben Dearg
3547
Ben Wyvis 3429
Dingwall
L. Fannich
Dornoch Firth
Tarbat Ness
Tain
Cromarty
Cromarty Firth
Beauly
Fort Augustus
Kingussie

INVERNESS

SCOTLAND

Skye
Portree
L. Snizort
Dunvegan
L. Bracadale
Cuillins
Rum
Canna
Eigg
Muck
Coll
Tiree
Ardnamurchan Pt
Staffa
Iona
Mull
Colonsay
Dubh Artach
Skerryvore

Ben Nevis
4406
L. Linnhe
Loch Ness
Kyle of Lochalsh
3383
Ben Attow
L. Mullardoch
Glen More
Invergarry
L. Garry
Ben Alder
3757
L. Ericht
L. Laggan
L. Rannoch
Schiehallion
3547
Ballachulish
Oban
Loch Awe
Blair Atholl
Pitlochry

Nairn
MORAY
Elgin
Forres
Lossiemouth
Buckie
BANFF
Keith
Banff
Macduff
Dufftown
Huntly

Cairngorm
Mts.
Braemar
ABERDEEN
Don
Dee

Fraserburgh
Rattray Hd
Peterhead
Buchan Ness

Aberdeen
Girdle Ness
Stonehaven

KINCARDINE
Ballater

Brechin
Forfar
ANGUS
Arbroath
Montrose
Dundee
Firth of Tay
PERTH
Perth
Crieff
Comrie
Ben Lawers
Killin
Loch Tay
Callander
Crianlarich
Loch Lomond

Stirling
STIRLING
Falkirk
Grangemouth
Alloa
Kincardine
Dunfermline
Kinross
Kirkcaldy
FIFE
St. Andrews
Fife Ness
Firth of Forth
North Berwick
Dunbar
EAST LOTHIAN
Haddington
MIDLOTHIAN
EDINBURGH
Leith
Linlithgow
Bathgate
Motherwell
Hamilton
GLASGOW
Paisley
RENFREW
Kilmarnock
Ayr

DUNBARTON
ARGYLL
Loch Fyne
Kintyre
Islay

BERWICK
Berwick-upon-Tweed
Eyemouth
Coldstream
Greenlaw
Duns
Peebles
Jedburgh
Hawick
Selkirk
Galashiels
Holy I.

Newcastle to Stavanger 346 m.
Newcastle to Bergen 410 m.
Hull to Trondheim 745 m.
Leith to Copenhagen 610 m.
Leith to Hamburg 495 m.

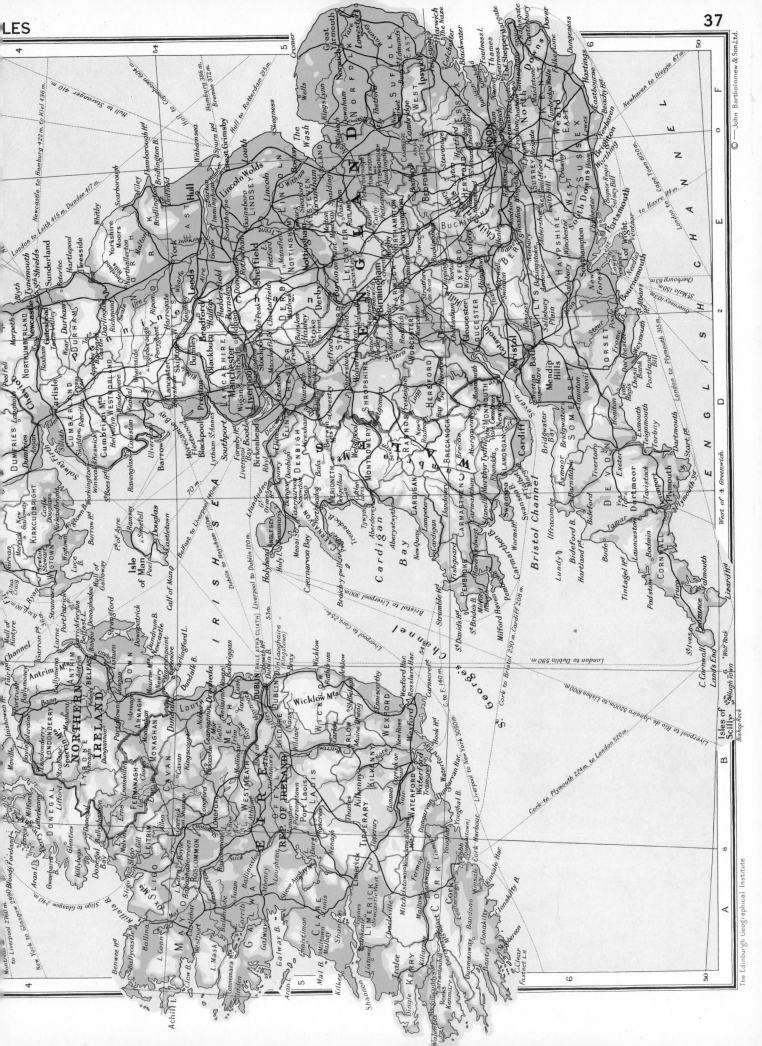

1:10 000 000
Statute Miles
0   50   100   150   200   250
Kilometres
0   100   200   300   400

REFERENCE TO COLOURING
12000 Feet
6000 "
3000 "
1500 "
600 "
SEA LEVEL
Land Depression
600 Feet
6000 "

UNITED KINGDOM OF
GREAT BRITAIN AND
N. IRELAND

ATLANTIC OCEAN

NORTH SEA

NORWAY

SCOTLAND

Aberdeen
Dundee
Glasgow Edinburgh
Newcastle
Sunderland
Carlisle
York
Leeds
Hull
Liverpool
Manchester
Sheffield
REP OF IRELAND
DUBLIN
BELFAST
NORTH IRELAND

IRISH SEA

ENGLAND
Birmingham
Nottingham
Leicester
Northampton
LONDON
Bristol
Cardiff
Swansea
Plymouth
Exeter
Southampton
Brighton
Dover

WALES

ENGLISH CHANNEL

Lands End
Isles of Scilly
Channel Is.

BAY OF BISCAY

FRANCE
PARIS
Rouen
Le Havre
Caen
Rennes
Nantes
Angers
Tours
Orleans
Bordeaux
Limoges
Clermont Ferrand
St Etienne
Lyons
Dijon
Toulouse
Montpellier
Marseilles
Nice
Perpignan

MASSIF CENTRAL

Pyrenees
Andorra

SPAIN
MADRID
Barcelona
Valencia
Saragossa
Valladolid
Salamanca
Seville
Cordoba
Granada
Malaga
Cadiz
Gibraltar
Murcia
Cartagena
Almeria

PORTUGAL
LISBON
Oporto
Coimbra

Balearic Islands
Majorca
Minorca
Iviza

Sa Nevada
Sa Morena

ATLANTIC

MEDITERRANEAN SEA

Algiers (Alger)
Tetuan
Oran

DENMARK
Jutland
Kiel
Hamburg
Bremen
Hanover

NETHERLANDS
AMSTERDAM
The Hague
Rotterdam
Antwerp
BELGIUM
BRUSSELS
Ghent
Lille

GERMANY
WEST GERMANY
BONN
Cologne
Dusseldorf
Essen
Dortmund
Frankfurt-on-Main
Mannheim
Heidelberg
Stuttgart
Nürnberg
Munich
Augsburg
Karl Marx Stadt
Leipzig
Magdeburg

SWITZERLAND
BERNE
Geneva
Zürich
Basle
Mont Blanc 15771

Milan
Turin
Genoa
Bologna
Florence
ROME
ITALY

CORSICA
SARDINIA
Cagliari

LIGURIAN SEA
TYRRHENIAN SEA

The Geographical Institute Edinburgh
5092
East of 8 Greenwich

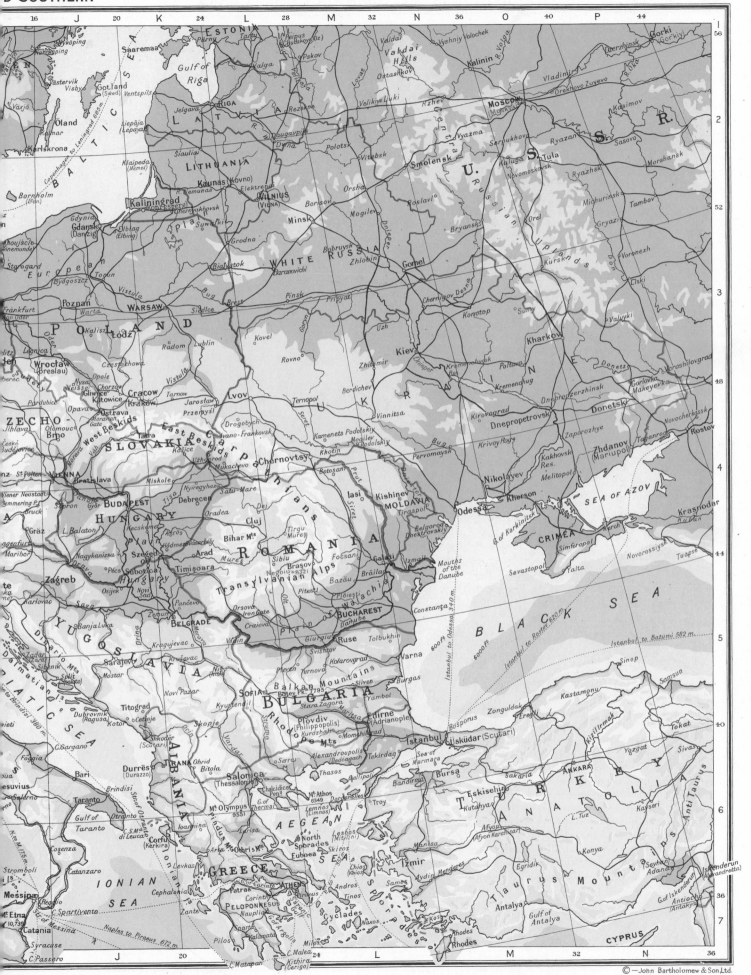

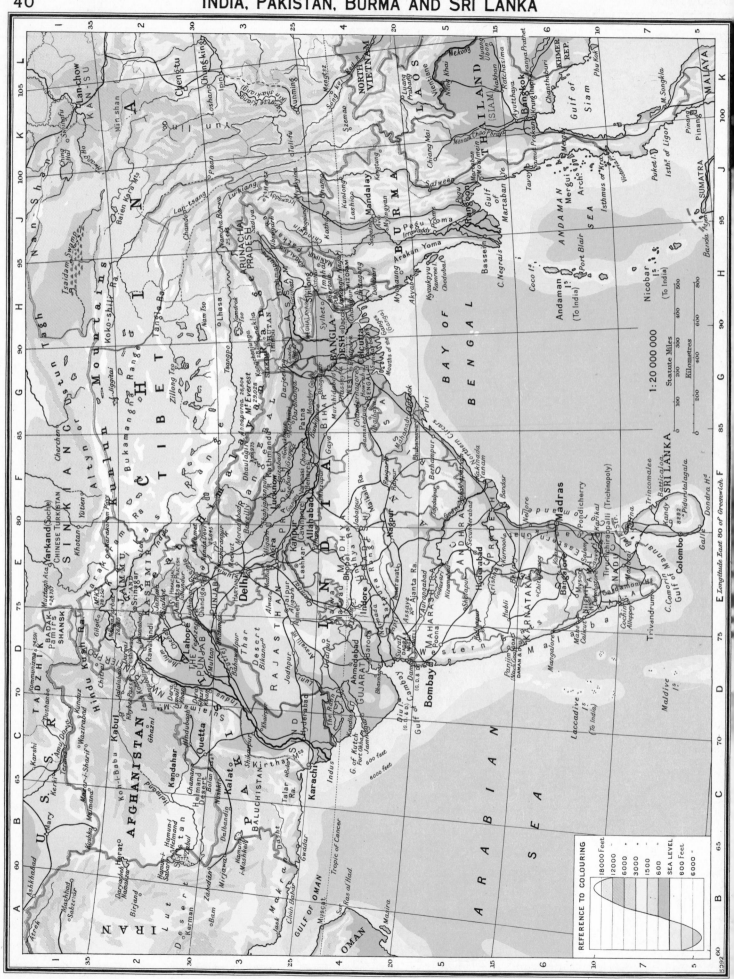

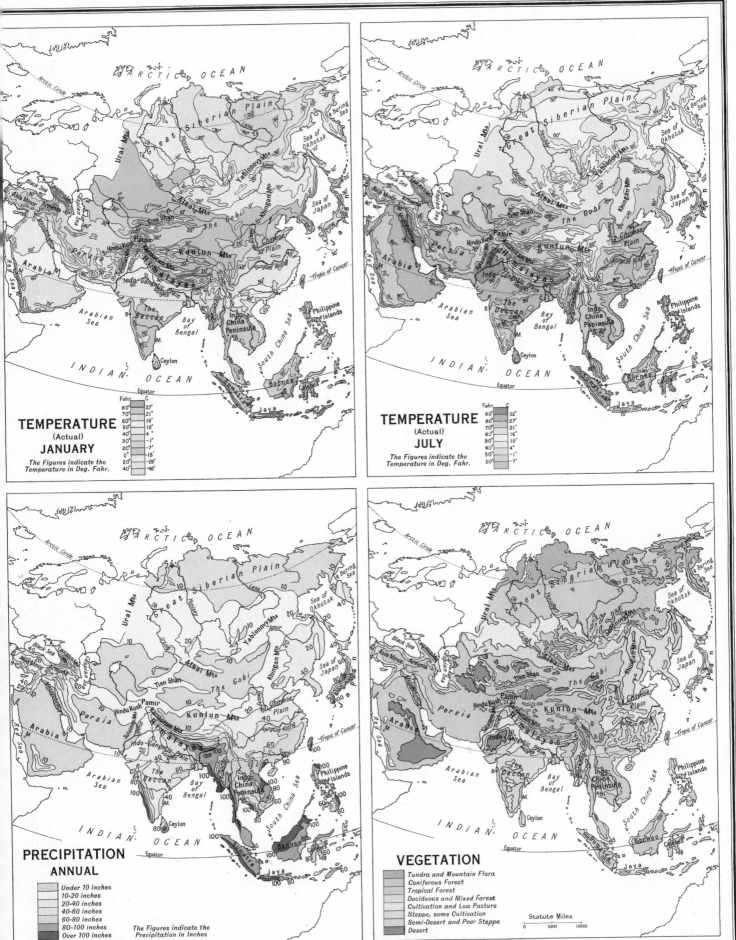

TEMPERATURE
(Actual)
JANUARY

The Figures indicate the
Temperature in Deg. Fahr.

Fahr.	C
80°	27°
70°	21°
60°	16°
50°	10°
40°	4°
30°	-1°
20°	-7°
0°	-18°
20°	-29°
40°	-40°

TEMPERATURE
(Actual)
JULY

The Figures indicate the
Temperature in Deg. Fahr.

Fahr.	C
90°	32°
80°	27°
70°	21°
60°	16°
50°	10°
40°	4°
30°	-1°
20°	-7°

PRECIPITATION
ANNUAL

Under 10 inches
10-20 inches
20-40 inches
40-60 inches
60-80 inches
80-100 inches
Over 100 inches

The Figures indicate the
Precipitation in Inches

VEGETATION

Tundra and Mountain Flora
Coniferous Forest
Tropical Forest
Deciduous and Mixed Forest
Cultivation and Low Pasture
Steppe, some Cultivation
Semi-Desert and Poor Steppe
Desert

Statute Miles

0   500   1000

1 : 105,000,000

ATLANTIC OCEAN

Arctic Circle

NORTH SEA

BALTIC SEA

EUROPE

MEDITERRANEAN SEA

AFRICA

ARCTI

Kara Sea

Weste Siberi Plain

U S S

BLACK SEA

CASPIAN SEA

Kirghiz Steppes

TURKEY

SYRIA
IRAQ
JORDAN
ISRAEL
LEBANON

Nafud Desert

SAUDI
ARABIA
Nejd

RED SEA

IRAN
(PERSIA)

AFGHANISTAN

PAMIR

Rub al Khali

OMAN

U.A.E.

YEMEN
DEM.REP.YEMEN
HADHRAMAUT

Gulf of Aden

Socotra I.
C. Guardafui

ARABIAN
SEA

INDIA

Laccadive Islands

Maldive Islands

REFERENCE TO COLOURING

18000 Feet
12000
6000
3000
1500
600
SEA LEVEL
Land Depression
600 Feet
6000

1:35 000 000

Statute Miles
0   200   400   600

Kilometres
0   500   1000

The Geographical Institute, Edinburgh

Longitude East 70 of Greenwich

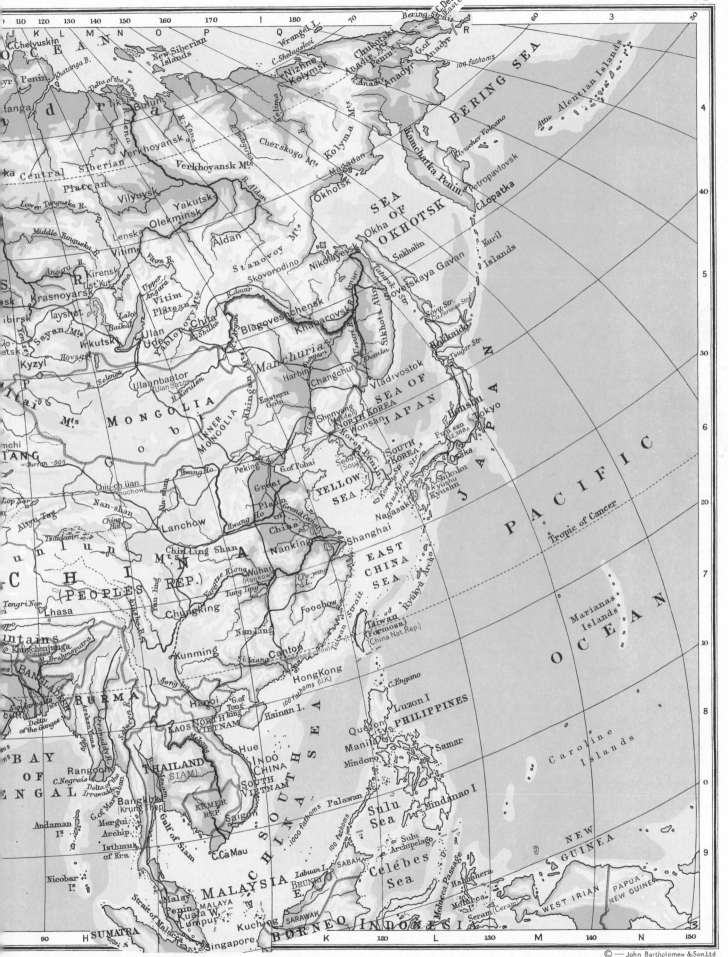

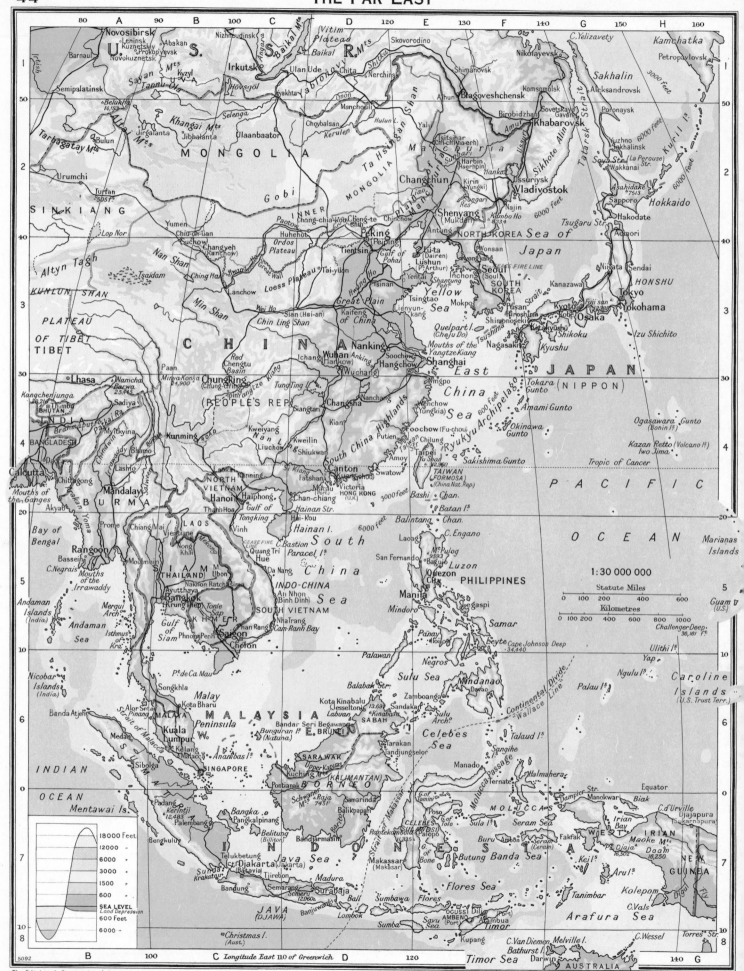

1:30 000 000

Statute Miles

0 100 200 400 600

Kilometres

0 100 200 400 600 800 1000

Challenger Deep 36,161 ft.

18000 Feet
12000 "
6000 "
3000 "
1500 "
600 "
SEA LEVEL
Land Depression
600 Feet
6000 "

5092

The Edinburgh Geographical Institute

Longitude East 110° of Greenwich

© – John Bartholomew & Son, Ltd.

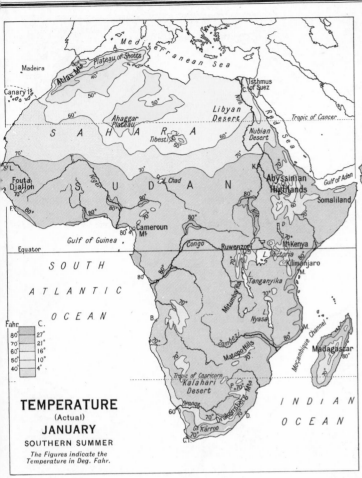

TEMPERATURE
(Actual)
JANUARY
SOUTHERN SUMMER
*The Figures indicate the
Temperature in Deg. Fahr.*

Fahr.	C.
80°	27°
70°	21°
60°	16°
50°	10°
40°	4°

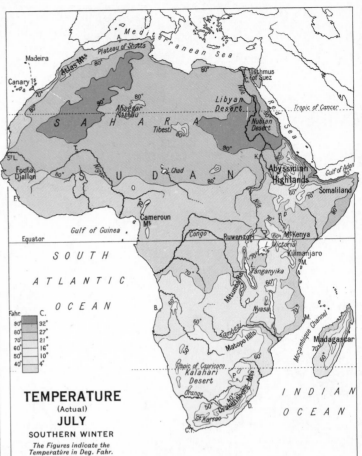

TEMPERATURE
(Actual)
JULY
SOUTHERN WINTER
*The Figures indicate the
Temperature in Deg. Fahr.*

Fahr.	C.
90°	32°
80°	27°
70°	21°
60°	16°
50°	10°
40°	4°

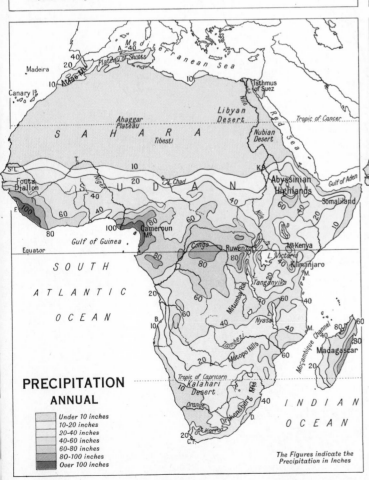

PRECIPITATION
ANNUAL

- Under 10 inches
- 10-20 inches
- 20-40 inches
- 40-60 inches
- 60-80 inches
- 80-100 inches
- Over 100 inches

*The Figures indicate the
Precipitation in Inches*

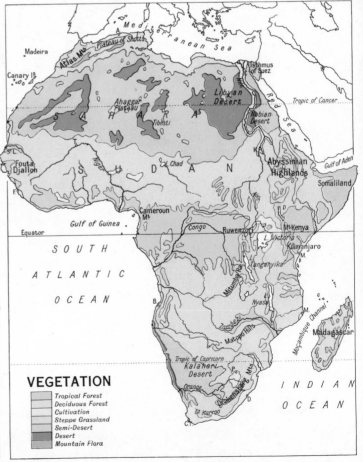

VEGETATION

- Tropical Forest
- Deciduous Forest
- Cultivation
- Steppe Grassland
- Semi-Desert
- Desert
- Mountain Flora

The Geographical Institute, Edinburgh

© — John Bartholomew & Son. Ltd.

1 : 77 000 000

Statute Miles
0   500   1000

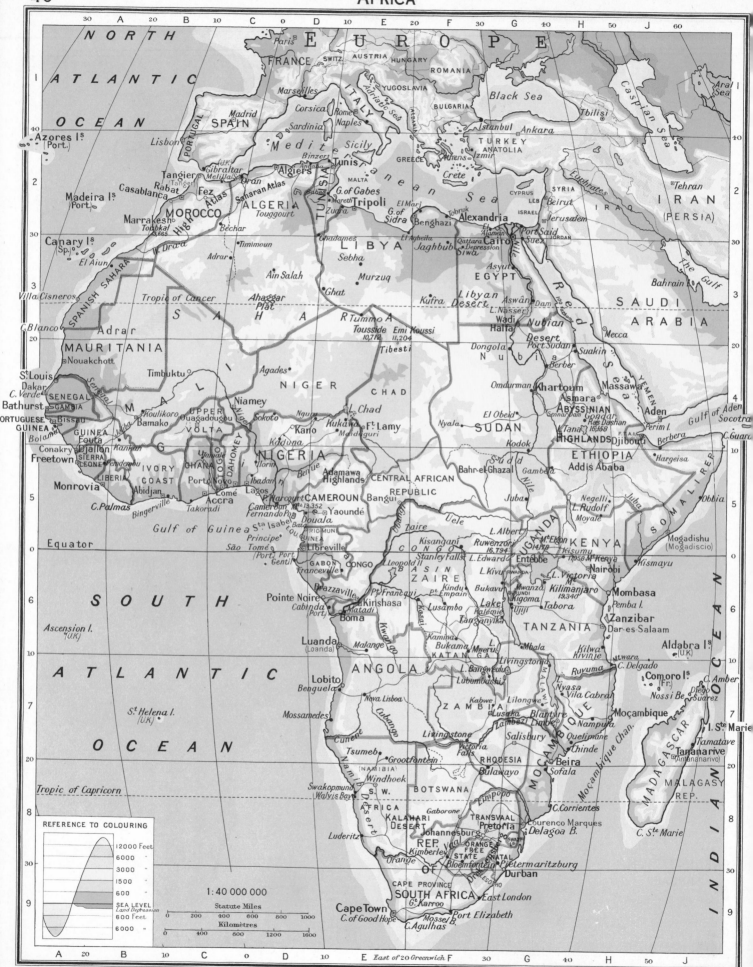

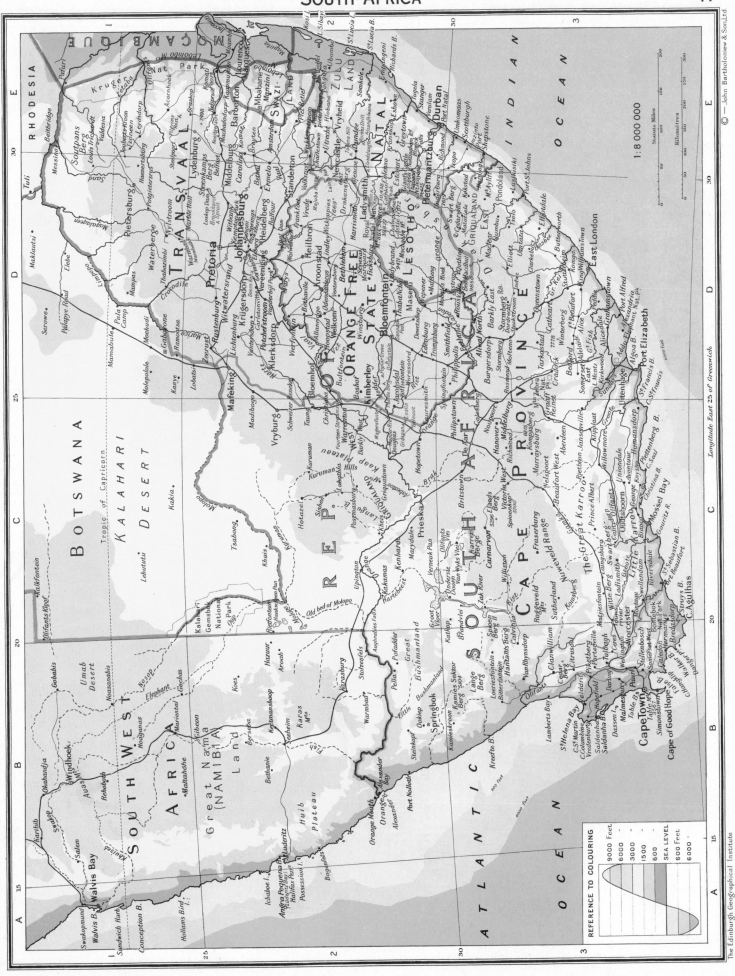

REFERENCE TO COLOURING

9000 Feet
6000 "
3000 "
1500 "
600 "
SEA LEVEL
600 Feet
6000 "

1:8 000 000

© — John Bartholomew & Son, Ltd.

The Edinburgh Geographical Institute

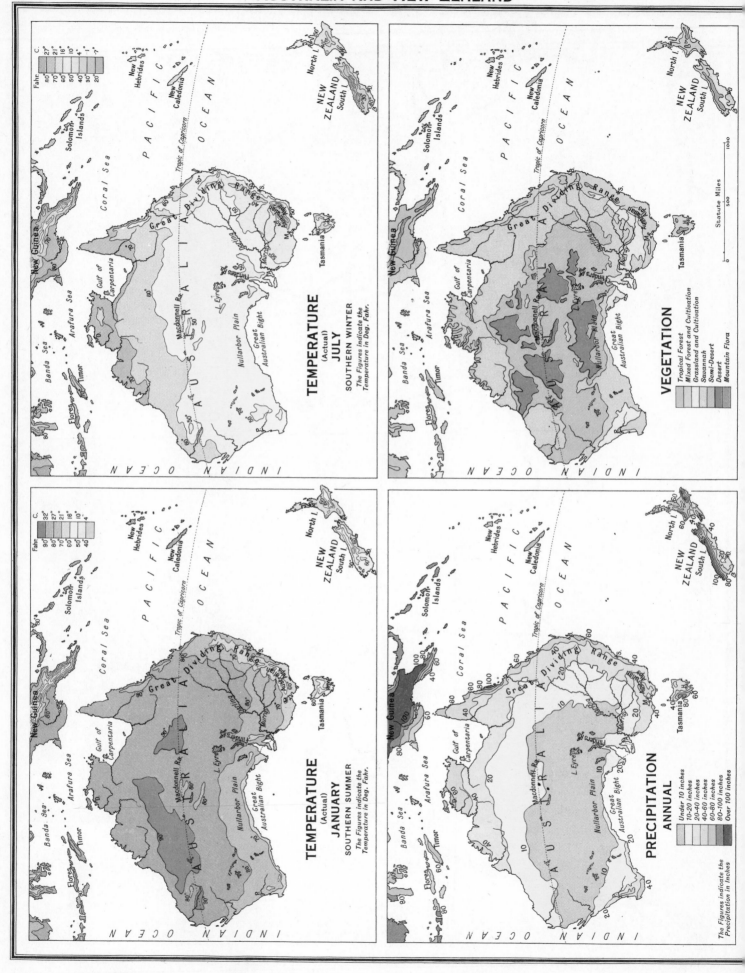

TEMPERATURE
(Actual)
JULY
SOUTHERN WINTER
The Figures indicate the
Temperature in Deg. Fahr.

TEMPERATURE
(Actual)
JANUARY
SOUTHERN SUMMER
The Figures indicate the
Temperature in Deg. Fahr.

VEGETATION

Tropical Forest
Mixed Forest and Cultivation
Grassland and Cultivation
Savannah
Semi-Desert
Desert
Mountain Flora

PRECIPITATION
ANNUAL

Under 10 inches
10–20 inches
20–40 inches
40–60 inches
60–80 inches
80–100 inches
Over 100 inches

The Figures indicate the
Precipitation in Inches

PACIFIC OCEAN

INDIAN OCEAN

Arafura Sea

Coral Sea

Timor Sea

Great Australian Bight

States and Territories

NEW GUINEA (PAPUA)

WESTERN AUSTRALIA

NORTHERN TERRITORY

SOUTH AUSTRALIA

QUEENSLAND

NEW SOUTH WALES

VICTORIA

TASMANIA

Cities and towns

Brisbane, Sydney, Newcastle, Wollongong, Canberra (Aust. Capital Terr.), Melbourne, Ballarat, Bendigo, Geelong, Adelaide, Port Pirie, Broken Hill, Perth, Fremantle, Kalgoorlie, Boulder, Coolgardie, Albany, Geraldton, Darwin, Alice Springs, Hobart, Launceston, Rockhampton, Townsville, Cooktown, Cairns, Bowen, Mackay, Bundaberg, Maryborough, Gympie, Ipswich, Toowoomba, Charleville, Longreach, Winton, Cloncurry, Normanton, Roma, Bourke, Wagga Wagga, Bathurst, Goulburn

Physical features

Great Barrier Reef, Cape York, Gulf of Carpentaria, Arnhem Land, Barkly Tableland, Great Sandy Desert, Gibson Desert, Great Victoria Desert, Simpson Desert, Nullarbor Plain, Hay Plain, Musgrave Ranges, Macdonnell Ra., Flinders Ra., Great Dividing Range, Australian Alps, L. Eyre, L. Torrens, L. Gairdner, L. Frome, Darling R., Murray R., Murrumbidgee, Lachlan, Cooper Cr., Diamantina R., Georgina R., Finke, Tropic of Capricorn

Mt. Kosciusko 7316, Mt. Bruce 4024, Mt. Woodroffe 4970, Cradle Mt. 5620, Bartle Frere 5287

C. York, C. Arnhem, C. Wessel, C. Leeuwin, C. Naturaliste, C. Catastrophe, C. Howe, Wilson's Prom.

Tasmania, Kangaroo I., Flinders I., King I., Melville I., Bathurst I., Groote Eylandt, Fraser or Gt. Sandy I.

AUSTRALIA
1:20 000 000

Statute Miles
0   100   200   300   400   500

Kilometres
0   200   400   600   800

REFERENCE TO COLOURING
6000 Feet
3000 "
1500 "
600 "
SEA LEVEL
Land Depression
600 Feet
6000 "

The Edinburgh Geographical Institute

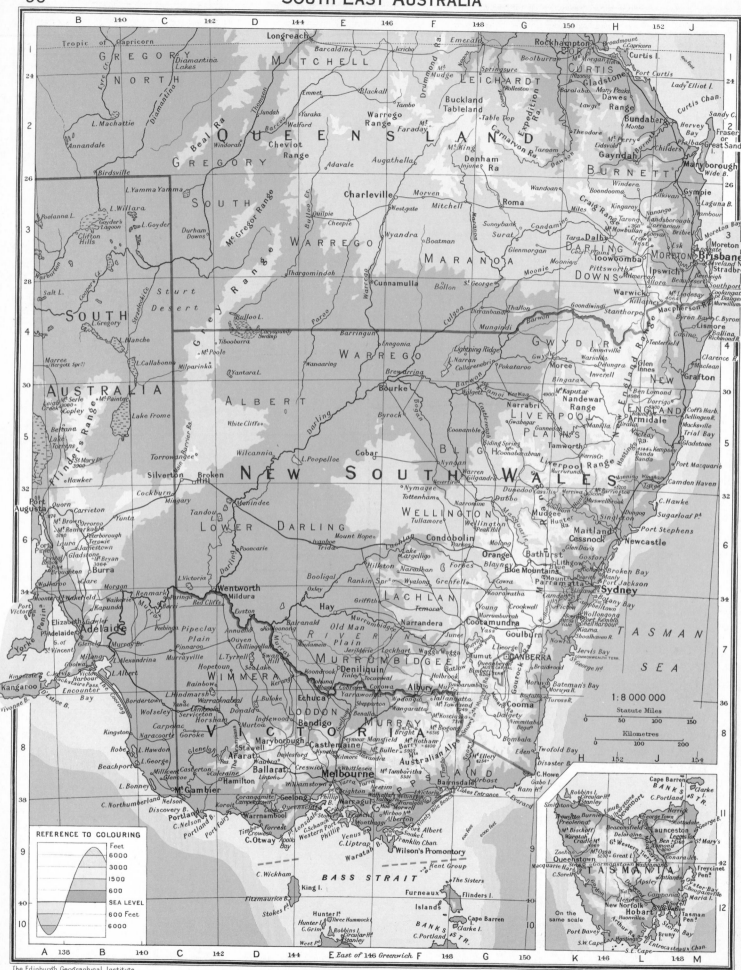

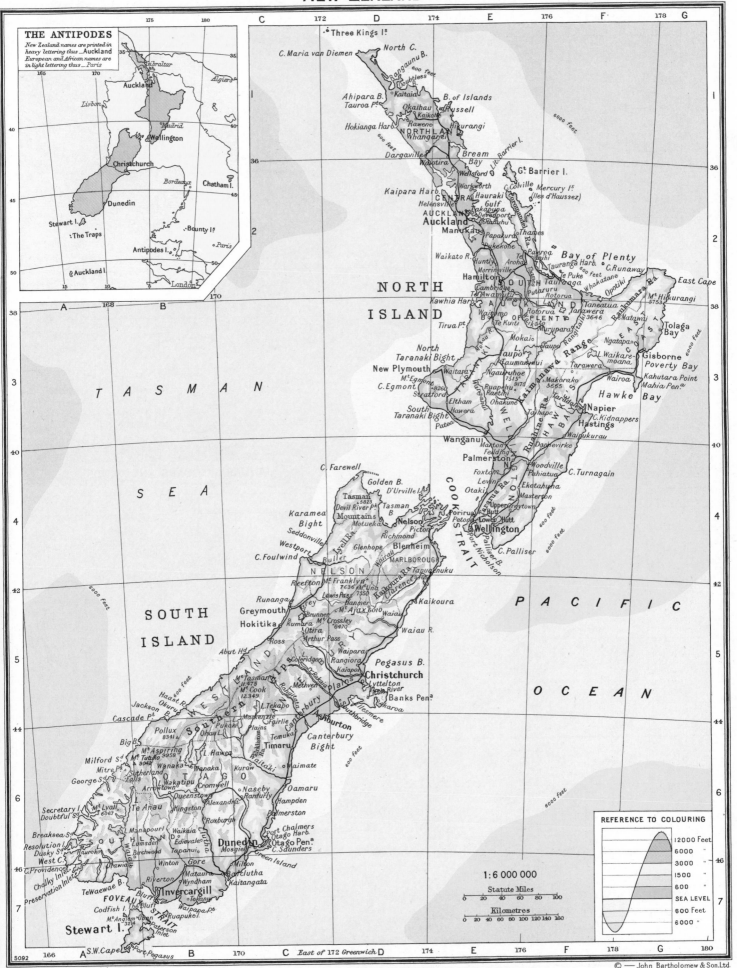

THE ANTIPODES

New Zealand names are printed in
heavy lettering thus — **Auckland**
European and African names are
in light lettering thus — *Paris*

TASMAN SEA

NORTH ISLAND

SOUTH ISLAND

PACIFIC OCEAN

1:6 000 000

Statute Miles

Kilometres

REFERENCE TO COLOURING

12000 Feet	
6000 "	
3000 "	
1500 "	
600 "	
SEA LEVEL	
600 Feet	
6000 "	

The Edinburgh Geographical Institute

5092

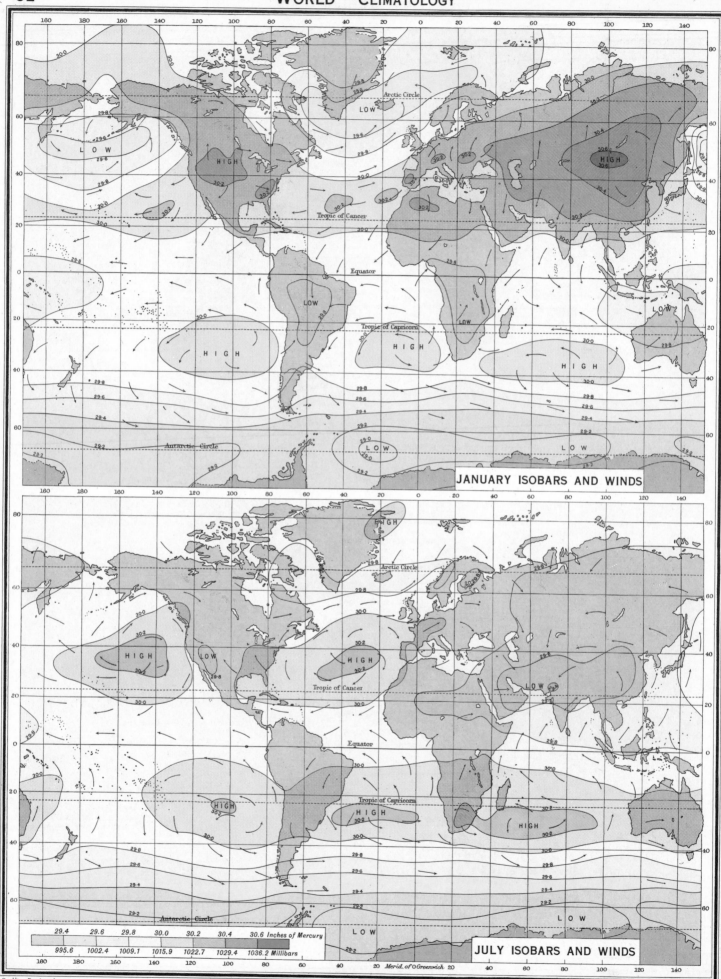

JANUARY ISOBARS AND WINDS

JULY ISOBARS AND WINDS

| 29.4 | 29.6 | 29.8 | 30.0 | 30.2 | 30.4 | 30.6 Inches of Mercury |
| 995.6 | 1002.4 | 1009.1 | 1015.9 | 1022.7 | 1029.4 | 1036.2 Millibars |

Merid. of 0 Greenwich

Gall's Projection

© — John Bartholomew & Son, Ltd., Edinburgh

GENERAL INDEX

The letters and figures following the map number correspond with those printed on the margins of the maps, and indicate the quadrilaterals, formed by the intersection of the lines of latitude and longitude, in which the names will be found

ABBREVIATIONS

Ala., Alabama
Arch., Archipelago
Ariz., Arizona
Ark., Arkansas
Aust., Australia
B., Bay
B.C., British Columbia
Brit., British
C., Cape
Cal., California
Can., Canal
Cent., Central
Chan., Channel
Co., County
Col., Colony
Colo., Colorado
Com. cap., Commonwealth capital
Conn., Connecticut
Cr., Creek
D.C., District of Columbia
Del., Delaware
Dep., Department
Dist., District
Div., Division
E., East, Eastern
Eng., England
Equat., Equatorial
Fd., Fjord
Fla., Florida
Fr., French
G., Gulf
Ga., Georgia
Ger., Germany

Gov., Government
Gt., Great
Harb., Harbour
Hd., Head
I., Island
Ia., Iowa
Ida., Idaho
Ill., Illinois
Ind., Indiana
Ind. Res., Indian Reservation
Ire., Ireland
Is., Islands
It., Italian
Junc., Junction
Kan., Kansas
Ky., Kentucky
L., Lake, Loch, Lac, Lago
La., Louisiana
Lab., Labrador
Ld., Land
Lit., Little
Man., Manitoba
Mass., Massachusetts
Md., Maryland
Me., Maine
Mich., Michigan
Minn., Minnesota
Miss., Mississippi
Mo., Missouri
Mont., Montana
Mt., Mountain, Mount
Mts., Mountains

N., North, Northern
N.B., New Brunswick
N.C., North Carolina
N. Dak., North Dakota
Neb., Nebraska
Nev., Nevada
Nfld., Newfoundland
N.H., New Hampshire
N. Ire., Northern Ireland
N.J., New Jersey
N. Mex., New Mexico
N.S., Nova Scotia
N.S.W., New South Wales
N.W.T., North-West Territory
N.Y., New York
N.Z., New Zealand
O., Ohio
Oc., Ocean
Okla., Oklahoma
Ont., Ontario
Orange F.S., Orange Free State
Ore., Oregon
Pa., Pennsylvania
Pak., Pakistan
Pan., Panama
P.E.I., Prince Edward Island
Penin., Peninsula
Plat., Plateau
Port., Portuguese
Pro., Protectorate
Prov., Province, Provincial
Pt., Point

Que., Quebec
R., River, Rio
Ra., Range
Rep., Republic
Res., Reservoir
R.I., Rhode Island
S., South, Southern
Sask., Saskatchewan
S.C., South Carolina
Sd., Sound
S. Dak., South Dakota
Sct., Settlement
Span., Spanish
St., Saint
Sta., Station
Ste., Sainte
Str., Strait
Tenn., Tennessee
Ter., Territory
Tex., Texas
Tn., Town
U.S.A., United States of America
U.S.S.R., Union of Soviet Socialist [Republics
Ut., Utah
Va., Virginia
Val., Valley
Vol., Volcano
Vt., Vermont
W., West, Western
Wash., Washington
Wis., Wisconsin
Wyo., Wyoming

Name	Map	Ref
Aachen, *Ger.*	38	F3
Aar R., *Switzerland*	38	G4
Abaco I., *Gt., Bahamas*	29	J2
Abakan, *U.S.S.R.*	44	B1
Abancay, *Peru*	30	C6
Abbotsford, *Que.*	20	C3
Abbey, *Sask.*	14	G5
Abee, *Alberta*	14	E3
Abenakis, *Que.*	20	D2
Aberdeen, *Cape Prov., Rep. of S. Africa*	47	C3
Aberdeen, *Sask.*	14	H4
Aberdeen, *S. Dak.*	24	G1
Aberdeen, *Wash.*	24	B1
Aberdeen, and co., *Scotland*	36	D3
Aberdeen L., *Keewatin, N.W.T.*	10	O5
Aberdovey, *Wales*	37	C5
Aberfeldy, *Scotland*	36	D3
Abergavenny, *Eng.*	37	D6
Aberystwyth, *Wales*	37	C5
Abidjan, *Ivory Coast, W. Africa*	46	C5
Abileno, *Tex.*	24	G4
Abingdon, *Eng.*	37	E6
Abingdon, *Va.*	25	K3
Abitibi L., *Ont.*	18	J4
Abitibi R., *Ont.*	18	H4
Abitibi R., Lit., *Ont.*	18	H3
Abrolhos I., *Brazil*	30	K7
Abunã, *Brazil*	30	E6
Abut Hd., *N.Z.*	51	C5
Abyssinian Highlands, *Ethiopia*	46	G4
Acadia National Park, *Me.*	24	D4
Acadia Valley, *Alberta*	14	F5
Acaponeta, *Mexico*	28	C3
Acapulco de Juarez, *Mexico*	28	D4
Acaraú, *Brazil*	30	K4
Accra, *Ghana*	46	D5
Achill I., *Eire*	37	A5
Achray, *Ont.*	17	H2
Acklins I., *Bahamas*	29	K3
Acme, *Alberta*	14	E5
Aconcagua, vol., *Argentina*	31	D10
Acornhoek, *Transvaal*	47	E1
Acre R., *Brazil*	30	D6
Actinolite, *Ont.*	17	H3
Acton, *Ont.*	16	E4
Acton Vale, *Que.*	20	C2
Acu, *Brazil*	30	K5
Adair C., *Baffin I., N.W.T.*	11	U3
Adam Mt., *Falkland Is.*	31	E14
Adamawa Highlands, *Cameroun*	46	E5
Adams I., *B.C.*	13	L7
Adams Landing, *Alberta*	14	D1
Adana, *Turkey*	39	N6
Adavale, *Queensland*	50	E2
Addis Ababa, *Ethiopia*	46	G5
Addo Elephant National Park, *Cape Prov., Rep. of S. Africa*	47	D3
Adelaer C., *Greenland*	11	Z5
Adelaide, *Cape Prov., Rep. of S. Africa*	47	D3
Adelaide, *S. Aust.*	50	B7
Adelaide I., *Antarctica*	3	H8
Adelaide Penin., *Keewatin, N.W.T.*	11	P4
Aden, *S. Yemen*	42	C7
Aden, G. of, *Arabia*	42	C7
Adirondack Mts., *N.Y.*	25	M2
Adlavik Is., *Lab.*	19	F2
Admiralty G., *W. Aust.*	49	D2
Admiralty I., *Alaska*	10	H6
Admiralty Sd., *Franklin, N.W.T.*	11	R3
Adolfo Alsina, *Argentina*	31	E11
Adrar, *Algeria*	46	C3
Adrar, *Mauritania, W. Africa*	46	B3
Adriatic Sea, *S. Europe*	39	H5
Advocate Harb., *N.S.*	21	B2
Aegadean Is., *Sicily*	38	H6
Aegean Sea, *Greece, etc.*	39	L6
Aero, *B.C.*	13	D6
Afars & Issas, French Ter. of the (*F.T.A.I.*), *N. E. Africa*	46	H4
Affabakka, *Surinam*	30	G3
Affonso Falls, *Brazil*	30	K5
Afghanistan, *S.W. Asia*	40	B2
Afognak I., *Alaska*	10	D6
Afyon Karanisar, *Turkey*	39	M6
Agades, *Niger, W. Africa*	46	D4
Agartala, *Tripura*	40	H4
Agawa, and R., *Ont.*	18	F5
Agen, *France*	38	E4
Agotawekami L., *Que.*	18	J4
Agra, *India*	40	E3
Agrigento, *Sicily*	38	H6
Aguadoe, *Brazil*	31	H8
Aguanehy R., *Brazil*	31	H8
Aguanish, *Que.*	22	F1
Aguapey R., *Argentina*	31	F9
Aguascalientes, *Mexico*	28	D3
Aguja C., *Peru*	30	A5
Agulhas C., *Cape Prov., Rep. of S. Africa*	47	C3
Ahaggar Plat., *Algeria*	46	D3
Ahipara B., *N.Z.*	51	D1
Ahmedabad, *India*	40	D4
Aigle, L. l', *Que.*	22	E1
Aigles, L. des, *Que.*	20	C2
Aihun, *China*	44	E2
Aillik, *Coast of Lab.*	19	F2
Ailsa Craig, *Ont.*	16	D4
Ailsa Craig, *Scotland*	37	C4
Ain Salah, *Algeria*	46	D3
Ainslie, L., *N.S.*	21	F1
Aiquile, *Bolivia*	30	D7
Airão, *Brazil*	30	E4
Airdrie, *Alberta*	14	E5
Aire R., *Eng.*	37	E5
Air Force I., *Franklin, N.W.T.*	11	U4
Aishihik L., *Yukon*	10	G5
Aiun, El, *Span. Sahara*	46	B3
Aiyansh, *B.C.*	12	F5
Ajaccio, *Corsica*	38	G5
Ajanta Ra., *India*	40	E4
Ajax, *Ont.*	17	F4
Ajmer, *India*	40	D3
Akaroa, *N.Z.*	51	D5
Akimiski I., *James B.*	18	G4
Aklavik, *Mackenzie, N.W.T.*	10	G4
Akpatok I., *Keewatin, N.W.T.*	19	D1
Akron, *N.Y.*	17	G4
Akron, *O.*	25	K2
Akureyri, *Iceland*	35	C2
Akyab, *Burma*	40	H4
Alabama, state, *U.S.A.*	25	J4
Alagoas, *Brazil*	30	K5
Alajuela, *Costa Rica*	29	H5
Alakurtti, *U.S.S.R*	35	N2
Alameda, *Sask.*	15	K6
Alamos, *Mexico*	28	C2
Aland Is., *Finland*	35	K3
Ala-shan, *China*	43	J5
Alaska, *U.S.A.*	10	C5
Alaska, G. of, *Alaska*	10	E6
Alaska Highway, *Yukon*	12	C2
Alaska Penin., *Alaska*	10	C6
Alaska Ra., *Alaska*	10	D5
Alay Tag, mts., *U.S.S.R.*	42	F5
Albacete, *Spain*	38	D6
Alban, *Ont.*	16	E1
Albanel L., *Que.*	19	C3
Albania, rep., *Europe*	39	K5
Albany, *Ga.*	25	K4
Albany, *N.Y.*	25	M2
Albany, *N.S.*	21	B3
Albany *W. Aust.*	49	B6
Albany, *James B.*	18	H2
Albany R., *Ont.*	18	G3
Alberga R., *S. Aust.*	49	E5
Alberni, *Vancouver I., B.C.*	13	K7
Albert, *N.B.*	21	C2
Albert L., *S. Aust.*	50	B7
Albert L., *Uganda*	46	G5
Alberta, prov., *Canada*	10	L7
Alberta Mt., *Alberta*	14	C4
Alberton, *P.E.I.*	21	C1
Alberton, *Victoria*	50	E9
Albert Shoal, *James B.*	18	H2
Alborg, *Denmark*	38	G1
Albreda, *B.C.*	13	L6
Albuquerque, *N. Mex.*	24	E3
Albury, *N.S.W.*	50	F7
Alcantara, *Brazil*	30	H4
Alcira, *Spain*	38	D6
Alcoa, *Tenn.*	25	K3
Aldabra Is., *Indian Oc.*	46	H6
Aldan R., *U.S.S.R.*	43	M2
Aldershot, *Eng.*	37	E6
Aldred, *Que.*	20	C2
Aleksandrovsk, *U.S.S.R.*	44	G1
Aleppo, *Syria*	42	B5
Alert Bay, *B.C.*	13	G7
Alessandria, *Italy*	38	G4
Alesund, *Norway*	35	H6
Aleutian Is., *Alaska*	43	Q3
Aleutian Ra., *Alaska*	10	C6
Alexander Arch., *Alaska*	10	G6
Alexander B., *Cape Prov., Rep. of S. Africa*	47	B2
Alexander Selkirk I. (Más Afuera I.), *S. Pacific Oc.*	31	A10
Alexandra, *N.Z.*	51	B6
Alexandra Fd., *Franklin, N.W.T.*	11	T2
Alexandra R., *Victoria*	50	E8
Alexandria, *B.C.*	13	J6
Alexandria, *Cape Prov., Rep. of S. Africa*	47	D3
Alexandria, *Egypt*	46	F2
Alexandria, *La.*	25	H4
Alexandria, *Ont.*	17	L2
Alexandria, *Va.*	25	L3
Alexandria Falls, *Mackenzie, N.W.T.*	12	M2
Alexandrina L., *S. Aust.*	50	B7
Alexandroupolis (Dedé Agach), *Greece*	39	L5
Alexis Cr., *B.C.*	13	J6
Alexis R., *Lab.*	19	F3
Algciras, *Spain*	38	C6
Algoma, *Mich.*	16	A3
Algeria, *N. Africa*	46	D2
Algiers, *Algeria*	46	D2
Algoa B., *Cape Prov., Rep. of S. Africa*	47	D3
Algoma, *Ont.*	16	C1
Algoma, dist. *Ont.*	18	F4
Algonquin, *Ont.*	17	G2
Algonquin Park, *Ont.*	17	G2
Alicante, *Spain*	38	D6
Alice, *Cape Prov., Rep. of S. Africa*	47	D3
Alice Arm, *B.C.*	12	F5
Alicedale, *Cape Prov., Rep. of S. Africa*	47	D3
Alice Springs (Stuart), *N. Ter., Aust.*	49	E4
Alida, *Sask.*	15	L6
Aligarh, *Rajasthan, India*	40	E3
Aligargh, *Ut. Pra., India*	40	E3
Alison B., *Greenland*	11	X3
Aliwal North, *Cape Prov., Rep. of S. Africa*	47	D3
Alkali Lake, *B.C.*	13	J7
Allahabad, *India*	40	F3
Allanridge, *Orange F.S.*	47	D2
Allan Water, *Ont.*	18	C3
Allard Lake, *Que.*	22	F1
Allen, Bog of, *Eire*	37	B5
Allen L., *Eire*	37	B4
Allende, *Mexico*	28	D2
Allenford, *Ont.*	16	D3
Alleppey, *India*	40	E7
Alliance, *Neb.*	24	F2
Allier R., *France*	38	E4
Allison Harb., *B.C.*	13	G7
Alliston, *Ont.*	16	F3
Alloa, *Scotland*	36	D3
Allora, *Queensland*	50	J3
Allumette I., *Que.*	17	H2
Allumettes, *Que.*	17	H2
Alma, *N.B.*	21	C2
Alma, *Que.*	22	B2
Alma l., *Que*	20	D1
Almaden, *Spain*	38	C6
Almaville, *Que.*	20	C2
Almeirim, *Brazil*	30	G4
Almeria, *Spain*	38	D6
Almonte, *Ont.*	17	J2
Alnwick, *Eng.*	37	E4
Alonsa, *Man.*	15	M5
Alpen, *Alberta*	14	B2
Alpena. *Mich.*	25	K1
Alps, The, *Cent. Europe*	38	F4
Alright I., *Que.*	23	G3
Alsask, *Sask.*	14	G5
Alsek R., *Yukon*	13	A3
Altagracia, *Venezuela*	30	C1
Altai Mts., *Mongolia*	43	G4
Altar, *Mexico*	28	B1
Altata, *Mexico*	28	C3
Alten E. R., *Norway*	35	L2
Altona, *Man.*	15	N6
Altoona, *Pa.*	25	L2

Place	No.	Ref.
Alto Trombetas R., Brazil	30	F3
Altyn or Ustun Tag, mts., China	40	F1
Alvena, Sask.	14	H4
Alvinston, Ont.	16	D5
Alwar, India	40	E3
Alward, N.B.	22	
Amadjuak L., Baffin I.	11	V5
Amalie I., W. Indies	29	M4
Amami Gunto, Japan	44	E4
Amapá, Brazil	30	G3
Amapu R., Brazil	30	G4
Amarante, Brazil	30	J5
Amaranth, Man.	15	M5
Amaravati, India	40	E4
Amarillo, Tex.	24	F3
Amatigue, G. of, Guatemala	28	G4
Amazon R., Brazil	30	E4
Amazon, Mouths of the R., Brazil	30	H3
Ambato, Ecuador	30	B4
Ambeno (Port. Ter.), Timor I., Indonesia	49	C1
Amber C., Madagascar	46	H7
Ambergris I., Brit. Honduras	28	G4
Amberley, Ont.	16	D3
Ambon I., Indonesia	44	E7
Ameca, Mexico	28	D3
Amery, Man.	15	O2
Ames Sd., N.S.	21	D2
Amherst, N.S.	21	C2
Amherst I., Ont.	17	J3
Amherst I., Que.	22	F3
Amherstburg, Ont.	16	B5
Amiens, France	38	E3
Amirantes Is., Indian Oc.	3	M5
Amisk L., Sask.	15	K3
Amisted Res., Tex.	28	D2
Amos, Que.	19	B4
Amoy, China	44	D4
Amqui, Que.	22	D2
Amritsar, India	40	E2
Amsterdam, Netherlands	38	E2
Amsterdam, Transvaal	47	E5
Amsterdam I., Indian Oc.	3	N6
Amu-Darya, Cent. Asia	42	E5
Amu Dar'ya, R., U.S.S.R.	40	C1
Amund Ringnes I., N.W.T.	11	P2
Amundsen G., N.W.T.	10	K3
Amur R., E. Asia	44	F2
Amyot, Ont.	18	F4
Anaconda, Mont.	24	D1
Anadyr, and G., U.S.S.R.	43	Q2
Anadyr, R., and Mts., U.S.S.R.	43	Q2
Anahim, and L., B.C.	13	H6
Anambas Is., Indonesia	44	C6
Anapolis, Brazil	30	H7
Anchieta, Brazil	31	J8
Anchor Pt., Nfld.	23	J1
Anchorage, Alaska	10	E5
Ancohuma Mt., Bolivia	30	D7
Ancona, Italy	38	H5
Ancud, and G. de, Chile	31	C12
Andaman Is., B. of Bengal	40	H6
Andersan L., B.C.	13	J7
Anderson Chan., N.W.T.	19	E1
Anderson R., Mackenzie, N.W.T.	10	J4
Andes, Cord de los, S. America	31	C12
Andes de Caravaya (Mts.), Peru	30	C6
Andhra Pradesh, state, India	40	F5
Andizhan, U.S.S.R.	42	F4
Andlesnes, Norway	35	H3
Andorra, and rep., Pyrenees	38	E5
Andover, Eng.	37	E6
Andreafski, Alaska	10	B5
Andreas, Peru	30	C4
Andrew Gordon B., Keewatin, N.W.T.	11	T5
Andros I., Greece	39	L6
Andros Is., Bahamas, W. Indies	29	J3
Androscoggin R., Me.	22	B4
Aneroid, Sask.	14	H6
Angangueo, Mexico	28	D4
Angara R., U.S.S.R.	43	J3
Angara R. Upper, U.S.S.R.	43	K3
Angel Falls, Venezuela	30	E2
Angerman Alv, Sweden	35	K3
Angers, France	38	D4
Angikuni L., Keewatin, N.W.T.	10	O5
Anglesey, Wales	37	C5
Angliers, Que.	18	J5
Angmagssalik, Greenland	11	Z4
Angol, Chile	31	C11
Angola, N.Y.	17	G5
Angola, S.W. Africa	46	E7
Angoulême, France	38	E4
Angra Pequena B., S.W. Africa	47	A2
Anguilla I., W. Indies	29	M4
Anguille C., Nfld.	23	H3
Angus, Ont.	16	F3
Angus, co., Scotland	36	D3
Anicuns, Brazil	30	G7
Ankara, Turkey	39	N6
Anking, China	44	D3
Annaba, Algeria	46	D2
Annan, Scotland	37	D4
Annandale, Queensland	50	B2
Annapolis, Md.	25	L3
Annapolis R., N.S.	21	B3
Annapolis Royal, N.S.	22	E4
Annapurna, Nepal	40	F5
Ann Arbor, Mich.	16	B5
Annette and Is., Alaska	12	E5
An Nhon (Binh Dinh), S. Vietnam	44	C5
Anniston, Ala.	25	J4
Annootok, Greenland	11	U2
Annuello, Victoria	50	D7
Anse au Griffon, Que.	22	E2
Ansonville, Ont.	18	H4
Antakya (Antioch), Turkey	39	N6
Antalya, and G., Turkey	39	NC
Anthony, Kan.	24	G3
Anticosti I., Que.	22	F2
Antigonish, N.S.	21	E2
Antigua, Guatemala	28	F5
Antigua I., W. Indies	29	M4
Antilles, Greater, W. Indies	29	H3
Antilles, Lesser, W. Indies	29	M4
Antioquia, Colombia	30	B2
Antipodes I., S. Pacific Oc.	2	D7
Anti-Taurus Mts., Turkey	39	O6
Antler, Sask.	15	L6
Antofagasta, Chile	31	C8
Antostagan L., Que.	20	A2
Antrim, and co., N. Ire.	37	B4
Antrim Mts., N. Ire.	37	B4
Antung, China	44	E2
Antwerp, Belgium	38	F3
An Uaimh (Navan), Eire	37	B5
Anvik, Alaska	10	B5
Anyox, B.C.	12	F5
Aomori, Japan	44	G2
Apa R., Paraguay-Brazil	31	F8
Apalachee B., Fla.	25	K5
Apalachicola, Fla.	25	J5
Apaporis R., Colombia	30	C3
Apennine Mts., Italy	38	G4
Aperé, Brazil	30	G4
Apere R., Bolivia	30	D6
Apiai, Brazil	31	H8
Apiskigamish L., Que.	11	U6
Apody R., Brazil	30	K5
Apollo B., Victoria	50	D9
Apolobamba, Bolivia	30	D6
Aporé R., Brazil	30	G7
Appalachian Mts., U.S.A.	25	K3
Apple I., Que.	20	E1
Apple R., N.S.	21	C2
Appleby, Eng.	37	D4
Apple Hill, Ont.	20	B3
Apsley, Ont.	17	G3
Apsley, Tasmania	50	L12
Apucarana, Serra d', Brazil	31	G8
Apure R., Venezuela	30	D2
Apurimac R. Peru	30	C6
Aqaba, G. of, Arabia	42	B6
Aquadilla, Puerto Rico	29	L4
Aquanus R., Que.	22	G1
Aquarico R., Ecuador	30	B4
Aquidaban, R., Paraguay	31	F8
Aquidauana, Brazil	30	F8
Arabella, Peru	30	C4
Arabian Sea, S.W. Asia	42	E7
Aracajú, Brazil	30	K6
Aracati, Brazil	30	K4
Araçuai, Brazil	30	J7
Arad, Romania	39	K4
Arafura Sea, Indonesia	44	F7
Araguaia R., Brazil	30	H5
Araguari R., Brazil	30	G3
Arakan Yoma, Burma	40	H4
Aral Sea, U.S.S.R.	42	D4
Aran I., Donegal, Eire	37	A4
Aran I., Galway. Eire	37	A5
Aranya Prathet, Thailand	44	K6
Ararat, Victoria	50	D8
Ararat Mt., Turkey	42	C4
Arauca, Colombia	30	C2
Arauco, Chile	31	C11
Aravalli Hills, India	40	D3
Araya Penin., Venezuela	30	E1
Arborfield, Sask.	15	K4
Arborg, Man.	15	N5
Arbroath, Scotland	36	D3
Archainbault L., Que.	20	B2
Archangel, U.S.S.R.	35	F3
Archidona, Ecuador	30	B4
Arcola, Sask.	15	K6
Arctic Bay, Franklin, N.W.T.	11	S3
Arctic Harb., Baffin I., N.W.T.	11	V4
Arctic Red River, Mackenzie, N.W.T.	10	H4
Ardal, Norway	35	H3
Ardbeg, Ont.	16	E2
Arden, Ont.	17	J3
Ardmore, Okla.	24	G4
Ardnamurchan Pt., Scotland	36	B3
Ardoise L., N.S.	21	G2
Ardrossan, Scotland	36	C4
Arecibo, Puerto Rico	29	L4
Arendal, Norway	38	G1
Arequipa, Peru	30	C7
Argentia, Nfld.	23	L3
Argentina, rep., S. America	31	D11
Argentino L., Argentina	31	C14
Argolis, G. of, Greece	39	K6
Argun R., China-U.S.S.R.	43	K3
Argyle, N.S.	21	B4
Argyll co.. Scotland	36	C3
Århus, Denmark	38	G1
Arica, Chile	30	C7
Arichat, N.S	21	G2
Arinos R., Brazil	30	F6
Ariporo R., Colombia	30	C2
Aripuana R., Brazil	30	E5
Aristazabal I., B.C.	13	F6
Arizona, state, U.S.A.	24	D4
Arizpe, Mexico	28	B1
Arkansas, state, and R., U.S.A.	25	H4
Arkansas City, Ark.	25	H4
Arkansas City. Kan.	24	G3
Arkhangelsk, U.S.S.R.	42	C2
Arklow, Eire	37	B5
Arkona, Ont.	16	D4
Arles, France	38	F5
Armagh, Que.	20	D2
Armagh, and co., N. Ire.	37	B4
Armidale, N.S.W.	50	H5
Armit, Ont.	15	L4
Armstrong, B.C.	13	L7
Armstrong, Ont.	18	D3
Armstrong. Que.	20	D3
Arnaud R., Que.	19	C2
Arnhem C., N. Ter., Aust.	49	F2
Arnhem, Netherlands	38	F2
Arnhem Ld., N. Ter., Aust.	49	E2
Arnprior, Ont.	17	J2
Arnstein, Ont.	16	F2
Aroostook, N.B.	22	D3
Aroostook R., Me.	22	C3
Arran, Sask.	15	L5
Arran I., Scotland	36	C4
Arrandale, B.C.	12	F5
Arras, France	38	E3
Arrochar, Scotland	36	C3
Arrow L., Ont.	18	D4
Arrow L., Lower, B.C.	13	L8
Arrow L., Upper, B.C.	13	L7
Arrowhead, B.C.	13	L7
Arrowhead Park, Ont.	17	F2
Arrow Park, B.C.	13	L7
Arrowtown, N.Z.	51	B6
Arrowwood, Alberta	14	E5
Arta, Greece	39	K6
Arthabaska, Que.	20	D2
Arthur, Ont.	16	E4
Arthur Ra., Tasmania	50	L12
Arthurette, N.B.	22	D3
Artigas, Uruguay	31	F10
Artillery L., Mackenzie, N.W.T.	10	N5
Aru Is., Indonesia	44	F7
Aruanã, Brazil	30	G6
Aruba I. (Oruba), Caribbean Sea	30	D1
Arunachal Pradesh, state, India	40	H3
Arundel, Que.	20	B3
Arur Fd., Iceland	35	C2
Arvida, Que.	22	B2
Asahidake Mt., Japan	38	G2
Asbestos, Que.	20	C3
Asbestos Mts., Cape Prov. Rep. of S. Africa	47	C2
Ascension, B. del la, Mexico	28	G4
Ascension I., S. Atlantic Oc.	46	B6
Ascot, Que.	20	D3
Ascotan, Chile	31	D8
Ashburton, N.Z.	51	C5
Ashburton R., W. Aust.	49	B4
Ashcroft, B.C.	13	K7
Ashern, Man.	15	M5
Asheville, N.C.	25	K3
Asheweig R., Ont.	18	E2
Ashford, Ariz.	24	D3
Ashkhabad, U.S.S.R.	40	A1
Ashland, Me.	22	C3
Ashland, Wis.	25	H1
Ashmont, Alberta	14	F3
Ashton, Ont.	17	J2
Ashuanipi L., Lab.	19	D3
Ashuapmuchuan R., Que.	19	C4
Asmara, Ethiopia, E. Africa	46	G4
Aspy B., N.S.	21	G1
Asquith, Sask.	14	H4
Assam, state, India	40	H3
Assaye, India	40	E4
Assigny L., Que.	19	D3
Assiniboia, Sask.	14	H6
Assiniboine Mt., Alberta	14	D5
Assiniboine R., Sask.-Man.	15	L5
Assinika L., Que.	19	B3
Assomption, L', Que.	20	B2
Aston, Que.	20	C2
Astoria. Ore.	20	B1
Astorville, Ont.	17	F1
Astrakhan, U.S.S.R.	42	C4
Asuncion, Paraguay	31	F9
Aswân, Egypt	46	G3
Asyut, Egypt	46	G3
Atacama, Chile	31	D8
Atacama Desert, Chile	31	D9
Atalaia, Brazil	30	K5
Atambua, Timor I., Indonesia	44	E7
Athabasca, Alberta	14	E3
Athabasca L., Alberta-Sask.	14	G1
Athabasca R., Alberta	14	F2
Athabasca Mt., Alberta	14	C4
Athapupuskow L., Sask.	15	K3
Athenry, Eire	37	A5
Athens, Ga.	25	K4
Athens, Greece	39	K6
Athens, Ont.	17	K3
Atherley, Ont.	17	F3
Athlone, Eire	37	B5
Atholl C., Greenland	11	U2
Athos Mt., Greece	39	L5
Atico, Peru	30	C7
Atikameg, Alberta	14	D3
Atikameg L., and Park, Man.	15	L3
Atikokan, Ont.	18	C4
Atikwa L., Ont.	18	B4
Atlanta, Ga.	25	K4
Atlanta, Mich.	16	A3
Atlantic I., Pacific Oc.	3	J3
Atlantic City, N.J.	25	M3
Atlee, Alberta	14	F5
Atlin, and L., B.C.	12	D3
Atnarko, B.C.	13	H6
Atoka, Okla.	24	G4
Atrato R., Colombia	30	B2
Atrek R., Persia	40	A1
Attawapiskat, Ont.	18	G2
Attawapiskat L., Ont.	18	E2
Attawapiskat R., Ont.	18	F2
Attikonak L., Lab.	19	D3
Attikumagen L., Que.	19	D3
Attu, Aleutian Is.	43	Q3
Atuel R., Argentina	31	D11
Atwood, Ont.	16	E4
Auas Mts., S.W. Africa	47	B1
Aubrey, Que.	20	C3
Auburn, Me.	25	M2
Auckland, N.Z.	51	E2
Auckland I., S. Pacific Oc.	2	D7
Auden, Ont.	18	E3
Augathella, Queensland	50	F2
Aughrabies Falls, Orange F.S.	47	C2
Augsburg, Ger.	38	G3
Augusta, Ga.	25	K4
Augusta, Me.	25	M2
Augusta, W. Aust.	49	A6
Augusta Fall, Brazil	30	F5
Augustus Mt., W. Aust.	49	B4
Auknak L., Lab.	19	E3
Aulatsivik I., Lab.	19	E2
Aulitivik I., Baffin I., N.W.T.	11	V4
Aulneau Penin., Ont.	18	A4
Aurangabad, India	40	E5
Aurora, Ill.	25	J2
Aurora, Ont.	16	F4
Au Sable, Mich.	16	A3
Au Sable Pt., Mich.	16	B3
Austin, Nev.	24	C3
Austin, Tex.	24	G4
Austin L., W. Aust.	49	B5
Australian Alps, Victoria	50	F8
Austria, rep., Europe	38	H3
Autlan de Navarro, Mexico	28	D4
Ava, Burma	40	J4
Avalon Penin., Nfld.	23	L3
Aveiro, Brazil	30	G4
Avellaneda, Argentina	31	E9
Aves, Is. de, Caribbean Sea	30	D1
Avia Teria, Argentina	31	E9
Avignon, France	38	F4
Avinof C., Alaska	10	B6
Avola, B.C.	13	L7
Avon R., Hants., Eng.	37	E6
Avon R., Worcs., etc., Eng.	37	E5
Avonlea, Sask.	14	J5
Avonmore, Ont.	20	B3
Avontuur, Cape Prov., Rep. of S. Africa	47	C3
Awe L., Scotland	36	C3
Axel Heiberg I., Franklin, N.W.T.	11	Q2
Ayabaca, Peru	30	B4
Ayacucho, Argentina	31	F11
Ayacucho, Peru	30	C6
Ayaviri, Peru	30	C6
Aydin, Turkey	39	L6
Aylen Lako, Ont.	17	H2
Aylesbury, Eng.	37	E6
Aylesbury, Sask.	14	J5
Aylesford, N.S.	21	B2
Aylmer, Ont.	16	E5
Aylmer, Que.	17	J2
Aylmer L., Mackenzie, N.W.T.	10	N5
Aylmer L., Que.	20	D3
Aylmer Sd., Que.	23	H1
Aylwin, Que.	17	J2
Aymorés, Serra Dos, Brazil	30	J7
Ayr, and co., Scotland	36	C4
Ayr R., Scotland	36	C4
Ayre, Pt. of, Isle of Man	37	C4
Aysen, prov., Chile	31	C13
Aysen R., Chile	31	C13
Ayutthaya, Thailand	44	C5
Azogues, Ecuador	30	B4
Azores Is., Atlantic Oc.	46	A2
Azouzetta L., B.C.	12	J5
Azov, Sea of, U.S.S.R.	39	O4
Azúcar, P. d. Mt., Colombia	29	H3
Azuero Penin., Pan.	28	H6
Azufre, vol., Chile	31	D9
Azul, Argentina	31	F11
Azure L., B.C.	13	L6
Baba C., Turkey	42	A5
Bab-el-Mandeb, Str. of, Arabia-Africa	42	C7

GENERAL INDEX 55

Babine, *B.C.* 12 G5
Babine Portage, *B.C.* 13 H5
Babine Ra., *B.C.* 12 G5
Babine, R., and L., *B.C.* 12 G5
Babohoyo, *Ecuador* 30 A4
Bacabal, *Brazil* 30 F5
Baccalieu I., *Nfld.* 23 L2
Baccaro Pt., *N.S.* 21 B4
Bache Penin., *Ellesmere Is.,*
N.W.T. 11 U2
Back R., *N.W.T.* 10 N4
Backstairs Passage, *S.*
Aust. 50 B7
Badajoz, *Spain* 38 C6
Badakshansk, *U.S.S.R.* 40 D1
Bad Axe, *Mich.* 16 B4
Baddeck, *N.S.* 21 F1
Badger, *Nfld.* 23 J2
Bad Hills, *Sask.* 14 G5
Baffin B., *Canada* 11 U3
Baffin I., *N.W.T.* 11 T4
Bage, *Brazil* 31 G10
Baghdad, *Iraq* 42 C5
Bagotville, *Que.* 22 B2
Baguio, *Luzon, Philippine*
Is. 38 E5
Bahama I., Gd., *Bahamas* 29 J2
Bahamas Is., *W. Indies* 29 J3
Bahawalpur, *W. Pak.* 40 D3
Bahia, *Is., Honduras* 29 G4
Bahia Blanca, *Argentina* 31 E11
Bahia de Caraquez, *Ecuador* 30 A4
Bahia Laura, *Argentina* 31 D13
Bahia Samborombon,
Argentina 31 F11
Bahrein I., *Persian G.* 42 C6
Bahr-el-Ghazal, *Sudan* 46 F5
Baie Comeau, *Que.* 22 C2
Baie Johan Beetz, *Que.* 22 F1
Baies, L. des, *Que.* 20 B2
Baie Ste. Claire, *Que.* 22 E2
Baie St. Paul, *Que.* 20 D2
Baie Trinité, *Que.* 22 D2
Baie Verte, *N.B.* 21 C1
Baie Verte, *Nfld.* 23 J2
Baikal L., and Mts.,
U.S.S.R. 44 C1
Bairanald, *N.S.W.* 50 D7
Baird Mts., *Alaska* 10 B4
Bairnsdale, *Victoria* 50 F8
Baker, *Ore.* 24 C2
Baker L., *Keewatin,*
N.W.T. 11 P5
Baker's Dozen Is.,
Hudson B. 19 B2
Bakersfield. *Cal.* 24 C3
Baku, *U.S.S.R.* 42 C4
Bala, *Ont.* 16 F2
Bala, *Wales* 37 D5
Balabak Str., *Philippine*
Is. 44 D6
Balaton L., *Hungary* 39 J4
Balboa, *Pan.* 29 J6
Balcarce, *Argentina* 31 F11
Balcarres, *Sask.* 15 K5
Balclutha, *N.Z.* 51 B7
Baldock L., *Man.* 15 M2
Baldur, *Man.* 15 M6
Balearic Is., *Spain* 38 E6
Balfour, *Transvaal* 47 D2
Balfour Mt., *Alberta* 14 D5
Balgonie, *Sask.* 15 J5
Bali I., *Indonesia* 44 D7
Balikpapan, *Borneo* 44 D7
Balintana Chan., *Philippine*
Is. 44 E5
Baljennie, *Sask.* 14 H4
Balkan Mts., *Bulgaria* 39 L5
Balkhash L., *Cent. Asia* 42 F4
Ballachulish, *Scotland* 36 C3
Ballaghaderreen, *Eire* 37 B4
Ballantyne B., *Sask.* 15 K3
Ballantyne Str., *Franklin,*
N.W.T. 10 K3
Ballarat, *Victoria* 50 D8
Ballard C., *Nfld.* 23 L3
Ballater, *Scotland* 36 D3
Ballenas, Bahia de, *Mexico* 28 B2
Ballina, *Eire* 37 A4
Ballinasloe, *Eire* 37 A5
Ballinrobe, *Eire* 37 A5
Ballycastle, *Eire* 37 B4
Ballymena, *N. Ire.* 37 B4
Ballymoney, *N. Ire.* 37 B4
Ballyshannon, *Eire* 37 A4
Balsam L., *Ont.* 17 F3
Balsas R., *Brazil* 30 H5
Balsas R., *Mexico* 28 D4
Baltic Sea, *Europe* 39 J2
Baltimore, *Md.* 25 L3
Baluchistan, prov., *Pak.* 40 B3
Balzapuerto, *Peru* 30 B5
Bamako, *Mali* 46 C4
Bamfield, *Vancouver I.,*
B.C. 13 H8
Banagher, *Eire* 37 B5
Bananal, Ilha do. *Brazil* 30 G6
Banco, L. de, *Chile* 31 C12
Bancroft, *Ont.* 17 H2
Banda Atjeh, *Sumatra* 44 B6
Bandar, *India* 40 F5
Bandara Seri Begawan,
Brunei 44 D6
Bandar Seri Begawan,
Indonesia 44 D6

Bandar Shah, prov. 42 D5
Bandar Shahpur, *Pak.* 42 D5
Banda Sea, *Indonesia* 44 F7
Banderas B., *Mexico* 28 C3
Bandirma, *Turkey* 39 L5
Bandjarmasin, *Borneo* 44 D7
Bandon, *Eire* 37 A6
Bandung, *Java* 44 C7
Banes, *Cuba* 29 J3
Banff, *Alberta* 14 D5
Banff, and co., *Scotland* 36 D3
Banff Park, *Alberta* 14 D5
Bangalore, *India* 40 E6
Bangka I., *Indonesia* 44 C7
Bangkok (Krung Thep),
Thailand 44 C5
Bangladesh, *Asia* 40 G4
Bangor, *Me.* 25 N2
Bangor, *N. Ire.* 37 C4
Bangor, *Sask.* 15 K5
Bangor, *Wales* 37 C5
Bangui, *Cent. African Rep.* 46 E5
Bangweulu L., *Zambia* 46 F7
Bani, *Dominican Rep.* 29 K4
Banja Luka, *Yugoslavia* 39 J4
Banjuwangi, *Java* 44 D7
Bankipore, *India* 40 G3
Banks Is., *B.C.* 13 E6
Banks I., *Franklin, N.W.T.* 10 K3
Bank L., *Wash.* 13 L9
Banks Penin., *N.Z.* 51 D5
Banks Str., *Tasmania* 50 F10
Bann R., *N. Ire.* 37 B4
Bannock, *Sask.* 15 K4
Bannockburn. *Ont.* 17 H3
Bantalor, *N.B.* 22 D3
Bantry, *Eire* 37 A6
Baptiste, *Ont.* 17 G2
Barachois, *N.S.* 21 G2
Barachois Pond Park, *Nfld.* 23 H2
Baracoa, *Cuba* 29 K3
Barahona, *Dominican Rep.* 29 K4
Barama R., *Guyana* 30 E2
Baranof I., *Alaska* 13 C4
Baranovichi, *U.S.S.R.* 39 L2
Barbacena, *Brazil* 31 J8
Barbados I., *W. Indies* 29 M5
Barberton, *Transvaal* 47 E2
Barbuda I., *W. Indies* 29 M4
Barcaldine, *Queensland* 50 E1
Barcelona, *Spain* 38 E5
Barcelona, *Venezuela* 30 E2
Barcelos, *Brazil* 30 E4
Barcoo R.. *Queensland* 50 D2
Bareilly, *India* 40 E3
Barents Sea, *Arctic Oc.* 3 M1
Barge B., *Coast of Lab.* 23 J1
Bar Harbor, *Me.* 22 C4
Bari, *Italy* 39 J5
Barinas, *Venezuela* 30 D2
Barito R., *Borneo* 44 D7
Bark L., *Labelle, Que.* 20 B2
Bariturite, *Brazil* 30 K4
Barker, *N.Y.* 17 G4
Barkerville, *B.C.* 13 K6
Barkley Sd., *Vancouver Is.,*
B.C. 13 H8
Barkly East, *Cape Prov.,*
Rep. of S. Africa 47 D3
Barkly Highway, *N. Ter.,*
Queensland 49 F3
Barkly Tableland, *N. Ter.,*
Queensland 49 F3
Barkly West, *Cape Prov.,*
Rep. of S. Africa 47 C2
Barlee L., *W. Aust.* 49 C5
Barlee Ra., *W. Aust.* 49 B4
Barn Mt., *Que.* 22 D2
Barnaby I., *Que.* 20 E1
Barnaby River. *N.B.* 21 B1
Barnard Castle, *Eng.* 37 D4
Barnaul, *U.S.S.R.* 44 A1
Barnaul, *U.S.S.R.* 42 G3
Barnsley, *Eng.* 37 E5
Barnstaple, *Eng.* 37 C6
Baroda, *India* 40 D4
Barquisimeto, *Venezuela* 30 D2
Barra, *Brazil* 30 J6
Barra, and Is., *Hebrides,*
Scotland 36 B3
Barra Hd., *Hebrides, Scot-*
land 36 B3
Barra, Sd. of, *Hebrides,*
Scotland 36 B3
Barranca, *Peru* 30 B5
Barrancabermeja, *Colombia* 30 C2
Barranquilla, *Colombia* 30 C1
Barren I., *N.S.* 22 G4
Barretos, *Brazil* 31 H8
Barrhead, *Alberta* 14 D3
Barrie, *Ont.* 16 F3
Barrie I., *Ont.* 16 C2
Barriere, *B.C.* 13 K7
Barrington, *N.S.* 21 B4
Barrington, *Que.* 20 C3
Barrington L., *Man.* 15 L2
Barrington Passage *N.S.* 21 B4
Barringun, *N.S.W.* 50 E4
Barrow, *Alaska* 10 C3
Barrow I., *W. Aust.* 49 A4
Barrow Pt., *Alaska* 10 C3
Barrow R.. *Eire* 37 B5
Barrow Str., *N.W.T.,*
Canada 11 P3
Barrow Creek, *N.Ter., Aust.* 49 E4
Barrow-in-Furness, *Eng.* 37 D4
Barry Mts., *Victoria* 50 F8

Barrys Bay, *Ont.* 17 H2
Bartibog, *N.B.* 22 E3
Bartica, *Guyana* 30 F2
Bartle Frere Mt., *Queens-*
land 49 G3
Bartlett L., *Mackenzie,*
N.W.T. 12 L1
Bartletts Harb., *Nfld.* 23 J1
Barton, *Eng.* 37 E5
Barton City, *Mich.* 16 B3
Barwon R., *N.S.W.-Queens-*
land 50 G4
Bashaw, *Alberta* 14 E4
Bashee R., *Cape Prov.,*
Rep. of S. Africa 47 D3
Bashi Chan., *Taiwan* 44 E4
Basildon, *Eng.* 37 F6
Basin L., *Sask.* 14 J4
Basingstoke, *Eng.* 37 E6
Baskatong Res., *Que.* 20 B2
Basle, *Switzerland* 38 F4
Basque I., *Que.* 20 E1
Bass Str., *Victoria-Tas-*
mania 50 E9
Bassano, *Alberta* 14 E5
Bassein, *Burma* 40 H5
Basse Terre, *Guadeloupe,*
W. Indies 29 M4
Bass River, *N.S.* 21 D2
Bastia, *Corsica* 38 G5
Bastion C., *China* 44 C5
Basutoland, see Lesotho
Bata, *Rio Muni* 46 D5
Batabano, G. of, *Cuba* 29 H3
Batan Is., *Philippine Is.* 44 E4
Batchawana, *Ont.* 18 F5
Bateman's B., *N.S.W.* 50 H7
Bath, *Eng.* 37 D6
Bath, *Ont.* 17 J3
Bathurst, *Gambia* 46 B4
Bathurst, *N.B.* 22 D3
Bathurst, *N.S.W.* 50 G6
Bathurst C., *Mackenzie,*
N.W.T. 10 J3
Bathurst I., *Franklin,*
N.W.T. 10 O2
Bathurst I., *N. Ter., Aust.* 49 D2
Bathurst Inlet, *Mackenzie,*
N.W.T. 10 N4
Batiscan L., *Que.* 20 D2
Batiscan, and R., *Que.* 20 C2
Batlow, *N.S.W.* 50 G7
Baton Rouge. *La.* 25 H4
Batteau, *Coast of Lab.* 19 F3
Batticaloa, *Sri Lanka* 40 F7
Battle Cr., *Mich.* 25 J2
Battle Cr., *Sask.* 14 G6
Battle R., *Alberta-Sask.* 14 F4
Battleford, *Sask.* 14 G4
Battle Harbour, *Lab.* 19 F3
Batum, *U.S.S.R.* 42 C4
Baturite, *Brazil* 30 K4
Baudo, *Colombia* 30 B2
Bauld C., *Nfld.* 23 K1
Bauma, *Finland* 35 L3
Baumann Fd., *Franklin,*
N.W.T. 11 R2
Bay Fd., *Franklin, N.W.T.* 11 S2
Bay Bulls, *Nfld.* 23 L3
Bay City, *Mich.* 25 K2
Bay des Rochers, *Que.* 20 E2
Bay de Verde, *Nfld.* 23 L2
Bayfield, *Ont.* 16 D4
Bayfield Mt., *Que.* 22 D2
Bay of Fundy, *N.B.-N.S.* 21 B2
Bay of Islands, *N.Z.* 51 E1
Baykonyr, *U.S.S.R.* 42 E4
Bayonne, *France* 38 D5
Bay Port, *Mich.* 16 B4
Bay Roberts, *Nfld.* 23 L3
Bays, L. of, *Ont.* 17 F2
Baysville, *Ont.* 17 F2
Bazin R., *Que.* 20 B2
Beachburg, *Ont.* 17 H4
Beachport, *S. Aust.* 50 B8
Beachy Hd., *Eng.* 37 F6
Beaconsfield, *Tasmania* 50 L11
Beal Ra., *Queensland* 50 C2
Beale C., *Vancouver I.,B.C.* 13 H8
Beamsville, *Ont.* 16 F4
Bear C., *P.E.I.* 22 F4
Bear I., *Barents Sea* 3 L1
Bear C., *James B.* 18 H1
Bear I., *Nfld.* 23 J3
Bear L., *B.C.* 12 G4
Bear L., *Man.* 15 H3
Bear L., Great, *N.W.T.* 10 K4
Bear R., *Alberta* 14 D1
Bear Hills, *Sask.* 14 G5
Bear River, *N.S.* 21 B3
Bearskin Lake, *Ont.* 18 C1
Beata C., *San Domingo* 29 K4
Beaton, *B.C.* 13 M7
Beatrice, *Neb.* 24 G2
Beatton River, *B.C.* 12 K4
Beattyville, *Que.* 19 B4
Beau, *Que.* 20 B3
Beaucanton, *Que.* 18 J4
Beauceville, *Que.* 20 D2
Beauchene I., *Falkland Is.* 31 F14
Beaudesert, *Queensland* 50 J3
Beaudet, *Que.* 20 C2
Beaufort Sea, *N.W.T.* 10 F3
Beaufort West, *Cape Prov.*
Rep. of S. Africa 47 C3
Beauharnois, *Que.* 20 C3

Beauly, *Scotland* 36 C3
Beaumaris, *Wales* 37 C5
Beaumont, *Que.* 20 D2
Beaumont, *Tex.* 25 H4
Beauport, *Que.* 20 D2
Beaurivage, *Que.* 20 D2
Beausejour, *Man.* 15 N5
Beauval, *Sask.* 14 H3
Beaver R., *Alberta* 14 F3
Beaver R., *Ont.* 15 R3
Beaver R., *Yukon* 12 H2
Beaver Bank, *N.S.* 21 C3
Beaverde, *B.C.* 13 L8
Beaverhill L., *Alberta* 14 E4
Beaverhill L., *Man.* 15 O3
Beaver Hills, *Sask.* 15 K5
Beaverlodge, *Alberta* 14 B3
Beaverton, *Ont.* 17 F3
Becancour. and R., *Que.* 20 C2
Bechar, *Algeria* 46 C2
Bechuanaland, see Botswana
Bedford, *Cape Prov., Rep.*
of S. Africa 47 D3
Bedford, *N.S.* 21 D3
Bedford, *Que.* 20 C3
Bedford, and co., *Eng.* 37 E5
Beecher Falls, *Que.* 20 D3
Beechey L., *Mackenzie,*
N.W.T. 10 N4
Beechy, *Sask.* 14 H5
Beenleigh, *Queensland* 50 J3
Bega, *N.S.W.* 50 G8
Beira, *Mozambique* 46 G7
Beirût, *Lebanon* 46 G2
Beitbridge, *Rhodesia* 47 E1
Beja, *Portugal* 38 C6
Beja'ïa (Bougie), *Algeria* 38 F6
Bela, *W. Pak.* 40 C3
Belair, *Que.* 20 D2
Belanger R., *Man.* 15 N4
Belcher Chan., *Franklin,*
N.W.T. 11 P2
Belcher Is., *Hudson B.* 11 S6
Belém, *Brazil* 30 H4
Belen, *Argentina* 31 D9
Belfast, *N. Ire.* 37 B4
Belfast, *P.E.I.* 21 E1
Belfast, *Transvaal* 47 E2
Belfast L., *N. Ire.* 37 C4
Belfort, *France* 38 F4
Belgium, kingdom, *W.*
Europe 38 F3
Belgorod Dnestrovskiy,
Ukraine 39 M4
Belgrade, *Yugoslavia* 39 K4
Belisle L., *Que.* 20 B2
Belitung I. (Billiton),
Indonesia 44 C7
Belize, and R., *Brit. Hon-*
duras 28 G4
Bell I., *Alaska* 12 E5
Bell I., *Nfld.* 23 K1
Bell I., *Nfld.* 23 L3
Bell R., *Que.* 19 B4
Bella Bella, *B.C.* 13 F6
Bella Coola, and R., *B.C.* 13 G6
Bellary, *India* 40 E5
Bellavista, *Argentina* 31 F9
Bellburns, *N.S.* 23 J1
Belledune, *N.B.* 22 D3
Belle Isle, *Nfld.* 23 K1
Belleisle Cr., *N.B.* 22 D4
Belle Isle, Str. of, *Nfld.* 23 J1
Belleoram, *Nfld.* 23 K3
Bellerive, *Tasmania* 50 L12
Belleville, *Ill.* 25 J3
Belleville, *Ont.* 17 H3
Bellevue, *Ont.* 18 F5
Bellin (Payne Bay), *Que.* 19 D1
Bellingham, *Wash.* 24 B1
Bell-Irving R., *B.C.* 12 F4
Belly R., *Alberta* 14 E6
Belmont, *Cape Prov., Rep.*
of S. Africa 47 C2
Belmont, *Nev.* 24 C3
Belmont, *N.S.* 21 D2
Belmont, *Ont.* 16 D5
Belmonte, *Bahia, Brazil* 30 D5
Belmonte, *Minas Gerais,*
Brazil 30 K7
Belmopan, *Brit. Honduras* 28 G4
Beloe L., *U.S.S.R.* 35 O3
Belo Horizonte, *Brazil* 30 H7
Belomorsk, *U.S.S.R.* 35 N3
Beloud Post, *Yukon* 13 B2
Beloye L., *U.S.S.R.* 35 O3
Beltana, *S. Aust.* 50 B5
Belukha Mt., *U.S.S.R.* 44 A2
Bemis. *Me.* 22 B4
Benalla, *Victoria* 50 E8
Ben Attow, *Scotland* 36 C3
Benbecula, *Hebrides, Scot-*
land 36 B5
Bend, *Ore.* 24 B3
Ben Dearg, *Scotland* 36 C2
Bendigo, *Victoria* 50 E8
Bengal, Bay of, *India* 40 G8
Benghazi, *Libya* 46 F5
Bengkulu, *Sumatra* 44 C2
Benguela, *Angola* 46 E7
Ben Hope, *Scotland* 36 C7
Beni R., *Bolivia* 30 D2
Ben Lawers. *Scotland* 36 C6
Ben Lomond, *N.S.W.* 50 H3
Ben Macdhui, *Lesotho* 47 D3

Ben Macdui, *Scotland* 36 D3
Bennett. and L., *B.C.* 12 C3
Ben Nevis, *Scotland* 36 C2
Benoni, *Transvaal* 47 D5
Benue R., *Macdui* 46 D3
Benwee Hd., *Eire* 37 A4
Ben Wyvis, *Scotland* 36 C3
Berber, *Sudan* 46 G4
Berbera, *Somali Rep.* 46 H4
Berbice R., *Guyana* 30 F2
Berdichev (Ossipevsk), *Ukraine* 39 M3
Berdyansk, *Ukraine* 35 O6
Berens I., *Man.* 15 N4
Berens L., and R., *Ont.* 18 B3
Berens River, tn., and R., *Man.* 15 N4
Beresford Lake, *Man.* 15 O5
Berezuik L., *Que.* 19 B3
Bergen, *Norway* 35 H3
Berger, *Tex.* 24 F3
Berhampur, *India* 40 F5
Bering Sea & Str., *Asia-N. America* 43 Q2
Berkeley, *Cal.* 24 B3
Berkshire, co., *Eng.* 37 E6
Berland R., *Alberta* 14 C4
Berlin, *Germany* 38 H2
Berlin, *N.H.* 22 B4
Bermejo R., *Formosa, Argentina* 31 E8
Bermejo R., *San Juan, Argentina* 31 D10
Bermudas Is., *N. Atlantic Oc.* 29 M1
Berne, *Switzerland* 38 F4
Berri, *S. Aust.* 50 C7
Berry Cr., *Alberta* 14 F5
Berry Is., *Bahamas* 29 J2
Berseba. *S.W. Africa* 47 B2
Berté L., *Que.* 22 C1
Berthierville, *Que.* 20 C2
Bertram, *Ont.* 18 F4
Berwick, *N.S.* 21 C2
Berwick, co., *Scotland* 36 D4
Berwick Fall, *Man.* 15 O3
Berwick-upon-Tweed, *Eng.* 36 E4
Berwyn, *Alberta* 14 C2
Berwyn Mts., *Wales* 37 D5
Besançon, *France* 38 F4
Beskids, East, Mts., *Czechoslovakia* 39 K3
Beskids, West, Mts., *Czechoslovakia* 39 J3
Besnard L., *Sask.* 14 H3
Bessemer, *Ont.* 17 H2
Bethal, *Transvaal* 47 D2
Bethanie, *S.W. Africa* 47 B2
Bethany, *Ont.* 17 G3
Bethel, *Alaska* 10 B5
Bethel, *Me.* 22 B4
Bethlehem, *Orange F.S.* 47 D2
Bethulie, *Orange F.S.* 47 D3
Bethune, *Sask.* 14 J5
Betsiamites, and R., *Que.* 22 C2
Bett's Cove, *Nfld.* 23 K2
Beulah, *Man.* 15 L5
Beverley Hd., *Nfld.* 23 H2
Beware, Pta., *Peru* 30 C7
Bezhetsk, *U.S.S.R.* 35 O4
Béziers, *France* 38 E5
Bhagalpur, *India* 40 G4
Bhamo, *Burma* 40 J4
Bhatinda, *India* 40 D2
Bhatpara, *India* 40 G4
Bhavnagar, *India* 40 D4
Bhopal, *India* 40 E4
Bhubaneswar, *India* 40 G4
Bhutan, state. *N. India* 40 H3
Biak, Is., *New Guinea* 44 F7
Bialystok, *Poland* 39. K2
Biarritz, *France* 38 D5
Bic, *Que.* 22 C2
Biche, L. la, *Que.* 14 E3
Biddeford, *Me.* 22 B5
Bideford, and B., *Eng.* 37 C6
Bienfait, *Sask.* 15 K6
Bienville L., *Que.* 19 C2
Big B., *N.Z.* 51 B6
Big Cr., *B.C.* 13 J7
Big I., *Keewatin, N.W.T.* 19 C1
Big I., *Mackenzie, N.W.T.* 12 M2
Big I., *Ont.* 18 A4
Big I., *Ungava B.* 19 D2
Big R., *Sask.* 14 H4
Big Beaver, *Sask.* 14 J6
Big Beaver House, *Ont.* 18 C2
Big Bell, *W. Aust.* 49 B5
Bigelow, *Me.* 22 B4
Biggar, *Sask.* 14 G4
Big Horn R., and Mts., *Wyo.* 24 E2
Big Lake, *Ont.* 16 C2
Big Muddy L., *Sask.* 14 J6
Big Pond, *N.S.* 21 G2
Big Quill L., *Sask.* 15 J5
Big River, *Sask.* 14 H4
Big Salmon, and R., *Yukon* 12 C2
Big Sand L., *Man.* 15 M2
Big Sandy L., *Sask.* 15 J3
Bigsby I., *Ont.* 18 A4
Big Stick L., *Sask.* 14 G5
Bigstone R., *Man.* 15 O3
Big Trout L., *Ont.* 18 C2
Big Trout L., *Ont.* 18 D2
Big Turtle L., *Ont.* 18 B4
Big Valley, *Alberta* 14 E4

Bigwood, *Ont.* 16 E1
Bihar, state, *India* 40 G4
Bihar Mts., *Romania* 39 K4
Bikaner, *India* 40 D3
Bikini I., *Pacific Oc.* 2 D4
Bilbao, *Spain* 38 D5
Billings, *Mont.* 24 E1
Bilodeau, *Que.* 20 C1
Bingara, *N.S.W.* 50 H4
Bingerville, *Ivory Coast, W. Africa* 46 C5
Bingham, *Me.* 22 B4
Binghampton, *N.Y.* 25 L2
Bingle, *Ont.* 18 H4
Binscarth, *Man.* 15 L5
Binzert, *Tunisia* 46 D2
Birch I., *Man.* 15 M4
Birch L., *Alberta* 14 F4
Birch L., *Mackenzie, N.W.T.* 14 M1
Birch L., *N. Ont.* 18 B3
Birch Mt., *Alberta* 14 D2
Birch R., *Alberta* 14 E1
Birch Hills, *Alberta* 14 B3
Birch Lake, *Sask.* 15 J1
Birchwood, *N.Z.* 51 A6
Bird, *Man.* 15 O2
Bird Rock, *Cabot Str.* 23 G3
Birdsville, *Queensland* 50 B2
Birdum, *N. Ter., Aust.* 49 E3
Birjand, *Iran* 40 A2
Birkenhead, *Eng.* 37 D5
Birmingham, *Ala.* 25 J4
Birmingham, *Eng.* 37 E5
Birobidzhan, *U.S.S.R.* 44 F2
Birtle, *Man.* 15 L5
Biscay, B. of, *France, etc.* 38 C4
Biscotasing, *Ont.* 18 G5
Bishop Rock I., *Eng.* 37 B7
Bishop's Falls, *Nfld.* 23 K2
Bismark, *N. Dak.* 24 F1
Bison L., *Alberta* 14 C2
Bissau, *Port. Guinea* 46 B4
Bissett, *Man.* 15 O5
Bistcho L., *Alberta* 12 L3
Bitola, *Yugoslavia* 39 K5
Bitterfontein, *Cape Prov., Rep. of S. Africa* 47 B2
Bittern L., *Alberta* 14 E4
Bitumount, *Alberta* 14 F2
Black B., *Ont.* 18 D4
Black L., *Man.* 15 N5
Black L., *Mich.* 16 A2
Black L., *Que.* 20 D2
Black L., *Sask.* 14 J1
Black L. Park, *Ont.* 17 J3
Blackall, *Queensland* 50 E2
Black Bear I. Lake, *Sask.* 14 H3
Blackburn, *Eng.* 37 D5
Black Donald Mines, *Ont.* 17 J2
Black Duck R., *Ont.* 15 R2
Blackfoot (Ind. Res.), *Alberta* 14 E5
Black Forest, *Ger.* 38 G3
Black Hills, *S. Dak.* 24 F2
Black Pool, *B.C.* 13 K7
Blackpool, *Eng.* 37 D5
Black Rock Pt., *Lab.* 19 E1
Black Rocks, *W. Aust.* 49 C3
Black Sea, *Europe-Asia* 39 M5
Black Sturgeon L., *Ont.* 18 D4
Blackville, *N.B.* 21 B1
Blackwater, *Eng.* 37 F6
Blackwater L., *Mackenzie, N.W.T.* 12 J1
Blackwater R., *Eire* 37 A5
Bladworth, *Sask.* 14 H5
Blagoveshchensk, *U.S.S.R.* 44 E1
Blair Athol, *Queensland* 49 H4
Blair Atholl, *Scotland* 36 D3
Blairmore, *Alberta* 14 D6
Blanc L., *Que.* 20 C2
Blanc, Mont, *France* 38 F4
Blanca B., *Argentina* 31 E11
Blanca L., *Chile* 31 C14
Blanca Peak, *Colo.* 24 E3
Blanca Encalada, *Chile* 31 C8
Blanche, *Que.* 17 K2
Blanche L., *S. Aust.* 50 B4
Blanche R., *Que.* 20 B3
Blanco, *Cape Prov., Rep. of S. Africa* 47 C3
Blanco C., *Argentina* 31 D13
Blanco C., *Costa Rica* 29 G6
Blanco C., *Ore.* 24 B2
Blanco C., *Peru* 30 A4
Blanco C., *Span. Sahara* 46 B3
Blanc Sablon, *Que.* 23 J1
Blandford, *Que.* 20 D2
Blandford B., *Baffin I.* 19 C1
Blanquilla I., *Venezuela* 30 E1
Blantyre Limbe, *Malawi* 46 G7
Blayney, *N.S.W.* 50 G6
Blenheim, *N.Z.* 51 D4
Blenheim, *Ont.* 16 D5
Blewet, *Sask.* 15 K6
Blind River, *Ont.* 16 B1
Bloedel, *Vancouver I., B.C.* 13 H7
Bloemfontein, *Orange F.S.* 47 D2
Bloemhof, *Transvaal* 47 D2
Blois, *France* 38 E4
Blood (Ind. Res.), *Alberta* 14 E6
Blood Indian Cr., *Alberta* 14 F5
Bloodvein R.. *Man.* 15 N5
Bloody Falls, *Mackenzie, N.W.T.* 10 L4

Bloody Foreland, *Eire* 37 A4
Bloomfield, *Ont.* 17 H3
Bloomington, *Ill.* 25 J2
Blue R., *B.C.* 12 F3
Blueberry, and R., *B.C.* 12 K4
Bluefields, *Nicaragua* 29 H5
Blue Hills of Coteau, *Nfld.* 23 J3
Blue Mountains, *N.S.W.* 50 H6
Blue Ridge, *Va.* 25 K3
Blue River, *B.C.* 13 L6
Blue Sea L., *Que.* 17 J1
Bluff, *Alaska* 10 B5
Bluff, *N.Z.* 51 B7
Bluff, *Ut.* 24 E3
Blumenau. *Brazil* 31 H9
Blumenhof, *Sask.* 14 H5
Blyth, *Eng.* 37 E4
Blyth, *Ont.* 16 D4
Boakview, *Ont.* 16 F2
Boat Basin, *Vancouver I., B.C.* 13 G8
Boatman, *Queensland* 50 F3
Boa Vista, *Brazil* 30 E3
Bobcaygeon, *Ont.* 17 G3
Bobi, *Paraguay* 31 F9
Bobruyk, *U.S.S.R.* 39 M2
Bocas del Toro, *Pan.* 29 H6
Bodalla, *N.S.W.* 50 G8
Bodmin, *Eng.* 37 C6
Bodmin, *Sask.* 14 H4
Bodo, *Alberta* 14 F4
Bodö, *Norway* 35 J2
Bogan R., *N.S.W.* 50 F5
Bogenfels, *S.W. Africa* 47 B2
Bognor Regis, *Eng.* 37 E6
Bogota, *Colombia* 30 C3
Bohemian Forest, *Ger.* 38 H3
Boiestown, *N.B.* 22 D3
Bois, R. dos, *Brazil* 30 G7
Bois Blanc I., *Mich.* 16 A2
Boisdale, *N.S.* 21 G1
Boisé, *Ida.* 24 C2
Boissevain, *Man.* 15 L6
Boisvert L., *Que.* 20 B2
Bökn Fd., *Norway* 35 H4
Boksburg, *Transvaal* 47 D2
Bolama, *Port. Guinea* 46 B4
Bolan Pass, *W. Pak.* 40 C3
Bolduc, *Que.* 20 D3
Bolger, *Que.* 20 A1
Bolivar, dept., *Colombia* 30 B2
Bolivia, rep., *S. America* 30 D7
Bollon, *Queensland* 50 F4
Bologna, *Italy* 38 G4
Bolson de Mapimi, *Mexico* 28 D2
Boma, *Zaire* 46 E6
Bombala, *N.S.W.* 50 G8
Bombay, *India* 40 D5
Bonaire I., *Caribbean Sea* 31 D1
Bonaparte Arch., *W. Aust.* 49 C2
Bonaparte L., *B.C.* 13 K7
Bonarlaw, *Ont.* 17 H3
Bonaventure, *Nfld.* 23 K2
Bonaventure, *Que.* 22 E2
Bonaventure I., *Que.* 22 E2
Bonavista, *Nfld.* 23 L2
Bonavista B., and C., *Nfld.* 23 L2
Bone, G. of, *Celebes* 44 E7
Bonfield, *Ont.* 17 F1
Bonheur, *Ont.* 18 C4
Bonifacio, Str. of, *Corsica-Sardinia* 38 G5
Bonn, *W. Ger.* 38 F3
Bonne B., *Nfld.* 23 H2
Bonners Ferry, *Ida.* 24 C1
Bonnet, Lac du, *Man.* 15 N5
Bonnet, L., *Man.* 15 O5
Bonney L., *S. Aust.* 50 B8
Bonnyville, *Alberta* 14 F3
Bontebok National Park, *Cape Prov., Rep. of S. Africa* 47 C3
Boolburra, *Queensland* 50 H2
Booligal, *N.S.W.* 50 E6
Boonville, *N.Y.* 17 K4
Boothia, G. of, *Franklin, N.W.T.* 11 Q3
Boothia Isthmus, *Keewatin, N.W.T.* 11 Q4
Boothia Penin., *Franklin, N.W.T.* 11 P3
Borås, *Sweden* 38 H1
Borba, *Brazil* 30 F4
Bordeaux, *France* 38 D4
Borden, *P.E.I.* 21 D1
Borden I., *Franklin, N.W.T.* 10 M2
Borden Penin., *Franklin, N.W.T.* 11 S3
Bordertown, *S. Aust.* 50 C8
Bordeyri, *Iceland* 35 B2
Borneo I., *Indonesia* 44 D6
Bornholm (I.), *Denmark* 39 H2
Borosiv, *U.S.S.R.* 39 M2
Boshof, *Orange F.S.* 47 D2
Bosporus, *Turkey* 39 M5
Boston, *Eng.* 37 E5
Boston. *Mass.* 25 M2
Boston Bar, *B.C.* 13 K8
Bostonnais R., *Que.* 20 C2
Botany B., *N.S.W.* 50 H7
Bothaville, *Orange F.S.* 47 D2
Bothnia, G. of, *Sweden-Finland* 35 K3

Bothwell. *Ont.* 16 D5
Botosani, *Romania* 39 L4
Botswana (Bechuanaland), *S. Africa* 47 C1
Botucatu, *Brazil* 31 H8
Botwood, *Nfld.* 23 K2
Bouchery, *Que.* 20 C3
Bouchette, *Que.* 17 K1
Bouchette L., *Que.* 20 C1
Bougainville C., *Tasmania* 50 M12
Boularderie I., *N.S.* 23 G2
Boulder, *W. Aust.* 49 C6
Boulogne, *France* 38 E3
Bounty, *Sask.* 14 H5
Bounty I., *S. Pacific Oc.* 2 D7
Bourges, *France* 38 E4
Bourget, *Ont.* 17 K2
Bourke, *N.S.W.* 50 F5
Bourkes, *Ont.* 18 H4
Bourmont, *Que.* 20 B1
Bournemouth, *Eng.* 37 E6
Bouvet I., *S. Atlantic Oc.* 3 L7
Bow R., *Alberta* 14 E5
Bow R., Lit., *Alberta* 14 E5
Bowden, *Alberta* 14 E5
Bowdoin Canyon, *Lab.* 19 E3
Bowen, *Queensland* 49 H3
Bow Island, *Alberta* 14 F6
Bowling Green, *Ky.* 25 B4
Bowmanville. *Ont.* 17 H4
Bowral, *N.S.W.* 50 H7
Bowron R., *B.C.* 13 K6
Bowron Lake Park, *B.C.* 13 K6
Bowsman River, *Man.* 15 L4
Bowser L., *B.C.* 12 E4
Boyd, *Man.* 15 N3
Boyd L., *Que.* 19 B3
Boyer R., *Alberta* 14 C1
Boyer Rapids, *Alberta* 14 E1
Boyle, *Eire* 37 A5
Boylston, *N.S.* 21 F2
Boyne R., *Eire* 37 B5
Boynton, *Que.* 20 C3
Bozeman, *Mont.* 24 D1
Bracadale L., *Skye I., Scotland* 36 B3
Bracebridge, *Ont.* 17 F2
Bracken, *Sask.* 14 G6
Brackettville, *Tex.* 24 F5
Bradford, *Eng.* 37 E5
Bradford, *Ont.* 16 F3
Braga, *Portugal* 38 B5
Bragado, *Argentina* 31 E11
Bragança, *Brazil* 30 H4
Bragança, *Portugal* 38 C5
Brahmaputra R., *India, etc.* 40 H3
Braich-y-pwll, *Wales* 37 C5
Braidwood, *N.S.W.* 50 G7
Bráila, *Romania* 39 L4
Brak R., *Cape Prov., Rep. of S. Africa* 47 C2
Bralorne, *B.C.* 13 J7
Brampton, *Ont.* 16 F4
Branch, *Nfld.* 23 L3
Branch R., *Que.* 22 G1
Branch W., R., *Sask.-Mont.* 14 H6
Branco C., *Brazil* 30 K5
Branco R., *Brazil* 30 E3
Brandon. *Man.* 15 M6
Brandvlei, *Cape Prov., Rep. of S. Africa* 47 C3
Brant, *Alberta* 14 E5
Brant, co., *Ont.* 16 E4
Brantford, *Ont.* 16 E4
Bras d'Apic, *Que.* 20 D2
Bras d'Or, *N.S.* 21 G1
Bras d'Or L., *N.S.* 21 G2
Brasilia, *Brazil* 30 D6
Brasilia Legal, *Brazil* 30 F4
Brasov, *Romania* 39 L4
Bratislava, *Czechoslovakia* 39 J3
Bray, *Eire* 37 B5
Brazeau, and R., *Alberta* 14 C4
Brazeau (Nordegg P.O.), *Alberta* 14 C4
Brazeau Mt., *Alberta* 14 C4
Brazil, rep., *S. America* 30 F6
Brazilian Guiana, *Brazil* 30 E3
Brazil Lake, *N.S.* 21 B4
Brazos R., *Tex.* 24 G4
Brazzaville, *Congo, Africa* 46 E6
Breaksea Sd., *N.Z.* 51 A6
Bream B., *N.Z.* 51 E1
Brechin, *Ont.* 17 F3
Brechin, *Scotland* 36 D3
Brecknock, co., *Wales* 37 D6
Brecon, *Wales* 37 D6
Bredasdorp, *Cape Prov., Rep. of S. Africa* 47 B3
Bredenbury, *Sask.* 15 L5
Breidha Fd., *Iceland* 35 B2
Brejó, *Brazil* 30 J4
Brem River, *B.C.* 13 H7
Bremen, *Ger.* 38 G2
Bremerhaven, *Ger.* 38 H5
Brent, *Ont.* 16 G1
Brescia, *Italy* 38 G4
Breslau. See Wrocław
Bressay Is., (Shetland Is.), *Scotland* 36 E1
Brest, *France* 38 C3
Brest, *U.S.S.R.* 39 K2
Breton C.. *N.S.* 23 H4
Breves, *Brazil* 30 G4
Brewarrina, *N.S.W.* 50 F4
Brewer, *Me.* 22 C4

Name	Page	Ref
Brewton, *Ala.*	25	J4
Breyten, *Transvaal*	47	E2
Bribie I., *Queensland*	50	J3
Bridgeport, *Conn.*	25	M2
Bridgetown, *N.S.*	21	B3
Bridgetown, *Windward Is.*	29	M5
Bridgeville, *N.S.*	21	E2
Bridgewater, *N.S.*	21	C3
Bridgton, *Me.*	22	B5
Bridgwater, and B., *Eng.*	37	D6
Bridlington, and B., *Eng.*	37	E4
Brier I., *N.S.*	21	A3
Brigden, *Ont.*	16	C5
Bright, *Victoria*	50	F8
Brighton, *Eng.*	37	E6
Brighton, *Ont.*	17	H3
Brighton, *Victoria*	50	E8
Brigus Junc., *Nfld.*	23	L3
Brilliant, *B.C.*	13	M8
Brindisi, *Italy*	39	J5
Brion I., *Que.*	22	G3
Brisbane, *Queensland*	50	J3
Brisco, *B.C.*	13	M7
Bristol, *Eng.*	37	D6
Bristol, *N.B.*	22	G3
Bristol, *Que.*	17	J2
Bristol B., *Alaska*	10	C6
Bristol Chan., *England-Wales*	37	C6
Britannia, *B.C.*	13	J8
British Columbia, prov., *Canada*	10	J6
British Honduras, *Cent. America*	28	G4
British Isles, *W. Europe*	35	E4
British Mts., *Alaska-Yukon*	10	F4
Briton Cove, *N.S.*	21	G1
Britstown, *Cape Prov., Rep. of S. Africa*	47	C3
Britt, *Ont.*	16	E2
Brno, *Czechoslovakia*	39	J3
Broad B., *Hebrides, Scotland*	36	B2
Broad R., *Man.*	15	P1
Broad R., *Man.*	15	Q2
Broadback R., *Que.*	19	B3
Broad Law, *Scotland*	36	D4
Broadmount, *Queensland*	50	H1
Broadview, *Sask.*	15	K5
Brochet, *Man.*	15	L2
Brochet, *Que.*	20	C2
Brochet L., *Man.*	15	L1
Brochu L., *Que.*	20	B1
Brock, *Sask.*	14	G5
Brockport, *N.Y.*	17	H4
Brockton, *Mass.*	25	M2
Brockville, *Ont.*	17	J3
Brodeur Penin., *Franklin, N.W.T.*	11	R3
Brodick, *Arran I., Scotland*	36	C4
Broken B., *N.S.W.*	50	H6
Broken Hill. *N.S.W.*	50	C5
Brome, *Que.*	20	C3
Bromtonville, *Que.*	20	C3
Bronkhorst Spruit, *Transvaal*	47	D2
Bronte, *Ont.*	16	F4
Brookbury, *Que.*	20	D3
Brookfield, *N.S.*	21	D2
Brookfield Mines, *N.S.*	21	B3
Brookhaven, *Miss.*	25	H4
Brooklin, *Ont.*	17	G4
Brooklyn, *N.Y.*	25	M2
Brooklyn, *N.S.*	21	C3
Brookmere, *B.C.*	13	K8
Brookport, *Que.*	20	C3
Brooks, *Alberta*	14	F5
Brooks B., *Vancouver I., B.C.*	13	G7
Brooks Ra., *Alaska*	10	B4
Brooks Brook, *Yukon*	12	D2
Broom L., *Scotland*	36	C3
Broome, *W. Aust.*	49	C3
Broquerie, La, *Man.*	15	N6
Brora, *Sask.*	14	J5
Broughton, E., *Que.*	20	D2
Brown Mt., *Que.*	14	B4
Browning Entrance, *B.C.*	13	E6
Brownsburg, *Que.*	20	B3
Brownsville, *Tex.*	24	G5
Brownville, *Me.*	22	C4
Broyle C., *Nfld.*	23	L3
Bruce, co., *Ont.*	16	E3
Bruce Mt., *W. Aust.*	49	B4
Bruce Penin., *Ont.*	16	D2
Brucefield, *Ont.*	16	D4
Bruce Mines, *Ont.*	16	B4
Bruck, *Ger.*	39	H4
Brule, *Alberta*	14	B4
Brule Lake, *Ont.*	17	G2
Brunette I., *Nfld.*	23	J3
Brunner L., *N.Z.*	51	C5
Bruno, *Sask.*	14	J4
Brunswick, *Ga.*	25	K4
Brunswick, *Ger.*	38	G2
Brunswick, *Me.*	22	B5
Brunswick L., *Ont.*	18	G4
Brunswick Penin., *Chile*	31	C14
Bruny I., *Tasmania*	50	L12
Brussels, *Belgium*	38	E3
Brussels, *Ont.*	16	D4
Brussels Mt., *Alberta*	14	C4
Bruton L., *Que.*	19	B3
Bryansk, *U.S.S.R.*	39	N2
Brydges Mt., *Ont.*	16	D5
Bryson, *Que.*	20	A3
Bucaramanga, *Colombia*	30	C2
Buchanan, *Sask.*	15	K5
Buchan Ness, *Scotland*	36	E3
Buchans, *Nfld.*	23	J2
Bucharest, *Romania*	39	L4
Buck L., *Alberta*	14	D4
Buckie, *Scotland*	36	D3
Buckingham, *Que.*	17	K2
Buckingham, and co., *Eng.*	37	E5
Buckland Tableland, *Queensland*	50	F2
Bucksport, *Me.*	22	C4
Buctouche, *N.B.*	21	C1
Budapest, *Hungary*	39	J4
Bude, *Eng.*	37	C6
Buenaventura, *Colombia*	30	B3
Buenos Aires, *Argentina*	31	F10
Buenos Aires L., *Chile-Argentina*	31	C13
Buffalo, *Alberta*	14	F5
Buffalo, *N.Y.*	25	L2
Buffalo, *Wyo.*	24	E2
Buffalo L., *Alberta*	14	E4
Buffalo L., *Mackenzie, N.W.T.*	10	L5
Buffalo Head Hills, *Alberta*	14	C2
Buffalo Narrows, *Sask.*	14	G3
Buffalo Park, *Alberta*	14	F4
Buffalo Pound L., *Sask.*	14	J5
Buffalo River, *Mackenzie, N.W.T.*	12	N2
Bug R., *Poland*	39	K2
Bug R., *Ukraine*	39	M3
Bukama, *Zaire*	46	F6
Bukamangna Ra., *Tibet*	40	F2
Bukavu, *Zaire*	46	F6
Bukhara, *U.S.S.R.*	42	E5
Bulawayo, *Rhodesia*	46	F8
Bulgaria, rep., *Europe*	39	K5
Bulkley R., *B.C.*	12	G5
Bulldog I., *Lab.*	19	F3
Buller R., *N.Z.*	51	C4
Bullmoose Mt., *B.C.*	12	K5
Bulloo Cr., *Queensland*	50	E3
Bulloo L., *Queensland*	50	D4
Bullpound Cr., *Alberta*	14	F5
Bull River, *B.C.*	13	N8
Bull Shoals Res., *Mo.-Ark.*	25	H3
Buloke L., *Victoria*	50	D8
Bulstrode, *Que.*	20	C2
Bulun, *U.S.S.R.*	44	A2
Bulyea, *Sask.*	14	J5
Bunbury, *W. Aust.*	49	B6
Bundaberg, *Queensland*	50	J2
Bunguran Is. (Natuna), *Indonesia*	44	C6
Burdekin R., *Queensland*	49	H3
Burden Mt., *B.C.*	12	J4
Burdett, *Alberta*	14	F6
Bureau L., *Que.*	20	B1
Burford, *Ont.*	16	E4
Burgaz, *Bulgaria*	39	L5
Burgeo, and Is., *Nfld.*	23	J3
Burgersdorp, *Cape Prov. Rep. of S. Africa*	47	D3
Burgos, *Spain*	38	D5
Burgoyne B., *Que.*	19	C1
Burica Pt., *Pan.*	29	H6
Burin, and Penin., *Nfld.*	23	K3
Burke Chan., *B.C.*	13	G6
Burks Falls, *Ont.*	17	F2
Burlington, *Ia.*	25	H2
Burlington, *Ont.*	16	F4
Burlington, *Vt.*	25	M2
Burma, *Asia*	40	J4
Burnett R., *Queensland*	50	H2
Burnie, *Tasmania*	50	K11
Burnley, *Eng.*	37	D5
Burns Lake, *B.C.*	13	H5
Burnt Is., *Nfld.*	23	H3
Burnt L., *Lab.*	19	E3
Burnt R., *Alberta*	14	B3
Burntisland, *Scotland*	36	D3
Burnt River, *Ont.*	17	G3
Burntwood R., *Man.*	15	M3
Burra, *S. Aust.*	50	B6
Burrinjuck, *N.S.W.*	50	G7
Burrow Hd., *Scotland*	37	C4
Bursa (Brusa), *Turkey*	39	M5
Burslem, *Eng.*	37	D5
Burton-on-Trent, *Eng.*	37	E5
Buru I., *Indonesia*	44	E7
Burundi, *Cent. Africa*	46	G6
Burwash, *Ont.*	16	D1
Burwash (Estaire), *Ont.*	16	D1
Bury, *Que.*	20	D3
Bury St. Edmunds, *Eng.*	37	F5
Bushmanland, Gt., and Lit., *Cape Prov., Rep. of S. Africa*	47	B2
Busselton, *W. Aust.*	49	B6
Bute, *Scotland*	36	C4
Butedale, *B.C.*	13	F6
Bute Inlet, *B.C.*	13	H7
Butte, *Mont.*	24	D1
Butter Pot Park, *Nfld.*	23	L3
Butterworth, *Cape Prov., Rep. of S. Africa*	47	D3
Butt of Lewis, *Scotland*	36	B2
Button B., *Man.*	15	O1
Button Is., *N.W.T.*	19	E1
Butung I., *Indonesia*	44	E7
Buzău, *Rumania*	39	L4
Bwahit Mt., *Ethiopia*	46	G4
Byam Martin C., *Franklin, N.W.T.*	11	T3
Byam Martin Chan., *Franklin, N.W.T.*	10	N2
Byam Martin I., *Franklin, N.W.T.*	10	O2
Bydgoszcz, *Poland*	39	J2
Bylot I., *Franklin, N.W.T.*	11	T3
Byng Inlet, *Ont.*	16	E2
Byrock, *N.S.W.*	50	F5
Byron B., *Lab.*	19	F3
Byron C., *N.S.W.*	50	J4
Byron Bay, *N.S.W.*	50	J4
Caa Cati, *Argentina*	31	F9
Caamaño Sd., *B.C.*	13	F6
Caanan R., *N.B.*	21	B2
Caatinga, *Brazil*	30	F5
Cabanas, *Cuba*	29	H3
Cabimas, *Venezuela*	30	C1
Cabonga Res., *Que.*	20	A2
Cabot Hd., *Ont.*	16	D2
Cabot I., *Nfld.*	23	L2
Cabot Str., *Nfld., etc.*	23	G3
Cabri, *Sask.*	14	G5
Cacequi, *Brazil*	31	G9
Caceres, *Brazil*	30	F7
Caceres, *Spain*	38	C6
Cache Bay, *Ont.*	16	E1
Cache Cr., *B.C.*	13	K7
Cachoeira, *Brazil*	30	L6
Cactus L., *Sask.*	14	G4
Cadereyta, *Mexico*	28	E2
Cader Idris, Mt., *Wales*	37	D5
Cadillac, *Sask.*	14	H6
Cadiz, and G. of, *Spain*	38	C6
Cadomin, *Alberta*	13	M6
Cadotte R., *Alberta*	14	C2
Caen, *France*	38	D3
Caernarvon, and co., *Wales*	37	C5
Caernarvon B., *Wales*	37	C5
Cagliari, *Sardinia*	38	G6
Caguan R., *Colombia*	30	C3
Caicara, *Venezuela*	30	D2
Caicos Is., *W. Indies*	29	K3
Cailloma, *Peru*	30	C7
Cains R., *N.B.*	21	A1
Cairngorm Mts., *Scotland*	36	D3
Cairns, *Queensland*	49	H3
Cairo, *Egypt*	46	F3
Cairo, *Ill.*	25	J3
Caithness, *Scotland*	36	D2
Cajamarca, *Peru*	30	B5
Cajatambo, *Peru*	30	B6
Calabogie, *Ont.*	17	J3
Calabozo, *Venezuela*	30	D2
Calais, *France*	38	E3
Calais, *Me.*	25	N1
Calama, *Brazil*	30	E5
Calama, *Chile*	31	D8
Calamar, *Magdalena, Colombia*	30	C1
Calamar, *Vaupés, Colombia*	30	C3
Calatayud, *Spain*	38	D5
Calate, *Chile*	31	D8
Calcutta, *India*	40	G4
Caldera, *Chile*	31	C9
Caledon, *Cape Prov., Rep. of S. Africa*	47	B3
Caledonia, *N.S.*	21	B3
Caledonia, *Ont.*	16	F4
Calgary, *Alberta*	14	D5
Cali, *Colombia*	30	B3
Calicut, *India*	40	D6
California, state, *U.S.A.*	24	B3
California, G. of, *Mexico*	28	B2
California, Lower, *Mexico*	28	B2
Calitzdorp, *Cape Prov., Rep. of S. Africa*	47	C3
Callabonna L., *S. Aust.*	50	C4
Callander, *Ont.*	16	F1
Callao, *Peru*	30	B6
Callaria, *Peru*	30	C5
Calling L., *Alberta*	14	E3
Callison Ranch, *B.C.*	12	E3
Calstock, *Ont.*	18	F1
Calumet, *Mich.*	25	J1
Calumet, *Que.*	17	L2
Calvert I., *B.C.*	13	F7
Calvinia, *Cape Prov., Rep. of S. Africa*	47	B3
Camachigama L., *Que.*	20	A2
Camagüey, *Cuba*	29	J3
Camamu, *Brazil*	30	K6
Camana, *Peru*	30	C7
Camaquam R., *Brazil*	31	G10
Camargo, *Bolivia*	31	D8
Camarones B., *Argentina*	31	E12
Camarones R., *Chile*	30	C7
Camarron R., *Okla., etc.*	24	G3
Ca Mau, C., *Vietnam*	43	J8
Cambay, G. of, *India*	40	D4
Cambrian Mts., *Wales*	37	D5
Cambridge, *Eng.*	37	F5
Cambridge, *N.Z.*	51	E2
Cambridge B., *Victoria I., N.W.T.*	10	O4
Cambridge G., *W. Aust.*	49	D2
Camden, *Ark.*	25	H4
Camden, *Me.*	22	C4
Camden, *N.S.W.*	50	H7
Camden B., *Alaska*	10	F3
Camden Haven, *N.S.W.*	50	J5
Cameron Falls, *Ont.*	18	D4
Cameroun, *W. Africa*	46	E5
Cameroun Mt., *Cameroun*	46	D5
Cameta, *Brazil*	30	G4
Camlaren, *Mackenzie, N.W.T.*	12	O1
Camocim, *Brazil*	30	J4
Campana, *Argentina*	31	E10
Campaña I., *Chile*	31	B13
Campanha, *Brazil*	31	J8
Campania, *Tasmania*	50	L12
Campbell I., *S. Pacific Oc.*	2	D7
Campbellford, *Ont.*	17	H3
Campbellpore, *W. Pak.*	40	D2
Campbell Island, *B.C.*	13	F6
Campbell River, *B.C.*	13	H7
Campbell's B., *Que.*	17	J2
Campbellton, *N.B.*	22	D3
Campbellton, *Nfld.*	23	K2
Campbelltown, *N.S.W.*	50	H7
Campbelltown, *Scotland*	36	B4
Campeche, Bank of, *Mexico*	28	F3
Campeche, and G. of, *Mexico*	28	F3
Camperdown, *Victoria*	50	D9
Campina Grande, *Brazil*	30	K5
Campinas, *Brazil*	31	H8
Campobello I., *N.B.*	22	D4
Campo Gallo, *Argentina*	31	E9
Campo Grande, *Brazil*	30	F8
Campo Maior, *Brazil*	30	J4
Campos, *Brazil*	31	J8
Campos de Vacarias, *Brazil*	31	G8
Cam Ranh B., *Vietnam*	44	C5
Camrose, *Alberta*	14	E4
Camsell Mt., *Mackenzie, N.W.T.*	12	J1
Camsell Bend, *Mackenzie, N.W.T.*	12	J1
Camsell Portage, *Sask.*	14	G1
Canaan, *N.B.*	21	B1
Canada B., *Nfld.*	23	K1
Cañada Quemada R., *Argentina*	31	E8
Canadian R., *Tex., etc.*	24	F3
Canadian Shield, *Canada*	11	P5
Cañadón Leon, *Argentina*	31	D13
Canairtok R., *Lab.*	19	E3
Canal Flats, *B.C.*	13	N7
Cananea, *Mexico*	28	B1
Canary Is., *Atlantic Oc.*	46	B3
Canavieras, *Brazil*	30	K7
Canberra, *Capital Ter., Australia*	50	G7
Candelaria, *Brazil*	31	F9
Candle L., *Sask.*	14	J4
Canelones, *Uruguay*	31	F10
Cañete, *Peru*	30	B6
Cangallo, *Peru*	30	C6
Canim, L., *B.C.*	13	K7
Canmore, *Alberta*	13	N7
Cann, *Que.*	20	C2
Canna I., *Scotland*	36	B3
Cannes, *France*	38	F5
Canning, *N.S.*	21	C2
Cannington, *Ont.*	17	F3
Canoe L., *Sask.*	14	G3
Canoe Lake, *Sask.*	14	G3
Canoe R., *B.C.*	13	L6
Canora, *Sask.*	15	K5
Canrobert, *Que.*	20	C3
Canso, *N.S.*	21	G2
Canso C., *N.S.*	21	G2
Canso Str., *N.S.*	21	F2
Canta, *Peru*	30	B6
Cantabrian Mts., *Spain*	38	C5
Canterbury, *Eng.*	37	F6
Canterbury Bight, *N.Z.*	51	C6
Canterbury Plains, *N.Z.*	51	C6
Cantley, *Que.*	20	B3
Canton (Kuang-chou), *China*	44	D4
Canton, *N.Y.*	17	K3
Canton, *O.*	25	K2
Canton I., *Pacific Oc.*	2	E5
Canvey I., *Eng.*	37	F6
Canwood, *Sask.*	14	H4
Caopacho R., *Que.*	22	D1
Cap à l'Aigle, *Que.*	22	D2
Capanaparo R., *Venezuela*	30	D2
Cap-aux-Meules, *Que.*	22	G3
Cap Chat, *Que.*	22	D2
Cap de la Madeleine, *Que.*	22	E2
Cap de Rabast, *Que.*	22	F2
Cape Barren I., *Tasmania*	50	G10
Cape Breton, *N.S.*	21	G2
Cape Breton I., *N.S.*	21	F1
Cape Breton Highlands National Park, *N.S.*	21	G1
Cape Broyle, *Nfld.*	23	L3
Cape Girardeau, *Mo.*	25	J3
Cape Kennedy, *Fla.*	25	K5
Cape Pembroke, *Coats I., N.W.T.*	19	A1
Cape Province, *S. Africa*	47	C3
Cape Sable I., *N.S.*	21	B4
Cape St Lawrence, *N.S.*	21	G1
Cape St Mary, *N.S.*	21	A3
Cape Town, *Cape Prov., Rep. of S. Africa*	47	B3
Cape Van Diemen, *Melville I., N. Aust.*	49	E2
Cape Verde Is., *Atlantic Oc.*	3	K4
Cape York Penin., *Queensland*	44	G2
Cap-Haiten, *Haiti*	29	K4
Capitachouane L., *Que.*	20	B1
Capitachouane R., *Que.*	20	A2

Caplan, Que. 22 E2
Capreol, Ont. 18 H5
Cap St. Ignace, Que. 20 D2
Cap Santa, Que. 20 D2
Capstick, N.S. 21 G1
Capua, Italy 39 H5
Caqueta R., Colombia 30 C4
Caracas, Venezuela 31 D1
Caramat, Ont. 18 E4
Carapegua, Paraguay 31 F9
Caraquet, N.B. 22 E3
Caras, Peru 30 B5
Caratasca Lagoon, Honduras 29 H4
Caravelas, Brazil 30 K7
Carberry, Man. 15 M6
Carbonear, Nfld. 23 L3
Carcajou, Alberta 14 C2
Carcross, Yukon 12 C2
Cardamon Hills, India 40 E6
Cardeñas, Cuba 29 H3
Cardenas, Mexico 28 F4
Cardiff, Wales 37 D6
Cardigan, and B., P.E.I. 21 E1
Cardigan, and co., Wales 37 C5
Cardigan B., Wales 37 C5
Cardinal. Ont. 17 K3
Cardinal L., Alberta 14 C2
Cardross, Sask. 14 J6
Cardston, Alberta 14 E6
Cargellico, N.S.W. 50 F6
Cargill, Ont. 16 D3
Caribbean Sea, Cent. America 29 J5
Cariboo Mts., B.C. 13 K6
Caribou, Man. 15 N1
Caribou, Me. 22 C3
Caribou I., L. Superior 18 F5
Caribou I., N.S. 21 E2
Caribou I., Ont. 18 D3
Caribou Mts., Alberta 14 C1
Caribou R., Mackenzie, N.W.T. 12 G2
Caribou R., Man. 15 O1
Caribou Hide, B.C. 12 G4
Carinhanha, Brazil 30 J6
Carinhanha R., Brazil 30 H6
Carleton, Que. 22 D2
Carleton, co., Ont. 17 K2
Carleton Mt., N.B. 22 D3
Carleton Place. Ont. 17 J2
Carletonville, Transvaal 47 D2
Carlingford L., Eire-N. Ire. 37 C5
Carlisle, Eng. 37 D4
Carlow, and co., Eire 37 B5
Carlton, Sask. 14 H4
Carlyle, Sask. 15 K6
Carmacks, Yukon 12 B1
Carman, Man. 15 N6
Carmangay, Alberta 14 E5
Carmanville, Nfld. 23 K2
Carmarthen, and co., Wales 37 C6
Carmarthen B., Wales 37 C6
Carmen, Bolivia 30 D6
Carmen, Colombia 30 B1
Carmen, Mexico 28 F4
Carmen I., Mexico 28 B2
Carmen de Mojos, Bolivia 30 E6
Carmen de Patagones, Argentina 30 E12
Carmichael, Sask. 14 G5
Carnarvon, Cape Prov., Rep. of S. Africa 47 C3
Carnarvon, W. Aust. 49 A4
Carnarvon Ra., Queensland 50 G2
Carnatic, region, India 40 E6
Carnduff, Sask. 15 L6
Carnsore Pt., Eire 37 B5
Caro, Alaska 10 E4
Caro, Mich. 16 B4
Carolina, Brazil 30 H5
Carolina, Transvaal 47 E2
Caroline I., Micronesia, Pacific Oc. 2 F5
Caroline Is., Pacific Oc. 44 G6
Caron, Sask. 14 J5
Caroni R., Venezuela 30 E2
Carora, Venezuela 30 C1
Carp, Ont. 17 J2
Carp L., B.C. 12 J5
Carpathian Mts., Europe 39 K3
Carpentaria, G. of, Queensland, etc. 50 F2
Carpolac, Victoria 50 C8
Carrantuohill Mt.. Eire 37 A6
Carrickfergus, N. Ire. 37 C4
Carrick-on-Shannon, Eire 37 B5
Carrick-on-Suir, Eire 37 B5
Carrieton, S. Aust. 50 B6
Carriso Mt.. Ariz. 24 E3
Carrot River, tn. and R., Sask. 15 K4
Carruthers, Sask. 14 G4
Carson City, Nev. 24 C3
Carson Sink, Nev. 24 C3
Carstairs, Alberta 14 D5
Cartagena, Colombia 30 B1
Cartagena, Spain 38 D6
Cartago, Costa Rica 29 H6
Carthage, Mo. 25 H3
Carthage, N.Y. 17 K4
Cartier, Ont. 18 H5
Cartmel Mt.. B.C. 12 F4
Cartwright, Lab. 19 F3
Carupano, Venezuela 30 E1
Cary Is., Franklin, N.W.T. 11 U2
Caryapundy Swamp, N.S.W. 50 D4

Casablanca, Morocco 46 B2
Cascade Ra., Oregon-Washington 24 B2
Cascade Pt., N.Z. 51 B5
Cascapedia R., Que. 22 D2
Cascavel, Brazil 30 K4
Casco B., Me. 22 C5
Casey, Que. 20 B2
Casino, N.S.W. 50 J4
Casma, Peru 30 B5
Casper, Wyo. 24 E2
Caspian Sea, Europe-Asia 42 C4
Cass R., Mich. 16 B4
Casselman, Ont. 17 K2
Cassiar Mts., B.C. 12 F3
Cassiar, B.C. 12 F3
Cassilis, N.S.W. 50 G6
Cassiporé R., Brazil 30 G3
Castanheiro, Brazil 30 D4
Castellon de La Plana, Spain 38 D5
Casterton, Victoria 50 C8
Castine, Me. 22 C4
Castleavery, Man. 15 L5
Castlebar, Eire 37 A5
Castle Douglas, Scotland 37 C4
Castlegar, B.C. 13 M8
Castlemaine, Victoria 50 E8
Castlerea, Eire 37 A5
Castlereagh R., N.S.W. 50 G5
Castletown, Isle of Man 37 C4
Castor. Alberta 14 F4
Castries St. Lucia, W. Indies 29 M5
Castro, Brazil 31 G8
Castro, Chile 31 C12
Cat I., Bahamas 29 J3
Cat L., and R., Ont. 18 C3
Cat Lake, Ont. 18 C3
Catalão, Brazil 30 H7
Catalina, Nfld. 23 L2
Catamarca, Argentina 31 D9
Catania, Sicily 39 H6
Catanzaro, Italy 39 J6
Catastrophe C., S. Aust. 49 F7
Catatumbo R., Colombia-Venezuela 30 C2
Cathcart, Cape Prov. 47 D3
Cathkin Peak, Basutoland 47 D2
Catoche C., Mexico 29 G3
Catorce, Mexico 28 D3
Catrimani R., Brazil 30 E3
Catua, Argentina 31 D8
Cauca R., Colombia 30 B3
Caucasus Mts., U.S.S.R. 42 C4
Cauquenes, Chile 31 C11
Caura R., Venezuela 30 E2
Causapscal, Que. 22 D2
Cauvery R., India 40 E6
Cavan, and co., Eire 37 B5
Cave I., Ont. 16 D2
Cavell, Ont. 18 E3
Caviana I.. Brazil 30 G3
Cawood, Que. 17 J2
Caxias, Brazil 30 J4
Caxias do Sul, Brazil 31 G9
Cayapo, Serra do, Brazil 30 G7
Cayenne, Fr. Guiana 30 G2
Cayman Is., W. Indies 29 H4
Cayo Romano, Cuba 29 J3
Cayuga, Ont. 16 F5
Ceannanus Mór (Kells), Eire 37 B5
Cebo, Philippine Is. 44 E5
Cecil Plains, Queensland 50 H3
Cedar L., Kenora, Ont. 18 C4
Cedar L., Man. 15 L4
Cedar Berg, Cape Prov., Rep. of S. Africa 47 B3
Cedar Keys, Fla. 25 K5
Cedar Rapids, Ia. 25 H2
Cedar Springs, Ont. 16 C5
Cedarvale. B.C. 12 F5
Cedarville, Cape Prov., Rep. of S. Africa 47 D3
Cedoux, Sask. 15 K6
Cedros I., Mexico 28 A2
Ceduna, S. Aust. 49 E6
Celaya, Mexico 28 D3
Celebes I., Indonesia 44 D7
Celebes Sea, Indonesia 44 E6
Cenis, Mont, France 38 F4
Central African Rep., Africa 46 E5
Central Auckland, N.Z. 51 E2
Centralia, Ont. 16 D4
Centreville, N.B. 22 C4
Centreville, N.S. 21 A3
Cephalonia I.. Greece 39 J6
Ceres, Cape Prov., Rep. of S. Africa 47 B3
Cerf, L. du, Que. 17 K1
Cerralvo, Mexico 28 E2
Cerralvo I., Mexico 28 C3
Cerro de Pasco, Peru 30 B6
České Budějovice, Czechoslovakia 35 K6
Cessnock, N.S.W. 50 H6
Cetinje, Yugoslavia 39 J5
Ceuta, Span. Morocco 38 C7
Cévennes Mts., France 38 E4
Ceylon. See Sri Lanka
Chaapo, R. de, Chile 31 C10
Chaca, Chile 30 D7
Chachapoyas, Peru 30 B5
Chaco, prov., Argentina 31 E9
Chaco Boreal, Paraguay 31 E8

Chacon C., B.C. 12 D5
Chad, Cent. Africa 46 D4
Chad L., W. Cent. Africa 46 E4
Chadron, Neb. 24 F2
Chagos Arch., Indian Oc. 3 N5
Chāhbār, Iran 40 B3
Chaibasa, India 40 G4
Chakonipau L., Que. 19 D2
Chalcidice Penin., Greece 39 K5
Chaleur B., N.B. 22 E3
Chalkar Tengis, U.S.S.R. 42 E4
Chalk River, Ont. 17 H1
Chalky Inlet, N.Z. 51 A7
Challis, Ida. 24 D2
Challhuanca, Peru 30 C6
Chamberlain, Sask. 14 J5
Chamberlain, S. Dak. 24 G2
Chamberlain L., Me. 22 C3
Chambly, Que. 20 C3
Chambord, Que. 22 A2
Chamical, Argentina 31 D10
Chamiss Bay, B.C. 13 G7
Champdare L., Que. 19 D2
Champlain, Que. 20 C2
Chañaral, Chile 31 C9
Chan-chiang, China 44 D4
Chandernagore, India 40 G4
Chandigarh. India 40 E2
Chandler, Que. 22 E2
Chandpur, Bangladesh 40 H4
Chang-chia-k'ou, China 44 D2
Changchun, China 44 E2
Changsha, China 44 D4
Changyeh (Kanchow), China 44 C3
Channel Is., Cal. 26 B4
Channel Is., English Chan. 38 D3
Channel—Port aux Basques, Nfld. 23 H3
Chanthaburi, Thailand 40 K6
Chantrey Inlet, Keewatin 11 P4
Chapais, Que. 19 C4
Chapala L., Mexico 28 D3
Chapeau, Que. 17 H2
Chapel I., Nfld. 23 K3
Chapleau, Ont. 18 G5
Chaplin, Sask. 14 H5
Chapra, India 40 F3
Chaput Hughes, Ont. 18 H4
Charcoal L., Sask. 15 K1
Charette, Que. 20 C2
Charlemagne, Que. 20 C3
Charles C., Va. 25 L3
Charles I., Hudson Str. 19 C1
Charles L., La. 25 H4
Charlesbourg, Que. 20 D2
Charleston, Mo. 25 J3
Charleston, S.C. 25 L4
Charleston, W. Va. 25 K3
Charlestown, Natal 47 E2
Charleville, Eire 37 A5
Charleville, Queensland 50 F3
Charlie L., B.C. 12 K4
Charlotte, N.C. 25 K3
Charlotte I., W. Indies 29 M4
Charlotte L., B.C. 13 H6
Charlottetown, P.E.I. 21 D1
Charlotte Waters, N. Ter., Aust. 49 E5
Charlton, Ont. 18 H5
Charlton I., James B. 18 J2
Charny, Que. 20 D2
Charter's Towers, Queensland 49 H3
Chartierville, Que. 20 D3
Chartres, France 38 E3
Chascomus, Argentina 31 F11
Chase, B.C. 13 L7
Chatanika, Alaska 10 E4
Chateauguay, Que. 20 C3
Chateau Richer, Que. 20 D2
Chatham, Eng. 37 F6
Chatham, N.B. 22 E3
Chatham, Ont. 16 C5
Chatham Is., Pacific Oc. 2 E7
Chatham Str., Alaska 12 C4
Chatia O'Shehuen R., Argentina 31 C13
Chatsworth, Ont. 16 E3
Chattanooga, Tenn. 25 J3
Chaud L., Que. 20 B2
Chaudiere, and R., Que. 20 D2
Chauvin, Alberta 14 F4
Chavantes, Serra dos, Brazil 30 H6
Chaves, Brazil 30 H4
Cheboygan, Mich. 16 A2
Chedabucto B., N.S. 21 F2
Cheduba I., Burma 40 H5
Cheecham, Alberta 14 F2
Cheepie, Queensland 50 E3
Chelmsford, Eng. 37 F6
Chelsea, Mich. 16 A5
Chelsea, Que. 20 B3
Cheltenham, Eng. 37 D6
Chelyuskin, C., U.S.S.R. 43 J1
Chemainus, B.C. 13 J8
Chena, Alaska 10 E4
Chenab R., India-Pak. 40 D2
Chénéville, Que. 17 K2
Cheng-te Shih, China 44 D2
Chengtu, China 44 C3
Cher R., France 38 E4

Cherbourg, France 38 D3
Cherchen, Sinkiang 40 G1
Chernigov, Ukraine 39 M3
Chernovsty, Ukraine 39 L3
Chernyakhovsk, U.S.S.R. 39 K2
Cherokee, Ia. 24 G2
Cherrepe, Peru 30 B5
Cherryfield, Me. 22 C4
Cherskogo Mts., U.S.S.R. 43 N2
Chesapeake B., Md. 25 L3
Cheshire, co., Eng. 37 D5
Chesil Bank, Eng. 37 D6
Cheskaya B., U.S.S.R. 35 Q2
Cheslatta L., B.C. 13 H6
Chesley, Ont. 16 D3
Chesnaye, Man. 15 O1
Chester, Eng. 37 D5
Chester, N.S. 21 C3
Chester Basin, N.S. 21 C3
Chesterfield, Eng. 37 E5
Chesterfield, and Inlet, Keewatin, N.W.T. 11 Q5
Chesterville, Ont. 17 K2
Chesuncook L.. Me. 22 C3
Cheticamp, N.S. 21 F1
Chetumal, and B., Mexico 28 G4
Cheverie, N.S. 22 E4
Cheviot, The, Eng. 36 D4
Cheviot Hills, Scot.-Eng. 37 D4
Cheviot Ra., Queensland 50 D2
Cheyenne, Wyo. 24 F2
Chezacut. B.C. 13 H6
Chiang Mai, Thailand 44 B5
Chiapa, Chile 30 D7
Chibougamau, Que. 19 C3
Chibougamau L., Que. 19 C4
Chibougamau Park, Que. 19 C4
Chicago, Ill. 25 J2
Chichagof, and I., Alaska 13 C4
Chichester, Eng. 37 E6
Chickasha, Okla. 24 G4
Chiclayo, Peru 30 A5
Chico R., Argentina 31 D13
Chicoana, Argentina 31 D9
Chicoutimi, and R., Que. 20 D1
Chicoutimi Park, Que. 22 B2
Chidley C., Lab. 19 E1
Chief B., Ont. 18 D4
Chiefs Pt., Ont. 16 D3
Chieti, Italy 39 H5
Chignecto B., N.B.-N.S. 21 C2
Chihuahua, Mexico 28 C2
Chilako R., B.C. 13 J6
Chilanko Forks, B.C. 13 H6
Chilapa de Alvarez, Mexico 28 E4
Chilcotin R., B.C. 13 J6
Childers, Queensland 50 J2
Childress, Tex. 24 G4
Chile, rep., S. America 31 C12
Chilecito, Argentina 31 D9
Chilko L., and R., B.C. 13 H7
Chilkoot Pass, B.C.-Alaska 12 C3
Chillan, Chile 31 C11
Chillicothe, Mo. 25 H3
Chillingollah, Victoria 50 D7
Chilliwack, B.C. 13 K8
Chiloé I., Chile 31 B12
Chilpancingo de los Bravos, Mexico 28 E4
Chiltern Hills, Eng. 37 E6
Chilung, Formosa 44 E4
Chimborazo Mt., Ecuador 30 B4
Chimbote, Peru 30 B5
Chimo, Que. 11 V6
Chin C., Ont. 16 D2
China, People's Rep. E. Asia 43 G5
China, Gt. Plain of, China 44 D3
Chinandega, Nicaragua 28 G5
Chincha, and Is., Peru 30 B6
Chinchaga R.. Alberta 14 B2
Chinchow, China 44 E2
Chin Coulee, Alberta 14 F6
Chinde, Mozambique 46 G7
Chindwin R., Burma 40 J4
Ching Hai, China 44 C3
Chin Lien Shan Mts., China 44 C2
Chinook Valley, Alberta 14 C2
Chios (Khios), Greece 39 L6
Chipewyan Lake, Alberta 14 E2
Chipie R., Ont. 18 G3
Chip L., Alberta 14 D4
Chipman, N.B. 22 B1
Chipman R., Sask. 14 J1
Chipp R., Alaska 10 D3
Chippawa, Ont. 17 F4
Chipping Norton, Eng. 37 E6
Chiputneticook Ls., N.B., etc. 22 C4
Chiquinquira, Colombia 30 B2
Chira R., Peru, etc. 30 A4
Chirikof I., Alaska 10 C6
Chiriqui Lagoon, Pan. 29 H6
Chisholm, Alberta 14 D3
Chita, U.S.S.R. 44 D1
Chita Mt., Colombia 30 C2
Chitaldroog, India 40 E6
Chitek, and L., Sask. 14 H4
Chitral, W. Pak. 40 D1
Chittagong, Bangladesh 40 H4
Chiu-ch'üan (Suchow), China 44 B3
Chivilcoy, Argentina 31 E10
Choapo, R. de, Chile 31 C10
Choco, B. del, Colombia 30 B3

Choele Choel, *Argentina* 31 D11
Choix, *Mexico* 28 C2
Cholon, *S. Vietnam* 44 C5
Chonos Arch., *Chile* 31 B12
Chorrillos, *Peru* 30 B6
Chorzów, *Poland* 39 J3
Chos Malal, *Argentina* 31 D11
Chouteca, *Honduras* 28 G5
Choybalsan, *Mongolia* 44 D2
Christchurch, *N.Z.* 51 D5
Christian C., *Baffin I., N.W.T.* 11 V3
Christian I.. *Ont.* 16 E3
Christiana, *Cape Prov., Rep. of S. Africa* 47 C2
Christianshåb, *Greenland* 11 Y4
Christie B., *Mackenzie, N.W.T.* 10 M5
Christie Mt., *Yukon* 12 F1
Christina B., *Cape Prov., Rep. of S. Africa* 47 C3
Christina R., *Alberta* 14 F2
Christmas I., *Indian Oc.* 44 C8
Christmas I., *Pacific Oc.* 2 E4
Chu, *U.S.S.R.* 42 E4
Chubb Crater, *Que.* 19 C1
Chubut R., *Argentina* 31 D12
Chuchi, *B.C.* 12 H5
Chu Chua, *B.C.* 13 K7
Chugach Mts.. *Alaska* 10 E5
Chukotat R., *Que.* 19 B1
Chukotsk Penin., *U.S.S.R.* 43 Q2
Chukotsk Sea, *U.S.S.R.* 2 E1
Chumbicha, *Argentina* 31 D9
Chungking, Ch'ung-ch'ing, *China* 44 C4
Church Pt., *N.S.* 21 A3
Churchill, and C., *Man.* 15 P1
Churchill Falls, *Lab.* 19 E3
Churchill L., *Sask.* 14 G2
Churchill R., *Lab.* 19 E3
Churchill R., *Sask.-Man.* 14 J3
Churchill R., Lit., *Man.* 15 O2
Churchill Peak, *B.C.* 12 H3
Chute-aux-Outardes, *Que.* 20 C2
Chute des Passes, *Que.* 22 B2
Ciconcine L., *Que.* 20 C2
Cienfuegos, *Cuba* 29 H3
Cilician Gate, *Turkey* 42 B5
Cincinnati, *O.* 25 K3
Cinto Mt., *Corsica* 38 G5
Circars, Northern, *India* 40 F5
Circle, *Alaska* 10 E3
Circular Head, *Tasmania* 50 K11
Cirque Mt., *Lab.* 19 E2
Cisco. *Tex.* 24 G4
Citlaltepec, mt., *Mexico* 28 E4
Citrosdal, *Cape Prov., Rep. of S. Africa* 47 B3
Ciudad Acuña, *Mexico* 28 D2
Ciudad Bolivar, *Venezuela* 30 E2
Ciudad Camargo, *Mexico* 28 C2
Ciudad de Valles, *Mexico* 28 E3
Ciudad Guerrero, *Mexico* 28 C2
Ciudad Guzman, *Mexico* 28 D4
Ciudad Juarez, *Mexico* 28 C1
Ciudad Lerdo, *Mexico* 28 D2
Ciudad Madero, *Mexico* 28 E3
Ciudad Obregon, *Mexico* 28 C2
Ciudad Victoria, *Mexico* 28 E3
Civita Vecchia, *Italy* 38 G5
Clair L., *Que.* 20 C2
Claire L., *Alberta* 14 E1
Clairmont, *Alberta* 14 B3
Clanwilliam *Cape Prov., Rep. of S. Africa* 47 B3
Clare, *S. Aust.* 50 B6
Clare, co., *Eire* 37 A5
Clarence Head, *Ellesmere I., N.W.T.* 11 T2
Clarence R., *N.S.W.* 50 J4
Clarence R., *N.Z.* 51 D5
Clarence Str., *Alaska* 12 D5
Clarendon, *Ont.* 17 H3
Clarenville, *Nfld.* 23 K4
Claresholm, *Alberta* 14 E6
Clark L., *Alaska* 10 D3
Clark Pt., *Ont.* 16 D3
Clarke I., *Tasmania* 50 G10
Clarkebury, *Cape. Prov., Rep. of S. Africa* 47 D3
Clarke City, *Que.* 23 H3
Clark Hill Reservoir, *Ga.-S.C.* 25 K4
Clarksburg, *W. Va.* 25 K3
Clark's Harb., *N.S.* 22 E5
Clarkson, *Ont.* 16 F4
Clarkson Valley, *Alberta* 12 M5
Clarksville, *Tenn.* 25 J3
Claxton, *B.C.* 13 E5
Clayoquot, and Sd., *Vancouver I., B.C.* 13 G8
Clear C., *Eire* 37 A6
Clear L., *Algonquin Park, Ont.* 17 H2
Clear L., *Man.* 15 L5
Clear R., *Alberta* 14 B2
Cleare C., *Montague I., Alaska* 10 E6
Clear Hills, *Alberta* 14 B2
Clear Hills, *B.C.. etc.* 12 K4
Clear Prairie, *Alberta* 14 B2
Clearwater, *B.C.* 13 K7
Clearwater L.. *B.C.* 13 K6
Clearwater Pk.. *Man.* 15 L3
Clearwater R., *Alberta* 14 D5

Clearwater R., *Alberta-Sask.* 14 G2
Clemens, Mt., *Mich.* 16 B5
Clementsport, *N.S.* 21 B3
Clementsville, *N.S.* 21 B3
Clermont, *Que.* 22 B3
Clermont, *Queensland* 49 H4
Clermont Ferrand, *France* 38 E4
Cleveland, *O.* 25 K2
Cleveland, *Queensland* 50 J3
Cleveland Hills, *Eng.* 37 E4
Clew B., *Eire* 37 A5
Clifden, *Eire* 37 A5
Clifford, *Mich.* 16 B4
Clifford, *Ont.* 16 E3
Clifton, *Que.* 20 D3
Clifton Hills, *S. Aust.* 50 C1
Clinton, *B.C.* 13 K7
Clinton, *Ia.* 25 H2
Clinton, *Ont.* 16 D4
Clinton Golden L., *Mackenzie, N.W.T.* 10 N5
Clipperton I., *Pacific Oc.* 2 G4
Clive L., *Mackenzie, N.W.T.* 12 L1
Cloan, *Sask.* 14 G4
Clonakilty, and B., *Eire* 37 A6
Cloncurry, *Queensland* 49 G4
Clones, *Eire* 37 B4
Clonmel, *Eire* 37 B5
Clo-oose, *Vancouver I., B.C.* 13 H8
Cloud Peak, *Wyo.* 24 E2
Clouston, *Sask.* 14 J4
Clova, *Que.* 20 B1
Cluculz L., *B.C.* 13 J6
Cluj, *Romania* 39 K4
Clutha R., *N.Z.* 51 B6
Clyde, *Alberta* 14 E3
Clyde, Firth of, *Scotland* 37 C4
Clyde R., *N.S.* 21 B3
Clyde R., *Scotland* 36 D4
Clyde Forks, *Ont.* 17 J2
Coal R., *Yukon* 12 G2
Coal River, *B.C.* 12 G3
Coalspar, *Alberta* 14 C4
Coari, *Brazil* 30 E4
Coast Mts., *B.C.* 12 D3
Coast Ra., *Ccl., etc.* 24 B3
Coatbridge, *Scotland* 36 D4
Coaticook, *Que.* 20 D3
Coats I., *Keewatin, N.W.T.* 11 S5
Coatzacoalcos, *Mexico* 28 E4
Cobalt, *Ont.* 18 H5
Coban, *Guatemala* 28 F4
Cobar, *N.S.W.* 50 E5
Cobble Hill, *Vancouver I., B.C.* 13 J8
Cobden, *Ont.* 17 J2
Cobequid Bay, *N.S.* 21 D2
Cobequid Mts., *N.S.* 21 C2
Cobh (Queenstown), *Eire* 37 A6
Cobham R., *Man.-Ont.* 15 O4
Cobija, *Bolivia* 30 D6
Cobija, *Chile* 31 C8
Coblenz, *Ger.* 38 F3
Coboconk, *Ont.* 17 F3
Cobourg, *Ont.* 17 G4
Cobram, *Victoria* 50 E7
Coburg, *Ger.* 38 G3
Coburg I., *Franklin, N.W.T.* 11 T2
Coburg Penin., *N. Ter., Aust.* 49 E2
Coca R., *Ecuador* 30 B4
Cocamá, *Peru* 30 C6
Cochabamba, *Bolivia* 30 D7
Cochin, *India* 40 E7
Cochrane, *Alberta* 14 D5
Cochrane, *Ont.* 18 H4
Cochrane, dist., *Ont.* 18 F3
Cochrane R., *Sask.-Man.* 15 K1
Cockburn, *S. Aust.* 50 C6
Cockburn Chan., *Chile* 31 C14
Cockburn I., *Ont.* 16 B1
Cockburn Island, *Ont.* 16 B2
Coco Is., *Andaman Is.* 40 H6
Coco R., *Cent. America* 29 H5
Cocos I., *Pacific Oc.* 2 G4
Cocos-Keeling Is., *Indian Oc.* 2 B5
Cod I. (Ogualik), *Lab.* 19 E1
Codajas, *Brazil* 30 E4
Codfish I., *N.Z.* 51 A7
Codroy, and R., *Nfld.* 23 H3
Codroy Pond, *Nfld.* 23 H2
Codys, *N.B.* 21 B2
Coe Hill, *Ont.* 17 G3
Coffin I., *Que.* 23 G3
Coff's Harb., *N.S.W.* 50 J5
Coguar, *Que.* 50 B1
Cohuna, *Victoria* 50 E7
Coiba I., *Pan.* 29 H6
Coimbatore, *India* 40 E6
Coimbra, *Portugal* 38 B5
Colac, *Victoria* 50 D9
Colborne, *Ont.* 17 G3
Colby, *Kan.* 24 F3
Colchester, *Eng.* 37 F6
Cold L., *Alberta* 14 F3
Coldstream, *Scotland* 36 D4
Coldwater, *Ont.* 16 E3
Coldwell, *Ont.* 18 E4
Colebrook, *N.H.* 22 B4
Coleman, *Alberta* 14 D6
Coleman Mt., *Alberta* 14 C4
Colenso, *Natal* 47 D2
Coleraine, *N. Ire.* 37 B4

Coleraine, *Que.* 20 D3
Coleraine, *Victoria* 50 C8
Coleridge L., *N.Z.* 51 C5
Coles C., *Peru* 30 C7
Colesberg, *Cape Prov., Rep. of S. Africa* 47 D3
Colhué Huapi L., *Argentina* 31 D13
Colima, *Mexico* 28 D4
Colinet, *Nfld.* 23 L3
Colinton, *Alberta* 14 E3
Colinton, *Queensland* 50 J3
Coll I., *Scotland* 36 B3
Collarenebri, *N.S.W.* 50 G4
College, *Alaska* 10 E5
Collie, *W. Aust.* 49 B6
Collier B., *W. Aust.* 49 C3
Collingwood, *Ont.* 16 E3
Colmena, *Argentina* 31 E9
Cologne, *Ger.* 38 F3
Colombia, rep., *S. America* 30 C3
Colombia Pt., *Colombia* 30 B1
Colombo, *Sri Lanka* 40 E7
Colon, *Cuba* 29 H3
Colon, *Pan.* 29 H6
Colonia, *Uruguay* 31 F10
Colonsay I., *Scotland* 36 B3
Colorado, state, *U.S.A.* 24 E3
Colorado Plat., *Ariz.* 24 D3
Colorado R., *Argentina* 31 D11
Colorado R., *Tex.* 24 G4
Colorado R., *U.S.A.* 24 D3
Colorado City, *Tex.* 24 F4
Colorado Desert, *Cal.* 24 C4
Colorado Springs, *Colo.* 24 F3
Colpoys B., *Ont.* 16 E3
Colquechaca, *Bolivia* 30 D7
Columbia, *Ala.* 25 J4
Columbia, *S.C.* 25 K4
Columbia, *Tenn.* 25 J3
Columbia C., *Ellesmere I., N.W.T.* 1 H1
Columbia L., *B.C.* 13 N7
Columbia Mt., *Alberta* 14 C4
Columbia Mts., *B.C.* 13 L6
Columbia R., *B.C.* 13 L7
Columbia R.. *Wash., etc.* 24 B1
Co umbine C., *Cape. Prov., Rep. of S. Africa* 47 B3
Columbus, *Ga.* 25 K4
Columbus, *O.* 25 K3
Columbus, *Tex.* 24 G5
Colupo, *Chile* 31 D8
Colville C., *N.Z.* 51 E2
Colville R., *Alaska* 10 D4
Comayagua, *Honduras* 28 G5
Combarbala, *Chile* 31 C10
Comber, *Ont.* 16 C5
Combermere, *Ont.* 17 H2
Comet R., *Queensland* 50 G2
Comitan de Dominguez, *Mexico* 28 F4
Commanda, *Ont.* 16 F2
Commissaires, L. des, *Que.* 20 C1
Commissioner I., *Man.* 15 N4
Committee B., *N.W.T.* 11 R4
Como, and L., *Italy* 38 G4
Como L., *Ont.* 18 G5
Comodoro Rivadavia, *Argentina* 31 D13
Comondu, *Mexico* 28 B2
Comorin C., *India* 40 E7
Comoro Is., *Indian Oc.* 46 H7
Comox, *Vancouver I., B.C.* 13 H8
Compostela, *Mexico* 28 D3
Compton, *Que.* 20 D3
Comrie, *Scotland* 36 C3
Conakry, *Guinea* 46 B5
Conara Junc., *Tasmania* 50 L11
Concepcion, *Argentina* 31 F10
Concepcion, *Chile* 31 C11
Concepcion, *Colombia* 30 B4
Concepción, *Paraguay* 31 F8
Concepcion L., *Bolivia* 30 E7
Conception, *Nfld.* 23 L3
Conception B., *Nfld.* 23 L3
Conception B., *S.W. Africa* 47 A1
Conchas R., *Mexico* 28 C2
Conche, *Nfld.* 23 J1
Concord, *N.H.* 25 M2
Concordia, *Argentina* 31 F10
Condamine R., *Queensland, etc.* 50 G3
Condobolin, *N.S.W.* 50 F6
Condon Cr., *W. Aust.* 49 B3
Conestago Lake, *Ont.* 16 E4
Congo, rep., *Cent. Africa* 46 E6
Congo R., *W. Africa* 46 F5
Congo Basin, *Africa* 46 E5
Coniston, *Eng.* 37 D4
Coniston, *Ont.* 16 E1
Conklin, *Alberta* 14 F3
Conn L., *Eire* 37 A4
Connecticut, state, *U.S.A.* 25 M2
Connemara Mts., *Eire* 37 A5
Connoire B., *Nfld.* 23 H3
Connors, *N.B.* 22 C3
Conquest, *Sask.* 14 H5
Consecon, *Ont.* 17 H3
Consort, *Alberta* 14 F5
Constance L., *Ger.-Switz.* 38 G4
Constanta, *Romania* 39 M4
Constantine C.. *Alaska* 10 C6
Constitucion, *Chile* 31 C11
Consul, *Sask.* 14 G6
Contamana, *Peru* 30 C5
Contrecœur, *Que.* 20 C3
Contus R., *Brazil* 30 J6

Conway, *N.H.* 22 B4
Conway, *Wales* 37 D5
Coober Pedy, *S. Aust.* 49 E5
Cooch Behar, *India* 40 G3
Cook C., *Vancouver I., B.C.* 13 F7
Cook Inlet, *Alaska* 10 D6
Cook Is., *Pacific Oc.* 2 E5
Cook Mt., *N.Z.* 51 C5
Cook Str., *N.Z.* 51 E4
Cooks Harb., *Nfld.* 23 K1
Cookshire, *Que.* 20 D3
Cookstown, *Ont.* 16 F3
Cooktown, *Queensland* 49 G3
Coolangatta, *Queensland* 50 J4
Coolgardie, *W. Aust.* 49 B6
Cooma, *N.S.W.* 50 G8
Coonabarabran, *N.S.W.* 50 G5
Coonamble, *N.S.W.* 50 G5
Cooper's Cr., *S. Aust.-Queensland* 50 B4
Coorong, The, *S. Aust.* 50 B8
Cootamundra, *N.S.W.* 50 G7
Cooyar, *Queensland* 50 J3
Copenhagen, *Denmark* 38 H2
Copiapo, *Chile* 31 C9
Copley, *S. Aust.* 50 B5
Copp L., *Mackenzie, N.W.T.* 12 N2
Copper R., *Alaska* 10 F5
Copper Cliff, *Ont.* 16 D1
Coppermine, and R., *Mackenzie, N.W.T.* 10 L4
Coppermine Pt., *Ont.* 18 F5
Copper Mountain, *B.C.* 13 K8
Coprapo, vol., *Chile* 31 D9
Coquet Hd., and R., *Eng.* 37 E4
Coquimbo, *Chile* 31 C10
Coracora, *Peru* 30 C6
Coral Rapids, *Ont.* 18 H3
Coral Sea, *Pacific* 2 C5
Corangamite L., *Victoria* 50 D9
Corbetton, *Ont.* 16 E3
Corbin, *B.C.* 13 N8
Corby, *Eng.* 37 E5
Corcaigh (Cork), *Eire* 37 A6
Corcovado, G. del, *Chile* 31 C12
Cordillera Central, *Colombia* 30 B3
Cordillera Central, *Peru* 30 B4
Cordillera de los Andes, *Argentina-Chile* 31 D10
Cordillera Occidental, *Peru* 30 B6
Cordillera of Merida, *Venezuela* 30 C2
Cordillera Oriental, *Peru* 30 B5
Cordillera Real, *Argentina* 31 D9
Cordillera Real, *Bolivia* 30 D7
Cordoba, *Argentina* 31 E10
Córdoba, *Spain* 38 C6
Cordoba, dept., *Colombia* 30 B2
Cordova, *Alaska* 10 E5
Cordova Mines, *Ont.* 17 G3
Corfu (Kerkira), *Greece* 39 J6
Corinth, and G. of, *Greece* 39 K6
Coripós, *Brazil* 30 K5
Cork (Corcaigh), co., *Eire* 37 A6
Cork Harb., *Eire* 37 A6
Cormorant L., *Man.* 15 L3
Cornell Grinnell B., *N.W.T.* 19 E1
Corner Brook, *Nfld.* 23 H2
Cornes, L. des, *Que.* 20 B2
Cornwall, *Ont.* 17 L2
Cornwall, co., and C., *England* 37 C6
Cornwall I., *Franklin, N.W.T.* 11 Q2
Cornwallis I., *Franklin, N.W.T.* 11 P2
Coro, *Venezuela* 30 D1
Corocoro, *Bolivia* 30 D7
Coromandel, *India* 40 F6
Coromandel Ra., *N.Z.* 51 E2
Coronados, G. de, *Chile* 31 B12
Coronation, *Alberta* 14 F4
Coronation G., *N.W.T.* 10 M4
Coronation I., *Alaska* 13 C5
Coronda, *Argentina* 31 E10
Coronel, *Chile* 31 C11
Coronie, *Surinam* 30 F2
Corowa, *N.S.W.* 50 E7
Corpus Christi, *Tex.* 24 G5
Corrente R., *Brazil* 30 H6
Corrib L., *Eire* 37 A5
Corrientes, *Argentina* 31 F9
Corrientes C., *Argentina* 31 F11
Corrientes C., *Colombia* 30 B2
Corrientes C., *Mexico* 28 C3
Corrientes C., *Mozambique* 46 G8
Corse C., *Corsica* 38 G5
Corsica I., *France* 38 G5
Corsicana, *Tex.* 24 G4
Corumba, *Brazil* 30 F7
Corunna, *Mich.* 16 A5
Corunna, *Spain* 38 B5
Corvallis, *Ore.* 24 B2
Cosala, *Mexico* 28 C3
Cosenza, *Italy* 39 J6
Cosquin, *Argentina* 31 D10
Costa Rica, rep., *Cent. America* 29 G5
Cotagaita, *Bolivia* 31 D8
Coté, *Sask.* 15 L5
Coteau, *Que.* 20 B3
Coteau, The, *Sask.* 14 H5
Cotopaxi, vol., *Ecuador* 30 B4
Cotswold Hills, *Eng.* 37 D6

Cottel I., *Nfld.*	23	L2	
Cottonwood, *B.C.*	13	J6	
Coudres, I. aux, *Que.*	20	D2	
Council Bluffs, *Ia.*	24	G2	
Courantyne R., *Guyana/Surinam*	30	F2	
Course, Lac la, *Sask.*	15	L5	
Courtenay, *Vancouver I., B.C.*	13	H8	
Courtright, *Ont.*	16	C5	
Coutts, *Alberta*	14	E6	
Couture L., *Que.*	19	C1	
Coventry, *Eng.*	37	E5	
Covington, *Ky.*	25	J3	
Cowan L., *W. Aust.*	49	C6	
Cowansville, *Que.*	20	C3	
Cowes, *Eng.*	37	E6	
Cowichan L., *Vancouver I., B.C.*	13	H8	
Cowra, *N.S.W.*	50	G6	
Cox's Cove, *N.S.*	23	H2	
Cozomel I., *Mexico*	29	G3	
Cracow, *Poland*	39	J3	
Cradle Mt., *Tasmania*	50	H11	
Cradock, *Cape Prov., Rep. of S. Africa*	47	D3	
Craig, *Alaska*	12	D5	
Craig Ra., *Queensland*	50	H3	
Craik, *Sask.*	14	J5	
Craiova, *Romania*	39	K4	
Cranberry L., *Man.*	15	L3	
Cranberry L., *N.Y.*	17	K3	
Cranberry Portage, *Man.*	15	L3	
Cranbrook, *B.C.*	13	M8	
Crane L., *Sask.*	14	G5	
Crateus, *Brazil*	30	J5	
Crato, *Brazil*	30	K5	
Craven, *Sask.*	14	J5	
Cree L., *Sask.*	14	H2	
Cree R., *Sask.*	14	H1	
Creemore, *Ont.*	16	E3	
Creighton Mine, *Ont.*	16	D1	
Cremona, *Alberta*	14	D5	
Crescent City, *Cal.*	24	B2	
Cressman, *Que.*	20	C2	
Crest, *Que.*	18	J5	
Creston, *B.C.*	13	M8	
Creswick, *Victoria*	50	E8	
Crete I., *Greece*	42	A5	
Crewe, *Eng.*	37	D5	
Crianlarich, *Scotland*	36	C3	
Crib Pt., *Victoria*	50	E9	
Cribano, *Que.*	20	E2	
Crieff, *Scotland*	36	D3	
Crimea, *U.S.S.R.*	39	N4	
Croche R., *Que.*	20	C2	
Crocodile R., *Transvaal*	47	D1	
Croix, Lac la, *Minn.-Ont.*	15	P6	
Croker C., *Ont.*	16	E3	
Cromarty, *Man.*	15	O1	
Cromarty, *Scotland*	36	C3	
Cromer, *Eng.*	37	F5	
Cromwell, *N.Z.*	51	B6	
Crooked I., *Bahamas*	29	K3	
Crooked L., *Minn.-Ont.*	15	Q6	
Crooked L., *Nfld*	23	J2	
Crooked R., *B.C.*	13	J5	
Crooks Inlet, *Baffin B.*	19	C1	
Crookston, *Minn.*	24	G1	
Crookwell, *N.S.W.*	50	G7	
Cross L., *Man.*	15	M4	
Cross L., *Man.*	15	N3	
Cross L., *Ont.*	17	H3	
Cross Sd., *Alaska*	13	B3	
Cross Fell, *Eng.*	37	D4	
Crossfield, *Alberta*	14	D5	
Crossley Mt., *N.Z.*	51	D5	
Crow R., *Yukon*	12	H2	
Crowes, *Victoria*	50	D9	
Crown Prince Frederik I., *Franklin, N.W.T.*	11	R3	
Crow's Nest, *Queensland*	50	H3	
Crowsnest Pass, *Alberta-B.C.*	14	D6	
Croydon, *Eng.*	37	E6	
Croydon, *Queensland*	49	G3	
Crozet Is., *Indian Oc.*	3	M7	
Crozier Chan., *Franklin, N.W.T.*	10	K2	
Cruz, C., *Cuba*	29	J4	
Cruz Alta, *Argentina*	31	E10	
Cruz Alta, *Brazil*	31	G9	
Cruzeiro do Sul, *Brazil*	30	C5	
Cruz Grande, *Chile*	31	C9	
Crysler, *Ont.*	20	B3	
Crystal Beach, *Ont.*	17	F5	
Crystal Brook, *S. Aust.*	50	B6	
Crystal City, *Man.*	15	M6	
Crystal Falls, *Ont.*	16	F1	
Cuayabero R., *Colombia*	30	C3	
Cub I., E. and W., *James B.*	18	H1	
Cuba I., *W. Indies*	29	H3	
Cubango R., *Angola*	46	E7	
Cucuta, *Venezuela*	30	C2	
Cue, *W. Aust.*	49	B5	
Cuenca, *Ecuador*	30	B4	
Cuenca, *Spain*	38	D5	
Cuernavaca, *Mexico*	28	E4	
Cuiaba, *Brazil*	30	F7	
Cuiaba R., *Brazil*	30	F6	
Cuicuina, *Nicaragua*	29	H5	
Cuillin Sd., *Scotland*	36	B3	
Cuillins, *Skye I., Scotland*	36	B3	
Culgoa R., *N.S.W., etc.*	50	F4	
Culiacan, *Mexico*	28	C3	
Culotte, L. la, *Que.*	20	B2	
Culp, *Alberta*	14	C3	
Culter Fell, *Scotland*	36	D4	
Cumana, *Venezuela*	30	E1	
Cumberland, *Pa.*	25	L3	
Cumberland, *Que.*	20	D2	
Cumberland, *Vancouver I., B.C.*	13	H8	
Cumberland, co., *Eng.*	37	D4	
Cumberland L., *Sask.*	15	K3	
Cumberland Penin., *Baffin I., N.W.T.*	11	V4	
Cumberland R., *Ky.-Tenn.*	25	J3	
Cumberland Sd., *Baffin I.*	11	V4	
Cumberland House, *Sask.*	15	K4	
Cumbrian Mts., *Eng.*	37	D4	
Cumnock, *Scotland*	36	C4	
Cunany, *Brazil*	30	G3	
Cunene R., *Angola*	46	E7	
Cunnamulla, *Queensland*	50	E4	
Cunningham L., *B.C.*	13	H5	
Cupar, *Scotland*	36	D3	
Curaçao I., *Dutch W. Indies*	30	D1	
Curaray R., *Peru, etc.*	30	B4	
Curico, *Chile*	31	C10	
Curitiba, *Brazil*	31	H9	
Curling, *Nfld.*	23	J2	
Curry, *Alaska*	10	E5	
Curtis Chan., *Queensland*	50	J2	
Curtis I., *Queensland*	50	H1	
Curua, *Brazil*	30	G3	
Curupachi. *Brazil*	30	F5	
Cururupu, *Brazil*	30	J4	
Cutaway R., *Man.*	15	P2	
Cuthbert Mt., *Queensland*	49	F3	
Cutlor. *Ont.*	16	C1	
Cuttack, *India*	40	G4	
Cut Throat Harb., *Coast of Lab.*	19	E2	
Cuxhaven, *Ger.*	38	G2	
Cuyuni R., *Guyana*	30	F2	
Cuzco (Cusco), *Peru*	30	C6	
Cyclades Is., *Greece*	39	L6	
Cypress L., and Hills, *Sask.*	14	G6	
Cypress Hills Pk., *Sask.*	14	G6	
Cyprus I., *Mediterranean Sea*	42	B5	
Cyrus Field B., *N.W.T.*	19	E1	
Czar, *Alberta*	14	F4	
Czechoslovakia, state, *Europe*	39	H3	
Czestochowa, *Poland*	39	J3	
Dacca (Jahangir Nagar), *Bangladesh*	40	H4	
Dade City, *Fla.*	25	K5	
Dadquam R., *Que.-Me.*	20	D2	
Dadra & Nagar Haveli, terr., *India*	40	D4	
Dafter, *Mich.*	16	A1	
Dahadinni R., *Mackenzie, N.W.T.*	12	H1	
Dahana, *Arabia*	42	C6	
Dahomey, *W. Africa*	46	D5	
Dairen, *Japan*	44	E3	
Dajarra, *Queensland*	49	F4	
Dakar, *Senegal, Africa*	46	B4	
Dakota R., *N. and S. Dak.*	24	G1	
Dalai Nor (Hulun L.), *Inner Mongolia*	44	D2	
Dal Alv, *Sweden*	35	K3	
Dalby, *Queensland*	50	H3	
Dalgety, *N.S.W.*	50	G8	
Dalhousie, *N.B.*	22	D2	
Dalhousie C., *Mackenzie, N.W.T.*	10	H3	
Dall I., *Alaska*	12	D5	
Dallas, *Tex.*	24	G4	
Dalmatian Is., *Yugoslavia*	39	H5	
Dalry. *Scotland*	36	C4	
Dalrymple Mt., *Queensland*	49	H4	
Dalton, *Ga.*	25	K4	
Dalton, *Ont.*	18	G4	
Daly B., *Keewatin, N.W.T.*	11	R5	
Daly R., *N. Ter., Aust.*	49	E2	
Daly Waters, *N. Ter., Aust.*	49	E3	
Daman, *India*	40	D4	
Damascus, *Syria*	42	B5	
Damase, *Que.*	20	C3	
Damavand Mt., *Iran*	42	D5	
Dampier Arch., *W. Aust.*	49	B3	
Dampier Ld., *W. Aust.*	49	C3	
Dampier Str., *Indonesia*	44	F7	
Da Nang, *S. Vietnam*	44	C5	
Dandurand L., *Que.*	20	B2	
Danforth, *Me.*	22	C4	
Daniel's Harb., *Nfld.*	23	J1	
Danish Str., *Franklin, N.W.T.*	10	O2	
Danneville, *N.Z.*	51	F4	
Danube R., *Cent. Europe*	39	J4	
Danville, *Ill.*	25	J2	
Danville, *Que.*	20	D3	
Danville, *Va.*	25	K3	
Danzig. See Gdansk			
Daphne, *Ala.*	52	J4	
Darbhanga, *India*	40	G3	
D'Arcy, *B.C.*	13	J7	
Dardanelle, *Ark.*	25	H3	
Dardanelles, *Turkey*	39	L5	
Dar-es-Salaam, *Tanzania*	46	H6	
Dargai, *W. Pak.*	40	D2	
Dargaville, *N.Z.*	51	D1	
D'Argent, L., *Que.*	20	B2	
Darien, *Ga.*	25	K4	
Darien, G. of, *Pan-Colombia*	30	B2	
Darjeeling, *India*	40	G3	
Darling, *Cape Prov., Rep. of S. Africa*	47	B3	
Darling Ra., *W. Aust.*	49	B6	
Darling R., *N.S.W.*	50	E5	
Darling Downs, *Queensland*	50	H3	
Darlington, *Eng.*	37	E4	
Darlington Park, *Ont.*	17	G4	
Dartmoor, *Eng.*	37	C6	
Dartmouth, *Eng.*	37	D6	
Dartmouth, *N.S.*	21	D3	
Darwin, *N. Ter., Aust.*	49	E2	
Darwin, Mt., *Chile*	31	C14	
Daryacheh Namakzer (L.), *Persia-Afghanistan*	40	B2	
Dashwood, *Ont.*	16	D4	
Dassen I., *Cape Prov., Rep. of S. Africa*	47	B3	
Daugavpils, *Latvia*	39	L1	
Dauphin, and L., *Man.*	15	M5	
Daveluyv, *Que.*	20	C2	
Davenport, *Ia.*	25	H2	
David, *Pan.*	29	H6	
Davidson, *Sask.*	14	H5	
Davis Inlet, *Lab.*	19	E2	
Davis Str., *N.W.T.-Greenland*	11	X4	
Davy L., *Sask.*	14	G1	
Dawes Ra., *Queensland*	50	H2	
Dawson, *Yukon*	10	G5	
Dawson B., *Man.*	15	L4	
Dawson Cr., *B.C.*	12	K5	
Dawson Mt., *B.C.*	13	M7	
Dawson R., *Queensland*	50	G2	
Dawson Landing, *Mackenzie, N.W.T.*	12	O2	
Daylesford. *Victoria*	50	E8	
Dayton, *N.Y.*	17	G5	
Dayton, *O.*	25	K3	
Daytona Beach, *Fla.*	25	K5	
De Aar, *Cape Prov., Rep. of S. Africa*	47	C3	
Deadman, *Mackenzie, N.W.T.*	12	H2	
Dead Moose L., *Sask.*	14	J4	
Dead River, *Me.*	22	B4	
Dead Sea, *Jordan-Israel*	42	B5	
Deadwood L., *B.C.*	12	F3	
Dean Chan., and R., *B.C.*	13	G6	
Dean Funes, *Argentina*	31	E10	
Dease Arm, *Mackenzie, N.W.T.*	10	L4	
Dease L., and R., *B.C.*	12	F3	
Dease Str., *N.W.T.*	10	N4	
Dease Lake, *B.C.*	12	E3	
Death Valley, *Cal.*	24	C3	
Debden, *Sask.*	14	H4	
Debec, *N.B.*	22	D3	
Debrecen, *Hungary*	39	K4	
Decatur, *Ala.*	25	J4	
Deception B., *Que.*	11	B1	
Decker Lake, *B.C.*	13	H5	
Dede Agach (Alexandroupolis), *Greece*	39	L5	
Dee R., *Eng.*	37	D5	
Dee R., *Scotland*	36	D3	
Deep B., *Sask.*	15	K2	
Deep Brook, *N.S.*	21	B3	
Deep River, *Ont.*	17	H1	
Deer I., *Me.*	22	C4	
Deer L., *Ont.*	18	A2	
Deer Lake, *Nfld.*	23	J2	
Deer Lake, *Ont.*	15	P4	
Deferiet, *N.Y.*	17	K3	
De Grey R., *W. Aust.*	49	B4	
Dej, *Romania*	39	K4	
Delagoa B., *Mozambique*	46	G8	
Delahey, L., *Que.*	20	A2	
Delano Peak, *Ut.*	24	D3	
Delaronde L., *Sask.*	14	H3	
Delaware, state, *U.S.A.*	25	L3	
Delaware B., *Del.-N.J.*	25	M3	
Delgado C., *Tanzania*	46	H7	
Delhi, *India*	40	E3	
Delhi, *Ont.*	16	E5	
Delisle, *Sask.*	14	H5	
Del Norte, *Col.*	24	E3	
De Long Mts., *Alaska*	10	B4	
Deloraine, *Man.*	15	L6	
Deloraine, *Tasmania*	50	L11	
Delorme L., *Que.*	19	C3	
Del Rio, *Tex., U.S.A.*	28	D2	
Delta Beach, *Man.*	15	M5	
Delungra, *N.S.W.*	50	H4	
Demerara R., *Guyana*	30	F2	
Deming, *N. Mex.*	24	E4	
Demini R., *Brazil*	30	E3	
Democratic Republic of Yemen, *S.W. Asia*	42	C7	
Denbigh, *Ont.*	17	H2	
Denbigh, and co., *Wales*	37	D5	
Denham Ra., *Queensland*	50	G2	
Deniliquin, *N.S.W.*	50	E7	
Denison, *Tex.*	24	G4	
Denmark, kingdom, *Europe*	38	G2	
Denmark, *N.S.*	21	D2	
Denmark Str., *Greenland, etc.*	11	Z5	
Denver, *Colo.*	24	F3	
Depot Harbour, *Ont.*	16	E2	
Dera Ghazi Khan, *W. Pak.*	40	D2	
Dera Ismail Khan, *W. Pak.*	40	D2	
Derby, *W. Aust.*	49	C3	
Derby, and co., *Eng.*	37	E5	
Derg L., *Eire*	37	A5	
Derrynasaggart Mts., *Eire*	37	A6	
Derryveagh Mts., *Eire*	37	A4	
Derwent R., *Eng.*	37	E5	
Derwent R., *Tasmania*	50	L12	
Desaguadero R., *Bolivia*	30	D7	
Desbarats, *Ont.*	16	A1	
Deschaillons, *Que.*	20	C2	
Deschambault L., *Sask.*	15	K3	
Deseado, *Argentina*	31	D3	
Deseado R., *Argentina*	31	D13	
Deseronto, *Ont.*	17	H3	
Desert L., *Que.*	20	A2	
Desert R., *Que.*	20	B2	
Des Moines, *Ia.*	25	H2	
Desna R., *U.S.S.R.*	39	N3	
Desolacion I., *Chile*	31	B14	
Desolate B., *Chile*	31	C14	
Desolation C., *Greenland*	11	Z5	
Despair C., *Que.*	22	E2	
D'Estree B., *S. Aust.*	50	A7	
Destruction, *Yukon*	10	G5	
Detlor, *Ont.*	17	H2	
Detour, *Mich.*	16	A1	
Detroit, *Mich.*	25	K2	
Deux Montagnes, *Que.*	20	B3	
Deux Rivières, *Ont.*	17	G1	
Devil R., *Que.*	20	B2	
Devils Lake, *N. Dak.*	24	G1	
Devil's Thumb, *Alaska*	12	E4	
Devil's Thumb Fd., *Greenland*	11	X3	
Devizes, *Eng.*	37	D6	
Devon, *N.B.*	22	D4	
Devon, co., *Eng.*	37	D6	
Devon I., *Franklin, N.W.T.*	11	R2	
Devonport, *Eng.*	37	C6	
Devonport, *N.Z.*	51	E2	
Devonport, *Tasmania*	50	L11	
Dewetsdorp, *Orange F.S.*	47	D2	
Dexter, *Me.*	22	C4	
Dezhneva (East) C., *U.S.S.R.*	43	R2	
Dhaulagiri Mt., *Nepal*	40	F3	
Diamante R., *Argentina*	31	D10	
Diamantina, *Brazil*	30	J7	
Diamantina Ls., *Queensland*	50	C1	
Diamantina R., *S. Aust.-Queensland*	49	G4	
Diamantino, *Brazil*	30	F6	
Diamond City, *Alberta*	14	E6	
Diana B., *Que.*	19	C1	
Dibrugarh, *India*	40	G3	
Dickinson, *N. Dak.*	24	F1	
Dickinson, *Ont.*	20	B3	
Didsbury, *Alberta*	14	D5	
Diefenbaker L., *Sask.*	14	H5	
Diego Ramirez Is., *Chile*	31	C15	
Diego Suarez, *Madagascar*	46	H7	
Dieppe, *France*	38	E3	
Digby, *N.S.*	21	B3	
Digby Neck, *N.S.*	21	A3	
Digges Is., *Hudson B., N.W.T.*	19	B1	
Dijon, *France*	38	F4	
Dillingham, *Alaska*	10	C6	
Dillon, *Mont.*	24	D1	
Dimboola, *Victoria*	50	D8	
Dinaric Mts., *Yugoslavia*	39	H4	
Dingle, *Eire*	37	A5	
Dingwall. *Scotland*	36	C3	
Dingwall, *N.S.*	23	G3	
Dinosaur Park, *Alberta*	14	F5	
Dirk Hartogs I., *W. Aust.*	49	A5	
Dirranbandi, *Queensland*	49	G4	
Disappointment C., *Wash.*	24	B1	
Disappointment L., *W. Austr.*	49	C4	
Disaster B., *N.S.W.*	50	H8	
Discovery, *Mackenzie, N.W.T.*	12	O1	
Discovery B., *Victoria*	50	C9	
Disko I., and B., *Greenland*	11	Y4	
Disraeli, *Que.*	20	D3	
Ditchfield, *Que.*	20	D3	
Diu I., *India*	40	D4	
Diver, *Ont.*	16	E2	
Diver L., *Que.*	20	B2	
Dix, *Que.*	20	A1	
Dixon Entrance, *B.C.*	12	D5	
Dixonville, *Alberta*	12	M4	
Dixville, *Que.*	20	D3	
Djajapura, *W. Irian*	44	F7	
Djakarta, *Java*	44	C7	
Djaja Pk., *W. Irian*	44	F7	
Djajapura, *W. Irian*	44	F7	
Djibouti, *T.F.A.I.*	46	H4	
Djúpivogur, *Iceland*	35	D3	
Dneprodzerzhinsk, *Ukraine*	39	N3	
Dnepropetrovsk, *Ukraine*	39	N3	
Dnieper R., *U.S.S.R., etc.*	39	M2	
Dniester R., *Ukraine, etc.*	39	M4	
Doaktown, *N.B.*	21	A1	
Doce R., *Brazil*	30	K7	
Doctor Arroyo, *Mexico*	28	D3	
Dodge City, *Kan.*	24	F3	
Dog L., *Algoma, Ont.*	18	F4	
Dog L., *Man.*	15	M5	
Dog L., *Thunder B., Ont.*	18	D4	
Dog Creek, *B.C.*	13	J7	
Dogger Bank, *North Sea*	38	E2	
Dohazari, *Bangladesh*	40	H4	
Doig R., *B.C.*	12	K4	
Dolbeau, *Que.*	22	A2	
Dolgellau, *Wales*	37	C5	

Name	Map	Ref
Dolores, *Argentina*	31	F11
Dolphin and Union Str., *N.W.T.*	10	L4
Dolphin C., *Falkland Is.*	31	F14
Dome Cr., *B.C.*	13	K6
Dome Peak, *Mackenzie, N.W.T.*	12	G2
Domes, The (Mts.), *Lab.*	20	E2
Dominica I., *W. Indies*	29	M4
Dominican Republic, *W. Indies*	29	K4
Dominion, *N.S.*	21	G1
Dominion City, *Man.*	15	N6
Domremy, *Sask.*	14	J4
Don R., *Scotland*	36	D3
Don R., *U.S.S.R.*	39	O3
Donaghadee, *N. Ire.*	37	C4
Donald, *B.C.*	13	M7
Donald, *Ont.*	17	G3
Donald, *Queensland*	50	D8
Donalda, *Alberta*	14	E4
Donaldsonville, *La.*	25	H4
Doncaster, *Eng.*	37	E5
Dondra Hd., *Sri Lanka*	40	F7
Donegal, and co., *Eire*	37	A4
Donegal B., *Eire*	37	A4
Doneny, *Que.*	20	C2
Donetsk, *Ukraine*	39	O3
Donetz R., *Ukraine*	39	O3
Dongola, *Sudan*	46	F4
Donnacona, *Que.*	20	D2
Doorn Kop, *Transvaal*	47	D2
Dorchester, *Eng.*	37	D6
Dorchester, *N.B.*	21	C2
Dorchester Sta., *Ont.*	16	D5
Dordogne R., *France*	38	E4
Dordrecht, *Cape Prov., Rep. of S. Africa*	47	D3
Dore L., *Que.*	20	B2
Dore L., *Sask.*	14	H3
Dore, Mont, *France*	38	E4
Dornoch, *Scotland*	36	C3
Dornoch Firth, *Scotland*	36	D3
Dorreen, *B.C.*	12	F5
Dorrigo, *N.S.W.*	50	J5
Dorset, *Ont.*	17	G2
Dorset, co., *Eng.*	37	D6
Dortmund, *Ger.*	38	F3
Dorval, *Que.*	20	C3
Dos Pozos, *Argentina*	31	D12
Doting Cove, *Nfld.*	23	L2
Douala, *Cameroun*	46	E5
Doubtful Sd., *N.Z.*	51	A6
Doubtless B., *N.Z.*	51	D1
Doucet Landings, *Que.*	20	C2
Douglas, *Alaska*	12	C3
Douglas, *Cape Prov., Rep. of S Africa*	47	C2
Douglas, *Isle of Man*	37	C4
Douglas, *Ont.*	17	J2
Douglas, *Wyo.*	24	E2
Douglas Chan., *B.C.*	13	F6
Douglas Mt., *Mont.*	24	D1
Douglas Pt., *Ont.*	16	D3
Douglastown, *Que.*	22	E2
Dounreay, *Scotland*	36	D2
Douro R., *Spain-Portugal*	38	C5
Dover, *Del.*	25	L3
Dover, *Eng.*	37	F6
Dover, *Me.*	22	C4
Dover, *N.H.*	25	M2
Dover R., *Alberta*	14	E2
Dover, Str. of, *Eng.*	38	E3
Dover Foxcroft, *Me.*	22	C4
Dover West, *N.S.*	21	D3
Dovre Fjell, *Norway*	35	H3
Dowling L., *Alberta*	14	F5
Down, co., *N. Ire.*	37	B4
Downham, *Eng.*	37	F5
Downpatrick, *N. Ire.*	37	C4
Doyles, *Nfld.*	23	H3
Dozois Res., *Que.*	19	B4
Dra'a, Wady, *Morocco*	46	C3
Drake Str., *S. America*	3	H7
Drakensberg, *S. Africa*	47	D3
Drammen, *Norway*	35	J4
Drava R., *Hungary, etc.*	39	J4
Drayton, *Ont.*	16	E4
Dresden, *Ger.*	39	H3
Dresden, *Ont.*	16	C5
Driefontein, *Orange F.S.*	47	D2
Driftpile R., *Alberta*	14	D3
Drin R., *Albania*	39	K5
Drina R., *Yugoslavia*	39	J4
Drinkwater, *Sask.*	14	J5
Drogheda, *Eire*	37	B5
Drogobych, *Ukraine, U.S.S.R.*	39	K3
Drowning R., *Ont.*	18	F3
Drumbo, *Ont.*	16	E4
Drumheller, *Alberta*	14	E5
Drummond I., *Mich.*	16	B1
Drummond Ra., *Queensland*	50	F2
Drummondville, *Que.*	20	D3
Dry B., *Alaska*	13	A3
Dryberry L., *Ont.*	18	B4
Drybrough, *Man.*	15	L2
Dryden, *Ont.*	18	B4
Dry Lake, *Coast of Lab.*	19	D3
Dubawnt R., and L., *N.W.T.*	10	O5
Dubbo, *N.S.W.*	50	G6
Dubh Artach I., *Scotland*	36	B3
Dublin (Baile Atha Cliath), *Eire*	37	B5
Dublin, *Ga.*	25	K4
Dublin, *Ont.*	16	D4
Dublin B., *Eire*	37	B5
Dubrovnik (Ragusa), *Yugoslavia*	39	J5
Dubuque, *Ia.*	25	H2
Ducie I., *Pacific Oc.*	2	F6
Duck Mt., *Man.*	15	L5
Duck Mt. Park, *Sask.*	15	L5
Dudley, *Eng.*	37	D5
Dudswell, *Que.*	20	D3
Dufferin, co., *Ont.*	16	E3
Dufferin C., *Que.*	19	B2
Dufftown, *Scotland*	36	D3
Dufresne Lake, *Que.*	19	D3
Duguesclin, *Que.*	20	D2
Duhamel, *Que.*	17	K2
Duke I., *Alaska*	12	E5
Dulbandin, *W. Pak.*	40	B3
Dulce, G. of, *Costa Rica*	29	H6
Duluth, *Minn.*	25	H1
Dumbarton, *Scotland*	36	C4
Dumfries, and co., *Scotland*	37	D4
Dumont L., *Que.*	17	J1
Dún Laoghaire, *Eire*	37	B5
Dunbar, *Scotland*	36	D3
Dunbarton, co., *Scotland*	36	C3
Dunblane, *Sask.*	14	H5
Dunblane, *Scotland*	36	D3
Duncan, *Vancouver I., B.C.*	13	J8
Duncan L., *B.C.*	13	M7
Duncansby Hd., *Scotland*	36	D2
Dunchurch, *Ont.*	16	F2
Dundalk, *Eire*	37	B4
Dundalk, *Ont.*	16	E3
Dundalk B., *Eire*	37	B5
Dundas, *Ont.*	16	E4
Dundas, co., *Ont.*	17	K2
Dundas, I., *B.C.*	12	E5
Dundee, *Natal*	47	E2
Dundee, *Que.*	20	D3
Dundee, *Scotland*	36	D3
Dundrum B., *N. Ire.*	37	C4
Dundurn, *Sask.*	14	H5
Dunedin, *N.Z.*	51	C6
Dunedin R., *B.C.*	12	H3
Dunedoo, *N.S.W.*	50	G6
Dunfermline, *Scotland*	36	D3
Dungannon, *N. Ire.*	37	B4
Dungannon, *Ont.*	16	D4
Dungarvan, and Harb., *Eire*	37	B5
Dungeness, *Eng.*	37	F6
Dungog, *N.S.W.*	50	H6
Dunham, *Que.*	20	C3
Dunkeld, *Scotland*	36	D3
Dunkirk, *France*	38	E3
Dunkirk, *N.Y.*	16	F5
Dunlaoghaire (Kingstown), *Eire*	37	B5
Dunlop, *Man.*	15	M3
Dunlop, *Ont.*	16	D4
Dunmanway, *Eire*	37	A6
Dunmore, *Alberta*	14	F6
Dunnet Hd., *Scotland*	36	D2
Dunn Valley, *Ont.*	16	B1
Dunnville, *Ont.*	16	F5
Duns, *Scotland*	36	D4
Dunster, *B.C.*	13	K6
Duntroon, *Ont.*	16	E3
Dunvegan, *Alberta*	14	B3
Dunvegan L., *Skye I., Scotland*	36	B3
Du Quoin, *Ill.*	25	J3
Durango, *Colo.*	24	E3
Durazno, *Uruguay*	31	F10
Durban, *Natal*	47	E2
Durham, *Eng.*	37	E4
Durham, *N.C.*	25	L3
Durham, *Ont.*	16	E3
Durham, co., *Eng.*	37	D4
Durham, co., *Ont.*	17	G3
Durham Downs, *Queensland*	50	C3
Durrës (Durazzo), *Albania*	39	J5
D'Urville I., *N.Z.*	51	D4
Dushanbe, *U.S.S.R.*	40	C1
Dusky Sd., *N.Z.*	51	A6
Düsseldorf, *Ger.*	38	F3
Dutch Harb., *Aleutian Is.*	2	E2
Dutton, *Ont.*	16	D5
Duval L., *Que.*	17	H1
Dvina, G. of, *U.S.S.R.*	35	O2
Dvina R., *U.S.S.R.*	35	P3
Dyce, *Man.*	15	L3
Dyer B., *Prince Patrick I., N.W.T.*	10	K2
Dyer C., *Baffin I., N.W.T.*	11	W4
Dyer Bay, *Ont.*	16	D2
Dyke L., *Lab.*	19	D3
Dzerzhinsk, *U.S.S.R.*	39	P1
Dzungarian Gate, *U.S.S.R.*	42	G4
Eabamet L., *Ont.*	18	E3
Eagle, *Alaska*	10	F5
Eagle L., *Ont.*	18	B4
Eagle L., *Ont.*	18	A3
Eagle Ls., *Me.*	22	C3
Eagle R., *Lab.*	19	F3
Eagle R., *Que.*	20	A2
Eagle Depot, *Que.*	17	J1
Eagle Lake, *Ont.*	17	G3
Eagle Pass. *Tex.*	24	F5
Eagle Plains, *Yukon*	10	G4
Eardley, *Que.*	20	A3
Ear Falls, *Ont.*	18	B3
Earn L., *Yukon*	12	C1
East C., *N.Z.*	51	G2
East Pt., *Anticosti I.*	22	F2
East Pt., *P.E.I.*	21	F1
East Angus, *Que.*	20	D3
East Bay, *N.S.*	21	G1
East Bluff, *Baffin I.*	19	D1
Eastbourne, *Eng.*	37	F6
East China Seas, *China*	44	E3
East Coast, *N.Z.*	51	F3
East End, *Sask.*	14	G6
Easter I., *Pacific Oc.*	2	G6
East Indies Is., *S.E. Asia*	2	C4
East Jeddore, *N.S.*	22	F4
East Jordan, *N.S.*	21	B4
East Kemptville, *N.S.*	21	B3
East London, *Cape Prov.*	47	D3
East Lothian, co., *Scotland*	36	D4
East Main, *Que.*	19	B3
Eastmain R., *Que.*	19	B3
Eastman, *Que.*	20	C3
East Pine, *B.C.*	12	K5
Eastport, *Me.*	22	D4
East Pubnico, *N.S.*	21	B4
East Retford, *Eng.*	37	E5
East Siberian Sea, *Arctic Oc.*	2	D1
East Spit, *Sable I., N.S.*	23	H4
Eaton Canyon, *Que.*	19	D2
Eau Claire, *Wis.*	25	H2
Eau Claire, L. l', *Que.*	19	B2
Ebbw Vale, *Wales*	37	D6
Eboulement Mt., *Que.*	20	D2
Ebro R., *Spain*	38	D5
Echo Bay, *Ont.*	16	A1
Echoing R., *Man.*	15	Q3
Echuca, *Victoria*	50	E6
E. C. Manning Park, *B.C.*	13	K8
Ecorce, L. de l', *Que.*	20	A2
Ecorce R., *Que.*	20	D1
Ecorces, L. aux, *Que.*	20	D2
Ecuador, rep., *S. America*	30	B4
Ecum Secum, *N.S.*	21	E3
Eddontenajon L., *B.C.*	12	E4
Eden, *Man.*	15	M5
Eden, *Me.*	22	C4
Eden, *N.S.W.*	50	G8
Eden R., *Eng.*	37	D4
Edenburg, *Orange F.S.*	47	D2
Edenhurst, *Ont.*	16	D3
Edge I., *Spitsbergen*	3	L1
Edgecumbe C., *Alaska*	13	C4
Edgell I., *N.W.T.*	19	E1
Edievale, *N.Z.*	51	B6
Edinburgh, *Scotland*	36	D4
Edirne, *Turkey*	39	L5
Edith Cavell Mt., *Alberta*	14	D2
Edith River, *N. Ter., Aust.*	49	E2
Edmonton, *Alberta*	14	E4
Edmund L., *Man.*	15	P3
Edmundston, *N.B.*	22	C3
Edouard L., *Que.*	20	C2
Edrachillis B., *Scotland*	36	C2
Edson, *Alberta*	14	C4
Edward I., *L. Superior, Ont.*	18	D4
Edward L., *Cent. Africa*	46	E4
Edziza Peak, *B.C.*	12	E4
Egedo Ld., *Greenland*	11	Z4
Egedesminde, *Greenland*	11	Y4
Egenolf L., *Man.*	15	L1
Egersund, *Norway*	35	H4
Egg L., *Que.*	19	C3
Eglinton I., *Franklin, N.W.T.*	10	K2
Egmont B., *P.E.I.*	21	C1
Egmont Mt., and C., *N.Z.*	51	D3
Egridir, *Turkey*	39	M6
Egypt, Arab Rep. of, *N. Africa*	46	F3
Eidsvold, *Queensland*	50	H2
Eigg I., *Scotland*	36	B3
Eire. See Ireland, Rep. of		
Eisenhower Mt., *Alberta*	14	D5
Eketahuna, *N.Z.*	51	E4
Ekwan R., *Ont.*	18	G2
El Agheila, *Libya*	46	E2
El Alamein, *Egypt*	46	F2
Eiands Berg, *Cape Prov., Rep. of S. Africa*	47	C3
Elandslaagte, *Natal*	47	E2
Elba I., *Italy*	38	G5
Elbe R., *Ger.*	38	G2
Elbert Mt., *Col.*	24	E3
Elblag, *Poland*	39	J2
Elbow, *Sask.*	14	H5
Elbow L., *Ont.*	18	D3
Elbrus Mt., *Caucasus*	42	C4
Elburz Mts., *Iran*	42	D5
El Callao, *Venezuela*	30	E2
El Cardón, *Venezuela*	30	C1
Elche, *Spain*	38	D6
El Cuyo, *Mexico*	28	G3
Eldon, *Alberta*	14	D5
Eldorado, *Sask.*	14	G1
El Dorado, *Venezuela*	30	E2
Elebe, *Botswana*	47	D1
Elektrenai, *Lithuania, U.S.S.R.*	39	L2
Elephant R., *S.W. Africa*	47	B1
Eleuthera I., *Bahamas*	29	J2
Elgin, *Ill.*	25	J2
Elgin, *N.B.*	21	B2
Elgin, *Scotland*	36	D3
Elgin, co., *Ont.*	16	D5
Elgon Mt., *Uganda*	46	G5
El Gran Chaco, *Argentina-Paraguay*	31	E9
El Hamad, *Arabia*	42	B5
Elias Mts., *Alaska-B.C.*	10	G5
Elizabeth, *S. Australia*	49	F6
Elizabeth C., *N.C.*	25	L3
Elk I., *Man.*	15	N5
Elk R., *B.C.*	13	N8
Elkhorn, *Man.*	15	L5
Elk Island National Park, *Alberta*	14	E4
Elk Lake, *Ont.*	18	H5
Elko, *B.C.*	13	N8
Elko, *Nev.*	20	C2
Ellef Ringnes I., *Franklin, N.W.T.*	10	O2
Ellerslie, *P.E.I.*	22	F3
Ellesmere I., *Franklin, N.W.T.*	11	S1
Ellesmere L., *N.Z.*	51	D5
Ellice Is., *Pacific Oc.*	2	D5
Elliot, *Cape Prov., Rep. of S. Africa*	47	D3
Elliot L., *Ont.*	16	C1
Elliotdale, *Cape Prov., Rep. of S. Africa*	47	D3
Elliot Lake, *Ont.*	18	G5
Ellis B., *Anticosti I., Que.*	22	E2
Ellis R., *Alberta*	14	E2
Ellsworth, *Me.*	22	C4
Elm Creek, *Man.*	15	N6
Elmira, *N.Y.*	25	L2
Elmira, *Ont.*	16	E4
Elmira, *P.E.I.*	21	E1
Elmsdale, *N.S.*	21	D3
Elmsvale, *N.S.*	21	D2
Elmvale, *Ont.*	16	E3
Elmwood, *Ont.*	16	D3
Elnora, *Alberta*	14	E5
El Obeid, *Sudan*	46	G4
Elora, *Ont.*	16	E4
El Paso, *Tex.*	24	E4
El Pintado, *Argentina*	31	E8
Elrose, *Sask.*	14	G5
Elsa, *Yukon*	10	G5
El Salto, *Mexico*	28	C3
Elsas, *Ont.*	18	G4
Elsburg, *Transvaal*	47	D2
Eltham, *N.Z.*	51	E3
El Tigre, *Venezuela*	30	E2
El Toco, *Chile*	31	D8
El Turbio, *Argentina*	31	C14
Elu Inlet, *N.W.T.*	10	N4
Ely, and Isle of, *Eng.*	37	F5
Embar, *Lab.*	19	D3
Embarcacion, *Argentina*	31	E8
Embarras, L., *Que.*	20	A2
Embarras Portage, *Alberta*	14	F1
Embira R., *Brazil*	30	C5
Embro, *Ont.*	16	D4
Embrun, *Ont.*	17	K2
Emerald, *Queensland*	50	G1
Emerald I., *Franklin, N.W.T.*	10	M2
Emeril, *Lab.*	19	D3
Emerson, *Man.*	15	N6
Emi Koussi Mt., *Chad, Cent. Africa*	46	E3
Emily Park, *Ont.*	17	G3
Emmaville, *N.S.W.*	50	H4
Emmet, *Queensland*	50	E2
Emo, *Ont.*	18	B4
Empangeni, *Natal*	47	E2
Empedrado, *Argentina*	31	F9
Emporia, *Kan.*	24	G3
Emsdale, *Ont.*	16	F2
Emu B., *Tasmania*	50	K11
Encantada, Cerro de la, mt., *Mexico*	28	A1
Encarnacion, *Paraguay*	31	F9
Encarnacion de Diaz, *Mexico*	28	D3
Encontrados, *Venezuela*	30	C2
Encounter B., *S. Aust.*	50	B7
Endako, *B.C.*	13	H5
Enderby, *B.C.*	13	L7
Enderby Ld., *Antarctica*	3	M8
Endicott Ra., *Alaska*	10	D4
Enfield, *N.S.*	21	D3
Engano, C., *Dominican Rep.*	29	L4
Engaño C., *Philippine Is.*	44	E5
England, *Brit. Isles*	37	E5
Englee, *Nfld.*	23	K1
Englefield C., *Franklin, N.W.T.*	11	R4
Englehart, *Ont.*	18	J5
Englewood, *Vancouver I., B.C.*	13	G7
English Chan., *Eng.-France*	38	D3
English R., *Ont.*	18	A3
Enid, *Okla.*	24	G3
Ennadai, *Keewatin, N.W.T.*	10	O5
Enngonia, *N.S.W.*	50	E4
Ennis, *Eire*	37	A5
Enniscorthy, *Eire*	37	B5
Enniskillen, *N. Ire.*	37	B4
Ennistimon, *Eire*	37	A5
Ensagami L., *Ont.*	18	E3
Ensenada, *Argentina*	31	F10
Ensenada, *Mexico*	28	A1
Enslin, *Cape Prov., Rep. of S. Africa*	47	C2
Entebbe, *Uganda*	46	G6
Enterprise, *B.C.*	13	K6

Entry	Page	Grid
Enterprise, *Mackenzie, N.W.T.*	12	N2
Enterprise, *Ont.*	17	J3
Entiako L., *B.C.*	13	H6
Entrance, *Alberta*	14	B4
Entry I., *Que.*	23	G3
Entwistle, *Alberta*	14	D4
Epsom, *Eng.*	37	E6
Equatorial Guinea, *W. Africa*	46	D5
Erale, *Brazil*	30	G3
Erciyas Dagi, mt. (Argaeus, Mt.), *Turkey*	42	B5
Eregli, *Turkey*	39	M5
Erfurt, *Ger.*	38	G3
Eriboll L., *Scotland*	36	C2
Ericht L., *Scotland*	36	C3
Erie, *Pa.*	25	L2
Erie L., *Canada-U.S.A.*	16	D5
Erieau, *Ont.*	16	C5
Erin, *Ont.*	16	E4
Erlandson L., *Que.*	19	D2
Ermelo, *Transvaal*	47	D2
Erne L., *N. Ire.*	37	B4
Erne L., Upper, *N. Ire.*	37	B4
Errigal, *Eire*	37	A4
Erwood, *Sask.*	15	K4
Erz Gebirge, *Ger.-Czecho-slovakia*	38	H3
Esbjerg, *Denmark*	38	F2
Escalon, *Mexico*	28	D2
Escoumains, Les, *Que.*	20	E1
Escoumains R., *Que.*	20	E1
Escuminac Pt., *N.B.*	22	E3
Esfahan, *Iran*	42	D5
Eshowe, *Natal*	47	E2
Esk, *Queensland*	50	J3
Eskimo C., *Keewatin, N.W.T.*	11	Q5
Eskimo C., *Man.*	15	O1
Eskimo Ls., *Mackenzie, N.W.T.*	10	H4
Eskimo Pt., *Keewatin, N.W.T.*	11	Q5
Eskisehir, *Turkey*	39	M6
Eskwahani L., *Que.*	20	B2
Esla Res., *Spain*	38	C5
Esmeraldas, *Ecuador*	30	B3
Espanola, *Ont.*	16	D1
Española I., *Galapagos Is., S. Pacific Oc.*	31	O17
Esperance, *W. Aust.*	49	C6
Espiritu Santo, B. de, *Mexico*	28	G4
Espiritu Santo I., *Mexico*	28	G3
Esquel, *Argentina*	31	E10
Esquimalt, *Vancouver I., B.C.*	13	J8
Essen, *Ger.*	38	F3
Essequibo R., *Guyana*	30	F2
Essex, co. and tn., *Ont.*	16	C5
Essex, co., *Eng.*	37	F6
Est, L. de l', *Que.*	20	E2
Estcourt, *Natal*	47	D2
Estcourt, *Que*	20	E2
Esteli, *Nicaragua*	29	G5
Esterhazy, *Sask.*	15	K5
Estevan, *Sask.*	15	K6
Estevan Is., *B.C.*	13	F6
Eston, *Sask.*	14	G5
Estonia, rep., *Europe*	39	L1
Estoril, *Portugal*	38	B6
Etah, *Greenland*	11	U2
Etchemin R., *Que.*	20	D2
Ethiopia, *E. Africa*	46	G5
Etna, Mt., *Sicily*	39	H6
Etolin Str., *Alaska*	10	A5
Etomami R., *Sask.*	15	K5
Etomami R., N., *Sask.*	15	K4
Ettrick Pen Mt., *Scotland*	37	D4
Etzikom Coulee, *Alberta*	14	F6
Euboea (Negropont) I., *Greece*	39	K6
Euchiniko Cr., *B.C.*	13	H6
Euchu L., *B.C.*	13	H6
Eucla, *W. Aust.*	49	D6
Eugene, *Ore.*	24	B2
Eugenio, Pta., *Mexico*	28	A2
Euphrates R., *Iraq*	42	C5
Eureka, *Cal.*	24	B2
Eureka, *Ellesmere-N.W.T.*	11	R1
Eureka, *Nev.*	24	C3
Eureka Sd., *Franklin, N.W.T.*	11	R2
Eureka River, *Alberta*	12	L4
Euston, *N.S.W.*	50	D7
Eutsuk L., *B.C.*	13	G6
Evans L., *Que.*	19	B3
Evans Str., *Keewatin, N.W.T.*	11	S5
Evanston, *Wyo.*	24	D2
Evansville, *Ind.*	25	J3
Evansville, *Ont.*	16	C2
Everard C., *Victoria*	50	G8
Everest Mt., *Nepal-Tibet*	40	G3
Everett, *Wash.*	24	B1
Evora, *Portugal*	38	C6
Exaltacion, *Bolivia*	30	D6
Exe R., *Eng.*	37	D6
Exeter, *Eng.*	37	D6
Exeter, *Ont.*	16	D4
Exmoor, *Eng.*	37	D6
Exmouth, *Eng.*	37	D6
Exmouth G., *W. Aust.*	49	A4
Expanse, *Sask.*	14	J6
Expedition Ra., *Queensland*	50	G2
Exshaw, *Alberta*	13	N7
Exstew, *B.C.*	13	F5
Exuma Sd., *Bahamas*	29	J3
Eye Penin., *Hebrides, Scotland*	36	B2
Eye Hill Cr., *Alberta*	14	F4
Eyemouth, *Scotland*	36	D4
Eyre, *W. Aust.*	49	D6
Eyre Cr., *S. Aust.-Queensland*	49	F5
Eyre L., *S. Aust.*	49	F5
Eyre Penin., *S. Aust.*	49	F6
Faber L., *Mackenzie, N.W.T.*	12	M1
Facatativa, *Colombia*	30	B2
Faden, *Coast of Lab.*	19	D3
Faeroes, The, *Atlantic Oc.*	35	E3
Faillon L., *Que.*	20	A1
Fair Hd., *N. Ire.*	37	B4
Fair I., *Shetland Is., Scotland*	36	E2
Fairbanks, *Alaska*	10	L5
Fairfield, *Me.*	22	C4
Fairford, *Man.*	15	M5
Fairlie, *N.Z.*	51	C6
Fairloch, *Ont.*	18	E4
Fairport, *N.Y.*	17	H4
Fairview, *Alberta*	14	B2
Fairview, *Mich.*	16	B3
Fairweather L., *Yukon*	12	D1
Fairweather Mt., *Alaska*	13	B3
Faizabad, *India*	40	F3
Fakfak, *W. Irian*	44	F7
Falcon I., *Ont.*	18	A4
Falcon Res., *Tex.*	24	G5
Falconbridge, *Ont.*	16	E1
Falkenburg, *Ont.*	17	F2
Falkirk, *Scotland*	36	D3
Falkland E., *S. Atlantic Oc.*	31	F14
Falkland Is., *S. Atlantic Oc.*	31	E14
Falkland Sd., *Falkland Is.*	31	E14
Falkland W., *S. Atlantic Oc.*	31	E14
Fall River, *Mass.*	25	M2
Falmouth, *Eng.*	37	C6
Falmouth, *Jamaica*	29	J4
False B., *Cape Prov., Rep. of S. Africa*	47	B3
Falster I., *Denmark*	38	H2
Falun, *Sweden*	35	K3
Famatina, *Argentina*	31	D9
Fame Pt., *Que.*	22	G2
Family L., *Man.*	15	O5
Fanning I., *Pacific Oc.*	2	E4
Far Mt., *B.C.*	13	H6
Farewell C., *Greenland*	11	Z6
Farewell C., *N.Z.*	51	D4
Fargo, *N. Dak.*	24	G1
Farley, *Que.*	17	K1
Farmington, *Me.*	22	B4
Farnham, *Que.*	20	C3
Farnham Mt., *B.C.*	13	M7
Faro, *Portugal*	38	C6
Farrell Cr., *B.C.*	12	K4
Farrellton, *Que.*	17	J2
Farrington, *Ont.*	18	B4
Farwell, *Tex.*	26	F4
Fassett, *Que.*	20	B3
Fast L., *Que.*	22	G1
Father L., *Que.*	19	B4
Father Pt., *Que.*	22	C2
Fatsham, *China*	44	D4
Fauresmith, *Orange F.S.*	47	D2
Faust, *Alberta*	14	D3
Favourable L., *Ont.*	18	B2
Fawcett, *Alberta*	14	E3
Fawcett, *Ont.*	15	Q5
Fawn L., *Mackenzie, N.W.T.*	12	M1
Faxa Fd., *Iceland*	35	B3
Fayetteville, *Ark.*	25	H3
Fayetteville, *N.C.*	25	L3
Fed. of Malaya, *S. Asia*	44	C6
Feia L., *Brazil*	31	J8
Feilding, *N.Z.*	51	E4
Felipe Cartillo Pto., *Mexico*	28	G4
Felixstowe, *Eng.*	37	F6
Feller Heights, *B.C.*	12	K5
Fenelon Falls, *Ont.*	17	G3
Fenton, *Mich.*	16	B5
Fenwick, *Ont.*	16	F4
Fergus, *Ont.*	16	E4
Ferguson, *Que.*	20	C2
Fermanagh, co., *N. Ire.*	37	B4
Ferme Neuve, *Que.*	20	B2
Fermoy, *Eire*	37	A5
Fernandina, *Fla.*	25	K4
Fernandina I., *Galapagos Is., S. Pacific Oc.*	31	N17
Fernando Póo, I., *Equat. Guinea*	46	D5
Fernie, *B.C.*	13	N8
Ferole Pte., *Nfld.*	23	J1
Ferozepore, *India*	40	D2
Ferryland, *Nfld.*	23	L3
Fetlar, *Scotland*	36	E1
Fez, *Morocco*	46	C2
Ficksburg, *Orange F.S.*	47	D2
Field, *B.C.*	13	M7
Field, *Ont.*	16	F1
Fielding, *Sask.*	14	H4
Fife, co., *Scotland*	36	D3
Fife Ness, *Scotland*	36	D3
Figueira, *Brazil*	30	J7
Fiji Is., *Pacific Oc.*	2	D5
File L., *Man.*	15	L3
Filey, *Eng.*	37	E4
Fillmore, *Ut.*	24	D3
Filyos, *Turkey*	39	M5
Finch, *Ont.*	17	K2
Findhorn R., *Scotland*	36	C3
Findlater, *Sask.*	14	J5
Findlay Is., *Franklin, N.W.T.*	10	O2
Finger L., *Ont.*	18	B2
Finisterre C., *Spain*	38	B5
Finke R., *N. Ter., Aust.*	49	E5
Finland, rep., *N.E. Europe*	35	L3
Finland, G. of, *Finland, etc.*	35	M3
Finlay R., *B.C.*	12	H4
Finlay Forks, *B.C.*	12	J5
Finlayson L., *Yukon*	12	E2
Finley, *N.S.W.*	50	E7
Finmoore, *B.C.*	13	J6
Firebag R., *Alberta*	14	F2
Fire River, *Ont.*	18	G4
Firmat, *Argentina*	31	E10
Firmo R., *Brazil*	30	G6
Fish, *S.W. Africa*	47	B2
Fish L., *Mackenzie, N.W.T.*	12	J1
Fishburn, *Alberta*	14	E6
Fisher B., *Man.*	15	N5
Fisher Str., *N.W.T.*	11	S5
Fishguard, *Wales*	37	C6
Fishing L., *Man.*	18	A2
Fitzpatrick, *Que.*	20	C2
Fitzroy, *Ont.*	17	J2
Fitzroy R., *Queensland*	49	H4
Fitzroy R., *W. Aust.*	49	D3
Fitzwilliam I., *Ont.*	16	D2
Five Islands, *N.S.*	21	C2
Flagstaff L., *Me.*	22	B4
Flagstaff L., *Que.*	20	D3
Flaherty I., *Hudson B.*	19	A2
Flamand, and R., *Que.*	20	C2
Flamborough Hd., *Eng.*	37	E4
Flannan Is., *Hebrides, Scotland*	36	B2
Flat R., *Mackenzie, N.W.T.*	12	G2
Flathead L., *Mont.*	24	D1
Flattery C., *Wash.*	24	B1
Flaxcombe, *Sask.*	14	G5
Fleetwood, *Eng.*	37	D5
Fleming, *Sask.*	15	L5
Flesherton, *Ont.*	16	E3
Fleur de Mai L., *Lab.*	22	E1
Flinders I., *Tasmania*	50	G9
Flinders Ra., *S. Aust.*	50	B5
Flinders R., *Queensland*	49	G3
Flin Flon, *Man.*	15	K3
Flint, *Mich.*	16	B5
Flint, and co., *Wales*	37	D5
Flint R., *Mich.*	16	A4
Flintdale, *Ont.*	18	F3
Flodden, *Eng.*	36	D4
Florence, *Italy*	38	G5
Florence, *S.C.*	25	L4
Florencia, *Colombia*	30	B3
Flores I., *Vancouver I, B.C.*	13	G8
Flores I., and Sea, *Indonesia*	44	E7
Floriano, *Brazil*	30	J5
Florianópolis (Desterro), *Brazil*	31	H9
Florida, *Uruguay*	31	F10
Florida, state, *U.S.A.*	25	K5
Florida B., *Fla.*	25	K6
Florida Str., *Fla.*	25	L6
Florida Keys, *Fla.*	25	K6
Flowerpot I., *Ont.*	16	D2
Flowers C., *Nfld.*	23	J1
Fluor I., *L. Superior, Ont.*	18	D4
Flushing, *Netherlands*	38	E3
Fly R., *New Guinea*	44	G7
Focsani, *Romania*	39	L4
Foggia, *Italy*	39	H5
Fogo, and I., *Nfld.*	23	K2
Folda Fd., *Norway*	35	J3
Foleyet, *Ont.*	18	G4
Folkestone, *Eng.*	37	F6
Fond du Lac, *Minn.-Wis.*	18	C5
Fond-du-Lac, *Sask.*	14	H1
Fond-du-Lac R., *Sask.*	14	J1
Fonseca, G. of, *Honduras*	28	G5
Fontana L., *Argentina*	31	C12
Fontas, *B.C.*	12	K3
Fontas R., *B.C.*	12	K3
Fonte Boa, *Brazil*	30	D4
Fonteneau, *Que.*	23	G1
Foochow (Fu-chou), *China*	44	D4
Foothills, *Alberta*	14	C4
Forbes, *N.S.W.*	50	G6
Forbes, L., *Que.*	20	B2
Forbes Mt., *Alberta*	14	C5
Forel Mt., *Greenland*	11	Z4
Forest, *Ont.*	16	C4
Forestdale, *B.C.*	13	G5
Forestville, *Que.*	22	C2
Forfar, *Scotland*	36	D3
Forget, *Que.*	20	A1
Forget, *Sask.*	15	K6
Fork River, *Man.*	15	M5
Forks, The, *Ont.*	18	F3
Formby Hd., *Eng.*	37	D5
Formentera (I.), *Balearic Is.*	38	E6
Formosa, *Argentina*	31	F9
Forrest, *Victoria*	50	D9
Forsayth, *Queensland*	49	G3
Forsyth, *Mont.*	24	E1
Forsythe, *Que.*	20	A1
Fort à la Corne, *Sask.*	14	J4
Fort Albany, *Ont.*	18	H2
Fortaleza, *Brazil*	30	K4
Fort Anne Natural History Park, *N.S.*	21	B3
Fort Assiniboine, *Alberta*	14	D3
Fort Augustus, *Scotland*	36	C3
Fort Beaufort, *Cape Prov., Rep. of S. Africa*	47	D3
Fort Beauséjour Natural History Park, *N.B.*	21	C2
Fort Chimo, *Que.*	19	D2
Fort Chipewyan, *Alberta*	14	F1
Fort Coulonge, *Que.*	17	J2
Fort Daniel, *Que.*	22	E2
Fort de Coimbra, *Brazil*	30	F7
Fort Dodge, *Ia.*	25	H2
Forteau, *Que.*	23	J1
Fort Erie, *Ont.*	17	F5
Fortescue R., *W. Aust.*	49	B4
Fort Fairchild, *Me.*	22	D3
Fort Frances, *Ont.*	18	B4
Fort Franklin, *Mackenzie, N.W.T.*	10	K4
Fort Fraser, *B.C.*	13	H5
Fort George, *Que.*	19	B3
Fort Good Hope, *Mackenzie, N.W.T.*	10	J4
Fort Grahame, *B.C.*	12	H4
Forth, Firth of, *Scotland*	36	D3
Forth R., *Scotland*	36	C3
Fort Hertz, *Burma*	40	J3
Fort Hope, *Ont.*	18	D3
Forties Settlement, *N.S.*	21	C3
Fortin L., *Yukon*	12	E2
Fort Kent, *Me.*	22	C3
Fort Knox, *Ky.*	25	J3
Fort Lamy, *Chad, Africa*	46	E4
Fort Lavalle, *Argentina*	31	E8
Fort Liard, *Mackenzie, N.W.T.*	12	J2
Fort Mackay, *Alberta*	14	F2
Fort McKenzie, *Que.*	19	D2
Fort Mattagami, *Ont.*	18	H5
Fort Nelson, and R., *B.C.*	12	J3
Fort Norman, *Mackenzie, N.W.T.*	10	J5
Fort Olimpos, *Paraguay*	31	F8
Fort Peck Res., *Mont.*	24	E1
Fort Pelly, *Sask.*	15	K5
Fort Pierce, *Fla.*	27	K5
Fort Providence, *Mackenzie, N.W.T.*	12	M2
Fort Qu'Appelle, *Sask.*	15	K5
Fort Resolution, *Mackenzie, N.W.T.*	12	O2
Fortress of Louisbourg, Natural History Park, *N.S.*	21	G2
Fort Ross, *Franklin, N.W.T.*	11	Q3
Fort Rupert, *Que.*	19	B3
Fort St. James, *B.C.*	13	H5
Fort St. John, *B.C.*	12	K4
Fort Saskatchewan, *Alberta*	14	E4
Fort Scott, *Kan.*	25	H3
Fort Simpson, *Mackenzie, N.W.T.*	12	K2
Fort Smith, *Ark.*	25	H3
Fort Smith, *Mackenzie, N.W.T.*	10	M5
Fort Steele, *B.C.*	13	N8
Fort Teniente Montania, *Paraguay*	31	F8
Fortune, and B., *Nfld.*	23	K3
Fort Vermillion, *Alberta*	14	C1
Fort Walsh, *Sask.*	14	G6
Fort Wayne, *Ind.*	25	J2
Fort William, *Scotland*	36	C3
Fort Worth, *Tex.*	24	G4
Forty Mile, *Yukon*	10	F5
Fort Yukon, *Alaska*	10	F4
Foster, *Que.*	20	C3
Foster Ls., and R., *Sask.*	14	J2
Fosterton, *Sask.*	14	G5
Foula (I.), *Scotland*	36	D1
Foulness I., *Eng.*	37	F6
Foulwind C., *N.Z.*	51	C4
Fourchu, *N.S.*	21	G2
Fouta Djallon, *W. Africa*	46	B4
Foveaux Str., *N.Z.*	51	A7
Fowler B., *S. Aust.*	49	E6
Fox B., *Anticosti I., Que.*	22	F2
Fox C., *Nfld.*	23	K1
Fox R., *Man.*	15	O3
Foxe Chan., *Keewatin, N.W.T.*	11	S4
Foxe Penin., *Baffin I., N.W.T.*	11	T4
Foxe Basin, *Franklin, N.W.T.*	11	T4
Foxton, *N.Z.*	51	E4
Foxtrot, *Me.*	22	C4
Fox Valley, *Sask.*	14	G5
Foyle L., *N. Ire.*	37	B4
Foynes, *Eire*	37	A5
Framboise, *N.S.*	23	G4
Frampton, *Que.*	20	D2
France, rep., *Europe*	38	E4
Frances R., *Yukon*	12	F2
Frances Lake, *Yukon*	12	F2
Franceville, *Gabon, W. Africa*	46	E6
Francis, *Sask.*	15	J5

Francis Harb., *Lab.*	19	F3
Francis, L., *S. Dak.*	26	G2
Francois, *Nfld.*	23	J3
François L., *B.C.*	13	H6
François Lake, *B.C.*	13	H5
Frankford, *Ont.*	17	H3
Frankfort, *Ky.*	25	K3
Frankfort, *Orange F.S.*	47	D2
Frankfurt-on-Main, *Ger.*	38	G3
Frankfurt on Oder, *E. Ger.*	39	H4
Franklin, dist., *N.W.T.*	10	M3
Franklin B., *Mackenzie, N.W.T.*	10	J3
Franklin Chan., *Victoria*	50	F9
Franklin I., *Ont.*	16	E2
Franklin Str., *Franklin, N.W.T.*	11	P3
Franklin Falls, *N.H.*	22	B5
Franz, *Ont.*	18	F4
Fraser I., *Queensland*	49	J4
Fraser L., *B.C.*	13	H5
Fraser Plat., *B.C.*	13	J6
Fraser R., *B.C.*	13	K6
Fraserburg, *Cape Prov., Rep. of S. Africa*	47	C3
Fraserburgh, *Scotland*	36	E3
Fraserdale, *Ont.*	18	H4
Frater, *Ont.*	18	F5
Fray Bentos, *Uruguay*	31	F10
Fredericia, *Denmark*	38	G2
Frederick Sd., *Alaska*	12	C4
Frederick House, L. *Ont.*	18	H4
Fredericton, *N.B.*	19	D4
Frederiksdal, *Greenland*	11	Z6
Frederikshaab, *Greenland*	11	Y5
Frederikshavn, *Denmark*	38	G1
Frederikstad, *Norway*	35	J4
Fredonia, *N.Y.*	17	F5
Freeland, *Mich.*	16	A4
Freels C., *Nfld.*	23	L2
Freeman R., *Alberta*	14	D3
Freeport, *Ill.*	25	H2
Freeport, *N.S.*	21	A3
Freetown, *P.E.I.*	21	D1
Freetown, *Sierra Leone*	46	B5
Frelighsburg, *Que.*	20	C3
Fremantle, *W. Aust.*	49	B6
Fremont, *Neb.*	24	G2
Frémont L., *Lab.*	19	E3
French I., *Victoria*	50	E9
French R., *N. Ont.*	18	H3
French Guiana, *S. America*	30	G3
Frenchman R., *Sask.*	14	H6
Frenchman Butte, *Sask.*	14	G4
Fresco R., *Brazil*	30	G5
Fresnillo de Gonzalez, Echeverria, *Mexico*	28	D3
Fresno, *Cal.*	24	B3
Freycinet Penin., *Tasmania*	50	M12
Frias, *Argentina*	31	E9
Frio C., *Brazil*	31	J8
Frisian Is., *Netherlands*	38	F2
Frizzleton, *N.S.*	21	G1
Frobisher, *Sask.*	15	K6
Frobisher L., *Sask.*	14	G2
Frobisher Bay, *Baffin I., N.W.T.*	11	V5
Frog L., *Alberta*	14	F4
Frome L., *S. Aust.*	50	C5
Frome R., *Eng.*	37	D6
Frontenac, *Ont.*	17	H3
Frontera, *Mexico*	28	F4
Froward C., *Chile*	31	C14
Frozen Str., *Keewatin, N.W.T.*	11	R4
Fruitvale, *B.C.*	13	M8
Fryatt, *Ont.*	18	G4
Fuerte, and R., *Mexico*	28	C2
Fujisan, vol., *Japan*	44	F3
Fulton, *N.Y.*	17	J4
Fundy, B. of, *N.B., etc.*	22	G4
Fundy National Park, *N.B.*	21	B2
Fünen (Fyr) I., *Denmark*	38	G2
Funk I., *Nfld.*	23	L2
Furneaux Is., *Tasmania*	50	F9
Fury and Hecla Str., *Franklin, N.W.T.*	11	S4
Future, *Brazil*	30	H7
Fyne L., *Scotland*	36	C3
Gabarouse, *N.S.*	21	G2
Gabarus B., *N.S.*	21	G2
Gabes, *Tunisia*	46	D2
Gabes, G. of, *Tunisia*	46	E2
Gable Mt., *B.C.*	13	K5
Gabo I., *Victoria*	50	G8
Gabon, rep., *Africa*	46	E6
Gaborone, *Botswana*	47	D1
Gabriel Str., *N.W.T.*	19	D1
Gadsden, *Ala.*	25	J4
Gaeta, *Italy*	38	H5
Gage, *Alberta*	14	B2
Gage C., *P.E.I.*	21	C1
Gagetown, *N.B.*	22	D4
Gagnon, *Que.*	22	C1
Gagnon L., *Que.*	20	B2
Gaiman, *Argentina*	31	D12
Gainesville, *Fla.*	25	K5
Gainesville, *Ga.*	25	K4
Gainsboro', *Eng.*	37	E5
Gainsborough, *Sask.*	15	L6
Gainza, *Argentina*	31	E10
Gairdner L., *S. Aust.*	49	F6
Gairloch, *Scotland*	36	B3
Galahad, *Alberta*	14	F4
Galapagos Is. (Archipiélago de Colon), *Pacific Oc.*	31	N16
Galashiels, *Scotland*	36	D4
Galati, *Romania*	39	L4
Galdhöpiggen, *Norway*	35	H3
Galeana, *Mexico*	28	C1
Galena, *Alaska*	10	C5
Galle, *Sri Lanka*	40	E7
Gallegos R., *Argentina*	31	C14
Gallinas, Punta, *Colombia*	30	C1
Gallipoli, *Turkey*	39	L5
Gallivare, *Sweden*	35	L2
Galloway, Mull of, *Scotland*	37	C4
Galt, *Ont.*	16	E4
Galves, *Argentina*	31	E10
Galveston, *Tex.*	25	H5
Galway, and co., *Eire*	37	A5
Galway B., *Eire*	37	A5
Gambela, *Ethiopia*	46	G5
Gambia, *W. Africa*	46	B4
Gambo, *Nfld.*	23	K2
Gamka R., *Cape Prov., Rep. of S. Africa*	47	C3
Gamsby, *Ont.*	18	E4
Gananoque, *Ont.*	17	J3
Gander, and B., *Nfld.*	23	K2
Gander L., *Nfld.*	23	K2
Ganges (Ganga), R., *India*	40	G3
Gangtok, *India*	40	G3
Gannett Peak, *Wyo.*	24	D2
Gantheaume B., *W. Aust.*	49	A5
Gara L., *Eire*	37	A5
Garanhuns, *Brazil*	30	K5
Garda L., *Italy*	38	G4
Garden City, *Kan.*	24	F3
Garden River, *Ont.*	16	A1
Gardiner, *Me.*	22	C4
Gardner Can., *B.C.*	13	F6
Gargano C., *Italy*	39	J5
Gargantua C., *Ont.*	18	F5
Garibaldi Park, *B.C.*	13	J8
Garneau Junction, *Que.*	20	C2
Garner L., *Man.*	15	O5
Garnett, *Kan.*	24	G3
Garnish, *Nfld.*	23	K3
Garonne R., *France*	38	E4
Garrison Res., *N. Dak.*	24	F1
Garron Pt., *N. Ire.*	37	C4
Garry L., *N.W.T.*	11	P4
Garson, *Ont.*	16	E1
Garson L., *Alberta*	14	F2
Garthby, *Que.*	20	D3
Gary, *Ind.*	25	J2
Gascoyne R., *W. Aust.*	49	B5
Gasiquiare R., *Venezuela*	30	D3
Gasket Shoal, *James B.*	18	H2
Gaspé, and B., *Que.*	22	E2
Gaspé Penin., and C., *Que.*	22	E2
Gaspé Passage, *G. of St. Lawrence*	22	E2
Gaspereau Forks, *N.S.*	21	B1
Gaspésian Park, *Que.*	22	D2
Gata C., *Spain*	38	D6
Gataga R., *B.C.*	12	G3
Gatchina, *U.S.S.R.*	35	N4
Gate, The, *Mackenzie, N.W.T.*	12	H2
Gateshead, *Eng.*	37	E4
Gatineau, *Que.*	17	K2
Gatineau Park, *Que.*	17	K2
Gatineau R., *Que.*	17	K2
Gauhati, *India*	40	H3
Gävle, *Sweden*	35	K3
Gawler, *S. Aust.*	50	B7
Gawler Ra., *S. Aust.*	49	E6
Gaya, *India*	40	F4
Gayndah, *Queensland*	50	H2
Gdansk (Danzig), *Poland*	39	J2
Gdynia, *Poland*	39	J2
Gedeon, *Que.*	20	D3
Geelong, *Victoria*	50	E9
Geikie R., *Sask.*	14	J2
Gelert, *Ont.*	17	G3
Gem, *Alberta*	14	E5
General Acha, *Argentina*	31	D11
Genesee, *Mich.*	16	B4
Geneva, and L., *Switzerland*	38	F4
Gennargentu Mt., *Sardinia*	38	G6
Genoa, and G. of, *Italy*	38	G4
Genovesa I., *Galapagos Is., Pacific Oc.*	31	O16
Gens de Terre R., *Que.*	20	A2
Geographe B., *W. Aust.*	49	A6
George, *Cape Prov., Rep. of S. Africa*	47	C3
George B., *Nfld.*	21	F2
George B., *Tasmania*	50	M11
George C., *N.S.*	21	F2
George L., *N.S.W.*	50	G7
George L., *N.W.T.*	16	A1
George L., *S. Aust.*	50	C8
George Sd., *N.Z.*	51	A6
Goergetown, *Guyana*	30	F2
Georgetown, *Ont.*	25	K4
Georgetown, *Ont.*	16	F4
Georgetown, *P.E.I.*	21	E1
Georgetown, *Gd-Cayman, W. Indies*	29	H4
George Town, *Tasmania*	50	L11
Georgia, state, *U.S.A.*	25	K4
Georgia Str., *B.C.*	13	K8
Georgian B., *Ont.*	16	D2
Georgian Bay Is., National Park (Beausoleil I.), *Ont.*	16	E3
Georgina (Herbert) R., *Queensland*	49	F4
Geral, Serra, *Brazil*	31	G9
Geraldton, *Ont.*	18	E4
Geraldton, *W. Aust.*	49	A5
Germansen Landing, *B.C.*	12	H5
Germany, East, rep., *Europe*	38	H2
Germany, West, *Europe*	38	G3
Germiston, *Transvaal*	47	D2
Gerrard, *B.C.*	13	M7
Gethsemani, *Que.*	23	G1
Ghadames, *Libya*	46	D2
Ghana, *W. Africa*	46	C5
Ghat, *Libya*	46	E3
Ghats, Eastern, *S. India*	40	E6
Ghats, Western, *S. India*	40	D5
Ghazni, *Afghanistan*	40	C2
Ghent, *Belgium*	38	E3
Ghost L., *Mackenzie, N.W.T.*	12	N1
Ghost Mt., *B.C.*	13	L6
Ghost River, *Ont.*	18	G3
Gibeon, *S.W. Africa*	47	B2
Gibraltar, *Spain*	38	C6
Gibraltar, Str. of, *Spain-Morocco*	38	C7
Gibson Desert, *W. Aust.*	49	C4
Gibsons, *B.C.*	13	J8
Giessen, *Ger.*	38	G3
Gijon, *Spain*	38	C5
Gila R., *Ariz.*	24	D4
Gilbert Is., *Pacific Oc.*	2	D4
Gilbert Mt., *B.C.*	13	H7
Gilbert Plains, *Man.*	15	L5
Gilgandra, *N.S.W.*	50	G5
Gilgit, *Kashmir*	40	D1
Gill L., *Eire*	37	A4
Gillam, *Man.*	15	O2
Gillingham, *Eng.*	37	F6
Gilmour, *Ont.*	17	H3
Gimli, *Man.*	15	N5
Girardot, *Colombia*	30	C3
Girdle Ness, *Scotland*	36	E3
Gironde R., *France*	38	D4
Girvan, *Scotland*	37	C4
Girvin, *Sask.*	14	J5
Gisborne, *N.Z.*	51	G3
Giurgiu, *Romania*	39	L5
Glace Bay, *N.S.*	21	G1
Glacier B., *Alaska*	13	B3
Glacier Park, *B.C.*	13	M7
Gladstone, *Man.*	15	M5
Gladstone, *N.S.W.*	50	J5
Gladstone, *Queensland*	50	H1
Gladstone, *S. Aust.*	50	B6
Gladys L., *B.C.*	12	D3
Glamorgan, co., *Wales*	37	D6
Glasgow, *Scotland*	36	C4
Gleichen, *Alberta*	14	E5
Glen, *N.H.*	22	B4
Glen Almond, *Que.*	17	K2
Glenboro, *Man.*	15	M6
Glencoe, *Natal*	47	E2
Glencoe, *Ont.*	16	D5
Glencoe, *S. Aust.*	50	C8
Glendale Cove, *B.C.*	13	H7
Glen Davis, *N.S.W.*	50	H6
Glendive, *Mont.*	24	F1
Glenela R., *Victoria*	50	C8
Glenelg, *S. Aust.*	50	B7
Glengarry, co., *Ont.*	17	L2
Glenhope, *N.Z.*	51	D4
Glen Innes, *N.S.W.*	50	H4
Glen More, *Scotland*	36	C3
Glenora, *B.C.*	12	E4
Glenora, *Tasmania*	50	L12
Glen Robertson, *Ont.*	20	B3
Glenrothes, *Scotland*	36	D3
Glenties, *Eire*	37	A4
Glenwood, *Alberta*	14	E6
Glenwood, *Nfld.*	23	K2
Gliwice, *Poland*	39	J3
Glockner Mt., *Austria*	38	H4
Glomma R., *Norway*	35	J3
Gloucester, *N.B.*	22	D3
Gloucester, and co., *Eng.*	37	D6
Glover I., *Nfld.*	23	J2
Gloverton, *Nfld.*	23	K2
Goa, Daman & Diu, *India*	40	D5
Gobabis, *S.W. Africa*	47	B1
Gobi Desert, *Mongolia*	44	C2
Gochas, *S.W. Africa*	47	B1
Godavari R., *India*	40	F5
Godbout, *Que.*	22	D2
Goderich, *Ont.*	16	D4
Godfrey, *Ont.*	17	J3
God's L., *Man.*	15	O3
God's R., *Man.*	15	P3
Godthåb, *Greenland*	11	Y5
Goeland, L. au, *Que.*	18	H5
Gogama, *Ont.*	18	H5
Gogra R., *India*	40	F3
Goiânia, *Brazil*	30	H7
Goiás, *Brazil*	30	G7
Gold Bar, *B.C.*	12	J4
Goldboro, *N.S.*	21	F2
Golden, *B.C.*	13	M7
Golden B., *N.Z.*	51	D4
Golden Lake, *Ont.*	17	H2
Golden Prairie, *Sask.*	14	G5
Goldenville, *N.S.*	21	F2
Goldfields, *Sask.*	14	G1
Golfo Aranci, *Sardinia*	38	G5
Gollel, *Natal*	47	E2
Gomel, *U.S.S.R.*	39	M2
Gomez Palacio, *Mexico*	24	F5
Gonaïves, *Haiti*	29	K4
Gonave I., *Haiti*	29	K4
Gonazales I., *S. Pacific Oc.*	31	A9
Gondar, *Ethiopia*	46	G4
Goobies, *Nfld.*	23	L3
Goodall's Cataract, *Surinam*	30	F3
Gooderham, *Ont.*	17	G3
Good Hope, C. of, *Cape Prov., Rep. of S. Africa*	47	B3
Good Hope Mt., *B.C.*	13	H7
Good Spirit Lake Park, *Sask.*	15	K5
Goodwater, *Sask.*	15	K6
Goole, *Eng.*	37	E5
Goolwa, *S. Aust.*	50	B7
Goondiwindi, *Queensland*	50	H4
Goose L., *Man.*	15	L3
Goose L., *Ont.*	18	B3
Goose Bay, *Lab.*	19	E3
Gorakhpur, *India*	40	F3
Gordon L., *Alberta*	14	F2
Gordon R., *Tasmania*	50	K12
Gordonhorne Peak, *B.C.*	13	L7
Gore, *N.Z.*	51	B7
Gore Bay, *Ont.*	16	C2
Gorgona I., *Colombia*	30	B3
Gorki, *U.S.S.R.*	39	Q1
Görlitz, *Ger.*	39	H3
Gorlovka, *U.S.S.R.*	39	O3
Gormanstown, *Tasmania*	50	K11
Goroke, *Victoria*	50	C8
Gorrie, *Ont.*	16	D4
Goryn R., *Ukraine, etc.*	39	L3
Gosford, *N.S.W.*	50	H6
Gosford Mt., *Que.*	20	D3
Gota R., *Sweden*	38	G1
Göteborg, *Sweden*	38	G1
Gotland I., *Sweden*	39	J1
Gough I., *S. Atlantic Oc.*	3	K7
Gough L., *Alberta*	14	E4
Gouin, *Que.*	20	C2
Gouin Dam, and Res., *Que.*	20	B1
Goulburn, *N.S.W.*	50	G7
Goulburn R., *N.S.W.*	50	H6
Goulburn R., *Victoria*	50	E8
Gould, *Que.*	20	D3
Gould Dome, *Alberta*	14	D5
Gouritz R., *Cape Prov., Rep. of S. Africa*	47	C3
Gourock, *Scotland*	36	C4
Gourock Ra., *N.S.W.*	47	G7
Gouverneur, *N.Y.*	17	K3
Govan, *Sask.*	14	J5
Governador, Valadares, *Brazil*	30	J7
Governor Lake, *N.S.*	21	D2
Gowganda, *Ont.*	18	H5
Goya, *Argentina*	31	F9
Goyder L., *S. Aust.*	50	C3
Graaff Reinet, *Cape Prov., Rep. of S. Africa*	47	C3
Gracefield, *Que.*	17	J1
Gradaus, Serra dos, *Brazil*	30	G5
Grafton, *N.S.W.*	50	J4
Grafton C., *Queensland*	49	H3
Graham, *Ont.*	18	C4
Graham I., *B.C.*	13	D6
Graham L., *Alberta*	14	D2
Graham Ld., *Antarctica*	3	H8
Graham R., *B.C.*	12	J4
Grahamstown, *Cape Prov., Rep. of S. Africa*	47	D3
Grajaú R., *Brazil*	30	H4
Grampian Mts., *Scotland*	36	C3
Grampians, The, *Victoria*	50	D8
Granada, *Nicaragua*	29	G5
Granada, *Spain*	38	D6
Granby, *Que.*	20	C3
Gran Chaco, El, *Argentina-Paraguay*	31	E9
Grand Bank, *Nfld.*	23	K3
Grand Can., *China*	43	K5
Grand I., *Mich.*	18	E5
Grand I., *Ont.-N.Y.*	17	F4
Grand L., *Lab.*	19	E3
Grand L., *Me.*	22	C4
Grand L., *N.B.*	21	A2
Grand L., *N.B.-Me.*	22	D4
Grand L., *Nfld.*	23	J2
Grand Bahama I., *Bahamas*	29	J2
Grand Beach Park, *Man.*	15	N5
Grand Bend, *Ont.*	16	D4
Grand Bruit, *Nfld.*	23	H3
Grand Cache, *Alberta*	13	L6
Grand Canyon, *Ariz., etc.*	24	D3
Grand Centre, *Alberta*	14	F3
Grand Discharge, *Que.*	20	D1
Grande I., *Brazil*	31	J8
Grande L., *Argentina*	31	E9
Grande L., *Brazil*	30	H4
Grande R., *Argentina*	31	D11
Grande R., *Brazil*	30	H8
Grande, Bahia, *Argentina*	31	D14
Grande Anse, *N.B.*	22	E3
Grande Baie, *Que.*	20	D1
Grande O'Guapay, *Bolivia*	30	E7
Grande Prairie, *Alberta*	14	B3
Grande Rivière, *Que.*	22	E2
Grandes Bergeronnes, *Que.*	20	E1
Grande, Serra, *Brazil*	31	J5
Grand Etang, *N.S.*	21	F1
Grand Falls, *N.B.*	22	D3
Grand Falls, *Nfld.*	23	K2
Grand Forks, *B.C.*	13	L8
Grand Forks, *N. Dak.*	24	G1
Grandin, *Alberta*	14	F3

64 GENERAL INDEX

Grandin L., Mackenzie, N.W.T. 10 L5
Grand Island, Neb. 24 G2
Grand Junction, Colo. 24 E3
Grand Manan, I., N.B. 22 D4
Grand Mère, Que. 20 C2
Grand Pabos, R., Que. 22 E2
Grand Piles, Que. 20 C2
Grand Portage, Minn. 18 D5
Grand Rapids, Alberta 14 E2
Grand Rapids, Man. 15 M4
Grand Rapids, Mich. 25 J2
Grand River, N.S. 21 G2
Grand River, Que. 22 E2
Grand Valley, Ont. 16 E4
Grandview, Man. 15 L5
Grangeville, Ida. 24 C1
Granite Falls, Que. 19 D2
Gran Sasso, Italy 38 H5
Grant, Ont. 18 E3
Grantham, Eng. 37 E5
Granton, Ont. 16 D4
Grantown, Scotland 36 D3
Granum, Alberta 14 E6
Granville, Yukon 10 G5
Granville Ferry, N.S. 21 B3
Granville L., and Falls, Man. 15 L2
Gras, L. de, Mackenzie, N.W.T. 10 M5
Grasett, Ont. 18 F4
Grashop, Transvaal 47 E1
Graspan, Cape Prov., Rep. of S. Africa 47 C2
Grass R., Man. 15 N3
Grass River Park, Man. 15 L3
Grates Cove, Nfld. 23 L2
Gravelbourg, Sask. 14 H6
Gravenhurst, Ont. 17 F3
Gray Str., N.W.T. 19 D1
Grayson, Sask. 15 K5
Gräz, Austria 39 H4
Gready Harb., Lab. 19 F3
Greasy L., Mackenzie, N.W.T. 12 J1
Great I., Nfld. 23 L3
Great L., Man. 15 N1
Great L., Tasmania 50 L11
Great Abaco I., Bahamas 29 J2
Great Australian Basin, Aust. 49 G4
Great Australian Bight, Aust. 49 D6
Great Bahama Bank, W. Indies 29 J3
Great Barrier I., N.Z. 51 E2
Great Barrier Reef, Queensland 49 G2
Great Beaver L., B.C. 13 J5
Great Bend, Kan. 24 G3
Great Black R., Que.-Me. 20 E2
Great Burnt L., N.S. 23 J2
Great Central, Vancouver I., B.C. 13 H8
Great Cloche I., Ont. 18 H5
Great Driffield, Eng. 37 E4
Great Duck I., Ont. 16 B2
Greatest Cataract, Brazil 30 G4
Great Exuma I., Bahamas 29 J3
Great Falls, Man. 15 N5
Great Falls, Mont. 24 D1
Great Fish R., Cape Prov., Rep. of S. Africa 47 D3
Great Grimsby, Eng. 37 E5
Great Kei R., Cape Prov., Rep. of S. Africa 47 D3
Great Lowland Plain, Europe 35 K5
Great Nama Land, S.W. Africa 47 B2
Great Ormes Hd., Wales 37 C5
Great Plateau of Patagonia, Argentina 31 D12
Great Pubnico, N.S. 21 B4
Great Salt L., Ut. 24 D2
Great Sand Hills, Neb. 24 F2
Great Sandy I. (Fraser I.), Queensland 50 J2
Great Sandy Desert, W. Aust. 49 C3
Great Slave L., Mackenzie, N.W.T. 12 N2
Great Snow Mt., B.C. 12 H4
Great Village, N.S. 21 C2
Great Wass I., Me. 22 D4
Great Western Tiers, Tasmania 50 L11
Great Yarmouth, Eng. 37 F5
Greece, kingdom, Europe 39 K6
Green, Nfld. 23 J2
Green L., B.C. 13 K7
Green L., Sask. 14 H3
Green R., N.B. 22 C3
Green Bay, Wis. 25 J2
Greening, Que. 20 B1
Green Island, N.Z. 51 C6
Greenland, N. America 1 N2
Greenlaw, Scotland 36 D4
Greenly Is., Que. 23 J1
Greenock, Scotland 36 C4
Greenore, Eire 37 B4
Green River, Wyo. 24 E2
Greensboro, N.C. 25 L3
Greenspond, Nfld. 23 L2
Greenville, B.C. 12 F5
Greenville, Me. 22 B4
Greenville, Miss. 25 H4

Greenville, S.C. 25 K4
Greenville, Tex. 24 G4
Greenwater Lake Park, Sask. 15 K4
Greenwich, Eng. 37 F6
Greenwood, B.C. 13 L8
Greenwood, Miss. 25 H4
Gregory L., S. Aust. 50 B4
Grenada, Miss. 25 J4
Grenada I., W. Indies 29 M5
Grenfell, N.S.W. 50 G6
Grenfell, Sask. 15 K5
Grenoble, France 38 F4
Grenville, B.C. 20 B3
Grenville, co., Ont. 17 K3
Gretna, Man. 15 N6
Grey, co., Ont. 16 E3
Grey Is., Nfld. 23 K1
Grey Ra., Queensland 50 C4
Grey R., N.Z. 51 C5
Grey Goose I., James B. 18 H2
Greymouth, N.Z. 51 C5
Greytown, Natal 47 E2
Greytown, N.Z. 51 E4
Greytown, Nicaragua 29 H5
Griff, Ont. 18 D4
Griffith, N.S.W. 50 E7
Griffith, Ont. 17 H2
Grim C., Tasmania 50 E10
Grimsby, Ont. 16 F4
Grimshaw, Alberta 14 C2
Grindstone I., Que. 22 F3
Grinnell Glacier, Baffin I. 19 D1
Grinnell Penin., Franklin, N.W.T. 11 P2
Griqualand E., Cape Prov., Rep. of S. Africa 47 D3
Griqualand W., Cape Prov., Rep. of S. Africa 47 C2
Griquatown, Cape Prov., Rep. of S. Africa 47 C2
Griquet, Nfld. 23 K1
Grise Fiord, Ellesmere I., N.W.T. 11 S2
Griswold, Man. 15 L6
Grivel C., Greenland 11 Z4
Groai's I., Nfld. 23 K1
Grodno, Poland 39 L2
Groningen, Netherlands 38 F2
Gronlid, Sask. 15 J4
Groote R., Cape Prov., Rep. of S. Africa 47 C3
Groote Eylandt, N. Ter., Aust. 49 F2
Grootfontein, S.W. Africa 46 E7
Grosse I., Que. 20 D2
Grouard, Alberta 14 C3
Groundhog R., Ont. 18 G4
Grovedale, Alberta 12 L5
Grundy Lake Prov. Park, Ont. 16 E2
Gryazi, U.S.S.R. 39 O2
Grytviken, S. Georgia I., S. Atlantic Oc. 31 K14
Guacanayabo, G. de, Cuba 29 J3
Guachipas, Argentina 31 D9
Guadalajara, Mexico 28 D3
Guadalquivir R., Spain 38 C6
Guadalupe I., Pacific Oc. 24 C5
Guadarrama, Sierra, Spain 38 C5
Guadeloupe I., W. Indies 29 M4
Guadiana R., Spain 38 C6
Guafo I., Chile 31 B12
Guainia R., Colombia 30 D3
Guaira, Brazil 31 G8
Guaitecas Is., Chile 31 B12
Guajara Mirim, Brazil 30 D6
Guajira, Colombia 30 C1
Gualeguaychu, Argentina 31 F10
Gualfin, Argentina 31 D9
Guam I., Pacific Oc. 44 G5
Guamá R., Brazil 30 H4
Guanajuato, Mexico 28 D3
Guanape Is., Peru 30 B5
Guanare, Venezuela 30 D2
Guandacol, Argentina 31 D9
Guane, Cuba 29 H3
Guantanamo, Cuba 29 J3
Guaporé R., Bolivia-Brazil 30 E6
Guaqui, Bolivia 30 D7
Guaranda, Ecuador 30 B4
Guarapuava, Brazil 31 G9
Guarda, Portugal 38 C5
Guarda I., Mexico 28 B2
Guardafui C., Somali Rep. 46 J4
Guatemala, Guatemala 28 F5
Guatemala, rep., Cent. America 28 F4
Guaviare R. (R. de Lesseps), Colombia 30 C3
Guayama, Puerto Rico 29 L4
Guayanavieja, Venezuela 30 E2
Guayaquil, and G. of, Ecuador 30 A4
Guaymas, Mexico 28 B2
Guelph, Ont. 16 E4
Guenette, Que. 20 B2
Guildford, Eng. 37 E6
Guildford, Me. 22 C4
Guinea, rep., Africa 46 B4
Guinea, G. of, W. Africa 46 C5
Güines, Cuba 29 H4
Gujarat .state, India 40 D4
Gulf, The, S.W. Asia 42 C6
Gull I., Lab. 19 F2
Gull L., Alberta 14 D4

Gull Lake, Sask. 14 G5
Gull Rock L., Ont. 18 B3
Gunisso R., Man. 15 N4
Gunnar, Sask. 14 G1
Gunnedah, N.S.W. 50 H5
Guntersville Lake, Ala. 25 J4
Gurgueia R., Brazil 30 J5
Guriev, U.S.S.R. 42 D4
Gurupá, Para, Brazil 30 G4
Gurupa, and R., Maranhão, Brazil 30 H4
Gurupa C., Brazil 30 H4
Gustavus, Alaska 13 C3
Guthrie, Okla. 24 G3
Guyana, S. America 30 F3
Guysborough. N.S. 21 F2
Gwabegar, N.S.W. 50 G5
Gwadar, W. Pak. 40 B4
Gweebarra B., Eire 37 A4
Gwillim L., B.C. 12 K5
Gwydir R., N.S.W. 50 G4
Gympie, Queensland 50 J3
Györ, Hungary 39 J4
Gypsum Pt., Mackenzie, N.W.T. 12 N2
Gypsumville, Man. 15 M5

Haakscheen Pan, Cape Prov., Rep. of S. Africa 47 C2
Haast R., N.Z. 51 B5
Habay, Alberta 14 B1
Hache, Lac la, B.C. 13 K7
Haddington, Scotland 36 D4
Hadhramaut, S. Yemen 42 C7
Haenertsburg, Transvaal 47 D1
Hafnarfjördur, Iceland 35 B3
Hagemeister I., Alaska 10 B6
Hagensborg, B.C. 13 G6
Hagerstown, Md. 25 L3
Hagersville, Ont. 16 E4
Hague, Sask. 14 H4
Hague, The, Netherlands 38 F2
Ha Ha B., Que. 23 H1
Ha Ha R., and L., Que. 20 D1
Haifa, Israel 3 M3
Haig, W. Aust. 49 D6
Hai-k'ou, Hainan I., China 44 D5
Haileybury, Ont. 18 H5
Hainan (I.), China 44 D5
Hainan Str., China 44 D5
Haines, Alaska 12 C3
Haiphong, N. Vietnam 44 V4
Hair Cutting L., Que. 20 B1
Haiti, rep., W. Indies 29 K4
Hakodate, Japan 44 G2
Halbrite, Sask. 15 K6
Haldimand, co., Ont. 17 F4
Halfway R., B.C. 12 J4
Haliburton, Ont. 17 G2
Haliburton, co., Ont. 17 G2
Haliburton Highlands, Ont. 17 G2
Halifax, Eng. 37 E5
Halifax, N.S. 21 D3
Halifax Harb., N.S. 22 F4
Halkett C., Alaska 10 G4
Hall Lake, Franklin, N.W.T. 11 S4
Hall Penin., Baffin I., N.W.T. 19 D1
Halle, Ger. 38 G3
Hall's B., Nfld. 23 J2
Halmahera I., Indonesia 44 E6
Halmstad, Sweden 38 H1
Hälsingbörg, Sweden 38 H1
Halton, co., Ont. 16 F4
Hamar, Norway 35 J3
Hamber Park, B.C. 13 L6
Hamburg, Ger. 38 G2
Hamburg, N.Y. 17 F5
Hamilton, Ont. 51 E2
Hamilton, Ont. 16 F4
Hamilton, Scotland 36 C4
Hamilton, Victoria 50 D8
Hamilton Falls, Lab. 11 W7
Hamilton Inlet, Lab. 19 F3
Hammerfest, Norway 35 L1
Hammingford, Que. 20 C3
Hammondvale, N.B. 21 B2
Hampden, Nfld. 23 J2
Hampden. N.Z. 51 C6
Hampshire, co., Eng. 37 E6
Hampton, N.B. 21 B2
Ham Sud, Que. 20 D3
Hamun-I-Helmand, Persia 40 B2
Hamun-I-Mashkel, Pak.-Iran 40 B3
Hamun-I-Sabari (L.), Iran-Afghanistan 40 B2
Hanceville, B.C. 13 J7
Handsworth, Sask. 15 K6
Hangchow, China 44 D3
Hangklip C., Cape Prov., Rep. of S. Africa 47 B3
Hango (Hanko), Finland 35 L4
Hanley, Eng. 37 D5
Hanley, Sask. 14 H5
Hanmer, N.Z. 51 D5
Hanna, Alberta 14 E5
Hannah B., Ont. 18 H3
Hanoi, N. Vietnam 44 C4
Hanover, Cape Prov., Rep. of S. Africa 47 C3
Hanover, Ger. 38 G2
Hanover, Ont. 16 E3
Hanover I., Chile 31 B14
Hantams Berg, Cape Prov., Rep. of S. Africa 47 B3

Hantsport, N.S. 21 C2
Happy Valley, Coast of Lab. 19 E3
Har. L., Baffin I., N.W.T. 11 V5
Harbin (Haerhpin), China 44 E2
Harbor Beach, Mich. 16 C4
Harbour Breton, Nfld. 23 K3
Harbour Grace, Nfld. 23 L3
Harbourville, N.S. 21 B2
Harcourt, N.B. 21 B1
Hardisty, Alberta 14 F4
Hare B., Nfld. 23 K1
Hare I., Que. 20 E2
Harlow, Eng. 37 F6
Härnösänd, Sweden 35 K3
Harp L., Lab. 19 E2
Harricanaw R., Que. 19 B3
Harrington Harb., Que. 23 H1
Harris, Hebrides, Scotland 36 B3
Harris, Sd. of, Hebrides, Scotland 36 B3
Harrisburg, Pa. 25 L2
Harrismith, Orange F.S. 47 D2
Harrison C., Lab. 19 F2
Harrison L., B.C. 13 J8
Harrison Hot Springs, B.C. 13 K8
Harriston, Ont. 16 E4
Harrisville, Mich. 16 B3
Harrogate, B.C. 13 M7
Harrogate, Eng. 37 E4
Harrow, Mich. 16 B5
Harrowby, Man. 15 L5
Harry's Brook, N.S. 23 H2
Harspranget, Sweden 35 K2
Hartebeest R., Cape Prov., Rep. of S. Africa 47 C2
Hart Fell, Scotland 37 D4
Hartford, Conn. 25 M2
Hartland, B.C. 22 D3
Hartland Pt., Eng. 37 C6
Hartlepool, Eng. 37 E4
Hartley Bay, B.C. 13 F6
Hartney, Man. 15 L6
Harty, Ont. 18 G4
Hartz R., Transvaal 47 D2
Harvey, N.B. 22 D4
Harwell, Eng. 37 E6
Harwich, Eng. 37 F6
Haryana, state, India 40 E3
Harz Mts., Ger. 38 G3
Hassel Sd., Franklin, N.W.T. 11 P2
Hastings, Eng. 37 F6
Hastings, Neb. 24 G2
Hastings, N.Z. 51 F3
Hastings, Ont. 17 G3
Hastings, Ont. 17 H2
Hastings, Tasmania 50 L12
Hastings Ra., N.S.W. 50 H5
Hatchet L., Sask. 15 K1
Hatteras C., N.C. 25 L3
Hattiesburg, Miss. 25 J4
Hatton Headland, N.W.T. 19 E1
Haugesund, Norway 35 H4
Haultain R., Sask. 14 H2
Hauraki G., N.Z. 51 E2
Hauroko L., N.Z. 51 A6
Havana (Habana), Cuba 29 H3
Havasu L., Cal. 24 D3
Havelock, N.B. 21 B2
Havelock, Ont. 17 G3
Haverfordwest, Wales 37 C6
Havre, Le, France 38 E2
Havre, Mont. 24 E1
Havre Aubert, Que. 22 G3
Havre Boucher, N.S. 21 F2
Havre St. Pierre, Que. 22 F1
Hawaiian Is., Pacific Oc. 2 E3
Hawarden, Sask. 14 H5
Hawdon L., S. Aust. 50 C8
Hawea L., N.Z. 51 B6
Hawera, N.Z. 51 E3
Hawes, Alberta 14 C4
Hawick, Scotland 36 D4
Hawke B., N.Z. 51 F3
Hawke C., N.S.W. 50 J6
Hawke Harb., and I., Lab. 19 F3
Hawker, S. Aust. 50 B5
Hawkesbury, Ont. 17 L2
Hawk Junc., Ont. 18 F4
Hay, N.S.W. 50 E7
Hay, Wales 37 D5
Hay C., Bylot I., N.W.T. 11 T3
Hay Mt., B.C. 13 B3
Hayes Penin., Greenland 11 V2
Hayes R., Man. 15 P2
Hay River, Mackenzie, N.W.T. 12 N2
Hazelton, B.C. 12 G5
Hazen Str., Franklin, N.W.T. 10 M2
Hazuur, S.W. Africa 47 B2
Heard I., Indian Oc. 3 N7
Hearne, Tex. 24 G4
Hearst, Ont. 18 G4
Hearts Content, Nfld. 23 L3
Heath Pt., Anticosti I., Que. 22 F1
Hebrides, Outer, Scotland 38 C1
Hebron, Lab. 19 E2
Hebron, N.S. 21 A4
Hecate Str., B.C. 13 E6
Hecla I., Man. 15 N5
Hecla and Griper B., Franklin, N.W.T. 10 M2
Hectanooga, N.S. 21 A3
Hector Mt., Alberta 14 C5
Hedley, B.C. 13 K8

Place	Page	Grid
Heely Falls, *Ont.*	18	D2
Hegemann C., *Greenland*	11	Z4
Heidelberg, *Ger.*	38	G3
Heidelburg, *Transvaal*	47	D2
Heilbron, *Orange F.S.*	47	D2
Hoinsburg, *Alberta*	14	F4
Helda Mt., *Iceland*	35	C3
Helen L., *Ont.*	18	D4
Helena, *Mont.*	24	D1
Helensville, *N.Z.*	51	E2
Heligoland I., *Ger.*	38	F2
Hellvecia, *Argentina*	31	F10
Helmand R., and Desert, *Afghanistan*	40	B2
Helmsdale, *Scotland*	36	D2
Helsingør, *Denmark*	38	H1
Helsinki, *Finland*	35	L3
Helvellyn Mt., *Eng.*	37	D4
Hemaruka, *Alberta*	14	F5
Heming Lake, *Man.*	15	L3
Hemlo, *Ont.*	18	F4
Henderson, *Ky.*	25	J3
Henley, *Eng.*	37	E6
Henrietta Maria C., *Ont.*	11	S6
Henry Kater C., *Baffin I., N.W.T.*	11	V4
Hensall, *Ont.*	16	D4
Heppner, *Ore.*	24	C1
Hepworth, *Ont.*	16	D3
Herat, *Afghanistan*	40	B2
Herbert, *Queensland*	50	H1
Herbert, *Sask.*	14	H5
Herbert (Georgina) R., *Queensland*	49	F4
Herbertville, *Que.*	20	D1
Herb Lake, *Man.*	15	M3
Herchmer, *Man.*	15	O2
Herculania, *Brazil*	30	G7
Hereford, and co., *Eng.*	37	D5
Hermanus, *Cape Prov., Rep. of S. Africa*	47	B3
Hermitage B., *Nfld.*	23	J3
Hermosillo, *Mexico*	28	B2
Heron B., *Ont.*	18	E4
Herrick, *Tasmania*	50	L11
Herschel I., *Yukon*	10	G4
Hershel, *Sask.*	14	G5
Hertford, and co., *Eng.*	37	E6
Hervey B., *Queensland*	50	J2
Hervey Junc., *Que.*	20	C2
Hes d'Haussez, *N.Z.*	51	E2
Hespeler, *Ont.*	16	E4
Hess R., *Yukon*	12	D1
Hessel, *Mich.*	16	A1
Heughlin Mt., *N.Ter., Aust.*	49	E4
Hewett C., *Baffin I., N.W.T.*	11	V3
Hexham, *Eng.*	37	D4
Heysham, *Eng.*	37	D5
Hibbard, *Que.*	20	B2
Hibbing, *Minn.*	25	H1
Hickman Mt., *B.C.*	12	E4
Hickson, *Ont.*	16	E4
Hidalgo del Parral, *Mexico*	28	C2
Hiensburg, *Alberta*	14	F4
High I., *Lab.*	19	E2
High Atlas Mts., *Morocco*	46	C2
High Level, *Alberta*	12	M3
High Prairie, *Alberta*	14	C3
High River, *Alberta*	14	E5
Highrock L., *Man.*	15	L3
Highrock L., *Sask.*	14	J2
Highwood R., *Alberta*	14	D5
Hiiumaa, *Estonia*	35	L4
Hikurangi, *N.Z.*	51	E1
Hillier, *Ont.*	17	H4
Hillman, *Mich.*	16	A2
Hillsborough, *N.B.*	21	B2
Hillsborough Bay, *P.E.I.*	21	D1
Hillsburg, *Ont.*	16	E4
Hillsdale, *Ont.*	16	F3
Hillport, *Ont.*	18	F4
Hillston, *N.S.W.*	50	E6
Hilton Beach, *Ont.*	16	B1
Himāchal Pradesh, state, *India*	40	E2
Himalaya Mts., *Asia*	40	E2
Hindmarsh L., *Victoria*	50	C8
Hindubagh, *W. Pak.*	40	C2
Hindu Kush Ra., *Afghanistan*	40	D1
Hines Cr., *Alberta*	14	B2
Hiroshima, *Japan*	44	F3
Hispaniola I., *W. Indies*	29	K4
Hixon, *B.C.*	13	J6
Hlobane, *Natal*	47	E2
Hoaganas, *S.W. Africa*	47	B3
Hoare B., *Baffin I., N.W.T.*	11	W4
Hobart, *Tasmania*	50	J12
Hobson L., *B.C.*	13	K6
Hoch Elaga, *Que.*	20	C3
Hodges Hill, *Nfld.*	23	K2
Hodgson, *Man.*	15	N5
Hódmezővásárhely, *Hungary*	39	K4
Hof, *Ger.*	38	G3
Hokianga Harb., *N.Z.*	51	D1
Hokitika, *N.Z.*	51	C5
Hokkaido (I.), *Japan*	44	G2
Holberg, *Vancouver I., B.C.*	13	F7
Holden, *Alberta*	14	E4
Holguim, *Cuba*	29	J3
Hollam's Bird I., *S.W. Africa*	47	A1
Holland, *Man.*	15	M6
Holland, dist., *Eng.*	37	E5
Holland, kingdom. *See* Netherlands		
Holland Centre, *Ont.*	16	E3
Holliday, *Que.*	20	E2
Hollowell, *Me.*	22	B4
Holly Springs, *Miss.*	25	J4
Holo Arch., *Philippine Is.*	43	L8
Holstein, *Ont.*	16	E3
Holsteinsborg, *Greenland*	11	X4
Holton Harbour, *Lab.*	19	F3
Holy I., *Eng.*	36	E4
Holy I., *Wales*	37	C5
Holy Cross, *Alaska*	10	C5
Holyhead, *Wales*	37	C5
Holyrood, *Nfld.*	23	L3
Homathko R., *B.C.*	13	H7
Home B., *Baffin I., N.W.T.*	11	V4
Honda, *Colombia*	30	B2
Hondo R., *Mexico*	28	G4
Hondo R., *Paraguay*	31	F8
Honduras, rep., *Cent. America*	28	G5
Honduras, G. of, *Cent. America*	28	G4
Honeywood, *Ont.*	16	E3
Hong Kong, *China*	44	D4
Honiton, *Eng.*	37	D6
Honolulu, *Hawaiian Is.*	2	E3
Honshu (I.), *Japan*	44	G3
Hood Mt., *Ore.*	24	B1
Hook Hd., *Eire*	37	B5
Hoonah, *Alaska*	13	C3
Hooper C., *Baffin I., N.W.T.*	11	V4
Hoopstad, *Orange F.S.*	47	D2
Hoover Dam, *Nev.-Ariz.*	24	D3
Hope, *B.C.*	13	K8
Hope I., *B.C.*	13	F7
Hope Pt., *Alaska*	10	A4
Hopedale, *Lab.*	19	E2
Hopefield, *Cape Prov., Rep. of S. Africa*	47	B3
Hopes Advance B., *Que.*	19	D2
Hopes Advance C., *Que.*	19	D1
Hopetoun, *Victoria*	50	D7
Hopetown, *Cape Prov., Rep. of S. Africa*	47	C2
Hopewell, *N.S.*	21	E2
Hopkinsville, *Ky.*	25	J3
Hormuz, Str. of, *Arabia, etc.*	42	D6
Horn (North C.), *Iceland*	35	B2
Horn, C., *Chile*	31	D15
Horn Mts., *Mackenzie, N.W.T.*	12	L2
Horn R., *Mackenzie, N.W.T.*	12	L1
Horn-avan, *Sweden*	35	K2
Hornell L., *Mackenzie, N.W.T.*	12	L1
Hornepayne, *Ont.*	18	F4
Horsefly, and L., *B.C.*	13	K6
Horseshoe, *W. Aust.*	49	B5
Horsham, *Victoria*	50	D8
Hoste I., *Chile*	31	C15
Hotazel, *Cape Prov., Rep. of S. Africa*	47	C2
Hotchkiss, *Alberta*	12	M4
Hot Springs, *Ark.*	25	H4
Houghton, *Mich.*	18	D5
Houlton, *Me.*	22	C3
Houston, *B.C.*	13	G5
Houston, *Tex.*	24	G5
Houtman's Abrolhos, *W. Aust.*	49	A5
Hove, *Eng.*	37	E6
Hövsgöl, *Mongolia*	43	J3
Hövsgöl L., *Mongolia*	44	C1
Howe C., *N.S.W.*	50	H8
Howe Sd., *B.C.*	13	J8
Howell, *Mich.*	16	B5
Howick Falls, *Natal*	47	E2
Howley, *Nfld.*	23	J2
Howrah, *India*	40	G4
Howse Peak, *Alberta*	14	C5
Howser, *B.C.*	13	M7
Howth Hd., *Eire*	37	B5
Hoy, *Orkney Is., Scotland*	36	D2
Hoyt, *N.B.*	22	D4
Huacho, *Peru*	30	B6
Huallaga R., *Peru*	30	B5
Huamachuco, *Peru*	30	B5
Huanachache, *Argentina*	31	D10
Huancabamba, *Peru*	30	B5
Huancavelica, *Peru*	30	C6
Huancayo, *Peru*	30	C6
Huanchaca, *Bolivia*	30	D7
Huanuco, *Peru*	30	B5
Huanhuanu, *Peru*	30	C7
Huaras, *Peru*	30	B5
Huards, Lac aux, *Que.*	22	B2
Huari, *Chile*	30	D7
Huascaran, mt., *Peru*	30	B5
Huasco, *Chile*	31	C9
Hubbards, *N.S.*	21	C3
Hubbart Pt., *Man.*	15	O1
Huberdeau, *Que.*	17	L1
Hubli, *India*	40	E5
Huddersfield, *Eng.*	37	E5
Hudson, *Me.*	22	C4
Hudson, *Ont.*	18	B4
Hudson, *Que.*	20	B3
Hudson R., *N.W.T., Canada*	11	R6
Hudson R., *N.Y.*	25	M2
Hudson Str., *Que.-N.W.T., Canada*	11	U5
Hudson Bay, *Sask.*	15	K4
Hudson Hope, *B.C.*	12	J4
Hue, *Vietnam*	44	C5
Huelva, *Spain*	38	C6
Huesca, *Spain*	38	D5
Hughenden, *Queensland*	49	G4
Hugh Town, *Scilly Is.*	37	B7
Huhehot, *Inner Mongolia, China*	44	D2
Huib Plat., *S.W. Africa*	47	B2
Huixtla, *Mexico*	28	F4
Hull, *Eng.*	37	E5
Hull, *Que.*	17	K2
Hulan L., *China*	44	D2
Humahuaca, *Argentina*	31	D8
Humaita, *Brazil*	30	E5
Humansdorp, *Cape Prov., Rep. of S. Africa*	47	C3
Humar, *Norway*	35	J3
Humber R., *Eng.*	37	E5
Humbermouth, *Nfld.*	23	J2
Humboldt, *Sask.*	14	J4
Humboldt B., *Ont.*	18	E4
Humboldt R., *Nev.*	24	C2
Hume Reservoir, *Victoria*	50	F8
Humula, *N.S.W.*	50	F7
Huna Bay, *Iceland*	35	B2
Hundred Mile House, *B.C.*	13	K7
Hune, Cape la, *Nfld.*	23	J3
Hungabee Mt., *B.C.*	13	M7
Hungary, state, *Europe*	39	J4
Hunlen Falls, *B.C.*	13	HC
Hunt Mt., *Yukon*	12	F2
Hunter I., *B.C.*	13	F7
Hunter I., *Ont.*	18	C4
Hunter Is., *Tasmania*	50	E10
Hunter Ra., and R., *N.S.W.*	50	H6
Hunter River, *P.E.I.*	21	D1
Hunting I., *Que.*	22	F1
Huntingdon, *Eng.*	37	E5
Huntingdon, *Que.*	20	B3
Huntington, *W. Va.*	25	K3
Huntly, *N.Z.*	51	E2
Huntly, *Scotland*	36	D3
Hunts Pt., *N.S.*	21	C4
Huntsville, *Ala.*	25	J4
Huntsville, *Ont.*	17	F2
Huonville, *Tasmania*	50	L12
Hurd C., *Ont.*	16	D2
Hurkett, *Ont*	18	D4
Huron, *S. Dak.*	24	G2
Huron, co., *Ont.*	16	D4
Huron L., *Canada-U.S.A.*	16	B2
Huronia, *Ont.*	16	F3
Huronian, *Ont.*	18	C4
Hussar, *Alberta*	14	E5
Hutchinson, *Kan.*	24	G3
Hwang Ho (R.), *China*	44	D3
Hybla, *Ont.*	17	H2
Hydaburg, *Alaska*	12	D5
Hyder, *Alaska*	12	E5
Hyderabad, *W. Pak.*	40	C3
Hyderabad, *India*	40	E5
Hydraulic, *B.C.*	13	K6
Hyland R., *Yukon*	12	F2
Hyland Post, *B.C.*	12	F4
Hyndman Peak, *Ida.*	24	D2
Hythe, *Alberta*	12	L5
Iasi, *Romania*	39	L4
Ibadan, *Nigeria*	46	D5
Ibague, *Colombia*	30	B3
Ibarra, *Ecuador*	30	B3
Iberville, *Que.*	20	C3
Iberville, L. d', *Que.*	19	C2
Ibicuí R., *Brazil*	31	F9
Ibitinga, *Brazil*	31	G8
Ica, *Peru*	30	B6
Ica or Putumayo R., *Colombia-Peru*	30	C4
Iceland I., *N.W. Europe*	35	B3
Ichaboe I., *S.W. Africa*	47	A2
Ichang, *China*	44	D3
Ico, *Brazil*	30	K5
Icy C., *Alaska*	10	B3
Icy Pt., *Alaska*	13	B3
Icy Str., *Alaska*	13	C3
Icy Cove, *Baffin I., N.W.T.*	19	C1
Idaho City, and state, *U.S.A.*	24	C2
Idaho Falls, *Ida.*	24	D2
Igarape Miri, *Brazil*	30	H4
Igarka, *U.S.S.R.*	43	G2
Iglosatalialuk I., *Lab.*	19	E2
Iguaçu R., *Brazil*	31	G9
Iguaçu Falls, *Brazil*	31	G9
Iguala, *Mexico*	28	E4
Iguana, *Venezuela*	30	D2
Iguapé, *Brazil*	31	H8
Igugivik, *Que.*	19	B1
Iisalmi, *Finland*	35	M3
IJsselmeer (Zuider Zee), *Netherlands*	38	F2
Ilderton, *Ont.*	16	D4
Ile-à-la Crosse, L., *Sask.*	14	H3
Ilebo, *Zaire*	46	F6
Iles, L. des, *Que.*	20	B2
Iles, Lac des, *Ont.*	18	D4
Ilford, *Man.*	15	O2
Ilfracombe, *Eng.*	37	C6
Ilha do Bananal, *Brazil*	30	H6
Ilhéus, *Brazil*	30	K6
Ili R., *China-U.S.S.R.*	42	H4
Iliamna L., *Alaska*	10	C6
Illampu or Sorata Mt., *Bolivia*	30	D7
Illapel, *Chile*	31	C10
Illimani Mt., *Bolivia*	30	D7
Illinois, state, *U.S.A.*	25	H2
Illinois R., *Ill.*	25	J2
Ilmen L., *U.S.S.R.*	35	N4
Ilmzinto, *Natal*	47	E3
Ilo, *Peru*	30	C7
Iloilo, *Philippine Is.*	44	E5
Ilorin, *Nigeria*	46	D5
Imandra L., *U.S.S.R.*	35	N2
Imlay City, *Mich.*	16	B4
Immingham, *Eng.*	37	E5
Imperatriz, *Brazil*	30	H5
Imperia, *Italy*	38	G5
Imperial, *Sask.*	14	J5
Imperial R., *Chile*	31	C11
Imperoyal, *N.S.*	21	D3
Imphal, *India*	40	H4
Inagia Is., Lit. and Gt., *W. Indies*	29	K3
Inari L., *Finland*	35	M2
Inchon, *S. Korea*	44	E3
Incomati R., *Mozambique*	47	E2
India, rep., *S. Asia*	42	F6
Indian, *Ont.*	17	H2
Indian B., *Nfld.*	23	K2
Indian Harb., *Lab.*	19	F3
Indian Oc.	3	N5
Indian R., *N.Y.*	17	K3
Indiana, state, *U.S.A.*	25	J3
Indianapolis, *Ind.*	25	J3
Indian Brook, *N.S.*	21	G1
Indian Cabins, *Alberta*	12	M3
Indian Harbour, *N.S.*	21	D3
Indian Head, *Sask.*	15	K5
Indian House L., *Que.*	19	E2
Indigirka R., *U.S.S.R.*	43	N2
Indo-China, *E. Asia*	44	C5
Indonesia, *S.E. Asia*	44	D7
Indore, *India*	40	E4
Indus R., *India-Pak.*	40	D3
Indus Delta, *Pak.*	42	E6
Infiernillo, L., *Mex.*	28	D4
Ingenika R., *B.C.*	12	H4
Ingenika Mine, *B.C.*	12	H4
Ingersoll, *Ont.*	16	E4
Ingleborough, Mt., *Eng.*	37	D4
Inglefield G., *Greenland*	11	V2
Inglefield Ld., *Greenland*	11	W2
Inglewood, *Victoria*	50	D8
Inglis, *Man.*	15	L5
Ing Luiggi, *Argentina*	31	D11
Ingolf, *Ont.*	18	A4
Ingolfs Fd., *Greenland*	11	Z4
Ingonish, *N.S.*	21	G1
Ingramport, *N.S.*	21	C3
Inirida R., *Colombia*	30	D3
Inishowen Hd., *Eire*	37	B4
Injune, *Queensland*	50	F2
Inkerman, *N.B.*	22	E3
Inklin, and R., *B.C.*	12	D3
Inland L., *Man.*	15	M4
Inner Sd., *Scotland*	36	C3
Inner Mongolia, *China*	44	D2
Innetalling I., *Hudson B.*	19	B2
Innisfail, *Alberta*	14	E4
Innoko R., *Alaska*	10	C5
Innsbruck, *Austria*	38	G4
Inoucdjouac (Port Harrison), *Que.*	19	B2
International Falls, *Ont.-Minn.*	18	B4
Intersection Mt., *Alberta*	14	B4
Intersection Mt., *B.C.*	13	K6
Inuvik, *Mackenzie, N.W.T.*	10	H4
Inveraray, *Scotland*	36	C3
Invercargill, *N.Z.*	51	B7
Inverell, *N.S.W.*	50	H4
Inverhuron Nat. Park, *Ont.*	16	D3
Invermere, *B.C.*	13	M7
Inverness, *N.S.*	21	F1
Inverness, *Que.*	20	D2
Inverness, and co., *Scotland*	36	C3
Inwood, *Man.*	15	N5
Inwood, *Ont.*	16	C5
Inzana L., *B.C.*	12	H5
Ioannina, *Greece*	39	K6
Iona, *N.S.*	21	G2
Iona I., *Scotland*	36	B3
Ionian Is., *Greece*	39	J6
Ionian Sea, *Greece, etc.*	39	J6
Iowa, state, *U.S.A.*	25	H2
Ipiales, *Colombia*	30	B3
Ipin, *China*	44	K3
Ipperwash Prov. Park, *Ont.*	16	C4
Ipswich, *Eng.*	37	F5
Ipswich, *Queensland*	50	J3
Ipú, *Brazil*	30	J4
Iquique, *Chile*	30	C8
Iquitos, *Peru*	30	C4
Iran, *Asia*	42	D5
Irapuato, *Mexico*	28	D3
Iraq (Mesopotamia), *Asia*	42	C5
Ireland, Rep. of, *Brit. Isles*	37	B5
Irian B., *New Guinea*	44	F7
Iriari R., *Colombia*	30	C3
Irigoyen, *Argentina*	31	E10
Iriona, *Honduras*	29	G4
Iriri R., *Brazil*	30	G4
Irish Cove, *N.S.*	23	G4
Irish Sea, *Brit. Isles*	37	C5
Irkutsk, *U.S.S.R.*	44	C1
Irma, *Alberta*	14	F4
Iron Cr., *Alberta*	14	F4

Iron Bridge, *Ont.*	16	B1
Irondale, *Ont.*	17	G3
Iron Gate, *Rumania*	39	K4
Iron Knob, *S. Aust.*	49	F6
Iroquois, *Ont.*	17	K3
Iroquois Chute, *Que.*	20	C2
Iroquois Falls, *Ont.*	18	H4
Irrawaddy R., *Burma*	40	J4
Irtish R., *U.S.S.R.*	42	F3
Irvine, *Scotland*	36	C4
Isaac L., *B.C.*	13	K6
Isaac's Harb., *N.S.*	21	F2
Isachsen C., *Franklin, N.W.T.*	10	N2
Isafiödur, *Iceland*	35	B2
Isandhlwana, *Natal*	47	E2
Isère R., *France*	38	F4
Ishim R., *U.S.S.R.*	42	E3
Ishpeming, *Mich.*	18	D5
Iskenderun (Alexandretta), *Turkey*	39	O6
Iskenderun, G. of, *Turkey*	39	N6
Iskut R., *B.C.*	12	E4
Isla Isabela (Albemarle I.), *Pacific Oc.*	31	N17
Islamabad, *W. Pak.*	40	D2
Island L., *Man.*	15	O4
Island L., *Ont.*	16	F2
Island Falls, *Ont.*	18	H4
Island Falls, *Sask.*	15	K3
Island Lake, *Man.*	18	A1
Islands, B. of, *Nfld.*	23	H2
Islay, *Peru*	30	C7
Islay I., *Scotland*	36	B4
Isle au Haut, *Me.*	22	C5
Isle aux Morts, *Nfld.*	23	H3
Isle Royale, *Mich.*	25	J1
Isles, L. des, *Sask.*	14	G3
Isle Verte, *Que.*	20	E1
Isluga Mt., *Chile*	30	D7
Isolo, *Cape Prov.*	47	D3
Israel, rep., *W. Asia*	42	B5
Issiq Kol, *Cent. Asia*	42	F4
Istanbul, *Turkey*	39	M5
Isthmus Bay, *Ont.*	16	D2
Itabatisa, *Brazil*	30	H6
Itaboca Cataracts, *Brazil*	30	G4
Itacaré, *Brazil*	30	K6
Itacayunas R., *Brazil*	30	G5
Itacoai, *Brazil*	30	C5
Itacoatiara, *Brazil*	30	F4
Itaete, *Brazil*	30	J6
Itaituba, *Brazil*	30	F4
Itajai, *Brazil*	31	H9
Italy, rep., *Europe*	38	G5
Itany R., *Surinam*	30	G3
Itapecuru R., *Brazil*	30	J5
Itapetininga, *Brazil*	31	H8
Itapicuru R., *Brazil*	30	K6
Itapolis, *Brazil*	31	H8
Itapura, *Brazil*	30	G8
Itasca L., *Minn.*	24	G1
Itatiaia Mt., *Brazil*	31	H8
Itecoahy R., *Brazil*	30	C5
Ituaçú, *Brazil*	30	J6
Ituna, *Sask.*	15	K5
Ituxi R., *Brazil*	30	D5
Ivahi R., *Brazil*	31	G8
Ivanhoe, *N.S.W.*	50	E6
Ivano-Frankovsk, *Ukraine*	39	L3
Ivanovo, *U.S.S.R.*	35	P4
Ivigtut, *Greenland*	11	Z5
Iviza (I.), *Balearic Is.*	38	E6
Ivory Coast, *W. Africa*	46	C5
Ivugivik, *Quebec*	11	T5
Iwo Jima I., *Pacific Oc.*	44	G4
Ixmiquilpan, *Mexico*	28	E3
Ixopo, *Natal*	47	E3
Ixtlan, *Mexico*	28	E4
Izmail, *Rumania*	39	M4
Izmir, *Turkey*	39	L6
Izu, Schichito, *Japan*	44	G3
Jabalpur (Jubbulpore), *India*	40	E4
Jaboticabal, *Brazil*	31	H8
Jachal, *Argentina*	31	D10
Jack Fish, *Ont.*	18	E4
Jackfish L., *Sask.*	14	G4
Jackfish River, *Alberta*	14	E1
Jackson, *Mich.*	25	K2
Jackson, *Miss.*	25	H4
Jackson, *Tenn.*	25	J3
Jackson B., *N.Z.*	51	B5
Jacksonboro, *Ont.*	18	G4
Jackson's Arm, *N.S.*	23	J2
Jacksonville, *Fla.*	25	K4
Jacksonville, *N.C.*	25	L4
Jacmel, *Haiti*	29	K4
Jacob I., *James B*	18	J3
Jacobina, *Brazil*	30	J6
Jacobsdal, *Orange F.S.*	47	C2
Jacques Cartier L., and R., *Que.*	20	D2
Jacques Cartier Mt., *Que.*	22	E2
Jacques Cartier Passage, *St. Lawrence G.*	22	F1
Jacunda R., *Brazil*	30	G4
Jaffna, *Sri Lanka*	40	F7
Jagdalpur, *India*	40	F5
Jagersfontein, *Orange F.S.*	47	D2
Jaghbub, *Libya*	46	F3
Jaguaribe R., *Brazil*	30	K5
Jaipur, *India*	40	E3
Jakobshavn, *Greenland*	11	Y4

Jalalabad, *Afghanistan*	40	D2
Jalapa Enriquez, *Mexico*	28	E4
Jamaica I., *W. Indies*	29	J4
Jamanchim R., *Brazil*	30	F5
James B., *Canada*	11	S7
James Ross Str., *Franklin, N.W.T.*	11	P4
Jamestown, *N. Dak.*	24	G1
Jamestown, *S. Aust.*	50	B6
Jammu, *Kashmir*	40	E2
Jammu and Kashmir, state, *India*	40	E2
Jamnagar, *India*	40	C4
Jamshedpur, *India*	40	G4
Jamunda R., *Brazil*	30	F4
Janeville, *N.B.*	22	E3
Jan Mayen I., *Arctic Oc.*	35	E1
Janos, *Mexico*	28	C1
Jansenville, *Cape Prov., Rep. of S. Africa*	47	C3
Januaria, *Brazil*	30	J7
Japan, *E. Asia*	44	F3
Japan, Sea of, *Japan, etc.*	44	F2
Japura R., *Brazil, etc.*	30	D4
Jardines de la Reina, *W. Indies*	29	J3
Jari R., *Brazil*	30	G4
Jaroslaw, *Poland*	39	K3
Jarvis, *Ont.*	16	E5
Jarvis I., *Pacific Oc.*	2	E5
Jask, *Iran*	40	A3
Jason Is., *Falkland Is.*	31	E14
Jasper, *Alberta*	14	B4
Jasper, *Ont.*	17	J3
Jasper Park, *Alberta*	14	B4
Jatai, *Brazil*	30	G7
Jau, *Brazil*	31	H8
Jauja, *Peru*	30	B6
Jaumave, *Mexico*	28	E3
Java, and Sea, *Indonesia*	44	C7
Javari R., *Peru-Brazil*	30	C4
Jean Marie River, *Mackenzie, N.W.T.*	12	K2
Jeanotte, *Que.*	20	C2
Jean Péré, L., *Que.*	20	A2
Jebel Akhdar, *Oman*	42	D6
Jebel Shammar, *Saudi Ar.*	42	C6
Jebel Tuwaiq, *Saudi Arabia*	42	C6
Jedburgh, *Scotland*	36	D4
Jedway, *B.C.*	13	E6
Jefferson City, *Mo.*	25	H3
Jellicoe, *Ont.*	18	E4
Jemseg, *N.S.*	21	A2
Jennings R., *B.C.*	12	E3
Jequitinhonha R., *Brazil*	30	J7
Jérémie, *Haiti*	29	K4
Jerez, *Spain*	38	C6
Jericho, *Queensland*	50	F1
Jerilderie, *N.S.W.*	50	E6
Jersey City, *N.J.*	25	L2
Jerusalem, *Israel-Jordan*	42	B5
Jervis B., *N.S.W.*	50	H7
Jervis C., *S. Aust.*	50	B7
Jervis Inlet, *B.C.*	13	J8
Jesus I., *Que.*	20	C3
Jhansi, *India*	40	E3
Jhelum R., *W. Pak.*	40	D2
Jibhalanta, *Mongolia*	44	B2
Jiggitai L., *Tibet*	40	G1
Jihlava, *Czechoslovakia*	39	H3
Jimenez, Mapimi, *Mexico*	29	D2
Jinotega, *Nicaragua*	29	G5
Jipijapa, *Ecuador*	30	A4
Jirgalanta, *Mongolia*	44	B2
João Pessôa(Paraiba), *Brazil*	30	K5
Joaquin R., S., *Cal.*	24	B3
Jodhpur, *India*	40	D3
Joe Batt's Arm, *Nfld.*	23	K2
Joënsuu, *Finland*	35	N3
Joffre Mt., *B.C.*	13	N7
Joggins, *N.S.*	21	C2
Johannesburg, *Transvaal*	47	D2
John C., *N.S.*	21	D2
Johnny Hoe R., *Mackenzie, N.W.T.*	12	K1
John o' Groats, *Scotland*	36	D2
Johnson R., *Mackenzie, N.W.T.*	12	H1
Johnson City, *Tenn.*	25	K3
Johnson's Crossing, *Yukon*	12	D2
Johnston I., *Pacific Oc.*	2	E4
Johnstone Str., *B.C.*	13	G7
Johnstown, *Pa.*	25	L2
Johnswood, *Mich.*	16	B2
Joinville, *Brazil*	31	G9
Jökulsa R., *Iceland*	35	C2
Joliba R., *W. Africa*	46	C4
Joliet, *Ill.*	25	J2
Joliette, *Que.*	20	C2
Jolobert, L., *Que.*	20	D1
Jones C., *Ont.*	11	S7
Jones Sd., *N.W.T.*	11	R2
Jonesboro, *Ark.*	25	H3
Jonesport, *Me.*	22	D4
Jonesville, *Va.*	25	K3
Jönköping, *Sweden*	39	H1
Jonquière, *Que.*	22	B2
Joplin, *Mo.*	25	H3
Jordan, kingdom, *W. Asia*	42	B5
Jordan L., *N.S.*	21	B3
Jordan R., *Israel, etc.*	42	B5
Jorullo, vol., *Mexico*	28	D4
Joseph L., *Lab.*	19	E3
Joseph L., *Ont.*	16	E2
Joseph Bonaparte G., *N.W Aust.*	49	D2

Jostedals Breen, *Norway*	35	H3
Jouberts Kroon, *Transvaal*	47	E1
Joussard *Alberta*	14	D3
Joy B., *Que.*	19	C1
Juan de Fuca Str., *Wash.-Vancouver I.*	13	H8
Juan Fernandez Is., *S. Pacific Oc.*	31	A10
Juan Perez Sd., *B.C.*	13	E6
Juazeiro do Norte, *Brazil*	30	K5
Juazeiro, *Brazil*	30	J5
Juba, *Sudan*	46	G5
Juba R., *E. Africa*	46	H5
Jubilee L., *Nfld.*	23	K2
Jùcar R., *Spain*	38	D6
Juchitan, *Mexico*	28	E4
Judique, *N.S.*	21	F2
Juiz de Fóra, *Brazil*	31	J8
Jujuy, *Argentina*	31	D8
Julian L., *Que.*	19	B3
Julianehaab, *Greenland*	11	Z5
Julio de Castilhos, *Brazil*	31	G9
Jullundur, *India*	40	E2
Jumna R., *India*	40	E3
Junction, *Ut.*	24	D3
Junction City, *Kan.*	24	G3
Jundah, *Queensland*	50	E2
Jundiai, *Brazil*	31	H8
Juneau, *Alaska*	12	C3
Junee, *N.S.W.*	50	F7
Jungfrau, The, *Switzerland*	38	F4
Junin, *Argentina*	31	E10
Junin L., *Peru*	30	B6
Juniper, *N.B.*	22	D3
Jupiter R., *Anticosti I., Que.*	22	F2
Juquia, *Brazil*	31	H8
Jura, Sd. of, *Scotland*	36	C4
Jura I., *Scotland*	36	B4
Jura Mts., *Switzerland*	38	F4
Jurua R., *Brazil*	30	D4
Juruena R., *Brazil*	30	F6
Juskatla, *B.C.*	13	D6
Jutai R., *Brazil*	30	C5
Juticalpa, *Honduras*	29	G5
Jutland, *Denmark*	38	G1
Juuapa, *Guatemala*	28	G5
K2 (Godwin Austen) Mt., *Kashmir*	40	E1
Kaap Plat., *Cape Prov., Rep. of S. Africa*	47	C2
Kaapmuiden, *Transvaal*	47	E2
Kabatogama L., *Minn.*	18	B4
Kabir akagami L., and R., *Ont.*	18	F4
Kabinda, *Angola*	46	E6
Kabul, *Afghanistan*	40	C2
Kabwe, *Zambia*	46	F7
Kaduna, *Nigeria*	46	D4
Kagawong, and L., *Ont.*	16	C2
Kagianagami L., *Ont.*	18	E3
Kagsersuak, *Greenland*	11	X3
Kahnipiminanikok L., *Ont.*	18	C4
Kahntah, *B.C.*	12	K3
Kahutara Pt., *N.Z.*	51	G3
Kaiapoi, *N.Z.*	51	D5
Kaiashk B., *Ont.*	18	D4
Kaieteur Falls, *Guyana*	30	E2
Kaifeng, *China*	44	D3
Kaikohe, *N.Z.*	51	D1
Kaikoura, and Ra., *N.Z.*	51	D5
Kailas Ra., *Tibet, etc.*	40	E2
Kaimanawa Ra., *N.Z.*	51	E3
Kaipara Harb., *N.Z.*	51	D2
Kaiser Wilhelm II Ld., *Antarctica*	2	A8
Kaitaia, *N.Z.*	51	D1
Kaitangata, *N.Z.*	51	B7
Kajaani, *Finland*	35	M3
Kakamas *Cape Prov., Rep. of S. Africa*	47	C2
Kake, *Alaska*	12	D4
Kakhovsk Res., *Ukraine*	39	N4
Kakia, *Botswana*	47	C1
Kakinada, *India*	40	F5
Kakiska L., and R., *Mackenzie, N.W.T.*	12	L2
Kakwa R., *Alberta*	14	B3
Kaladar, *Ont.*	17	H3
Kalahari Desert, *S. Africa*	47	C1
Kalahari Gemsbok Nat. Park, *Cape Prov.*	47	C2
Kalamalka L., *B.C.*	13	L7
Kalamata, *Greece*	39	K6
Kalamazoo, *Mich.*	25	J2
Kalat, *W. Pak.*	40	C3
Kalémié, *Zaire*	46	F6
Kalgoorlie, *W. Aust.*	49	C6
Kalinin, *U.S.S.R.*	39	N1
Kaliningrad (Königsberg), *Lithuania*	39	K2
Kalisz, *Poland*	39	J3
Kalkfontein, *Botswana*	47	C1
Kalmar, *Sweden*	47	J1
Kaluga, *U.S.S.R.*	47	O2
Kama, *Ont.*	18	E4
Kama R., *U.S.S.R.*	42	D3
Kamanets Podolskiy, *Ukraine*	39	L3
Kambo Ho, Mt., *N. Korea*	44	E2
Kamchatka Penin., *U.S.S.R.*	43	P3
Kamet, mt., *India*	40	E2
Kamieskroon, *Cape Prov., Rep. of S. Africa*	47	B3

Kamies Sektor Berg, *Cape Prov., Rep. of S. Africa*	47	B3
Kamina, *Zaire*	46	F6
Kaministikwia, *Ont.*	18	D4
Kaminuriak L., *Keewatin, N.W.T.*	11	Q5
Kamloops, and L., *B.C.*	13	K7
Kamouraska, *Que.*	20	E2
Kamsack, *Sask.*	15	K5
Kamuchawie L., *Sask.*	15	K3
Kanaaupscow, and R., *Que.*	19	B3
Kananaskis L., *Alberta*	14	D5
Kanazawa, *Japan*	44	F3
Kandahar, *Afghanistan*	40	C2
Kandalaksha, and B., *U.S.S.R.*	35	N2
Kandla, *India*	40	D4
Kandy, *Sri Lanka*	40	F7
Kane Basin, *Franklin, N.W.T.*	11	U2
Kangaroo I., *S. Aust.*	50	A7
Kangatsiak, *Greenland*	11	Y4
Kanchenjunga, mt., *Nepal-Tibet*	40	G3
Kangerdlugsuak, *Greenland*	11	Z4
Kaniapiskua L., *Que.*	19	C3
Kaniapiskua R., *Que.*	19	D2
Kanin Penin., *U.S.S.R.*	35	Q2
Kanin Nos, *U.S.S.R.*	35	P2
Kankan, *Guinea*	46	C5
Kano, *Nigeria*	46	D4
Kanpur (Cawnpore), *India*	40	F3
Kansas, state, *U.S.A.*	24	G3
Kansas R., *Kan.*	24	G3
Kansas City, *Kan.*	25	H3
Kanye, *Botswana*	47	D1
Kapiskau, *Ont.*	18	H2
Kapiskau R., *Ont.*	18	G2
Kaposvar R., *Sask.*	15	K5
Kapuas Mts., Upper, *Borneo*	44	D6
Kapunda, *S. Aust.*	50	B7
Kapuskasing, *Ont.*	18	G4
Kapuskasing, L., and R., *Ont.*	18	G4
Kara, *U.S.S.R.*	42	D2
Kara Sea, *Arctic Oc.*	42	E1
Kara Str., *U.S.S.R.*	42	D1
Karachi, *W. Pak.*	40	C4
Karaganda, *U.S.S.R.*	42	F4
Karakoram Ra., and Pass, *Kashmir*	40	E1
Kara Kum, *U.S.S.R.*	42	D5
Karamea Bight, *N.Z.*	51	C4
Karapi, *N.Z.*	51	E3
Karas Mts., *S.W. Africa*	47	B2
Karasburg, *S.W. Africa*	47	B2
Karee Berge, *Cape Prov., Rep. of S. Africa*	47	C3
Karelia, *U.S.S.R.*	35	N3
Kargopol, *U.S.S.R.*	35	O3
Karibib, *S.W. Africa*	47	B1
Karikal, *India*	40	F6
Kariskrona, *Sweden*	39	H1
Karkinitsk, G. of, *U.S.S.R.*	39	N4
Karl Marx Stadt (Chemnitz), *E. Ger.*	38	H3
Karlovac, *Yugoslavia*	39	H4
Karlsruhe, *Ger.*	38	G3
Karlstad, *Sweden*	35	J4
Karnataka, state, *India*	40	E6
Karoo, Gt., *Cape Prov., Rep. of S. Africa*	47	C3
Karoo, Lit., *Cape Prov., Rep. of S. Africa*	47	C3
Karshi, *U.S.S.R.*	40	C1
Kartuk, *Kodiak I., Alaska*	10	D6
Kasai R., *Zaire*	46	F6
Kasba L., *Mackenzie, N.W.T.*	10	O5
Kashgar, *Sinkiang*	42	F5
Kasimov, *U.S.S.R.*	39	P2
Kaskattama R., *Man.*	15	Q2
Kaslo, *B.C.*	13	M8
Kasmere L., *Man.*	15	L1
Kassel, *Ger.*	38	G3
Kastamonu, *Turkey*	39	N5
Katahdin Mt., *Me.*	22	C4
Katahdin Iron Works, *Me.*	22	C4
Katha, *Burma*	40	J4
Katherine, *N. Ter., Aust.*	49	E2
Kathiawar, *India*	40	D4
Kathmandu, *Nepal*	40	G3
Kathovsk Res., *U.S.S.R.*	35	N6
Katkop, *Cape Prov., Rep. of S. Africa*	47	B2
Katmai, vol., *Alaska*	1	B4
Katowice, *Poland*	39	J3
Kattegat, *Denmark, etc.*	38	G1
Kaunas (Kovno), *Lithuania*	39	K2
Kausakuta L., *Que.*	20	C2
Kawa, *Ont.*	18	C3
Kawagama L., *Ont.*	17	G2
Kawartha Ls., *Ont.*	17	G3
Kawhia Harb., *N.Z.*	51	E3
Kayseri, *Turkey*	39	N6
Kazabazua, *Que.*	17	K2
Kazan, *U.S.S.R.*	42	C3
Kazan L., *Sask.*	14	G3
Kazan R., *Keewatin, N.W.T.*	10	O5
Kazan Retto, *Pacific Oc.*	44	G4
Kearney, *Neb.*	24	G2
Kearney, *Ont.*	17	F2
Kechika R., *B.C.*	12	G3
Kecskemet, *Hungary*	39	J4
Kedgwick, and R., *N.B.*	22	D3

Name	Page	Ref
Keele R., *Mackenzie, N.W.T.*	10	J5
Keele Peak, *Yukon*	12	E1
Keeley L., *Sask.*	14	G3
Keetmanshoop, *S.W. Africa*	47	B2
Keewatin, *Ont.*	18	A4
Keewatin, dist., *N.W.T.*	11	Q5
Keflavik, *Iceland*	35	B3
Keg R., *Alberta*	14	B2
Kegaska, *Que.*	23	G1
Keglo B., *Que.*	19	D2
Keg River Post, *Alberta*	14	B2
Kei Is., *Indonesia*	44	F7
Keighley, *Eng.*	37	E5
Keith, *Scotland*	36	D3
Keith Arm, *Mackenzie, N.W.T.*	10	K4
Keithley Cr., *B.C.*	13	K6
Kejimkujik L., *N.S.*	21	B3
Kekertuk, *Baffin I., N.W.T.*	11	W4
Kelfield, *Sask.*	14	G5
Keller L., *Mackenzie, N.W.T.*	12	K1
Kellett C., *Banks I., N.W.T.*	10	J3
Kellett Str., *Franklin, N.W.T.*	10	L2
Kelloselka, *Finland*	35	M2
Kelowna, *B.C.*	13	L8
Kelsey, *Man.*	15	N2
Kelsey Bay, *Vancouver I., B.C.*	13	H7
Kelso, *Scotland*	36	D4
Kelvin I., *Ont.*	18	D4
Kelvington, *Sask.*	15	K4
Kelwood, *Man.*	15	M5
Kem, and R., *U.S.S.R.*	35	N3
Kemano, *B.C.*	13	G6
Kemi R., *Finland*	35	M2
Kemp Ld., *Antarctica*	3	M8
Kempsey, *N.S.W.*	50	J5
Kempt L., *Ont.*	20	B2
Kempton Park, *Transvaal*	47	D2
Kemptville, *N.S.*	22	E4
Kemptville, *Ont.*	17	K2
Kenai, and Penin., *Alaska*	10	D5
Kenaston, *Sask.*	14	H5
Kendal, *Eng.*	37	D4
Kendal, *Sask.*	15	K5
Kendall N.Y.	17	G4
Kendall C., *Keewatin, N.W.T.*	11	Q5
Kendra, *Ont.*	18	B4
Kenhardt, *Cape Prov., Rep. of S. Africa*	47	C2
Kenmare, *Eire*	37	A6
Kennebec R., *Me.*	22	C4
Kennebunk, *Me.*	22	B5
Kennedy, *Sask.*	15	K5
Kennetcook, *N.S.*	21	C2
Kennicot, *Alaska*	10	F5
Keno Hill, *Yukon*	10	G5
Kenogami, and L., *Que.*	22	B2
Kenogami R., *Ont.*	18	F3
Kenogaming L., *Ont.*	18	H4
Kenora, *Ont.*	18	A4
Kenora (Patricia Portion), *Ont.*	18	D2
Kenosha, *Wis.*	25	J2
Kensington, *P.E.I.*	21	D1
Kent, co., *Eng.*	37	F6
Kent, co., *Ont.*	16	C5
Kent Penin., *Mackenzie, N.W.T.*	10	N4
Kent Bridge, *Ont.*	16	C5
Kent Group (Is.), *Victoria*	50	F9
Kent Junc., *N.B.*	22	E3
Kentucky, state, *U.S.A.*	25	J3
Kentucky Lake, *Ky.-Tenn.*	25	J3
Kentville, *N.S.*	21	C2
Kenya, col., *E. Africa*	46	G5
Kenya Mt., *Kenya*	46	G5
Keokuk, *Ia.*	25	H2
Kerala, state, *India*	40	E6
Kerang, *Victoria*	50	D7
Kerch, *U.S.S.R.*	39	O4
Keremeos, *B.C.*	13	K8
Kerguelen I., *Indian Oc.*	3	N7
Kerki, *U.S.S.R.*	40	C1
Kermadec Is., *Pacific Oc.*	2	E6
Kerman, *Iran*	40	A2
Kerr L., *Ont.*	18	J5
Kerrobert, *Sask.*	14	G5
Kerrville, *Tex.*	24	G4
Kerry, co., *Eire*	37	A5
Kersley, *B.C.*	13	J6
Kerulen R., *Mongolia*	44	D2
Kesagami L., *Ont.*	18	H3
Kesagami R., *Ont.*	18	J3
Kesteven, Parts of. *Eng.*	37	E5
Keswick, *Eng.*	37	D4
Ketchikan, *Alaska*	12	E5
Kettering, *Eng.*	37	E5
Kettle R., *B.C.*	13	L8
Kettle R., *Man.*	15	R2
Kettle Rapids, *Man.*	15	O2
Kettle Stone B., *Que.*	19	B1
Keweenaw B., *Mich.*	18	D5
Key Harb., *Ont.*	16	E2
Key Junc., *Ont.*	16	D2
Key Largo, *Fla.*	25	K5
Keystone, *W. Va.*	25	K3
Key West, *Fla.*	25	K6
Khabarovsk, *U.S.S.R.*	44	F2
Khal'mer Yu, *U.S.S.R.*	3	N1
Khangai Mts., *Mongolia*	44	B2
Khanka, L., *U.S.S.R.*	44	F2
Kharkov, *Ukraine*	39	O3
Khartoum, *Sudan*	46	G4
Khatanga, *U.S.S.R.*	43	H1
Khatanga B., *U.S.S.R.*	43	K1
Kheis, *Cape Prov., Rep. of S. Africa*	47	C2
Kherson, *Ukraine*	39	N4
Khingan Mts., *Mongolia, etc.*	43	K4
Khiva, *U.S.S.R.*	42	E4
Khmer Rep., *S.E. Asia*	44	C5
Kholm, *U.S.S.R.*	35	N4
Khoqand, *U.S.S.R.*	42	F4
Khotan, *Sinkiang*	40	E1
Khotin, *Ukraine*	39	L3
Khuis, *Botswana*	47	C2
Khyber Pass, *W. Pak.*	40	D2
Kialinek, *Greenland*	11	Z4
Kiama, *N.S.W.*	50	H7
Kiamika, *Que.*	17	K1
Kiamika L., *Que.*	20	B2
Kian, *China*	44	D4
Kiang Kheng, *Burma*	40	J4
Kicking Horse Pass, *Alberta*	14	C5
Kidderminster, *Eng.*	37	D5
Kidnappers C., *N.Z.*	51	F3
Kiel, *Ger.*	38	G2
Kiev, *Ukraine*	39	M3
Kiglapait C., *Lab.*	19	E2
Kigoma, *Tanzania*	46	G6
Kikkertorsoak I., *Ungava B.*	19	D2
Kilback Mts., *Alaska*	10	B6
Kildare, *Que.*	20	C2
Kildare, and co., *Eire*	37	B5
Kildare, C., *P.E.I.*	21	D1
Kildonan, *Vancouver I., B.C.*	13	H8
Kilimanjaro Mt., *Tanzania*	46	G6
Kilkee, *Eire*	37	A5
Kilkenny, *Que.*	20	C3
Kilkenny, and co., *Eire*	37	B5
Kilkivan, *Queensland*	50	J3
Killala B., *Eire*	37	A4
Killaloe Sta., *Ont.*	17	H2
Killarney, *Eire*	37	A5
Killarney, *Man.*	15	M6
Killarney, *Ont.*	16	D2
Killarney, *Queensland*	50	J4
Killarney Prov. Park, *Ont.*	16	D1
Killbear Point Prov. Park, *Ont.*	16	E2
Killdeer, *Sask.*	14	H6
Killin, *Scotland*	36	C3
Killinek I., *Lab.*	19	E1
Killybegs, *Eire*	37	A4
Kilmarnock, *Scotland*	36	C4
Kilmore, *Victoria*	50	E8
Kilwa Kivinje, *Tanzania*	46	G6
Kilworthy, *Ont.*	17	F3
Kimberley, *B.C.*	13	M8
Kimberley, *Cape Prov., Rep. of S. Africa*	47	C2
Kimberley, *Ont.*	16	E3
Kinabalu Mt., *Sabah*	44	D6
Kinaskan, *B.C.*	12	F4
Kinbasket L., *B.C.*	13	M7
Kincardine, *Ont.*	16	D3
Kincardine, co., *Scotland*	36	D3
Kincolith, *B.C.*	12	F5
Kindersley, *Sask.*	14	G5
Kindu-Port Empain, *Zaire*	46	F6
Kineo, *Me.*	22	C4
Kineshma, *U.S.S.R.*	35	P4
King, *Victoria*	50	F8
King I., *Alaska*	10	A5
King I., *B.C.*	13	G6
King I., *Tasmania*	50	E9
King Sd., *W. Aust.*	49	C3
Kingaroy, *Queensland*	50	H3
King Christian IX Ld., *Greenland*	11	Z4
Kingcome Inlet, *B.C.*	13	G7
King Frederick VI Ld., *Greenland*	11	Z5
King George Is. *Hudson B.*	19	B1
King George Mt., *B.C.*	13	N7
King George's Sd., *W. Aust.*	49	B7
King Leopold Ra., *W. Aust.*	49	C3
Kingscote, *S. Aust.*	50	A7
Kingscourt, *Eire*	37	B5
Kings Cove, *Nfld.*	23	L2
Kingsgate, *B.C.*	14	C6
Kingsley, *Drummond, Que.*	20	C3
Kingsley, *Richmond, Que.*	20	D3
King's Lynn, *Eng.*	37	F5
Kings Peak, *Utah*	24	D2
Kingsport, *N.S.*	22	E4
Kingston, *Eng.*	37	E6
Kingston, *Jamaica*	29	J4
Kingston, *N.Y.*	25	L2
Kingston, *N.Z.*	51	B6
Kingston, *Ont.*	17	J3
Kingston, *S. Aust.*	50	B8
Kingstown (Dun Laoghaire), *Eire*	37	B5
Kingstown, St. Vincent, *W. Indies*	29	M5
Kingstown, *Windward Is.*	30	E1
Kingsvale, *B.C.*	13	K8
Kingsville, *Ont.*	16	C5
Kingussie, *Scotland*	36	C3
King William I., *Franklin, N.W.T.*	11	P4
King Williams Town, *Cape Prov., Rep. of S. Africa*	47	D3
Kinkora, *P.E.I.*	21	D1
Kinlochleven, *Scotland*	36	C3
Kinmount, *Ont.*	17	G3
Kinnaird Hd., *Scotland*	36	E3
Kinoosao, *Sask.*	15	K2
Kinosis, *Alberta*	14	F2
Kinosota, *Man.*	15	M5
Kinross, *Scotland*	36	D3
Kinsale, and Harb., *Eire*	37	A6
Kinshasa (Leopoldville), *Zaire*	46	E6
Kintyre, *Scotland*	36	C4
Kintyre, Mull of, *Scotland*	37	C4
Kinuso, *Alberta*	14	D3
Kiosk, *Ont.*	17	G1
Kipawa, and L., *Que.*	19	B4
Kipling, *Sask.*	15	K5
Kipp, *Alberta*	14	E6
Kippee, *Que.*	20	E2
Kippokok, and B.. *Lab.*	19	F2
Kirghiz Steppes, *U.S.S.R.*	42	D4
Kirin (Yungki), *China*	44	E2
Kirkcaldy, *Scotland*	36	D3
Kirkcudbright, and co., *Scotland*	37	C4
Kirkella, *Man.*	15	L5
Kirkland Lake, *Ont.*	18	H4
Kirkliston Ra., *N.Z.*	51	C6
Kirkpatrick L., *Alberta*	14	F5
Kirkwall, *Orkney Is., Scotland*	36	D2
Kirovograd, *Ukraine*	39	N3
Kirthar Mts., *W. Pak.*	40	C3
Kisangani (Stanleyville), *Congo*	46	F5
Kisgegas, *B.C.*	12	G5
Kishinev, *Moldavia*	39	M4
Kiska I., *Aleutian Is.*	2	D2
Kiskatinaw R., *B.C.*	12	K5
Kiskisink, *Que.*	20	C2
Kiskitto L., *Man.*	15	M3
Kiskittogisu L., *Man.*	15	M3
Kismayu, *Somali Rep.*	46	H6
Kispiox R., *B.C.*	12	F5
Kisseynew L., *Man.*	15	L3
Kissimmee, *Fla.*	25	K5
Kississing L., *Man.*	15	L3
Kistigan L., *Man.*	15	P3
Kisumu, *Kenya*	64	G5
Kitakyūshū, *Japan*	44	F3
Kitchener, *Ont.*	16	E4
Kitchener L., *B.C.*	12	G4
Kitchener Mt., *Alberta*	14	B4
Kithira (Cerigo) I., *Italy*	39	K6
Kitigan, *Ont.*	18	G4
Kitimat, *B.C.*	13	F5
Kitkatla, *B.C.*	13	E6
Kitwanga, *B.C.*	12	F5
Kivu L., *Cent. Africa*	46	F6
Kiwalik, *Alaska*	10	B4
Kiyiu L., *Sask.*	14	G5
Kizil Irmak (R.), *Turkey*	39	N5
Kjöge B., *Greenland*	11	Z5
Klagenfurt, *Austria*	39	H4
Klaipeda (Memel), *Lithuania*	39	K2
Klamath Falls, *Ore.*	24	B2
Klappan R., *B.C.*	12	F4
Klarälven R., *Sweden-Norway*	35	J3
Kleena Kleene, *B.C.*	13	H7
Klemtu, *B.C.*	13	F6
Klerksdorp, *Transvaal*	47	D2
Klinaklini R., *B.C.*	13	H7
Klipplaat, *Cape Prov., Rep. of S. Africa*	47	C3
Klock, *Ont.*	17	G1
Klondike, *Yukon*	10	G5
Kluane L., *Yukon*	10	G5
Klukshu, *Yukon*	13	B2
Klukwan, *Alaska*	13	C3
Klyuchev, vol., *U.S.S.R.*	43	P3
Knee L., *Man.*	15	O3
Knee L., *Sask.*	14	H3
Kneehill Creek, *Alberta*	14	E5
Knife L., N., *Man.*	15	N1
Knife R., N. and S., *Man.*	15	O1
Knight Inlet, *B.C.*	13	H7
Knockmealdown Mts., *Eire*	37	A5
Knowlton, *Que.*	20	C3
Knox C., *B.C.*	12	D5
Knoxville, *Tenn.*	25	K3
Knud Rasmussen Ld., *Greenland*	11	Z4
Knysna, *Cape Prov., Rep. of S. Africa*	47	C3
Koartak, *Que.*	19	C1
Koasoak, *Que.*	19	D2
Kobdo, Plat. of, *Mongolia*	43	H4
Kobe, *Japan*	44	F3
Kobuk R., *Alaska*	10	C4
Kodiak, and I., *Alaska*	10	D6
Kodok, *Sudan*	46	G4
Koes *S.W. Africa*	47	B2
Kofflefontein, *Orange F.S.*	47	D2
Kogaluk B., and R., *Que.*	19	B2
Koh-i-Baba, *Afghanistan*	40	B2
Koko-shili Ra., *China*	40	H1
Kokstad, *Cape Prov., Rep. of S. Africa*	47	D3
Kola, and B., *U.S.S.R.*	35	N2
Kola Penin., *U.S.S.R.*	35	O2
Kolar, *India*	40	E6
Kolarovgrad, *Bulgaria*	39	L5
Kolepom I., *W. Irian*	44	F7
Kolguev I., *U.S.S.R.*	35	Q2
Koihapur, *India*	40	D5
Kolima R., *U.S.S.R.*	43	O2
Kologriv, *U.S.S.R.*	35	P4
Kolyma Mts., *U.S.S.R.*	43	O2
Komandorskie Is., *Bering Sea*	2	D2
Komati R., *Transvaal*	47	E2
Komati Poort, *Transvaal*	47	E2
Komga, *Cape Prov., Rep. of S. Africa*	47	D3
Kommunisma, mt., *U.S.S.R.*	40	D1
Kompasberg, *Cape Prov., Rep. of S. Africa*	47	C3
Komsberg R., *Cape Prov., Rep. of S. Africa*	47	C3
Komsomolsk, *U.S.S.R.*	44	F1
Königsberg (Kaliningrad), *Lithuania*	39	K2
Konkib R., *S.W. Africa*	47	B2
Konosha, *U.S.S.R.*	35	P3
Konotop, *Ukraine*	39	N3
Konya, *Turkey*	39	N6
Kooloonong, *Victoria*	50	D7
Koondrook, *Victoria*	50	E7
Koorawatha, *N.S.W.*	50	G7
Kootenay L., *B.C.*	13	M8
Kootenay National Park, *B.C.*	13	M7
Kopet Mts., *U.S.S.R.*	42	D5
Koraluk R., *Lab.*	19	E2
Korea, N. & S., *E. Asia*	44	E3
Korea Str., and Penin., *Asia*	43	L5
Koroit, *Victoria*	50	D9
Korok R., *Que.*	19	D2
Korös R., *Hungary*	39	K4
Kos, G. of, *Turkey*	39	L6
Kosciusko Mt., *N.S.W.*	50	G8
Kosi L., *Natal*	47	E2
Košice, *Czechoslovakia*	39	K3
Kostroma, *U.S.S.R.*	35	P4
Kota Bharu, *Malaya*	44	C6
Kota Kinabalu (Jesselton), *Sabah*	44	D6
Kotcho L., and R.. *B.C.*	12	K3
Kotelnyi I.. *U.S.S.R.*	2	C1
Kotlas, *U.S.S.R.*	35	Q3
Kotor, *Yugoslavia*	39	J5
Kotzebue Sd., *Alaska*	10	A4
Koulikoro, *Mali, W. Africa*	46	C4
Kovel, *Ukraine, U.S.S.R.*	39	L3
Kovik B., *Que.*	19	B1
Kovrov, *U.S.S.R.*	35	P4
Koyukuk R., *Alaska*	10	C4
Kra, Isthmus of, *Malay Penin.*	40	J6
Kragujevac, *Yugoslavia*	39	K4
Krakatau I., *Indonesia*	44	C7
Kranskop, *Natal*	47	E2
Krasnodar, *U.S.S.R.*	39	O4
Krasnoyarsk, *U.S.S.R.*	43	H3
Kreefte B., *Cape Prov., Rep. of S. Africa*	47	B3
Kremenchug, *Ukraine*	39	N3
Kremenchugsk Res., *Ukraine*	39	N3
Krishna R., *India*	40	E5
Kristiansand, *Norway*	38	F1
Kristiansund, *Norway*	35	H3
Krivoy Rog, *U.S.S.R.*	39	N4
Kronshtadt, *U.S.S.R.*	35	M3
Kroonstad, *Orange F.S.*	47	D2
Kruger National Park, *Transvaal*	47	E1
Krugersdorp, *Transvaal*	47	D2
Kruzof, *Alaska*	13	C4
Kuala Lumpur, *Malaya*	44	C6
Kuban R., *U.S.S.R.*	39	O4
Kuching, *Borneo*	44	D6
Kufra, *Libya*	46	F3
Kugong I., *Hudson B.*	19	A2
Kuibyshev, *U.S.S.R.*	42	D3
Kuiu I., *Alaska*	12	C4
Kukatush, *Ont.*	18	G4
Kukawa, *Nigeria*	46	E4
Kukong, *China*	44	D4
Kuldo, *B.C.*	12	G5
Kuluene R., *Brazil*	30	G6
Kumara, *N.Z.*	51	C5
Kunduz, *Afghanistan*	40	C1
Kunghit I., *B.C.*	13	E6
Kunlong, *Burma*	40	J4
Kunlun Mts., *Tibet, etc.*	40	F1
Kunming, *China*	44	C4
Kuopio, *Finland*	35	M3
Kupang, *Timor I., Indonesia*	44	E8
Kupreanof I., *Alaska*	12	D4
Kura R., *U.S.S.R.*	42	C4
Kurdistan, *Iraq, etc.*	42	C5
Kurdzhali, *Bulgaria*	39	L5
Kuria Muria Is., *Arabia*	42	D7
Kuril Is., *Japan*	44	G2
Kurnool, *India*	40	E5
Kurow, *N.Z.*	51	C6
Kursk, *U.S.S.R.*	39	O3
Kuruman, and R., *Cape Prov., Rep. of S. Africa*	47	C2
Kuruman Hills, *Cape Prov., Rep. of S. Africa*	47	C2
Kusawa L., *Yukon*	13	B2
Kushka, *U.S.S.R.*	40	B1
Kuskokwim B., *Alaska*	10	B6
Kuskokwim Mts., *Alaska*	10	C5
Kuskokwim R., *Alaska*	10	C5
Kutahya, *Turkey*	39	M6
Kutch, G. of, *India*	40	C4

Kutch, Ranh of, *India* 40 C4
Kuyakuz L., *B.C.* 13 H6
Kwango R., *Congo, etc.* 46 E6
Kwataboahegan R., *Ont.* 18 G3
Kweilin, *China* 44 D4
Kweiyang, *China* 44 C4
Kwokwullie, L., *B.C.* 12 K3
Kyakhta, *U.S.S.R.* 44 C1
Kyaukpyu, *Burma* 40 H5
Kyle of Lochalsh, *Scotland* 36 C3
Kyneton, *Victoria* 50 E8
Kyoto, *Japan* 44 F3
Kyuquot, *Vancouver I., B.C.* 13 G7
Kyuquot Sd., *Vancouver I., B.C.* 13 G8
Kyushu (I.), *Japan* 44 F3
Kyzyl, *U.S.S.R.* 43 H4
Kyzyl Kum, *U.S.S.R.* 42 E3

La Baie, *Que.* 20 C2
La Grande Riviere, *Que.* 19 B3
Labelle, *Que.* 17 L1
Labelle, L., *Que.* 20 B2
Laberge L., *Yukon* 12 C2
Labos, *Argentina* 31 F11
Labrador, *Nfld.* 11 W7
Labrador, Coast of, *Nfld.* 19 E3
Labrador City, *Lab.* 19 D3
Labrea, *Brazil* 30 E5
Labrieville, *Que.* 22 C2
Labuan, *Sabah* 44 D6
Lac à la Tortue, *Que.* 20 C2
Lac au Saumon, *Que.* 22 D2
Lac Baker, *N.B.* 22 C3
Laccadive Is., *Arabian Sea* 40 D6
Lac Edouard, *Que.* 20 C2
La Ceiba, *Honduras* 28 G4
Lac Etehemin, *Que.* 20 D2
Lachlan R., *N.S.W.* 50 F6
Lachine, *Que.* 20 C3
Lachute, *Que.* 20 B3
Lac la Biche, *Alberta* 14 E3
Lac la Hache, *B.C.* 13 K7
Lac la Ronge Park, *Sask.* 15 J3
Lac la Martre, *Mackenzie* 12 M1
Lac Lavieille, *Ont.* 17 G2
Lac Long, *Que.* 20 C1
Lacolle, *Que.* 20 C3
Lacombe, *Alberta* 14 E4
La Conception, *Que.* 17 K1
Lacoste, *Que.* 20 B2
Lac Poisson Blanc, *Que.* 17 K1
La Crosse, *Wis.* 25 H2
Lac St Jean, *Que.* 20 C1
Lac Ste. Marie, *Que.* 17 K2
Lac St. Patrice, *Que.* 17 H1
Ladismith, *Cape Prov., Rep. of S. Africa* 47 C3
Ladoga L., *U.S.S.R.* 35 N3
Ladybrand, *Orange F.S.* 47 D2
Lady Elliot I., *Queensland* 50 J2
Lady Evelyn Falls, *Mackenzie, N.W.T.* 12 M2
Ladysmith, *Natal* 47 D2
Ladysmith, *Vancouver I., B.C.* 13 H8
Lae, *New Guinea* 2 C5
La Esperanza, *Honduras* 28 G5
La Fayette, *Ind.* 25 J2
Laferte R., *Mackenzie, N.W.T.* 12 L2
Lafontaine, *Que.* 20 E2
La Forest, *Ont.* 18 H5
Lagan R., *N. Ire.* 37 C4
Laggan L., *Scotland* 36 C3
Lagos, *Nigeria* 46 D5
Lagos de Moreno, *Mexico* 28 D3
La Grande, *Ore.* 24 C1
La Grande, *Que.* 19 C3
La Guaira, *Venezuela* 30 D1
Laguna, *Brazil* 31 H9
Laguna B., *Queensland* 50 J3
Lagunas, *Chile* 31 D8
Lagunillas, *Bolivia* 30 E7
La Have, *N.S.* 21 C3
Lahave Is., *N.S.* 21 C3
La Higuera, *Chile* 31 C9
Lahore, *W. Pak.* 40 D2
Laingsburg, *Cape Prov., Rep. of S. Africa* 47 C3
Laings Nek, *Natal* 47 D2
Laird, *Sask.* 14 H4
Lajes, *Brazil* 31 G9
La Junta, *Colo.* 24 F3
Lake Athabasca, *Alberta-Sask.* 14 G1
Lake Charles, *La.* 25 H4
Lake City, *Colo.* 24 E3
Lake City, *Fla.* 25 K5
Lake Claire National Park, *Alberta* 14 E1
Lake Cumberland, *Ky.* 25 J3
Lakefield, *Ont.* 17 G3
Lake Harb., *Baffin I., N.W.T.* 19 D1
Lake Leopold II, *Zaire* 46 E6
Lake Martin, *Ala.* 25 J4
Lake Nasser, *Egypt* 46 G3
Lake of the Ozarks, *Mo.* 25 H3
Lakeport, *Cal.* 24 B3
Lakeport, *Mich.* 16 C4
Lake Superior Park, *Ont.* 18 F5
Lake View, *Ore.* 24 B2
Lakewood, *O.* 25 K2

La Libertad, *Ecuador* 30 A4
La Libertad, *Guatemala* 28 F4
La Ligua, *Chile* 31 C10
La Loche & L., *Sask.* 14 G2
La Malbaie, *Que.* 20 D2
Lambayeque, *Peru* 30 A5
Lamberts Bay, *Cape Prov., Rep. of S. Africa* 47 B3
Lambeth, *Ont.* 16 D5
Lambton, *Que.* 20 D3
Lambton, co., *Ont.* 16 C5
Lambton C., *Banks I., N.W.T.* 10 K3
La Mocha I., *Chile* 31 B11
La Montana, *Peru* 30 C5
Lampeter, *Wales* 37 C5
Lampman, *Sask.* 15 K6
Lamprey, *Man.* 15 O1
Lanark, *Ont.* 17 J2
Lanark, co., *Ont.* 17 J3
Lanark, and co., *Scotland* 36 D4
Lancashire, co., *Eng.* 37 D5
Lancaster, *Eng.* 37 D4
Lancaster, *N.B.* 21 A2
Lancaster, *Ont.* 17 L2
Lancaster, *Pa.* 25 L2
Lancaster Sd., *Franklin, N.W.T.* 11 R3
Lanchow, *China* 44 C3
Landa, *Mexico* 28 E3
Lander, *Wyo.* 24 E2
Lander Cr., *N. Ter., Aust.* 49 E4
Landi Kotal, *W. Pak.* 40 D2
Landing L., *Man.* 15 N3
Landsborough, *Queensland* 50 J3
Land's End, *Eng.* 37 C6
Land's End, *Prince Patrick I., N.W.T.* 10 K2
Langanes, *Iceland* 35 D2
Lange B., *Cape Prov., Rep. of S. Africa* 47 C2
Lange Berg, *Cape Prov., Rep. of S. Africa* 47 B3
L'Ange Gardien, *Que.* 20 D2
Langelier, *Que.* 20 D2
Langenburg, *Sask.* 15 L5
Langham, *Sask.* 14 H4
Langholm, *Scotland* 37 D4
Langlade, *Que.* 19 B4
Langlade I., *St Pierre & Miquelon, Atlantic Oc.* 23 J3
Langraie, *Que.* 20 C3
Lanigan, *Sask.* 14 J5
Lanin Nat. Park, *Argentina* 31 11C
L'Annonciation, *Que.* 20 B2
Lansdowne, *Ont.* 17 K3
Lansdowne House, *Ont.* 18 D2
L'Anse St. Jean, *Que.* 20 D1
Lansing, *Mich.* 25 K2
Láoag, *Luzon* 44 E5
Laois, Co., *Eire* 37 A4
Laokai, *N. Vietnam* 44 C4
Laon, *France* 38 E3
La Oroya, *Peru* 30 B6
Laos, *S.E. Asia* 44 C5
La Pampa, prov., *Argentina* 31 D11
La Patrie, *Que.* 20 D3
La Paz, *Argentina* 31 F10
La Paz, *Bolivia* 30 D7
La Paz, *Mexico* 28 B3
Lapeer, *Mich.* 16 B4
La Perouse, *Man.* 15 N3
La Piedad, *Mexico* 28 D3
Lapland, *N. Europe* 35 L2
La Plata, prov., *Argentina* 31 F11
La Poile B., *Nfld.* 23 H3
Laprairie, *Que.* 20 C3
Laprida, *Argentina* 31 E11
Laptev Sea, *Arctic Oc.* 2 C1
La Puntilla, *Ecuador* 30 A4
L'Aradie, *Que.* 20 C3
Laramie, *Wyo.* 24 E2
Larch R., *Que.* 19 C2
Lardeau, *B.C.* 13 M7
Larder L., *Ont.* 18 J4
Larder Lake, *Ont.* 18 J4
Laredo, *Tex.* 24 G5
Laredo Sd., *B.C.* 13 F6
La Reine, *Que.* 18 J4
Largs, *Scotland* 36 C4
La Rioja, *Argentina* 31 D9
Larisa, *Greece* 39 K6
La Rivière, *Man.* 15 M6
Larne, *N. Ire.* 37 C4
La Rochelle, *France* 38 D4
La Romana, *Dominican Rep.* 29 L4
La Ronge, *Sask.* 14 J3
Larry's River, *N.S.* 21 F2
Larvik, *Norway* 35 J4
La Sabana, *Argentina* 31 E9
La Salle, *Mich.* 16 B5
Las Animas, *Colo.* 24 F3
La Sarre, *Que.* 19 B4
La Scie, *Nfld.* 23 K2
Las Cruces, *N. Mex.* 24 E4
La Seine, *Ont.* 18 B4
La Serena, *Chile* 31 C9
Las Flores, *Argentina* 31 E11
Lashburn, *Sask.* 14 G4
Las Heras, *Argentina* 31 D13
Lashio, *Burma* 40 J4
Lashkar, *India* 40 E3
Las Perlas Lagoon, *Nicaragua* 29 H5
Lassen Peak, *Cal.* 24 B2

L'Assomption, *Que.* 20 C3
Last Mountain L., *Sask.* 14 J5
Las Tres Marias, *Mexico* 28 C3
Las Vegas, *Nev.* 24 C3
Las Vegas, *N. Mex.* 24 E3
La Tabatière, *Que.* 23 H1
Latacunga, *Ecuador* 30 B4
Latchford, *Ont.* 18 H5
Laterrière, *Que.* 20 D1
La Tola, *Ecuador* 30 B3
Latultrie, *Que.* 20 C3
La Tuque, *Que.* 20 C2
La Verendrye Park, *Que.* 19 B4
Latvia, rep., *Europe* 39 K1
Lauder, *Man.* 15 L6
Launceston, *Eng.* 37 C6
Launceston, *Tasmania* 50 J11
Laura, *S. Aust.* 50 B6
Laurel, *Ont.* 16 E4
Laurentide Mts., *Que.* 20 C2
Laurentides, *Que.* 20 C2
Laurentides Park, *Que.* 20 D2
Laurie L. & River, *Man.* 15 L2
Laurier, *Man.* 15 M5
Laurier, *Que.* 20 D2
Laurier Mt., *B.C.* 12 J4
Lausanne, *Switzerland* 38 F4
Lauzon, *Que.* 20 D2
Laval B., *Que.* 22 C2
Lavant, *Ont.* 17 J2
La Vega, *Dominican Rep.* 29 K4
L'Avenir, *Que.* 20 C3
Laverton, *W. Aust.* 49 C5
Lavras, *Brazil* 31 H8
Lawashi R., *Ont.* 18 G2
Lawgi, *Queensland* 50 H2
Lawrence, *Kan.* 24 G3
Lawrence, *Mass.* 25 M2
Lawrencetown, *N.S.* 22 E4
Lawrencetown, *N.S.* 21 B3
Lawton, *Okla.* 24 G4
Lay Pt., *Alaska* 10 B4
Layfield, *Guyana* 30 F2
Lea R., *Eng.* 37 F6
Leach I., *L. Superior, Ont.* 18 F5
Lead, *S. Dak.* 24 F2
Leader, *Sask.* 14 G5
Leadville, *Colo.* 24 E3
Leaf B., *Que.* 19 D2
Leaf R., *Que.* 19 C2
Leamington, *Eng.* 37 E5
Loamington, *Ont.* 16 C5
Leaside, *Ont.* 17 F4
Leask, *Sask.* 14 H4
Lebanon, rep., *W. Asia* 42 B5
Lebanon Mts., *Syria* 42 B5
Lebombo Mts., *Transvaal, etc.* 47 E1
Lebu, *Chile* 31 C11
Le Cave, *Ont.* 17 G1
Ledesma, *Argentina* 31 D8
Leduc, *Alberta* 14 E4
Lee R., *Eire* 37 A6
Leeds, *Eng.* 37 E5
Leeds, *Que.* 20 D2
Leeds, co., *Ont.* 17 J3
Leeuwin C., *W. Aust.* 49 A6
Leeward Is., *W. Indies* 29 M4
Lefebvre, *Que.* 20 E2
Lefroy, *Ont.* 16 F3
Legal, *Alberta* 14 E4
Legaspi, *Philippine Is.* 44 E5
Legend L., *Alberta* 14 E2
Légère, *N.B.* 22 E3
Legges Tor Mt., *Tasmania* 50 L11
Leghorn, *Italy* 38 G5
Legnica, *Poland* 39 J3
Leh, *Kashmir* 40 E2
Lehututu, *Botswana* 47 C1
Leicester, and co., *Eng.* 37 E5
Leichardt R., *Queensland* 49 F3
Leigh Creek, *S. Aust.* 50 B5
Leipzig, *Ger.* 38 H3
Leiria, *Portugal* 38 B6
Leismer, *Alberta* 14 F3
Leith, *Scotland* 36 D4
Leith Hill, *Eng.* 37 E6
Leitrim, co., *Eire* 37 A4
Le Maire Str., *Argentina* 31 E14
Le Mans, *France* 38 E3
Lemberg, *Sask.* 15 K5
Lemieux, *Que.* 20 C2
Lemnos (Limnos), I., *Greece* 39 L6
Lempriere, *B.C.* 13 L6
Lena R., and Delta, *U.S.S.R.* 43 L1
Lençóis, *Brazil* 30 J6
Leningrad, *U.S.S.R.* 35 N3
Leninsk Kuznetskiy, *U.S.S.R.* 44 A1
Lennox and Addington, co., *Ont.* 17 H3
Lennoxville, *Que.* 20 D3
Lenore, *Man.* 15 L6
Lenore L., *Sask.* 14 J4
Leon, *Mexico* 28 D3
Leon, *Nicaragua* 28 G5
León, *Spain* 38 C6
Leonora, *W. Australia* 49 C5
Lenôtre, L., *Que.* 20 B2
Leopold Mc. Clintock C., *Prince Patrick I., N.W.T.* 10 L2
Leopoldville, *see Kinshasa*
L'Epiphanie, *Que.* 20 C3
Lepreau, *N.B.* 22 D4
Lerida, *Spain* 38 E5

Lerwick, *Shetland Is., Scotland* 36 E1
Lesbos I. (Mitilini), *Greece* 39 L6
Les Cayes, *Haiti* 29 K4
Les Eboulements, *Que.* 20 D2
Les Escoumins, *Que.* 22 B2
Lesotho, state, *S.E. Africa* 47 D2
Les Pélerins, *Que.* 20 D2
Lestock, *Sask.* 15 K5
Letaba R., *Transvaal, etc.* 47 E1
Lethbridge, *Alberta* 14 E6
Leticia, *Colombia* 30 C4
Letterkenny, *Eire* 37 B4
Letty Harbour, *Mackenzie, N.W.T.* 10 K4
Levack, *Ont.* 18 H5
Levanger, *Norway* 35 J3
Leven L., *Scotland* 36 D3
Levêque C., *W. Aust.* 49 C3
Levin, *N.Z.* 51 E4
Levis, *Que.* 20 D2
Levis L., *Mackenzie, N.W.T.* 12 M1
Levkás I., *Greece* 39 K6
Lewes, *Eng.* 37 F6
Lewis, *Scotland* 36 B2
Lewis Ra., *Mont.-B.C.* 24 D1
Lewis R., *Yukon* 10 G5
Lewisporte, *Nfld.* 23 K2
Lewiston, *Ida.* 24 C1
Lewiston, *Me.* 25 N2
Lexington, *Ky.* 25 K3
Leydsdorp, *Transvaal* 47 E1
Leyland, *Alberta* 14 C4
Leyson Pt., *Southampton I., N.W.T.* 19 A1
Leyte, *Philippine Is.* 44 E5
Lhasa, *Tibet* 40 H3
Liao-ho R., *China* 43 L4
Liard R., *B.C., etc.* 12 G3
Liard River, *B.C.* 12 G3
Liard River Hot Springs Park, *B.C.* 12 H3
Libby Res., *Mont.* 14 D6
Liberec, *Czechoslovakia* 39 H3
Liberia, *Costa Rica* 29 G5
Liberia, rep., *W. Africa* 46 B5
Libreville, *Gabon* 46 D5
Libya, rep., *N. Africa* 46 E3
Libyan Desert, *Libya* 46 F3
Lichfield, *Eng.* 37 D5
Lichtenau, *Greenland* 11 Z5
Lichtenburg, *Transvaal* 47 D2
Lichtenfels, *Greenland* 11 Y5
Liechtenstein, state, *Europe* 38 G4
Liége, *Belgium* 38 F3
Lienyun Kang, *China* 44 D3
Liepäja (Lepaya), *Latvia* 39 K1
Lièvre R., *Que.* 17 K2
Lievres, I. aux, *Que.* 20 E2
Liffey R., *Eire* 37 B5
Lifford, *Eire* 37 B4
Lightning Ridge, *N.S.W.* 50 F4
Ligor, Isthmus of, *Siam* 40 J7
Ligurian Sea, *Italy* 38 G5
Lille, *France* 38 E3
Lillooet, *B.C.* 13 K7
Lillooet R., and L., *B.C.* 13 J7
Lilm Fd., *Denmark* 38 G1
Lilongwe, *Malawi* 46 G7
Lima, *O.* 25 K2
Lima, *Peru* 30 B6
Limay R., *Argentina* 31 D11
Limerick, and co., *Eire* 37 A5
Limestone, *Me.* 22 D3
Limestone B., and Pt., *Man.* 15 M4
Limestone R., *Man.* 15 O2
Limestone Fall, *Que.* 19 D2
Limoges, *France* 38 E4
Limoges, *Ont.* 17 K2
Limon, *Colombia* 30 B3
Limon, *Costa Rica* 29 H5
Limpopo R., *S.E. Africa* 47 E1
Linares, *Chile* 31 C11
Linares, *Mexico* 28 E3
Linares, *Spain* 38 D6
Lincoln, *Me.* 22 C4
Lincoln, *Neb.* 24 G2
Lincoln, *N. Mex.* 24 E4
Lincoln, and co., *Eng.* 37 E5
Lincoln, co., *Ont.* 16 F4
Lincolnville, *N.S.* 21 F2
Lincoln Wolds, *Eng.* 37 E5
Lindenows Fd., *Greenland* 11 Z5
Lindesay Mt., *Queensland* 50 J5
Lindley, *Orange F.S.* 44 D2
Lindsay, *Ont.* 17 G3
Lindsey, Parts of, *Eng.* 37 E5
Linhares, *Brazil* 30 K7
Linlithgow, *Scotland* 36 D4
Linnhe L., *Scotland* 36 C3
Linton, *Que.* 20 C2
Linton, *Victoria* 50 D8
Linz, *Austria* 38 H3
Lions, G. of, *France* 38 E5
Lions Hd., *Ont.* 16 E3
Lipari Is., *Italy* 39 H6
Liptrap C., *Victoria* 50 E9
Lisbon, *Portugal* 38 B6
Lisburn, *N. Ire.* 37 B4
Lisburne C., *Alaska* 10 A4
Liscomb, *N.S.* 21 E2
L'Islet, *Que.* 20 D2
Lismore, *Eire* 37 A5
Lismore, *N.S.W.* 50 J4
Lismore, *N.S.* 21 E2

Listowel, *Eire* 37 A5
Listowel, *Ont.* 16 E4
Lithgow, *N.S.W.* 50 H6
Lithuania, rep., *Europe* 39 K2
Little Abitiba L., *Ont.* 18 H4
Little Barrier I., *N.Z.* 51 E2
Little Bay Islands, tn., and B., *Nfld.* 23 K2
Little Current, *Ont.* 16 C2
Little Current R., *Ont.* 18 F3
Little Grand Rapids, *Man.* 15 O4
Little Harbour Deep, *Nfld.* 23 J1
Little Longlac, *Ont.* 18 E4
Little Manicouagan L., *Que.* 22 D1
Little Mecatina, *Que.* 23 H1
Little Prairie, *B.C.* 12 K5
Little Quill L., *Sask.* 15 K5
Little Red River, *Alberta* 14 D1
Little River, *Nfld.* 23 H3
Little River, *N.Z.* 51 D5
Little Rock, *Ark.* 25 H4
Little Trout L., *Ont.* 18 A2
Little Whale R., *Que.* 19 B2
Liuchow, *China* 44 C4
Liverpool, *N.S.W.* 50 H6
Liverpool, *N.S.* 21 B3
Liverpool, and B., *Eng.* 37 D5
Liverpool B., *Mackenzie, N.W.T.* 10 J3
Liverpool Ra., *N.S.W.* 50 H5
Livingston, *Guatemala* 28 G4
Livingston, *Coast of Lab.* 19 D3
Livingston, *Zambia* 46 F7
Livingstone Cr., *Yukon* 12 C2
Livingstone Ra., *Alberta* 14 D5
Livingstonia, *Malawi* 46 G7
Livonia, *Mich.* 16 B5
Livramento, *Brazil* 31 F10
Lizard Hd., *Eng.* 37 C6
Lizotte, *Que.* 20 C1
Ljubljana, *Yugoslavia* 39 H4
Ljusne Alv, *Sweden* 35 K3
Llancaguelo L., *Argentina* 31 D11
Llandovery, *Wales* 37 C5
Llandudno, *Wales* 37 C5
Llanelli, *Wales* 37 C6
Llano Estacado, *Tex.*, etc. 24 F4
Llanos de Guarayos, *Bolivia* 30 E6
Llanos de Mojos, *Bolivia* 30 E6
Llanquihue L., *Chile* 31 C12
Lloyd George Mt., *B.C.* 12 H4
Lloydminster, *Alberta-Sask.* 14 F4
Llullaillaco, vol., *Chile* 31 D8
Lobatse, *Botswana* 47 D2
Lobito, *Angola* 46 E7
Lobster B., *Que.* 22 D2
Lobstick L., *Lab.* 19 D3
Lochaber Mines, *N.S.* 21 E2
Locnalsh, *Ont.* 18 F4
Lochgoilhead, *Scotland* 36 C3
Lochinver, *Scotland* 36 C2
Loch Lomond, *N.S.* 21 G2
Lochnagar, *Scotland* 36 D3
Lochy L., *Scotland* 36 C3
Lockeport, *N.S.* 21 B4
Lockhart, *N.S.W.* 50 F7
Lockport, *N.Y.* 17 G4
Lockwood, *Sask.* 14 J5
Lodge Cr., *Alberta* 14 F6
Łódź, *Poland* 39 J3
Loeriesfontein, *Cape Prov., Rep. of S. Africa* 47 B3
Loess Plat., *China* 44 C3
Lofoten Is., *Norway* 35 J2
Logan, *Ut.* 24 D2
Logan I., *Ont.* 18 D3
Logan Mt., *Que.* 22 D2
Logan Mt., *Yukon* 10 C2
Logansport, *Ind.* 25 J2
Lohathla, *Cape Prov., Rep. of S. Africa* 47 C2
Loire R., *France* 36 F4
Loja, *Ecuador* 30 B4
Loks Ld., *Baffin I., N.W.T.* 19 E1
Lolland, I., *Denmark* 38 G2
Lomas, Pto., *Peru* 30 B7
Lomé, *Togo, Africa* 46 D5
Lomond, *Alberta* 14 E5
Lomond, *Nfld.* 23 J2
Lomond L., *Scotland* 36 C3
Londesborough, *Ont.* 16 D4
London, *Eng.* 37 E6
London, *Ont.* 16 D5
Londonderry, *N.S.* 21 D2
Londonderry, and co., *N. Ire.* 37 B4
Londonderry C., *W. Aust.* 49 D2
Londonderry Is., *Chile* 31 C15
Londrina, *Brazil* 31 G8
Lone Butte, *B.C.* 13 K7
Lonely I., *Ont.* 16 D2
Long, B., *S.C.* 25 L4
Long Cr., *Sask.* 15 J6
Long I., *Bahamas* 29 K3
Long I., *Hudson B.* 19 B3
Long I., *Nfld.* 23 J3
Long I., *Notre Dame B., Nfld.* 23 K2
Long I., *N.Y.* 25 M2
Long I., *N.S.* 21 A3
Long L., *B.C.* 13 K6
Long L., *Me.* 22 C3
Long L., *Ont.* 18 E4
Long L., *Temiscouata, Que.* 20 E2
Long L., *Gt., Que.* 11 U6
Long Pt., *Man.* 15 M4

Long Pt., *Nfld.* 23 H2
Long Pt., *Ont.* 16 E5
Long Ra., *Nfld.* 23 J2
Long Beach, *Cal.* 24 C4
Longford, and co., *Eire* 37 B5
Longlac, *Ont.* 18 E4
Long-legged L., *Ont.* 18 A3
Long Pt. B., and Park, *Ont.* 16 E5
Long Range Mts., *N.S.* 23 J1
Longreach, *Queensland* 50 E1
Longs Peak, *Colo.* 24 E2
Longueuil, *Que.* 20 C3
Longview, *Tex.* 25 H4
Lookout C., *N.C.* 25 L4
Lookout C., *Ont.* 11 S6
Loon Cr., *Sask.* 15 J5
Loon Is., *James B.* 18 J2
Loon L., *Sask.* 15 K3
Loos, *B.C.* 13 K6
Lopatka C., *U.S.S.R.* 43 O3
Lop Nor, *Sinkiang* 44 B2
Lorain, *O.* 25 K2
Loran B., *Venezuela* 30 E2
Lord Howe I., *Pacific Oc.* 2 D6
Lorea, *Spain* 38 D6
Lorêto, *Brazil* 30 H5
Loretteville, *Que.* 20 D2
Lorica, *Colombia* 30 B2
Lorient, *France* 38 D4
L'Orignal, *Ont.* 17 L2
Lorn, Firth of, *Scotland* 36 C3
Loros, *Chile* 31 D9
Los Andes, *Chile* 31 C10
Los Alerces Nat. Park, *Argentina* 31 C12
Los Angeles, *Cal.* 24 C4
Los Angeles, *Chile* 31 C11
Loshan, *China* 40 K3
Los Mojis, *Mexico* 28 C2
Los Olmos, *Argentina* 31 E9
Los Roques Is., *Venezuela* 30 D1
Lossiemouth, *Scotland* 36 D3
Lost L., *Ont.* 15 P4
Lost L., *Ont.* 15 P5
Los Teques, *Venezuela* 30 D1
Los Vilos, *Chile* 31 C10
Lot R., *France* 38 E4
Lotbinière, *Que.* 20 D2
Lougheed I., *Franklin, N.W.T.* 10 O2
Loughrea, *Eire* 37 A5
Louisburg, *N.S.* 21 G2
Louisdale, *N.S.* 21 F2
Louise, *Alberta* 14 C5
Louise I., *B.C.* 13 E6
Louiseville, *Que.* 20 C2
Louisiade Arch., *New Guinea* 49 J2
Louisiana, state, *U.S.A.* 25 H4
Louis Trichardt, *Transvaal* 47 D1
Louisville, *Ky.* 25 J3
Lount L., *Ont.* 18 A3
Loup, R. du, *Kamouraska, etc., Que.* 20 E2
Loup, R. du, *St. Maurice, Que.* 20 C2
Lourenço Marques, *Mozambique* 47 E2
Louth, *Eng.* 37 F5
Louth, co., *Eire* 37 B5
Lovat R., *U.S.S.R.* 39 M1
Loverna, *Sask.* 14 G5
Low, *Que.* 17 J2
Low L., *Que.* 19 B3
Lowell, *Mass.* 25 M2
Lower California, state, *Mexico* 28 B2
Lower Hutt, *N.Z.* 51 E4
Lower Kiama, *N.S.W.* 50 H7
Lower Laberge, *Yukon* 12 C2
Lower Neguac, *N.B.* 22 E3
Lower Ohio, *N.S.* 21 B4
Lower Post, *B.C.* 12 F3
Lower Seal L., *Que.* 19 C2
Lower West Pubnico, *N.S.* 21 A4
Lower Wood Harbour, *N.S.* 21 A4
Lowestoft, *Eng.* 37 F5
Lowville, *N.Y.* 17 K4
Lozeau L., *Lab.* 19 E3
Luanda (Loanda), *Angola* 46 E6
Luang Prabang, *Laos* 40 K5
Lubbock, *Tex.* 24 F4
Lübeck, *Ger.* 38 G2
Lubicon L., *Alberta* 14 D2
Lublin, *Poland* 39 K3
Lubumbashi (Elisabethville), *Zaire* 46 F7
Lucan, *Ont.* 16 D4
Lucca, *Italy* 38 G5
Luce B., *Scotland* 37 C4
Lucerne, *B.C.* 13 L6
Lucerne, *Switzerland* 38 G4
Lucknow, *Ont.* 16 D4
Lucknow, *India* 40 F3
Lucky Lake, *Sask.* 14 H5
Lucyville, *Coast of Lab.* 19 F3
Luderitz, *S.W. Africa* 47 B2
Ludgate, *Ont.* 16 E2
Ludhiana, *India* 40 E2
Ludlow, *N.B.* 21 A1
Lufkin, *Tex.* 25 H4
Lugg R., *Eng.* 37 D5
Lugo, *Spain* 38 C5
Luleå, and Alv, *Sweden* 35 L2
Lumberton, *B.C.* 13 M8

Lumbok, *Indonesia* 44 D7
Lumby, *B.C.* 13 L7
Lumsden, *Nfld.* 23 L2
Lumsden, *N.Z.* 51 B6
Lumsden, *Sask.* 14 J5
Lundy I., *Eng.* 37 C6
Lune R., *Eng.* 37 D4
Lunenburg, *N.S.* 21 C3
Luni R., *India* 40 D3
Lurgan, *N. Ire.* 37 B4
Luro, *Argentina* 31 E11
Lusaka, *Zambia* 46 F7
Lusambo, *Zaire* 46 F7
Luscar, *Alberta* 14 C4
Lüshun (Port Arthur), *China* 44 E3
Lusikisiki, *Cape Prov., Rep. of S. Africa* 47 D3
Lusk, *Eire* 37 B5
Lü-ta, *China* 44 E3
Lut Desert, *Iran* 40 A2
Luton, *Eng.* 37 E6
Luxembourg, *Luxembourg* 38 F3
Luzon I., *Philippine Is.* 44 E5
Lvov, *Ukraine* 39 K3
Lybster, *Scotland* 36 D2
Lydenburg, *Transvaal* 47 E2
Lyell I., *B.C.* 13 E6
Lyell Mt., *Alberta* 14 C5
Lyell Mt., *Cal.* 24 C3
Lyell Ra., *N.Z.* 51 D4
Lyleton, *Man.* 15 L6
Lyme Regis, *Eng.* 37 D6
Lynchburg, *Va.* 25 L3
Lynden, *Ont.* 16 E4
Lynn Can., *Alaska* 12 C3
Lynn Lake, *Man.* 15 L2
Lyon, *Mich.* 16 B5
Lyons, *France* 38 F4
Lyons Falls, *N.Y.* 17 K4
Lytham St. Annes, *Eng.* 37 D5
Lyttleton, *N.Z.* 51 D5
Lytton, *B.C.* 13 K7

Maas R., *Netherlands, etc.* 38 F3
Mabel L., *B.C.* 13 L7
Maberly, *Ont.* 17 J3
Mabou, *N.S.* 21 F1
McAdam, *N.B.* 22 D4
Macaé, *Brazil* 31 J8
McAlester, *Okla.* 24 G4
MacAlpine L., *Mackenzie, N.W.T.* 10 O'
McAlves R., *Brazil* 30 H6
Macapá, *Brazil* 30 G3
Macas, *Ecuador* 30 B4
Macáu, *Brazil* 30 K5
Macau, *China* 44 D4
McAuley, *Man.* 15 L5
Macaza, and R., *Que.* 20 B2
McBride, *B.C.* 13 K6
Maccan, *N.S.* 21 C2
McCarthy, *Que.* 20 B2
Macclesfield, *Eng.* 37 D5
McClintock, *Man.* 15 O2
McClintock Chan., *Franklin, N.W.T.* 10 O3
McCook, *Neb.* 24 F2
McCreary, *Man.* 15 M5
McCusker L., *Ont.* 18 A3
McDame, *B.C.* 12 F3
Macdonald L., *W. Aust.* 49 D4
Macdonnell Ra., *N. Ter., Aust.* 49 E4
MacDowell L., *Ont.* 18 B2
Macduff, *Scotland* 36 D3
Macció, *Brazil* 30 K5
McFarlane R., *Sask.* 14 H1
Macgillycuddy's Reeks, *Eire* 37 A5
McGregor L., *Alberta* 14 E5
McGregor Ra., *Queensland* 50 D3
McGregor R., *B.C.* 13 K5
Machache Mt., *Lesotho* 47 D2
Machadodorp, *Transvaal* 47 E2
Machala, *Ecuador* 30 B4
Machattie L., *Queensland* 50 B2
Machawaian L., *Ont.* 18 E3
Machias, and B., *Me.* 22 D4
Machiasport, *Me.* 22 D4
Machichi R., *Man.* 15 P2
McInnes L., *Ont.* 15 P4
McIvor R., *Alberta* 14 F1
Mackay, *Queensland* 49 H4
MacKay L., *Mackenzie, N.W.T.* 10 M5
McKay L., *Ont.* 18 E4
MacKay R., *Alberta* 14 E2
Mackenzie, *Ont.* 18 D4
Mackenzie, dist., *N.W.T.* 10 K5
Mackenzie B., *N.W.T.* 10 G4
Mackenzie L., *Lab.* 19 E3
Mackenzie Mts., *Yukon-N.W.T.* 10 H5
Mackenzie R., *N.W.T.* 10 J4
Mackenzie Island, *Ont.* 18 B3
Mackenzie King I., *Franklin, N.W.T.* 10 M2
Mackenzie Plains, *N.Z.* 51 C6
Mackies, *Ont.* 18 C4
McKinley Mt., *Alaska* 10 D5
McKirdy, *Ont.* 18 D4
Mackinac I., *Mich.* 16 A2
Macklin, *Sask.* 14 G4

Macksville, *N.S.W.* 50 J5
Maclean, *N.S.W.* 50 J4
Maclear, *Cape Prov., Rep. of S. Africa* 47 D3
Macleay R., *N.S.W.* 50 H5
McLelan Str., *Lab.* 19 E1
McLennan, *Alberta* 14 C3
Macleod, *Alberta* 14 E6
McLeod B., *Mackenzie, N.W.T.* 10 M5
McLeod L., *B.C.* 12 J5
McLeod R., *Alberta* 14 C4
McLure, *B.C.* 13 K7
M'Clure Str., *Franklin, N.W.T.* 10 K3
MacMillan R., *Yukon* 12 C1
MacMillan Pass, *Yukon* 12 E1
McMorran, *Sask.* 14 G5
McMurray, *Alberta* 14 F2
McNutt I., *N.S.* 21 B4
Macon, *Ga.* 25 K4
Macoun, *Sask.* 15 K6
McPherson, *Mackenzie, N.W.T.* 10 G4
MacPherson Ra., *Queensland-N.S.W.* 50 J4
MacQuarie Harb., *Tasmania* 50 K12
Macquario I., *S. Pacific Oc.* 2 D7
Macquarie R., *N.S.W.* 50 G6
Macquarie R., *Tasmania* 50 L11
Mac Rae, *Yukon* 12 C2
McTavish Arm, *Mackenzie, N.W.T.* 10 L4
MacTier, *Ont.* 16 F2
McVicar B., *Mackenzie, N.W.T.* 10 L5
Madagascar (Malagasy Rep.), *Indian Oc.* 46 H8
Madagascar I., *Indian Oc.* 46 H8
Madame I., *N.S.* 23 G4
Madang, *New Guinea* 2 C5
Madawaska, *Ont.* 17 G2
Madawaska R., *Ont.* 17 H2
Madeira Is., *Atlantic Oc.* 46 B2
Madeira R., *and Falls, Brazil* 30 E5
Madcleine, Cap de la, *Que.* 22 E2
Madeleine R., *Que.* 22 E2
Madhya Pradesh, state, *India* 40 E4
Madibogo, *Cape Prov., Rep. of S. Africa* 47 D2
Madison, *Ga.* 25 K4
Madison, *Wis.* 25 H2
Madoc, *Ont.* 17 H3
Madonbaskika L., *Que.* 20 B2
Madras, *India* 40 F6
Madre, Laguna del, *Tex.* 24 G5
Madre, L. de la, *Mexico* 28 E3
Madre de Dios Arch., *Chile* 31 B14
Madre de Dios R., *Bolivia, etc.* 30 C6
Madrid, *Spain* 38 D5
Madura I., *Indonesia* 44 D7
Madurai, *India* 40 E7
Mafeking, *Cape Prov., Rep. o, S. Africa* 47 D2
Mafeking, *Man.* 15 L4
Mafeteng, *Lesotho* 47 D2
Magadan, *U.S.S.R.* 43 O3
Magalaqeen R., *Transvaal* 47 D1
Magallanes, prov., *Argentina* 31 C41
Magangue, *Colombia* 30 B2
Magdalen Is., *Que.* 22 F3
Magdalena I., *Chile* 31 C12
Magdalena R., *Colombia* 30 C2
Magdeburg, *Ger.* 38 G2
Magellan, Str. of, *S. America* 31 D14
Magersfontein, *Cape Prov., Rep. of S. A,rica* 47 C2
Maggiore L., *Italy* 38 G4
Maghera, *N. Ire.* 37 B4
Maghull, *Eng.* 19 B1
Magnet Pt., *Que.* 16 F2
Magnetawan, *Ont.* 16 F2
Magnetic Pole, N., *Franklin, N.W.T.* 10 O3
Magnitogorsk, *U.S.S.R.* 38 D3
Magog, and L., *Que.* 20 C3
Magpie, and L., *Que.* 22 E1
Magpie R., *Ont.* 18 F4
Magpie R., *Que.* 22 E1
Magrath, *Alberta* 14 E6
Maguary C., *Brazil* 30 H3
Maguse L., *Keewatin, N.W.T.* 11 P5
Mahai Penin., *N.Z.* 51 G3
Mahanadi R., *India* 40 F4
Maharashtra, state, *India* 40 E5
Mahé, *India* 40 D6
Mahone Bay, *N.S.* 21 C3
Mahood L., *B.C.* 13 K7
Maidstone, *Eng.* 37 F6
Maiduguri, *Nigeria* 46 E4
Maikala Ra., *India* 40 F4
Maillard C., *Que.* 20 D2
Main à Dieu, *N.S.* 21 G1
Mainana, *Afghanistan* 40 B1
Main Barrier Ra., *S. Aust.-N.S.W.* 50 C5
Main Centre, *Sask.* 14 H5
Main Duck I., *Ont.* 17 J4
Maine, state, *U.S.A.* 23 N1
Mainstream, *Me.* 22 C4

Mainz, *Ger.* 38 G3
Maipo, *Argentina* 31 D10
Maipu, *Argentina* 31 F11
Maisi C., *Cuba* 29 K3
Maitland, *N.S.W.* 50 H6
Maitland, *N.S.* 21 D2
Maitland Bridge, *N.S.* 21 B3
Majorca (I.), *Balearic Is.* 38 E6
Majuba Hill, *Natal* 47 D2
Makassar (Makasar), *Celebes* 44 D7
Makassar Str., *Indonesia* 44 D7
Makeyevka, *Ukraine* 39 O3
Makkovik, *Lab.* 19 F3
Maklautsi, *Botswana* 47 D1
Makokibatan L., *Ont.* 18 E3
Makoop L., *Ont.* 18 C2
Makran Dasht, *Iran-Afghanistan* 40 A3
Mal B., *Eire* 37 A5
Mal B., *Que.* 22 E2
Malacca, *Malaya* 44 C6
Malacca, Str. of, *Malaya-Sumatra* 44 B6
Malad City, *Ida.* 24 D2
Maladetta Mt., *Spain* 38 E5
Malaga, *Spain* 38 C6
Malagasy Rep., *Madagascar I.* 46 H8
Malaher L., *Ont.* 18 A3
Malakova, *B.C.* 13 L7
Malanzan, *Argentina* 31 D10
Mälarero L., *Sweden* 35 K4
Malartic, *Que.* 19 B4
Malawi, rep., *E. Africa* 46 G7
Malaya, *Malaysia* 44 C6
Malay Penin., *S. Asia* 44 C6
Malaysia, *S.E. Asia* 44 C6
Malbaie L., *Que.* 20 D2
Malden I., *Pacific Oc.* 2 E5
Maldive Is., *Indian Oc.* 40 D7
Maldonado, *Uruguay* 31 G10
Mâle, L. du, *Que.* 20 B1
Maléa C., *Greece* 39 K6
Malheur L., *Ore.* 24 C2
Mali, rep., *W. Africa* 46 C4
Malignant Cove, *N.S.* 21 E2
Maligne L., *Alberta* 14 C4
Malin Hd., *Eire* 37 B4
Mallaig, *Scotland* 36 C3
Malloch C., *Borden I., N.W.T.* 10 L2
Mallorytown, *Ont.* 17 K3
Mallow, *Eire* 37 A5
Malmesbury, *Cape Prov., Rep. of S. Africa* 47 B3
Malmö, *Sweden* 38 H2
Malo Pt., *Pan.* 29 J6
Malone, *Ont.* 17 H3
Malpeque B., *P.E.I.* 21 D1
Malta, *Mont.* 24 E1
Malta, I., *Mediterranean Sea* 46 E2
Maltahöhe, *S.W. Africa* 47 B1
Malton, *Eng.* 37 E4
Malton, *Ont.* 16 F4
Malvina, *Que.* 20 D3
Malwa Plat., *India* 40 E4
Mamabule, *Botswana* 47 D1
Mammamattawa, *Ont.* 18 F3
Mamore R., *Bolivia, etc.* 30 DC
Mampas, *Transvaal* 47 D1
Man, Calf of, *Isle of Man* 37 C4
Man, Isle of, *Brit. Isles* 37 C4
Mana R., *Fr. Guiana* 30 G3
Manacapura, *Brazil* 30 E4
Manado, *Celebes* 44 E6
Managua L., *Nicaragua* 29 G5
Manapouri L., *N.Z.* 51 A6
Manaus, *Brazil* 30 E4
Manchester, *Eng.* 37 D5
Manchester, *N.H.* 25 M2
Manchouli, *China* 44 D2
Manchuria, *China* 44 E2
Mandalay, *Burma* 40 J4
Mangalore, *India* 40 D6
Manglares C., *Ecuador* 30 B3
Mangles C., *Ecuador* 30 B3
Manicoré, *Brazil* 30 E5
Manicouagan, and R., *Que.* 22 C1
Manicouagan, L., *Que.* 19 D3
Manicouagan Penin., *Que.* 22 C2
Manicouagan, Petit Lac, *Que.* 22 D1
Manigotagan L., *Man.* 15 O5
Manihiki Is., *Pacific Oc.* 2 E5
Manila, *Philippine Is.* 44 E5
Manilla, *N.S.W.* 50 H5
Manipur, ter., *India* 40 H4
Manisa, *Turkey* 39 L6
Manistee, *Mich.* 25 J2
Manito L., *Sask.* 14 G4
Manitoba, prov., *Canada* 10 O7
Manitoba, L., *Man.* 15 M5
Manitou, *Man.* 15 M6
Manitou L., *Algonquin Park, Ont.* 16 D2
Manitou L., *Kendra, Ont.* 18 B4
Manitou L., *Que.* 22 E1
Manitou L., *Sask.* 14 J5
Manitou R., *Ont.* 15 P5
Manitoulin, co., and I., *Ont.* 16 C2
Manitouwadge, *Ont.* 18 E4
Manitowaning, and B., *Ont.* 16 D2
Maniwaki, *Que.* 17 J1
Manizales, *Colombia* 30 B2
Mankato, *Minn.* 25 H2
Mankota, *Sask.* 14 H6

Manly, *N.S.W.* 50 H6
Mannar. G. of, *Sri Lanka-India* 40 E7
Mannheim, *Ger.* 38 G3
Manning, *Alberta* 14 C2
Manning Pt., *Alaska* 10 F3
Manning R., *N.S.W.* 50 H7
Mannsville, *N.Y.* 17 J4
Manokwari I., *W. Irian* 44 F7
Manouane, L., and R., *Que.* 20 B2
Manouane L., *Que.* 22 B1
Manouane R., *Que.* 22 B2
Mansel I., *Keewatin, N.W.T.* 11 S5
Mansfield, *Eng.* 37 E5
Mansfield, *O.* 25 K2
Mansfield, *Victoria* 50 F8
Mansonville, *Que.* 20 C3
Manson Cr., *B.C.* 12 H5
Manta, *Ecuador* 30 A4
Manta, B. of, *Ecuador* 30 A4
Manukau, *N.Z.* 51 E2
Manybone Cr., *Sask.* 15 K5
Many Peaks, *Queensland* 50 H2
Manzanillo, *Cuba* 29 J3
Manzanillo, *Mexico* 28 D4
Manzini, *Swaziland* 47 E2
Maoke Mts., *W. Irian* 44 F7
Mapimi, *Mexico* 28 D2
Maple Creek, *Sask.* 14 G6
Mapleton, *N.S.* 21 C2
Maputa R., *Mozambique* 47 E2
Maquinchao, *Argentina* 31 D12
Maraã, *Brazil* 30 D4
Maraça I., *Brazil* 30 H3
Maraca L., *Brazil* 30 E3
Maracaibo, *Venezuela* 30 C1
Maracaibo, Lagoon of, *Venezuela* 30 C2
Maracás, *Brazil* 30 J6
Maracay, *Venezuela* 30 D1
Maragogipe, *Brazil* 30 J6
Marajo, I. of, *Brazil* 30 H4
Maralinga, *S. Aust.* 49 E6
Maranhão R., *Brazil* 30 H6
Maranon R., *Peru* 30 B5
Marañon R., *Peru* 30 C4
Mara Park, *Ont.* 17 F3
Marathon, *Ont.* 18 E4
Maraú, *Brazil* 30 K6
Marble I., *Keewatin, N.W.T.* 11 Q5
Marble Bar, *W. Aust.* 49 C4
Marble Hall, *Transvaal* 47 D2
Marbleton, *Que.* 20 D3
Marchena I., *Pacific Oc.* 31 N16
Mar Chiquita, *Buenos Aires, Argentina* 31 F11
Mar Chiquita, *Santa Fé, Argentina* 31 E10
Marcus I., *Pacific Oc.* 2 D3
Mar del Plata, *Argentina* 31 F11
Marechal Floriana, *Brazil* 30 K5
Maree L., *Scotland* 36 C3
Mareth, *Tunisia* 46 E2
Marfa, *Tex.* 24 F4
Margaree Harbour, *N.S.* 23 G3
Margaree Is., *N.S.* 21 F1
Margaret L., *Alberta* 14 D1
Margaret Bay, *B.C.* 13 G7
Margaretsville, *N.S.* 22 E4
Margarita I., *Venezuela* 30 E1
Margate, *Eng.* 37 F6
Margie, *Alberta* 14 F3
Margo, *Sask.* 15 K5
Marguerite R., *Que.* 22 D1
Marian L., *Mackenzie, N.W.T.* 12 M1
Marian Lake, *Mackenzie* 12 O1
Marianas Is., *Pacific Oc.* 44 G5
Mariato Pt., *Pan.* 29 H6
Maria Van Diemen C., *N.Z.* 51 D1
Marico R., *Transvaal* 47 D2
Maricourt (Wakeham Bay), *Que.* 19 C1
Maricourt L., *Que.* 19 C2
Marié R., *Brazil* 30 D3
Marie Galante I., *W. Indies* 29 M4
Mariental, *S.W. Africa* 47 B1
Maricoville, *Que.* 20 C3
Marinca, *Brazil* 31 G8
Marinette, *Wis.* 25 J1
Marion I., *Indian Oc.* 3 M7
Marion L., *Va.* 25 L3
Maripa, *Brazil* 30 E3
Maritsa R., *Bulgaria, etc.* 39 L5
Mariupol, *Ukraine* 39 O4
Marj, El, *Libya* 46 F2
Markdale, *Ont.* 16 E3
Markham, *Ont.* 17 F4
Markham B., *Baffin I., N.W.T.* 19 C1
Markstay, *Ont.* 16 E1
Marlbank, *Ont.* 17 H3
Marmara, Sea of, *Turkey* 39 M5
Marmora, *Ont.* 17 H3
Maroa, *Venezuela* 30 D3
Maroni R., *Fr. Guiana-Surinam* 30 G2
Marquesas Is., *Pacific Oc.* 2 F5
Marquette, *Ont.* 18 E5
Marrakesh, *Morocco* 46 C2
Mars R., *Que.* 20 D1
Marsala, *Sicily* 38 H6
Marseilles, *France* 38 F5
Marsh L., *Yukon* 12 C2

Marshall, *Sask.* 14 G4
Marshall Is., *Pacific Oc.* 2 D4
Marshalltown. *Ia.* 25 H2
Marshfield, *Ore.* 24 B2
Mars Hill, *Me.* 22 C3
Martaban, and G. of, *Burma* 40 J5
Martin Falls, *Ont.* 18 E3
Martinho, *Brazil* 30 F5
Martinique I., *W. Indies* 29 M5
Martius Cataract, *Brazil* 30 G5
Marton, *N.Z.* 51 E4
Mary, *U.S.S.R.* 40 B1
Maryborough, *Queensland* 50 J2
Maryborough, *Victoria* 50 D8
Marydale, *Cape Prov., Rep. of S Africa* 47 C2
Maryfield, *Sask.* 15 L6
Mary Henry Mt., *B.C.* 12 H3
Maryland, state, *U.S.A.* 25 L3
Marystown, *Nfld.* 23 K3
Marysville, *B.C.* 13 N8
Marysville, *N.B.* 22 D3
Marzo C., *Colombia* 30 B2
Masabi, *Bolivia* 30 E7
Masaya, *Nicaragua* 29 G5
Maseru, *Lesotho* 47 D2
Masham Mills, *Que.* 20 A3
Mashhad, *Iran* 42 D5
Masiati Mt., *Venezuela* 30 E3
Masira I., *Arabia* 40 A4
Mask L., *Eire* 37 A5
Maskinongé, and L., *Que.* 20 C2
Maskinongé R., *Que.* 20 C2
Mason Cr., *B.C.* 12 J4
Mason City, *Ia.* 25 H2
Massachusetts, state, *U.S.A.* 25 M2
Massawa, *Ethiopia* 46 G4
Massawippi, and L., *Que.* 20 D3
Massena, *N.Y.* 17 L3
Masset, *B.C.* 13 D6
Masset Inlet, *B.C.* 13 D6
Massey, *Ont.* 16 C1
Massif Central, *France* 38 E4
Masson, *Que.* 17 K2
Masterton, *N.Z.* 51 E4
Matachewan, *Ont.* 18 H5
Matadi, *Zaire* 46 E6
Matador, *Sask.* 14 H5
Matagalpa, *Nicaragua* 29 G5
Matagami L., *Que.* 19 B4
Matagorda I., *Tex.* 24 G5
Matamek Factory, *Que.* 22 E1
Matamoros, *Mexico* 28 E2
Matane, *Que.* 22 D2
Matanzas, *Cuba* 29 H3
Matapan C., *Greece* 39 K6
Matapedia, *Que.* 22 D3
Matapedia L., *Que.* 22 D2
Matarani, *Peru* 30 C7
Matatiele, *Cape Prov., Rep. of S. Africa* 47 D3
Mataura, *N.Z.* 51 B7
Matawai, *N.Z.* 51 F3
Matawin R., *Que.* 20 C2
Matchuala, *Mexico* 28 D3
Matheson, *Ont.* 18 H4
Matheson Island, *Man.* 15 N5
Mathura, *India* 40 E3
Matinenda L., *Ont.* 16 B1
Matjiesfontein, *Cape Prov., Rep. of S. Africa* 47 C3
Matlock, *Eng.* 37 E5
Mato Grosso, *Brazil* 30 F6
Mato Grosso, Plat. of, *Brazil* 30 G7
Matre, I. la, *Mackenzie, N.W.T.* 12 M1
Mattagami L., *Ont.* 18 G5
Mattagami R., *Ont.* 18 G4
Mattawa L., *N. Ont.* 18 C4
Mattawa, and R., *S. Ont.* 17 G1
Mattice, *Ont.* 18 G4
Maturin, *Venezuela* 30 E2
Maugerville, *N.B.* 22 D4
Mauritania, *W. Africa* 46 C4
Mauritius, *Indian Oc.* 3 M6
Maxcanu, *Mexico* 28 F3
Maxville, *Ont.* 17 L2
May, I. of, *Scotland* 36 D3
May Pt., *Nfld.* 23 J3
Mayaguana I., *Bahamas* 29 K3
Mayagüez, *Puerto Rico* 29 L4
Maybole, *Scotland* 37 C4
Mayerthorpe, *Alberta* 14 D4
Mayfair, *Sask.* 14 H4
Maynard L., *Ont.* 18 B3
Maynooth, *Eire* 37 B5
Maynooth, *Ont.* 17 G2
Mayo, *Yukon* 10 G5
Mayo. co., *Eire* 37 A5
Mayo R., *Argentina* 31 C13
Mayville, *N.Y.* 16 F5
Mazana L., *Que.* 20 D3
Mazapil, *Mexico* 28 D3
Mazar-i-Sharif, *Afghanistan* 40 C1
Mazatlan, *Mexico* 28 C3
Mazuruni R., *Guyana* 30 F2
Mbabane, *Swaziland* 47 E2
Mbala, *Zambia* 46 G6
Mead L., *Nev., etc.* 24 D3
Meadow L., *Sask.* 14 G3
Meadow Lake Park, *Sask.* 14 G3
Meaford, *Ont.* 16 E3
Meaghers Grant, *N.S.* 21 D3

Meander River, *Alberta* 14 C1
Mearim R., *Brazil* 30 H5
Meath, co., *Eire* 37 B5
Mecatina C., and I., *Que.* 23 H1
Mecatini I., and R., Lit., *Que.* 23 H1
Mecca, *Saudi Arabia* 42 C6
Medan, *Sumatra* 44 B6
Medanos, *Argentina* 31 E11
Medellin, *Colombia* 30 B2
Medford, *Ore.* 24 B2
Medicine R., *Alberta* 14 D4
Medicine Hat, *Alberta* 14 F5
Medicine Stone L., *Ont.* 18 A3
Medina, *N.Y.* 17 G4
Medinas, *Argentina* 31 D9
Mediterranean Sea, *Europe-Africa* 42 A5
Medstead, *Sask.* 14 H4
Meekatharra, *W. Aust.* 49 B5
Meelpaeg L., *Nfld.* 23 J2
Meerut, *India* 40 E3
Megantic, and L., *Que.* 20 D3
Megantic Mt., *Que.* 20 D3
Meghalaya, state, *India* 40 H3
Megiscane. L., *Que.* 20 B1
Meighen I., *Franklin, N.W.T.* 10 O1
Meilleur Cr., *N.W.T.* 12 H2
Mejillones, *Chile* 31 C8
Mekatina, *Ont.* 18 G5
Mekinac L., *Que.* 20 C2
Mekong R., *S.E. Asia* 44 C8
Melange, *Angola* 46 E2
Melbourne, *Que.* 20 C3
Melbourne, *Victoria* 50 E8
Melchor Ocanipo, *Mexico* 28 D4
Meldrum Bay, *Ont.* 16 B2
Melfort, *Sask.* 15 J4
Melgund, *Ont.* 18 E4
Melilla, *Morocco* 46 C2
Melita, *Man.* 15 L6
Melitopol, *Ukraine* 39 N4
Melo, *Uruguay* 31 G10
Melrose, *N.S.* 21 E2
Melrose, *Scotland* 36 D4
Melton Mowbray, *Eng.* 37 E5
Melville, *Sask.* 15 K5
Melville B., *Greenland* 11 W2
Melville C., *Queensland* 49 G2
Melville I., *Franklin, N.W.T.* 10 M2
Melville I., *N. Ter., Aust.* 49 E2
Melville L., *Lab.* 19 F3
Melville Penin., *Franklin, N.W.T.* 11 S4
Melville Sd., *Mackenzie, N.W.T.* 10 N4
Melvin L., *Eire* 37 A4
Memphis, *Mo.* 25 H2
Memphis, *Tenn.* 25 J3
Memphremagog L., *Que.* 20 C3
Memramcook, *N.B.* 21 C1
Menai Str., *Wales* 37 C5
Menam, R., *Thailand* 43 J7
Menam Chao Bhraya R., *Siam* 40 J5
Menderes R., *Turkey* 39 M6
Mendip Hills, *Eng.* 37 D6
Mendocino C., *Cal.* 24 B2
Mendoza, *Argentina* 31 D10
Menihek, *Coast of Lab.* 19 D3
Menindee, *N.S.W.* 50 D6
Mentawai Is., *Indonesia* 44 B7
Mentz L., *Cape Prov., Rep. of S. Africa* 47 D3
Menzies, *W. Aust.* 49 C5
Meota, *Sask.* 14 G4
Merashoen I., *Nfld.* 23 K3
Mercedes, *Buenos Aires, Argentina* 31 F10
Mercedes, *Corrientes, Argentina* 31 F9
Mercedes, *Uruguay* 31 F10
Merchant B., *Baffin I., N.W.T.* 11 W4
Mercoal, *B.C.* 13 L7
Mercy C., *Baffin I., N.W.T.* 11 W4
Mergui, *Burma* 40 J6
Mergui Arch., *Burma* 40 J6
Merida, *Mexico* 28 G3
Merida, *Venezuela* 30 C2
Meridian, *Miss.* 25 J4
Merioneth, co., *Wales* 37 C5
Merlin, *Ont.* 16 C5
Merrick Mt., *Scotland* 37 C4
Merrickville, *Ont.* 17 K3
Merritt, *B.C.* 13 K7
Merriwa, *N.S.W.* 50 H6
Merry C., *Man.* 15 O1
Mersey R., *Eng.* 37 D5
Merthyr Tydfil, *Wales* 37 D6
Merv, *U.S.S.R.* 42 E5
Meshed, *Persia* 40 A1
Mesilinka R., *B.C.* 12 H4
Mesopotamian Plains, *Iraq* 42 C5
Messina, *Transvaal* 47 E1
Messina, and Str. of, *Sicily* 39 H6
Messines, *Que.* 17 K1
Meta R., *Colombia* 30 C3
Metabetchouan, and R. *Que.* 20 D1
Metagama, *Ont.* 18 H5
Meta Incognita Penin., *Baffin I., N.W.T.* 19 D1
Metaripuá, *Brazil* 30 D5
Metaskuak L., *Que.* 20 D2

Place	Map	Ref
Meteghan Sta., *N.S.*	21	A3
Methil, *Scotland*	36	D3
Methven, *N.Z.*	51	C5
Metis Ls., *Que.*	22	D2
Metis sur Mer, *Que.*	22	C2
Metz, *France*	38	F3
Meuse R., *France*	38	F3
Mexiana I., *Brazil*	30	H3
Mexicali, *Mexico*	28	C4
Mexico, tn., *Mexico*	28	E4
Mexico, rep., *N. America*	28	C3
Mexico, G. of, *Mexico*	28	F2
Mezen, and G. of, *U.S.S.R.*	35	P2
Mezen R., *U.S.S.R.*	35	Q3
Meziadin L., *B.C.*	12	F4
Miami, *Fla.*	25	K5
Miami, *Man.*	15	M6
Michigan, state, *U.S.A.*	25	J2
Michigan L., *Canada-U.S.A.*	25	J2
Michigan City, *Ind.*	25	J3
Michikamau, *Lab.*	19	E3
Michipicoten, and B., *Ont.*	18	F5
Michipicoten Harb., *Ont.*	18	F4
Michipicoten I., *Ont.*	18	E5
Michurinsk, *U.S.S.R.*	39	P2
Micronesia, *Pacific Oc.*	2	C4
Middelburg, *Cape Prov., Rep. of S. Africa*	47	C3
Middelburg, *Transvaal*	47	D2
Middle L., *Sask.*	14	J4
Middle Musquodoboit, *N.S.*	21	D2
Middle River Village, *B.C.*	12	H5
Middle Savage Is., *Hudson Str.*	19	D1
Middlesex, co., *Ont.*	16	D4
Middleton, *N.S.*	21	B3
Midhurst, *Ont.*	16	F3
Midland, *Ont.*	16	E3
Midland, *Tex.*	24	F4
Midlothian, co., *Scotland*	36	D4
Midway I., *Pacific Oc.*	2	E3
Miguick, *Que.*	20	C2
Mikkeli, *Finland*	35	M3
Mikkwa R., *Alberta*	14	D2
Milagres, *Brazil*	30	K5
Milan, *Italy*	38	G4
Milan, *N.H.*	22	B4
Milan, *Tenn.*	25	J3
Milang, *S. Aust.*	50	M7
Milbanke Sd., *B.C.*	13	F6
Mildmay, *Ont.*	16	D3
Mildura, *Victoria*	50	D7
Miles, *Queensland*	50	H3
Miles City, *Mont.*	24	E1
Milestone, *Sask.*	14	J6
Milford, *Eire*	37	B4
Milford Sd., *N.Z.*	51	A6
Milford Haven, *Wales*	37	C6
Milieu, R. du, *Que*	20	B2
Milk R., *Alberta*	14	F6
Milk R., *Mont.*	24	E1
Mill I., *Keewatin, N.W.T.*	11	T5
Mill Brook, *Ont.*	17	G3
Millerton, *N.B.*	21	B1
Millertown, *Nfld.*	23	J2
Millertown Junction, *Nfld.*	23	J2
Millet, *Alberta*	14	E4
Millicent, *S. Aust.*	50	C8
Millinocket, *Me.*	22	C4
Millridge, *Me.*	22	D4
Mills L., *Mackenzie, N.W.T.*	12	L2
Milltown, *N.B.*	22	D4
Milltown, *Nfld.*	23	K3
Mill Village, *N.S.*	21	C3
Milne B., *New Guinea*	49	J1
Milne Ld., *Greenland*	11	Z3
Milo, *Me.*	22	C4
Milos I., *Greece*	39	K6
Milparinka, *N.S.W.*	50	C4
Milton, *N.Z.*	51	B7
Milton, *N.S.*	21	C3
Milton, *Ont.*	16	F4
Miltown Malbay, *Eire*	37	A5
Milverton, *Ont.*	16	E4
Milwaukee, *Wis.*	25	J2
Mimico, *Ont.*	16	F4
Miminiska L., *Ont.*	18	D3
Mina L., *Que.*	19	D2
Minago R., *Man.*	15	M3
Minaki, *Ont.*	18	A3
Minas, *Uruguay*	31	F10
Minas Basin, *N.S.*	21	C2
Minas Chan., *N.S.*	21	C2
Minas Gerais, *Brazil*	30	H7
Minas Novas, *Brazil*	30	J7
Minch, Lit., *Hebrides, Scotland*	36	B3
Minch, N., *Hebrides, Scotland*	36	B2
Mindanao I., *Philippine Is.*	44	E6
Minden, *Ont.*	17	G3
Mindoro I., *Philippine Is.*	44	E5
Mine Centre, *Ont.*	18	B4
Mingan, *Que.*	22	E1
Mingan Is., and R., *Que.*	22	F1
Mingary, *S. Aust.*	50	B6
Minho R., *Spain-Portugal*	38	C5
Miniota, *Man.*	15	L5
Minipi L., *Lab.*	19	E3
Mink L., *Que.*	20	C1
Minneapolis, *Minn.*	25	H1
Minnedosa, *Man.*	15	M5
Minnesota, state, *U.S.A.*	24	G1
Minnesota R., *Minn.*	24	G2
Minnitaki L., *Ont.*	18	A3
Minorca (I.), *Balearic Is.*	38	E5
Minot, *N. Dak.*	24	F1
Min Shan, *China*	44	C3
Minsk, *U.S.S.R.*	39	L2
Minto, *N.B.*	21	A1
Minto, *Yukon*	12	B1
Minto L., *Que.*	19	B2
Minton, *Sask.*	15	J6
Minya Konka Mt., *China*	44	C4
Mio, *Mich.*	16	A3
Miquelon & I., *Atlantic Oc.*	23	J3
Mira Gut, *N.S.*	21	G1
Miramichi B., *N.B.*	22	E3
Miramichi R., *N.B.*	21	A1
Miranda, *Brazil*	30	F8
Mirboo North, *Victoria*	50	F9
Mirim L., *Uruguay*	31	G10
Mirjawa, *Persia*	40	B3
Mirond L., *Sask.*	15	K3
Mirzapur, *India*	40	F4
Miscou I., *N.B.*	22	E3
Miscouche, *P.E.I.*	21	D1
Mishikamats L., *Lab.*	19	E3
Misiones, prov., *Argentina*	31	G9
Miskolc, *Hungary*	39	K3
Missanabie, *Ont.*	18	F4
Missinaibi L., and R., *Ont.*	18	G4
Mission, *B.C.*	13	J8
Missisa L., *Ont.*	18	F2
Mississagi Park, *Ont.*	18	G5
Mississagi R., *Ont.*	18	G5
Mississippi L., and R., *Ont.*	17	J2
Mississippi R., and state, *U.S.A.*	25	H4
Missoula, *Mont.*	24	D1
Missouri, state, *U.S.A.*	25	H3
Missouri Plat., *N. Dak.-Sask.*	24	F1
Missouri R., *U.S.A.*	24	E1
Mistake B., *Que.*	19	B2
Mistassibi R., *Que.*	22	A2
Mistassini, and R., *Que.*	22	A2
Mistassini L., *Que.*	19	C3
Mistastin L., *Lab.*	19	E2
Mistatim, *Sask.*	15	K4
Mistehae L., *Alberta*	14	D3
Misty L., *Man.*	15	L1
Mitchell, *Ont.*	16	D4
Mitchell, *Queensland*	50	F3
Mitchell, *S. Dak.*	24	G2
Mitchell L., *B.C.*	13	K6
Mitchell Mt., *N.C.*	25	K3
Mitchell R., *Queensland*	49	G3
Mitchelstown, *Eire*	37	A5
Mitchinamecus L., and R., *Que.*	20	B2
Mitkof I., *Alaska*	12	D4
Mituas, *Colombia*	30	D3
Mizoram, state, *India*	40	H4
Mjösa L., *Norway*	35	J3
Mo, *Norway*	35	J2
Moak L., *Man.*	15	N3
Moama, *N.S.W.*	50	E7
Moamba, *Mozambique*	47	E2
Moar L., *Que.*	15	O4
Moars B., *Que.*	18	J2
Moberly, *Mo.*	25	H3
Moberly L., *B.C.*	12	K5
Moberly R., *B.C.*	12	K4
Mobile, *Ala.*	25	J4
Mocajuba, *Brazil*	30	H4
Moçambique, *S. Africa*	46	G8
Moçambique, tn., *Moçambique*	46	H7
Moçambique Chan, *Indian Oc.*	46	G8
Moche, *Peru*	30	B5
Mochudi, *Botswana*	47	D1
Mocoa, *Colombia*	30	B3
Mocorito, *Mexico*	28	C2
Moctezuma, *Mexico*	28	C2
Modder R., *Orange F.S.*	47	C2
Modder River, *Cape Prov., Rep. of S. Africa*	47	C2
Modena, *Italy*	38	G4
Moe, *Victoria*	50	F9
Moffat, *Scotland*	37	D4
Mogadishu (Mogadiscio), *Somali Rep.*	46	H5
Mogaung, *Burma*	40	J3
Mogilev Podolskiy, *Ukraine*	39	L3
Mogilev, *U.S.S.R.*	39	M2
Mohale's Hoek, *Lesotho*	47	D3
Moine, L. du, *Que.*	19	B4
Moines R., *Ia.*	25	H2
Moisie, and B., *Que.*	22	D1
Moisie R., *Que.*	22	D1
Mojave Desert, *Cal.*	24	C4
Mokai, *N.Z.*	51	E3
Mokau R., *N.Z.*	51	E3
Mokomon, *Ont.*	18	D4
Mokpo, *S. Korea*	44	E3
Moldavia, rep., *U.S.S.R.*	39	M4
Molde, *Norway*	35	H3
Molepolole, *Bechuanaland*	47	D1
Mollendo, *Peru*	30	C7
Molong, *N.S.W.*	50	G6
Molopo R., *S. Africa*	47	C2
Molotov, *U.S.S.R.*	35	D3
Molson L., *Man.*	15	N3
Molteno, *Cape Prov., Rep. of S. Africa*	47	D3
Molucca Is., *Indonesia*	44	E7
Molucca Passage, *Indonesia*	43	L9
Mombasa, *Kenya*	46	H6
Mompós, *Colombia*	30	C2
Mona I., *W. Indies*	29	L4
Monaghan, and co., *Eire*	37	B4
Mona Passage, *W. Indies*	29	L4
Monarch Mt., *B.C.*	13	H7
Monaro Ra., *N.S.W.*	50	G8
Monashee Mts., *B.C.*	13	L7
Monclova, *Mexico*	28	D2
Moncouche L., *Que.*	22	B2
Moncton, *N.B.*	21	C1
Mondonac L., *Que.*	20	C2
Monet, *Que.*	20	B1
Monghyr, *India*	40	G3
Mongolia, rep., *Asia*	44	B2
Monk, *Que.*	20	E2
Monkton, *Ont.*	16	D4
Monmouth, and co., *Eng.*	37	D6
Monroe, *La.*	25	H4
Monroeville, *Ala.*	25	J4
Monrovia, *Liberia*	46	B5
Monsomshi L., *Ont.*	15	R3
Montagu, *Cape Prov., Rep. of S. Africa*	47	C3
Montague, *P.E.I.*	21	E1
Montague, *Yukon*	12	C2
Montague I., *Alaska*	10	E5
Montana, state, *U.S.A.*	24	D1
Montana, La, *Peru*	30	C5
Montcerf, *Que.*	20	A2
Montebello, *Que.*	17	K2
Monte Bello Is., *W. Aust.*	49	A4
Monte Carlo, *Monaco*	38	F5
Monte Caseros, *Argentina*	31	F9
Monte Christo, *Dominican Rep.*	29	J4
Montego Bay, *Jamaica*	29	J4
Montello, *Nev.*	24	D2
Montemorelos, *Mexico*	28	E2
Monte Nuevas, *Argentina*	31	D11
Monteria, *Colombia*	30	B2
Monterrey, *Mexico*	28	D2
Montes Claros, *Brazil*	30	J7
Montevideo, *Uruguay*	31	F11
Montfort, *Que.*	20	B3
Montgomery, *Ala.*	25	J4
Montgomery, and co., *Wales*	37	D5
Monticello, *Me.*	22	C3
Mont Joli, *Que.*	22	C2
Mont Laurier, *Que.*	20	B2
Mont Louis, *Que.*	22	E2
Montmagny, *Que.*	20	D2
Montmartre, *Sask.*	15	K5
Montmorency, and R., *Que.*	20	D2
Monto, *Queensland*	50	H2
Mont Orford Park, *Que.*	20	C3
Montpelier, *Vt.*	25	M2
Montpellier, *France*	38	E5
Montpellier, *Que.*	17	K2
Montreal, *Que.*	20	C3
Montreal I., *L. Superior, Ont.*	18	F5
Montreal Pt., *Man.*	15	H4
Montreal R., *Sudbury, Ont.*	18	F5
Montreal R., *Timiskaming, Ont.*	18	H5
Montreal R., and L., *Sask.*	14	J3
Montrose, *Colo.*	24	E3
Montrose, *Scotland*	36	D3
Montserrat I., *W. Indies*	29	M4
Mont Tremblant Park, *Que.*	20	B2
Moonbeam, *Ont.*	18	C4
Moonie, *Queensland*	50	H3
Moonie R., *N.S.W.-Queensland*	50	G3
Moonta, *S. Aust.*	50	A7
Moore L., *W. Aust.*	49	B5
Moorhead, *Minn.*	24	G1
Moor Lake Sta., *Ont.*	17	H1
Moose L., *B.C.*	13	L6
Moose L., *Man.*	15	M4
Moose Creek, *Ont.*	20	B3
Moose Factory, *Ont.*	18	H3
Moosehead L., *Me.*	22	B4
Moose Jaw, *Sask.*	14	J5
Moose Lake, *Man.*	15	L4
Moose Mountain Cr., *Sask.*	15	K5
Moose Mountain Park, *Sask.*	15	K6
Moose River, tn., and R., *Ont.*	18	H3
Moosomin, *Sask.*	15	L5
Moosonee, *Ont.*	18	H3
Moquegua, *Peru*	30	C7
Moradabad, *India*	40	E3
Morar L., *Scotland*	36	C3
Morava R., *Czechoslovakia*	39	J3
Moravian Gate, *Czechoslovakia*	39	J3
Morawhanna, *Guyana*	30	F2
Moray, co., *Scotland*	36	D3
Moray Firth, *Scotland*	36	D3
Morden, *Man.*	15	M6
Morden, *N.S.*	21	B2
Morecambe B., *Eng.*	37	D5
Moree, *N.S.W.*	50	G4
Morelia, *Mexico*	28	D4
Morena Serra, *Spain*	38	C6
Moresby I., *B.C.*	13	D6
Moreton I., *Queensland*	50	J3
Morgan, *S. Aust.*	50	B6
Morgan City, *La.*	25	H5
Morice L., *B.C.*	13	G6
Morice R., *B.C.*	13	G5
Moricetown, *B.C.*	12	G5
Morinville, *Alberta*	14	E4
Morkill R., *B.C.*	13	K6
Morley River, *Yukon*	12	D2
Morocco, *N. Africa*	46	C2
Moron, *Cuba*	29	J3
Morona R., *Peru*	30	B4
Morpeth, *Eng.*	37	E4
Morpeth, *Ont.*	16	D5
Morrinsville, *N.Z.*	51	E2
Morris, *Man.*	15	N6
Morrisburg, *Ont.*	17	K3
Morristown, *N.Y.*	17	K3
Morse, *Sask.*	14	H5
Morshansk, *U.S.S.R.*	39	P2
Mortes, R. das, *Brazil*	30	G6
Mortier B., *Nfld.*	23	K3
Mortlach, *Sask.*	14	H5
Moruya, and R., *N.S.W.*	50	H7
Morven, *Queensland*	50	F3
Morwell, *Victoria*	50	F9
Moscow, *U.S.S.R.*	39	O2
Moselle R., *Ger.*	38	F3
Mosers River, *N.S.*	21	E3
Mosgiel, *N.Z.*	51	C6
Mosquito B., *Que.*	19	B1
Mossamedes, *Angola*	46	D7
Mossel Bay, *Cape Prov., Rep. of S. Africa*	47	C3
Mossoro, *Brazil*	30	K5
Mossoro B., *Brazil*	30	K4
Moss Vale, *N.S.W.*	50	H7
Mossy Pt., *Man.*	15	N4
Mostar. *Yugoslavia*	39	J5
Mostardas, *Brazil*	31	G10
Mösting C., *Greenland*	11	Z5
Mosul, *Iraq*	42	C5
Motherwell, *Scotland*	36	D4
Motihari, *India*	40	G3
Motueka, *N.Z.*	51	D5
Motupe, *Peru*	30	B5
Mouchalagane L., *Que.*	22	C1
Moulin, L. du. *Que.*	20	B1
Moulmein, *Burma*	40	J5
Mountain Park, *Alberta*	14	C4
Mountain Zebra National Park, *Cape Prov., Rep. of S. Africa*	47	D3
Mount Assiniboine (Park), *Alberta*	14	D5
Mount Ayliff, *Cape Prov., Rep. of S. Africa*	47	D3
Mount Daam, *West Irian*	44	F7
Mount Desert I., *Me.*	22	C4
Mount Forest, *Ont.*	16	E3
Mount Gambier, *S. Aust.*	50	C8
Mount Hope, *N.S.W.*	50	E6
Mount Isa, *Queensland*	49	F4
Mount Kennedy, *Yukon*	10	G5
Mount Magnet, *W. Aust.*	49	B5
Mount Morgan, *Queensland*	50	H1
Mount Perry, *Queensland*	50	H2
Mount Revelstoke National Park, *B.C.*	13	L7
Mount Robson Park, *B.C.*	13	L6
Mount St. Gregory, *Nfld.*	23	J2
Mount Stewart, *P.E.I.*	21	E1
Mount Uniacke, *N.S.*	21	D3
Mount Washington, *N.H.*	22	B4
Moura, *Brazil*	30	E4
Mourne Mts., *N. Ire.*	37	B4
Mouton I., *N.S.*	21	C4
Moville, *Eire*	37	B4
Moy R., *Eire*	37	A5
Moyale, *Kenya*	46	G5
Moyobamba, *Peru*	30	B5
Mozambique. See Moçambique		
Mtwara, *Tanzania*	46	H6
Muchalat, *Vancouver I., B.C.*	13	G8
Mucuri, *Brazil*	30	K7
Muang Ubon, *Thailand*	40	K5
Muddy L., *Sask.*	14	G4
Mudgee, *N.S.W.*	50	G6
Mudjatik R., *Sask.*	14	H2
Mugford C., *Lab.*	19	E2
Muine Bheag, *Eire*	37	B5
Mukden (Shenyang), *China*	44	E2
Mukutawa R., *Man.*	15	N4
Mulege, *Mexico*	28	B2
Mulgrave, *N.S.*	21	F2
Mulhouse, *France*	38	F4
Mull I., *Scotland*	36	C3
Mullewa, *W. Aust.*	49	B5
Mullingar, *Eire*	37	B5
Multan, *W. Pak.*	40	D2
Muncho Lake Park, *B.C.*	12	H3
Muncie, *Ind.*	25	J2
Mungindi, *N.S.W.*	50	G4
Munich, *Ger.*	38	G3
Munk, *Man.*	15	O3
Munroe L., *Man.*	15	M1
Munson, *Alberta*	14	E5
Münster, *Ger.*	38	F3
Munyang Ra., *N.S.W.*	50	G8
Muong Aran Pratet, *Siam*	44	K6
Muong Songkla, *Siam*	40	K7
Murchison C., *N.W.T.*	19	E1
Murchison R., *W. Aust.*	49	B5
Murcia, *Spain*	38	D6
Murdale, *B.C.*	12	K4
Murdoch C., *Greenland*	11	X2
Murdochville, *Que.*	22	E2
Mures R., *Romania*	39	K4
Muriel L., *Alberta*	14	F3
Murillo, *Ont.*	18	D4
Murman Coast, *U.S.S.R.*	35	N2
Murmansk. *U.S.S.R.*	35	N2
Murphy, *Ida.*	24	C2
Murphy L., *B.C.*	13	K6
Murray Harb., *P.E.I.*	21	E1
Murray R., *B.C.*	12	K5

Name	Map	Ref.
Murray R., *Que.*	20	D2
Murray R., *S. Aust.*	50	C7
Murray Bridge, *S. Aust.*	50	B7
Murray Head, *P.E.I.*	21	E2
Murray River, *P.E.I.*	21	E2
Murraysburg, *Cape Prov., Rep. of S. Africa*	47	C3
Murrayville, *Victoria*	50	C7
Murrumbidgee R., *N.S.W.*	50	F7
Murrumburrah, *N.S.W.*	50	G7
Murrurundi, *N.S.W.*	50	H5
Murshidabad, *India*	40	G4
Murtle L., *B.C.*	13	K6
Murtoa, *Victoria*	50	D8
Murupara, *N.Z.*	51	F3
Murwillumbah, *N.S.W.*	50	J4
Murzuq, *Libya*	46	E3
Muscat, *Oman*	42	D6
Muscongus B., *Me.*	22	C5
Musgrave Ranges, *N. Ter.-S. Aust.*	49	E5
Musgravetown, *Nfld.*	23	L2
Muskeg R., *Mackenzie, N.W.T.*	12	J2
Muskegon, *Mich.*	25	J2
Muskogee, *Okla.*	24	G3
Muskoka, co., *Ont.*	16	F2
Muskoka R., and L., *Ont.*	16	F2
Muskrat Dam L., *Ont.*	15	P4
Muskrat Falls, *Lab.*	19	E3
Muskwa, and R., *B.C.*	12	J3
Muskwa L., *Alberta*	14	D2
Musquaro, *Que.*	23	G1
Musquaro L., *Que.*	19	E3
Musquodoboit Harb., *N.S.*	21	D3
Musters L., *Argentina*	31	C13
Muswellbrook, *N.S.W.*	50	H6
Mutton B., *Que.*	23	H1
Muzon C., *B.C.*	12	D5
Muztagh Ata, *Sinkiang*	40	E1
Mwanza, *Tanzania*	46	G6
Mweru L., *Zaire-Zambia*	46	F6
Myingyan, *Burma*	40	J4
Myitkyina, *Burma*	40	J3
Myohaung, *Burma*	40	H4
Myrtle, *Ont.*	17	G3
Mysore, tn., *India*	40	E6
Mystery L., *Man.*	15	N3
Naas, *Eire*	37	B5
Nabisipi R., *Que.*	22	F1
Nacaome, *Honduras*	28	G5
Nachikapau, L., *Que.*	19	D2
Nachvak, *Lab.*	11	W6
Nachvak B., *Lab.*	19	E2
Nadina River, *B.C.*	13	G6
Nafud Des., *Saudi Arabia*	42	C6
Nagagami, *Ont.*	18	F4
Nagagami L., and R., *Ont.*	18	F4
Nagaland, state, *India*	40	H3
Nagasaki, *Japan*	44	E3
Nagpur, *India*	40	E4
Nagykanizsa, *Hungary*	39	J4
Nahanni R., N., *Mackenzie, N.W.T.*	12	H1
Nahanni R., S., *Mackenzie, N.W.T.*	12	G1
Nahuel Huapi L., *Argentina*	31	C12
Nahuel Huapi Nat. Park, *Argentina*	31	C12
Naicam, *Sask.*	15	J4
Nain, *Lab.*	19	E2
Nairn, *Ont.*	16	D1
Nairn, and co., *Scotland*	36	D3
Nairobi, *Kenya*	46	G6
Najin, *N. Korea*	44	F2
Najwalwank L., *Que.*	20	C2
Nakhon Ratchasima, *Siam*	44	C5
Nakina, *B.C.*	12	D3
Nakina, *Ont.*	18	E3
Nakina R., *B.C.*	12	D3
Nakusp, *B.C.*	13	M7
Namakan L., *Ont.*	18	B4
Nambour, *Queensland*	50	J3
Namcha Barwa Mt., *Tibet*	44	B4
Namibia. *See S.W. Africa*		
Namew L., *Man.*	15	L3
Namoi R., *N.S.W.*	50	G5
Nampa, *Alberta*	12	M4
Nampula, *Mozambique*	46	G7
Namsos, *Norway*	35	J3
Nam Tso, *Tibet*	40	H2
Namu, *B.C.*	13	G7
Namur, *Belgium*	38	F3
Namur, *Que.*	17	L2
Namur L., *Alberta*	14	E2
Nanaimo, *Vancouver I., B.C.*	13	H8
Nanango, *Queensland*	50	H3
Nanchang, *China*	44	D4
Nancy, *France*	38	F3
Nanda Devi Mt., *India*	40	E2
Nandewar Ra., *N.S.W.*	50	H5
Nanga Parbat Mt., *Kashmir*	40	D1
Nanika L., *B.C.*	13	G6
Nanking, *China*	44	D3
Nan Ling (Mts.), *China*	44	C4
Nannine, *W. Aust.*	49	B5
Nanning, *China*	44	C4
Nanortalik, *Greenland*	11	Z5
Nansen Fd., *Greenland*	11	Z4
Nan Shan (Mts.), *China*	44	B3
Nantais L., *Que.*	19	C1
Nantel, *Que.*	20	B2
Nantes, *France*	38	D4
Nanticoke, *Ont.*	16	F5
Nanton, *Alberta*	14	E5
Nantwich, *Eng.*	37	D5
Nao C., *Spain*	38	E6
Naococane L., *Que.*	19	C3
Napanee, and R., *Ont.*	17	H3
Napier, *N.Z.*	51	F3
Napierville, *Que.*	20	C3
Napinka, *Man.*	15	L6
Naples ,and G. of, *Italy*	39	H5
Napo, *Ecuador*	30	B4
Napo, *Peru*	30	C4
Naracoorte, *S. Aust.*	50	C8
Naramata, *B.C.*	13	L8
Narmada R., *India*	40	D4
Narrabri, *N.S.W.*	50	G5
Narran L., *N.S.W.*	50	F4
Narrandera, *N.S.W.*	50	F7
Narromine, *N.S.W.*	50	G6
Narsarssuak, *Greenland*	11	Z5
Narva, *Estonia*	35	M4
Narvik, *Norway*	35	K2
Naryan Mar, *U.S.S.R.*	35	R2
Naseby, *N.Z.*	51	C6
Nashville, *Tenn.*	25	J3
Nashwaaksis, *N.B.*	22	D3
Naskaupi R., *Lab.*	19	E3
Nass R., *B.C.*	12	F4
Nassau, *Bahamas*	29	J2
Nassau, C., *Guyana*	30	F2
Nastapoka Is., *Keewatin, N.W.T.*	19	B2
Nátal, *Brazil*	30	K5
Natal, *B.C.*	13	N8
Natal, prov., *S. Africa*	47	E2
Natalkuz L., *B.C.*	13	H6
Natashquan, and R., *Que.*	22	F1
Natchez, *Miss.*	25	H4
Nation R., *B.C.*	12	J5
National Park, *P.E.I.*	21	D1
Natividade, *Brazil*	30	H6
Natla R., *Mackenzie, N.W.T.*	12	F1
Nattawa Falls, *Ont.*	15	Q5
Naturaliste C., *W. Aust.*	49	A6
Nauplia, *Greece*	39	K6
Naura I., *Pacific Oc.*	2	D5
Nauta, *Peru*	30	C4
Navarino I., *Chile*	31	D15
Navios, B. de, *Venezuela*	30	E2
Naxos I., *Greece*	39	L6
Nazare da Mata, *Brazil*	30	K5
Nazas R., *Mexico*	28	D2
Naze, The, *Eng.*	37	F6
Naze, The, *Norway*	38	F1
Nazko, and R., *B.C.*	13	J6
Neagh L., *N. Ire.*	37	B4
Neakongut B., *Que.*	19	B1
Neale R., *S. Aust.*	49	F5
Nebraska, *Neb.*	24	G2
Nebraska, state, *U.S.A.*	24	G2
Nechako R., *B.C.*	13	H6
Nechako Canyon Dam, *B.C.*	13	H6
Necochea, *Argentina*	31	F11
Needles, *B.C.*	13	L8
Needles, *I. of Wight, Eng.*	37	E6
Neepawa, *Man.*	15	M5
Neerin, *Victoria*	50	F8
Negelli, *Ethiopia*	46	G5
Negrais C., *Burma*	40	H5
Negro R., *Argentina*	31	E12
Negro R., *Mato Grosso, Brazil*	30	F7
Negro Rio (R.), *Brazil*	30	D4
Negros I., *Philippine Is.*	44	E6
Neidpath, *Sask.*	14	H5
Neils Harbour, *N.S.*	21	G1
Neiva, *Colombia*	30	B3
Nejanilini L., *Man.*	15	M1
Nejd, *Saudi Arabia*	42	C6
Nellore, *India*	40	F6
Nelson, *B.C.*	13	M8
Nelson, *N.Z.*	51	D4
Nelson, and C., *Victoria*	50	C9
Nelson I., *Alaska*	10	B5
Nelson R., *Man.*	15	O2
Nelson Forks, *B.C.*	12	J3
Nelson House, *Man.*	15	M3
Nelspruit, *Transvaal*	47	E2
Neman R., *Lithuania*	39	K2
Nemeiben L., *Sask.*	14	J3
Nemiscachingue, L., *Que.*	20	B2
Nemiscau, *Que.*	19	B3
Nen R., *Eng.*	37	F5
Nenagh, *Eire*	37	A5
Nenana, *Alaska*	10	E5
Neoskweskau, *Que.*	19	C3
Nepal, state, *Himalayas, Asia*	40	F3
Nepean R., *N.S.W.*	50	H7
Nephton, *Ont.*	17	G3
Neptune, *Sask.*	15	J6
Nerchinsk, *U.S.S.R.*	44	D1
Neret L., *Que.*	19	C3
Ness L., *Scotland*	36	C3
Nesselrode Mt., *Alaska-B.C.*	12	C3
Nesterville, *Ont.*	16	B1
Nestor Falls, *Ont.*	18	B4
Netherlands, *W. Europe*	38	F3
Nettilling L., *Baffin I., N.W.T.*	11	U4
Neuchâtel, *Switzerland*	38	F4
Neudorf, *Sask.*	15	K5
Neuquen, *Argentina*	31	D11
Nevada, *Mo.*	25	H3
Nevada, state, *U.S.A.*	24	C3
Nevada Serra, *Spain*	38	D6
Nevers, *France*	38	E4
Nevertire, *N.S.W.*	50	F5
Neville, *Sask.*	14	H6
Nevis I., *W. Indies*	29	M4
New R., *Guyana*	30	F3
New Albany, *Ind.*	25	J3
New Amsterdam, *Guyana*	30	F2
Newark, *Eng.*	37	E5
Newark. *N.J.*	25	L2
Newark. *N.Y.*	17	H4
New Bedford, *Mass.*	25	M2
New Bern, *N.C.*	25	L3
Newboro, and L., *Ont.*	17	J3
New Brunswick, prov., *Canada*	21	B1
Newburg, *N.B.*	22	D3
Newburgh, *N.Y.*	25	L2
Newbury, *Eng.*	37	E6
New Carlisle, *Que.*	22	E3
Newcastle, *Natal*	47	D2
Newcastle, *N.B.*	22	D3
Newcastle, *N.S.W.*	50	H6
Newcastle, *N. Ire.*	37	C4
Newcastle, *Ont.*	17	G4
New Castle, *Pa.*	25	K2
Newcastle Bridge, *N.B.*	21	B1
Newcastle-on-Tyne, *Eng.*	37	E4
Newcastle under Lyme, *Eng.*	37	D5
Newcastle West, *Eire*	37	A5
Newdale, *Man.*	15	L5
New Denver, *B.C.*	13	M8
Newell L., *Alberta*	14	E5
New England Ra., *N.S.W.*	50	H5
Newenham C., *Alaska*	10	B6
New Forest, *Eng.*	37	E6
Newfoundland, I. & prov., *Canada*	11	X8
New Galloway, *Scotland*	37	C4
Newgate, *B.C.*	13	N8
New Germany, *N.S.*	21	B3
New Glasgow, *N.S.*	21	D2
New Hamburg, *Ont.*	16	D4
New Hampshire, state, *U.S.A.*	25	M2
New Haven, *Conn.*	25	M2
Newhaven, *Eng.*	37	F6
New Hazelton, *B.C.*	12	G5
New Hebrides Is., *Pacific Oc.*	2	D5
New Jersey, state. *U.S.A.*	25	M2
New Liskeard, *Ont.*	18	J5
Newmarket, *Eng.*	37	F5
Newmarket, *Ont.*	17	F3
New Mexico, state, *U.S.A.*	24	E4
New Nickerie, *Surinam*	30	F2
New Norfolk, *Tasmania*	50	L12
New Orleans, *La.*	25	J5
New Plymouth, *N.Z.*	51	D3
Newport, *I. of Wight, Eng.*	37	E6
Newport, *Ky.*	25	K3
Newport, *Mo.*	25	H3
Newport, *Monmouth, Eng.*	37	D6
Newport, *Ore.*	24	B2
Newport, *Que.*	22	E2
Newport, *R.I.*	25	M2
Newport News, *Va.*	25	L3
New Providence I., *Bahamas*	29	J2
New Quay, *Wales*	37	C5
New Radnor, *Wales*	37	D5
New Richmond, *Que.*	22	E2
New Ross, *Eire*	37	B5
Newry, *N. Ire.*	37	B4
New Siberian Is., *U.S.S.R.*	43	N1
New South Wales, state, *Aust.*	50	D5
Newton Stewart, *Scotland*	37	C4
New Toronto, *Ont.*	16	F4
New Ulm, *Minn.*	24	G2
New Waterford, *N.S.*	21	G1
New Westminster, *B.C.*	13	J8
New World I., *Nfld.*	23	K2
New York, *N.Y.*	25	M2
New York, state, *U.S.A.*	25	L2
New Zealand, Dom. of, *S. Pacific Oc.*	2	DC
Ngatapa, *N.Z.*	51	F3
Ngulu Is.. *Pacific Oc.*	44	F6
Nguru, *Nigeria*	46	E4
Nha Trang, *S. Vietnam*	44	C5
Niagara, and R., *Ont.*	17	F4
Niagara Falls, *N.Y.*	17	G4
Niagara Falls, *Ont.*	16	F4
Niagara on the Lake, *Ont.*	17	F4
Niamey, *Niger, W. Africa*	46	D4
Niblock, *Ont.*	18	C4
Nicaragua, *Cent. America*	29	G5
Nicaragua L., *Nicaragua*	29	G5
Nice, *France*	38	F5
Nichikun L., *Que.*	19	C3
Nicholson, *Ont.*	18	G4
Nicman, *Que.*	22	D1
Nicobar Is.. *B. of Bengal*	40	H7
Nicola, and L., *B.C.*	13	K7
Nicolet, and R., *Que.*	20	C2
Nicoya, G. of, *Costa Rica*	29	H6
Nictaux Falls, *N.S.*	21	C3
Nictor, *N.B.*	22	D3
Nieves, *Mexico*	28	D3
Nigaluk, *Alaska*	10	D3
Niger, *W. Africa*	46	D4
Niger L., *W. Africa*	46	D4
Nigeria, *W. Africa*	46	D5
Nighthawk L., *Ont.*	18	H4
Niigata, *Japan*	44	G3
Nikolaevsk, *U.S.S.R.*	43	N1
Nikolayev, *Ukraine*	39	N4
Nile R., *Egypt, etc.*	46	G3
Nilgiri Hills, *India*	40	E6
Nimes, *France*	38	F5
Nimmitabel, *N.S.W.*	50	G8
Nimpkish R., and L., *Vancouver I., B.C.*	13	G7
Ninety Mile Beach, *Victoria*	50	F9
Ningpo, *China*	44	E4
Nioaque, *Brazil*	31	F8
Niobrara R., *Neb.*	24	F2
Nipawin, *Sask.*	15	J4
Nipawin Park, *Sask.*	15	K3
Nipigon, and L., *Ont.*	18	D4
Nipigon, B., and R., *Ont.*	18	D4
Nipigon House, *Ont.*	18	D4
Nipishish L., *Lab.*	19	E3
Nipisiguit R., *N.B.*	22	D3
Nipissing, co., *Ont.*	16	F1
Nipissing L., *Ont.*	16	F1
Nipissing Junc., *Ont.*	17	F1
Nipissis L., *Que.*	22	E1
Nippers Harb., *Nfld.*	23	J2
Niquelandia, *Brazil*	30	H7
Niriz L., *Persia*	42	D6
Niš (Nish), *Yugoslavia*	39	K5
Nisa (Neisse), *Poland*	39	J3
Niskibi R., *Ont.*	15	R2
Nisutlin R., *Yukon*	12	D2
Nitchequon, *Que.*	19	C3
Niterói, *Brazil*	31	J8
Nith R., *Scotland*	37	D4
Nitinat L., *Vancouver I., B.C.*	13	H8
Nizamabad, *India*	40	E5
Nizhne Kolymsk, *U.S.S.R.*	43	P2
Nizhneudinsk, *U.S.S.R.*	44	B1
Noasanabis, *S.W. Africa*	47	B1
Noatak R., *Alaska*	10	B4
Nobber, *Eire*	37	B5
Nobel, *Ont.*	16	E2
Noelville, *Ont.*	16	E1
Nogales, *Ariz.*	24	D4
Nogoa, *Queensland*	50	F1
Nokomis, *Sask.*	14	J5
Nokomis L., *Sask.*	15	K2
Nomansland Pt., *Ont.*	18	H2
Nome, *Alaska*	10	A5
Nominingue, and L., *Que.*	17	K1
Nonacho L., *Mackenzie, N.W.T.*	10	N5
Nonato, *Brazil*	30	J5
Nong Khai, *Thailand*	40	K5
Nooitgedacht, *Transvaal*	47	E2
Nootka, *Vancouver I., B.C.*	13	G8
Nootka I. and Sd., *Vancouver I., B.C.*	13	G8
Noradham, *N.S.W.*	50	F6
Noranda, *Que.*	19	B4
Nordegg R., *Alberta*	14	D4
Nordkyn, *Norway*	35	M1
Nore R., *Eire*	37	B5
Norembega, *Ont.*	18	H4
Norfolk, *Neb.*	24	G2
Norfolk, *Va.*	25	L3
Norfolk, co., *Eng.*	37	F5
Norfolk, co., *Ont.*	16	E5
Norfolk I., *Pacific Oc.*	2	D6
Norfolk L., *Ark.*	25	H3
Norland, *Ont.*	17	G3
Norman C., *Nfld.*	23	K1
Norman R., *Queensland*	49	G3
Normand L., *Que.*	20	C2
Normanton, *Queensland*	49	G3
Norman Wells, *Mackenzie, N.W.T.*	10	J4
Normetal, *Que.*	18	J4
Norris Arm, *Nfld.*	23	K2
Norrköping, *Sweden*	35	K4
North B., *Baffin I., N.W.T.*	19	C1
North C., *N.Z.*	51	D1
North C., *Norway*	35	M1
North C., *N.S.*	21	G1
North Chan., *Manitoulin I., Ont.*	25	K1
North Chan., *N. Ire.*	37	B4
North Chan., *Ont.*	16	B1
North I., *N.Z.*	51	D2
North Pt., *P.E.I.*	22	F3
North R., *Lab.*	19	E2
Northallerton, *Eng.*	37	E4
Northam, *W. Aust.*	49	B6
Northampton, and co., *Eng.*	37	E5
Northampton, *W. Aust.*	49	B5
Northan Bight, *Nfld.*	23	K2
North Arm, *Gt. Slave L., N.W.T.*	12	N1
North Battleford, *Sask.*	14	G4
North Bay, *Ont.*	16	F1
North Belcher Is., *Hudson B.*	19	A2
North Berwick, *Scotland*	36	D3
North Brook, *Ont.*	17	H3
North Caribou Lake, *Ont.*	18	C2
North Carolina, state, *U.S.A.*	25	L3
North Cruz, *Brazil*	30	K5
North Dakota, state, *U.S.A.*	24	F1
North Downs, *Eng.*	37	F6
Northern Indian L., *Man.*	15	N2

Northern Ireland, *Brit. Isles*	37	B4
Northern Rhodesia. *See Zambia*		
Northern Territory, *Aust.*	49	E3
North Fork R., *Alaska*	10	D5
Northgate, *Sask.*	15	K6
North Indian L., *Man.*	15	N2
North Lake, *Ont.*	18	C4
Northland, *N.Z.*	51	D1
North Magnetic Pole, *Franklin, N.W.T.*	10	O2
North Mills, *Que.*	20	B3
North Platte, *Neb.*	24	F2
North Point, *Mich.*	16	B2
North Point, *P.E.I.*	21	C1
Northport, *N.S.*	21	D2
North River Bridge, *N.S.*	21	F1
North Rona, *Hebrides, Scotland*	36	C2
North Rustico, *P.E.I.*	21	D1
North Sea, *N.W. Europe*	36	E3
North Seal R., *Man.*	15	M1
North Sporades Is., *Greece*	39	L6
North Stradbroke I., *Queensland*	50	J3
North Sydney, *N.S.*	21	G1
North Thompson R., *B.C.*	13	L7
North Twin, *James B.*	18	H2
Northumberland, co., *Eng.*	37	D4
Northumberland, co., *Ont.*	17	G3
Northumberland, C., *S. Aust.*	50	C9
Northumberland Is., *Queensland*	49	J4
Northumberland Str., *N.B.-N.S.*	21	C1
North Vancouver, *B.C.*	13	J8
North West C., *Axel Heiberg I., N.W.T.*	11	P1
North West C., *W. Aust.*	49	A4
North West Frontier Prov., *Pakistan*	40	D2
North West River, *Lab.*	19	E3
Northwest Territories, *Canada*	10	K5
Norton, *N.B.*	21	B2
Norton Sd., and B., *Alaska*	10	A5
Norway, kingdom, *Europe*	35	J3
Norway House, *Man.*	15	N4
Norwegian B., *Franklin, N.W.T.*	11	Q2
Norwegian Sea, *N. Europe*	35	F2
Norwich, *Eng.*	37	F5
Norwich, *Ont.*	16	E4
Norwood, *N.Y.*	17	L3
Norwood, *Ont.*	17	H3
Nosop R., *S.W. Africa*	47	B1
Nossi Be I., *Madagascar*	46	H7
Notikewin, and R., *Alberta*	14	C2
Notre Dame, *N.B.*	21	C1
Notre Dame B., *Nfld.*	23	K2
Notre Dame Mts., *Que.*	20	D2
Notre Dame de-la-Dore, *Que.*	20	C1
Notre Dame de Lourdes, *Man.*	15	M6
Notre Dame des Anges, *Que.*	20	C2
Notre Dame du Lac, *Que.*	20	E2
Notre Dame du Laus, *Que.*	17	K1
Nottawasaga B., and R., *Ont.*	16	E3
Nottaway R., *Que.*	19	B3
Nottingham, and co., *Eng.*	37	E5
Nottingham I., *Keewatin, N.W.T.*	11	T5
Nottingham Rd., *Natal*	47	E2
Notukeu Cr., *Sask.*	14	H6
Nouakchott, *Mauritania, W. Africa*	46	B4
Noupoort, *Cape Prov., Rep. of S. Africa*	47	C3
Nova Lisboa, *Angola*	46	E7
Nova Scotia, prov., *Canada*	21	B3
Novaya Sibir, *U.S.S.R.*	2	D1
Novaya Zemlya I., *U.S.S.R.*	42	D1
Novgorod, *U.S.S.R.*	35	N4
Novi Pazar, *Yugoslavia*	39	K5
Novita, *Colombia*	30	B3
Novo R., *Brazil*	31	J8
Novocherkassk, *U.S.S.R.*	39	P4
Novojoa, *Mexico*	28	C2
Novokuznetsk, *U.S.S.R.*	44	A1
Novomoskovsk, *U.S.S.R.*	39	O2
Novorossiysk, *U.S.S.R.*	39	O4
Novosibirsk, *U.S.S.R.*	44	A1
Nowra, *N.S.W.*	50	H7
Noyan, *Que.*	20	C3
Nubia, *Sudan*	46	F4
Nubian Desert, *Sudan*	46	G3
Nudo de Apolo, *Bolivia*	30	D6
Nueltin L., *Keewatin, N.W.T.*	10	O5
Nueva Rosita, *Mexico*	28	D2
Nuevo G., *Argentina*	31	E12
Nuevo Laredo, *Mexico*	28	E2
Nugsuak Penin., *Greenland*	11	Y3
Nulato, *Alaska*	10	C5
Nullarbor Plain, *W. Aust.*	49	D6
Nungesser L., *Ont.*	18	B3
Nunivak I., *Alaska*	10	A5
Nuovitas, *Cuba*	29	J3
Nurmes, *Finland*	35	M3
Nürnberg, *Ger.*	38	G3
Nushagak, *Alaska*	10	C6
Nushki, *W. Pak.*	40	C3
Nut L., *Sask.*	15	K4
Nutak, *Lab.*	19	E2
Nutarawit L., *Keewatin, N.W.T.*	11	P5
Nutrias, *Venezuela*	30	D2
Nuweveld Ra., *Cape Prov., Rep. of S. Africa*	47	C3
Nyala, *Sudan*	46	F4
Nyarling R., *Mackenzie, N.W.T.*	12	N2
Nyasa L., *E. Africa*	46	G7
Nyasaland. *See Malawi*		
Nyköping, *Sweden*	39	J1
Nylstroom, *Transvaal*	47	D1
Nymagee, *N.S.W.*	50	F6
Nyngan, *N.S.W.*	50	F5
Oahe Res., *N. Dak.*	24	F1
Oak L., *Ont.*	18	A3
Oakham, *Eng.*	37	E5
Oak Lake, *Man.*	15	L6
Oakland, *Cal.*	24	B3
Oak Ridge, *Tenn.*	25	K3
Oakville, *Ont.*	16	F4
Oamaru, *N.Z.*	51	C6
Oastler Prov. Park, *Ont.*	16	F2
Oatlands, *Tasmania*	51	L12
Oaxaca de Juarez, *Mexico*	28	E4
Ob, G. of, *U.S.S.R.*	42	F2
Ob, R., *U.S.S.R.*	42	E2
Oba, and L., *Ont.*	18	F4
Oban, *Scotland*	36	C3
Oban, *Stewart I., N.Z.*	51	B7
Obbia, *Somali Rep.*	46	H5
Obed, *Alberta*	14	C4
Obidos, *Brazil*	30	F4
Observatory Inlet, *B.C.*	12	F5
Ocala, *Fla.*	25	K5
Ocatol, *Nicaragua*	29	G5
Ocean I., *Pacific Oc.*	2	D5
Ocean Falls, *B.C.*	13	G6
Ochre, *Man.*	15	M5
Ocoa, B. de, *Dominican Rep.*	29	K4
Ocotepeque, *Honduras*	28	G5
Ocussi Ambeno, *Timor I., Indonesia*	44	E7
O'Day, *Man.*	15	O2
Odda, *Norway*	35	H3
Odendaalsrus, *Orange F.S.*	47	D2
Odense, *Denmark*	38	G2
Oder R., *Ger.*	39	J3
Odessa, *Ont.*	17	J3
Odessa, *Ukraine*	39	M4
Oeiras, *Brazil*	30	J5
Offaly, co., *Eire*	37	B5
Ogaki, *Ont.*	18	D3
Ogasawara Gunto (Bonin Is.), *Pacific Oc.*	44	G4
Ogden, *N.S.*	22	G4
Ogden, *Ut.*	24	D2
Ogden Mt., *Alaska-B.C.*	12	D3
Ogdensburg, *N.Y.*	17	K3
Ogoki, *Ont.*	18	F3
Ogoki L., *Ont.*	18	E3
Ogoki R., and Res., *Ont.*	18	D3
Ohakune, *N.Z.*	51	E3
Ohau L., *N.Z.*	51	B6
Ohio, state, *U.S.A.*	25	K2
Ohio R., *U.S.A.*	25	K3
Oies, L. aux, *Que.*	20	D2
Oil Springs, *Ont.*	16	C5
Oiseau B., *Ont.*	18	E4
Oiseau L., *Man.*	15	O5
Ojo de Agua, *Argentina*	31	E9
Oka R., *U.S.S.R.*	39	P2
Okahandja, *S.W. Africa*	47	B1
Okak, *Lab.*	11	W6
Okak Is., *Lab.*	19	E2
Okanagan Lake, *B.C.*	13	L7
Okanagan Lake Park, *B.C.*	13	L8
Okanagan Mission, *B.C.*	13	L8
Okathau, *N.Z.*	51	D1
Okeechobee L., *Fla.*	25	K5
Okha, *U.S.S.R.*	43	N3
Okhotsk, and Sea of, *U.S.S.R.*	43	N3
Okinawa Guntō, *Japan*	44	E4
Oklahoma, state, *U.S.A.*	24	G3
Oklahoma City, *Okla.*	24	G3
Okotoks, *Alberta*	14	D5
Okuru, *N.Z.*	51	B5
Oland I., *Sweden*	39	J1
Olavarria, *Argentina*	31	E11
Olbia, *Sardinia*	38	G5
Oldcastle, *Eire*	37	B5
Old Crow, *Yukon*	10	G4
Old Factory, *Que.*	19	B3
Old Fort Bay, *Que.*	23	H3
Oldham, *Eng.*	37	D5
Old Hogem, *B.C.*	12	H5
Old Man Plain, *N.S.W.*	50	E7
Old Orchard Beach, *Me.*	22	B5
Old Perlican, *Nfld.*	23	L2
Oldtown, *Me.*	22	C4
Old Shoes L., *Ont.*	18	A2
Olds, *Alberta*	14	D5
Old Wives L., *Sask.*	14	J5
O'Leary, *P.E.I.*	21	C1
Olekminsk, *U.S.S.R.*	43	K2
Olhue, *Chile*	31	C10
Olifants R., *Cape Prov., Rep. of S. Africa*	47	B3
Olifants R., *Cape Prov., Rep. of S. Africa*	47	C3
Olifants R., *Transvaal*	47	E1
Olifants Kloof, *Botswana*	47	C1
Olifants Vlei, *Cape Prov., Rep. of S. Africa*	47	C3
Oliver, *B.C.*	13	L8
Oliver, *Que.*	20	C3
Oliver L., *Sask.*	15	K2
Olmos L., *Argentina*	31	J3
Olney, *Ill.*	25	J3
Olomane R., *Que.*	23	G1
Olomouc, *Czechoslovakia*	39	J3
Olonets, *U.S.S.R.*	35	N3
Olt R., *Romania*	39	L4
Olympia, *Wash.*	24	B1
Olympus Mt., *Greece*	39	K5
Omagh, *N. Ire.*	37	B4
Omaha, *Neb.*	24	G2
Oman, G. of, *Arabia-Persia*	42	D6
Oman, *S.W. Asia*	42	D7
Ombabika B., *Ont.*	18	D3
Omdurman, *Sudan*	46	G4
Omemee, *Ont.*	17	G3
Omer, *Mich.*	16	B3
Omineca Mts., *B.C.*	12	G4
Omineca R., *B.C.*	12	H5
Ommaney C., *Alaska*	13	C4
Ommanney B., *Prince of Wales I., N.W.T.*	10	O3
Omsk, *U.S.S.R.*	42	F3
Onanam L., *Ont.*	18	E3
Onatchiway L., *Que.*	22	B2
Onaway, *Mich.*	16	A2
Onderste Doorn, *Cape Prov., Rep. of S. Africa*	47	C3
Onega, and R., *U.S.S.R.*	35	O3
Onega, G. of, *U.S.S.R.*	35	O3
Onega L., *U.S.S.R.*	35	O3
Onion Lake, *Sask.*	14	G4
Onon R., *U.S.S.R.*	44	D1
Onslow, *W. Aust.*	49	B4
Onslow B., *N.C.*	25	L4
Ontario, prov., *Canada*	17	F3
Ontario, prov., *Canada*	11	Q8
Ontario L., *Canada-U.S.A.*	17	G4
Ontonagon, *Mich.*	18	D5
Oodnadatta, *S. Aust.*	49	E5
Ookiep, *S. Africa*	47	B2
Ooldea, *S. Aust.*	49	E6
Oona River, *B.C.*	13	G6
Ootsa Lake, *B.C.*	13	G6
Opasatika L., *Que.*	18	J4
Opasatika L., and R., *Ont.*	18	G4
Opava, *Czechoslovakia*	39	J3
Opeongo L., *Ont.*	17	G2
Opinaka L., and R., *Que.*	19	B3
Opinnagau R., *Ont.*	18	G1
Opiskoteo L., *Que.*	19	D3
Opole, *Poland*	39	J3
Oponask L., *Ont.*	15	P3
Oporto, *Portugal*	38	B5
Opotiki, *N.Z.*	51	F2
Oradea, *Romania*	39	K4
Oraefa Jokull, *Iceland*	37	C3
Oran, *Algeria*	46	C2
Oran, *Argentina*	31	E8
Orange, *N.S.W.*	50	G6
Orange, *Tex.*	25	H4
Orange B., *Nfld.*	23	J1
Orange C., *Brazil*	30	G3
Orange R., *Cape Prov., Rep. of S. Africa, etc.*	47	C2
Orangeburg, *S.C.*	25	K4
Orangedale, *N.S.*	21	F2
Orange Free State, *S. Africa*	47	D2
Orange Mouth, *S.W. Africa*	47	D2
Orangeville, *Ont.*	16	E4
Orano, *Me.*	22	C4
Orawia, *N.Z.*	51	A7
Orbando, *Fla.*	25	K5
Orbost, *Victoria*	51	G8
Orchila I., *Caribbean Sea*	30	D1
Ordos Plat., *China*	44	C3
Orebro, *Sweden*	35	K4
Oregon, state, *U.S.A.*	24	B2
Orekhovo Zuyevo, *U.S.S.R.*	39	O2
Orel, *U.S.S.R.*	39	O2
Orenburg, *U.S.S.R.*	42	D3
Original C., *Que.*	20	E1
Orillia, *Ont.*	16	F3
Orinoco, Delta del, *Venezuela*	30	E2
Orinoco R., *Venezuela*	30	D3
Orissa, state, *India*	40	F4
Orkney Is., *Scotland*	36	D2
Orleans, *France*	38	E4
Orleans, I. de., *Que.*	20	D2
Orlov C., *U.S.S.R.*	35	P2
Ormsby, *Ont.*	17	H3
Ormstown, *Que.*	20	B3
Orono, *Ont.*	17	G4
Ororoo, *S. Aust.*	50	B6
Orsha, *U.S.S.R.*	39	M2
Orsova, *Romania*	39	K4
Ortegal C., *Spain*	38	B5
Ortiz, *Venezuela*	30	D2
Ortles, *Italy*	38	G4
Oruro, *Bolivia*	30	D7
Osage R., *Mo., etc.*	25	H3
Osaka, *Japan*	44	F3
Oscoda, *Mich.*	16	B3
Osgoode, *Ont.*	17	K2
Oshawa, *Ont.*	17	G4
Oshkosh, *Wis.*	25	J2
Oskelane, *Que.*	20	B1
Oslo, *Norway*	35	J3
Osnabrück, *Ger.*	38	G2
Osnaburgh House, *Ont.*	18	C3
Osorno, *Chile*	31	C12
Osoyoos, *B.C.*	13	L8
Ospika R., *B.C.*	12	H4
Ossa Mt., *Tasmania*	50	K11
Ossineke, *Mich.*	16	B3
Ossokmanuan L., *Lab.*	19	D3
Ostashkov, *U.S.S.R.*	39	N1
Ostend, *Belgium*	38	E3
Ostersund, *Sweden*	35	J3
Ostrava, *Czechoslovakia*	39	J3
Ostrov, *U.S.S.R.*	35	M4
Ostrova Novo Sibirskiye I., *U.S.S.R.*	2	C1
O'Sullivan L., *Ont.*	18	E3
O'Sullivan, L., *Que.*	20	A2
Oswego, *Kan.*	25	H3
Oswego, and R., *N.Y.*	17	J4
Oswestry, *Eng.*	37	D5
Otago Penin., and Harb., *N.Z.*	51	C6
Otahuhu, *N.Z.*	51	E2
Otaki, *N.Z.*	51	E4
Otelnuk L., *Que.*	19	D2
Othris Mts., *Greece*	39	K6
Otira, *N.Z.*	51	C5
Otis, *N.B.*	22	D3
Otoskwin R., *Ont.*	18	D3
Otranto, and Str. of, *Italy*	39	J5
Ottawa, *Ont.*	17	K2
Ottawa Is., *Hudson B., Canada*	11	S6
Ottawa R., *Ont.-Que.*	17	G1
Otter Hd., and I., *Ont.*	18	E4
Otter L., *Alberta*	14	D2
Otter L., *Ont.*	15	Q6
Otter Lake, *Ont.*	16	F2
Otter Lake, *Que.*	17	J2
Otto, *Man.*	15	N5
Ottumwa, *Ia.*	25	H2
Otukamamoan L., *Ont.*	18	B4
Otway C., *Victoria*	50	D9
Ouagadougou, *Upper Volta, Africa*	46	C4
Ouareau L., *Que.*	20	B2
Ouareau R., *Que.*	20	C2
Oudtshoorn, *Cape Prov., Rep. of S. Africa*	47	C3
Ouiteauguny R., *Que.*	20	B3
Oulu, *Finland*	35	M2
Oulu L., *Finland*	35	M3
Oup R., *Cape Prov., Rep. of S. Africa*	47	C2
Ouricuri, *Brazil*	30	J5
Ouro Preto, *Brazil*	30	J8
Ouse R., *Eng.*	37	F5
Outarde B., *Que.*	22	C2
Outardes R., *Que.*	22	C1
Outlook, *Sask.*	14	H5
Ouyen, *Victoria*	50	D7
Ovalle, *Chile*	31	C10
Oviedo, *Spain*	38	C5
Owensboro, *Ky.*	25	J3
Owen Sound, *Ont.*	16	E3
Owikeno L., *B.C.*	13	G7
Owl R., *Man.*	15	P2
Owosso, *Mich.*	16	A4
Owyhee R., *Ida., etc.*	24	C2
Ox Mts., *Eire*	37	A4
Oxbow, *Sask.*	15	K6
Oxford, *Mich.*	16	B5
Oxford, *N.S.*	21	C2
Oxford, and co., *Eng.*	37	E6
Oxford, co., *Ont.*	16	E4
Oxford L., *Man.*	15	N3
Oxford House, *Man.*	15	O3
Oxley, *N.S.W.*	50	E7
Oyama, *B.C.*	13	L7
Oyapok R., *Fr. Guiana-Brazil*	30	G3
Oyen, *Alberta*	14	F5
Oyster B., *Tasmania*	50	M12
Ozark Mts., *Mo., etc.*	25	H4
Ozhiska L., *Ont.*	18	D2
Paan, *China*	44	B3
Paarde Berg, *Orange F.S.*	47	D2
Paarl, *Cape Prov., Rep. of S. Africa*	47	B3
Pacaraima, Sa., *Venezuela*	30	E3
Pacasmayo, *Peru*	30	A5
Pachuca, *Mexico*	28	E3
Pacific, *B.C.*	12	F5
Pacific Oc.	2	D4
Packenham, *Ont.*	17	J2
Packs Harb., *Lab.*	19	F3
Pacofi, *B.C.*	13	E6
Padang, *Sumatra*	44	C7
Padauiri R., *Brazil*	30	E3
Paddle R., *Alberta*	14	D3
Paddle Prairie, *Alberta*	14	C2
Paddockwood, *Sask.*	14	J4
Padre I., *Tex.*	24	G5
Padstow, *Eng.*	37	C6
Padua, *Italy*	38	G4
Paducah, *Ky.*	25	J3
Paeroa, *N.Z.*	51	E2
Pafuri, *Mozambique*	47	E1
Pagwa River, *Ont.*	18	F3
Pagwachuan R., and L., *Ont.*	18	F4
Pahiatva, *N.Z.*	51	E4
Pai-ho R., *China*	43	K5
Paincourt, *Ont.*	16	C5
Paint L., *Man.*	15	M3

Name	Page	Grid
Painter, Mt., *S. Aust.*	50	B5
Paint Hills Is., *James B.*	18	J2
Paisley, *Ont.*	16	D3
Paisley, *Scotland*	36	C4
Paita, *Peru*	30	A5
Pakaraima Mts., *Guyana*	30	E2
Pakistan, *Asia*	40	
Pakowki, and L., *Alberta*	14	F6
Pakwash L., *Ont.*	18	B3
Pala Camp, *Botswana*	47	D1
Palapye Road, *Botswana*	47	D1
Palau Is., *Pacific Oc.*	44	F6
Palawan I., *Philippine Is.*	44	D6
Palembang, *Sumatra*	44	C7
Palena R., *Chile-Argentina*	31	C12
Palencia, *Spain*	38	C5
Palermo, *Ont.*	16	F4
Palermo, *Sicily*	38	H4
Palestina, *Chile*	31	D8
Palk Str., *India-Sri Lanka*	40	E7
Palliser C., and B., *N.Z.*	51	E4
Palma, *Majorca, Balearic Is.*	38	E6
Palmas, *Brazil*	31	G9
Palmas C., *Liberia*	46	C5
Palm Beach, *Fla.*	25	K5
Palmeira, *Brazil*	30	K5
Palmerston, *N.Z.*	51	C6
Palmerston, *Ont.*	16	D4
Palmerston, M., *N.Z.*	51	E4
Palms, *Mich.*	16	C4
Palmyra I., *Pacific Oc.*	2	E4
Palopo, *Celebes*	44	E7
Pamirs, *Cent. Asia*	42	F5
Pamlico Sd., *N.C.*	25	L3
Pamouscadhiou L., *Que.*	22	B2
Pampas, *Argentina*	30	D11
Pampas del Sacramento, *Peru*	30	B5
Pampiona, *Spain*	38	D5
Panache L., *Ont.*	16	D1
Panama, rep., *Cent. America*	29	H6
Panama, and G. of, *Cent. America*	29	J6
Panama Can., *Pan.*	29	J6
Panay I., *Philippine Is.*	44	D6
Pan de Azucar, *Chile*	31	C9
Panet, *Que.*	20	D2
Pangkai Pinang, *Indonesia*	44	C7
Pangnirtung, *Baffin I., N.W.T.*	11	V4
Panjim (Nova Goa), *India*	40	D5
Panny R., *Alberta*	14	D2
Paotow, *China*	44	C2
Papagaio R., *Brazil*	30	F6
Papagayo G., *Costa Rica*	28	G5
Papakura, *N.Z.*	51	E2
Papantla de Olarta, *Mexico*	28	E3
Papineau L., *Que.*	20	B3
Papineauville, *Que.*	17	K2
Paposo, *Chile*	31	C8
Papua and New Guinea, *Pacific Ocean*	2	C5
Paquette, *Que.*	20	D3
Para (Tocantins) R., *Brazil*	30	H4
Paracatu, and R., *Brazil*	30	H7
Paracel Is., *S. China Sea*	44	D5
Paradis, *Que.*	20	A1
Paradise Pt., *Coast of Lab.*	19	F3
Paradise Valley, *Alberta*	14	F4
Paragua R., *Venezuela*	30	E2
Paraguana Penin., *Venezuela*	30	D1
Paraguari, *Paraguay*	31	F9
Paraguassu R., *Brazil*	30	J6
Paraguay, rep., *S. America*	31	F8
Paraguay R., *Paraguay-Brazil*	30	F7
Paraiba R., *Brazil*	30	H5
Paraiba R., *Brazil*	31	J8
Paramaribo, *Surinam*	30	F2
Paramonga, *Peru*	30	B6
Parana, *Argentina*	31	E10
Paraná, and Serra do, *Brazil*	30	H6
Paraná R., *Paraguay, etc.*	31	F9
Paranaguá, *Brazil*	31	H9
Paranaiba, and R., *Brazil*	30	G7
Paranapanema R., *Brazil*	31	G8
Paranatinga R., *Brazil*	30	F6
Paraopeba R., *Brazil*	30	G5
Paratinga, *Brazil*	30	J6
Pardo R., *Minas Gerais, Brazil*	30	J7
Pardo R., *São Paulo, Brazil*	31	G8
Pardubice, *Czechoslovakia*	39	J3
Parecis, Serra dos, *Brazil*	30	E6
Parent, *Que.*	19	C4
Paria Penin., and G. of, *Venezuela*	30	E1
Paricutin, *Mexico*	28	D4
Parinas, Pta., *Peru*	30	A4
Paringa, *S. Aust.*	50	C7
Parintins, *Brazil*	30	F4
Paris, *France*	38	E3
Paris, *Me.*	22	B4
Paris, *Ont.*	16	E4
Paris, *Tenn.*	25	J3
Paris, *Tex.*	24	G4
Parkersburg, *W. Va.*	25	K3
Parkerview, *Sask.*	15	K5
Parkes, *N.S.W.*	50	G6
Park Hill. *Ont.*	16	D4
Parksville, *Vancouver I., B.C.*	13	H8
Parma, *Italy*	38	G4
Parnagua, *Brazil*	30	J5
Parnaiba, and R., *Brazil*	30	J4
Pärnu, *Estonia*	39	K1
Paroo R., *N.S.W.-Queensland*	50	E4
Parramatta, *N.S.W.*	50	H6
Parras, *Mexico*	28	D2
Parrsboro, *N.S.*	21	C2
Parry C., *Mackenzie, N.W.T.*	10	K3
Parry I., *Ont.*	16	E2
Parry Is., *Franklin, N.W.T.*	10	M2
Parry Sound, *Ont.*	16	E2
Parry Sound, co., and tn., *Ont.*	16	F2
Parsnip R. , *B.C.*	12	J5
Parson, *B.C.*	13	M7
Parsons Pond, *N.S.*	23	J1
Partridge Pt., *Nfld.*	23	J1
Paru R., *Brazil*	30	G4
Parys, *Orange F.S.*	47	D2
Pas, The, *Man.*	15	L4
Pasadena, *Cal.*	24	C4
Pasfield L., *Sask.*	14	J1
Pashkokogan L., *Ont.*	18	C3
Paska, *Ont.*	18	E3
Paso Robles, *Cal.*	24	B3
Parsonstown, *Eire*	37	B5
Paspébiac, *Que.*	22	E2
Pasquia R., *Man.-Sask.*	15	L4
Pasquia Hills, *Sask.*	15	K4
Passamaquoddy B., *N.B.*	22	D4
Passau, *Ger.*	38	H3
Passero C., *Sicily*	39	H6
Passes, L. des, *Que.*	20	C2
Passo Fundo, *Brazil*	31	G9
Passos, *Brazil*	31	H8
Pastaza R., *Peru*	30	B4
Paso, *Colombia*	30	B3
Patagonia, *Argentina*	31	C13
Patagonia, Gt. Plat. of, *Argentina-Chile*	31	D12
Patea, *N.Z.*	51	E3
Paterson, *N.J.*	25	M2
Paterson Inlet, *Stewart I., N.Z.*	51	B7
Patia R., *Colombia*	30	B3
Patillos, *Chile*	31	C8
Patkai Ra., *Burma, etc.*	40	J3
Patna, *India*	40	G3
Patos L., *Brazil*	31	G10
Patras, *Greece*	39	K6
Patten, *Me.*	22	C3
Patuca R., *Honduras*	29	H4
Pau, *France*	38	D5
Paugan Falls, *Que.*	17	J2
Pauillac, *France*	38	D4
Paul I., *Lab.*	19	E2
Paulatuk, *Mackenzie, N.W.T.*	10	K4
Pauline Mt., *Alberta*	14	B4
Paulistana, *Brazil*	32	E3
Paulo, *Brazil*	30	K5
Paulpietersburg, *Natal*	47	E2
Paute R., *Peru, etc.*	30	B4
Pavalion, *B.C.*	13	K7
Pavia, *Italy*	38	G4
Pavon, *Argentina*	31	E11
Payne B., *Que.*	19	C2
Payne L., *Que.*	19	C2
Paynton, *Sask.*	14	G4
Paysandu, *Uruguay*	31	F10
Paz L., *Argentina-Chile*	31	C12
Peace R., *Alberta*	14	D1
Peace River, *Alberta*	14	C2
Peachland, *B.C.*	13	L8
Peak, The, *Eng.*	37	E5
Peak Hill, *N.S.W.*	50	G6
Peard B., *Alaska*	10	B3
Pearl, *Ont.*	18	D4
Pearl Harb., *Hawaiian Is.*	2	E4
Pearl Lake, *Que.*	20	C2
Peary Chan., *Franklin, N.W.T.*	10	O2
Pebas, *Peru*	30	C4
Pechora R., *U.S.S.R.*	35	R2
Pecos, *Tex.*	24	F4
Pécs. *Hungary*	39	J4
Peddie, *Cape Prov., Rep. of S. Africa*	47	D3
Pedernales, *Ecuador*	30	B3
Pedernales, *Venezuela*	30	E2
Pedras, *Brazil*	30	K5
Pedro Afonso, *Brazil*	30	H5
Peebinga, *S. Aust.*	50	B7
Peebles, *Sask.*	15	K5
Peebles, and co., *Scotland*	36	D4
Peel, *Isle of Man*	35	C4
Peel, co., *Ont.*	16	F4
Peel R., *Yukon-N.W.T.*	10	H4
Peel Sd., *Franklin, N.W.T.*	11	P3
Peel Fell, *Eng.*	37	D4
Peerless L., *Alberta*	14	D2
Pegasus B., *N.Z.*	51	D5
Pegu, *Burma*	40	J5
Pei-ho, *China*	43	K4
Peipus L. (Chudskoye Oz), *Estonia-U.S.S.R.*	35	M4
Pekisko, *Alberta*	14	D5
Peking (Peiping), *China*	44	D2
Pelican L., *Man.*	15	M6
Pelican L., *Que.*	19	C1
Pelican Narrows, *Sask.*	15	K3
Pelican Portage, *Alberta*	14	E3
Pella, *Cape Prov., Rep. of S. Africa*	47	B2
Pelletier, *Que.*	20	E2
Pelly L., *N.W.T.*	10	O4
Pelly Mts., *Yukon*	12	D2
Pelly Pt., *Victoria I., N.W.T.*	10	O3
Pelly R., *Yukon*	10	H5
Pelly Bay, *Keewatin, N.W.T.*	11	R4
Pelly Crossing, *Yukon*	12	B1
Peioponnisos, *Greece*	39	K6
Pelotas, *Brazil*	31	G10
Pemba I., *Tanzania*	46	H6
Pemberton, *B.C.*	13	J7
Pembina R., *Alberta*	14	D4
Pembina R., *Man.-N. Dak.*	15	M6
Pembroke, *Ont.*	17	H2
Pembroke, and co., *Wales*	37	C6
Pemdembu, *Sierra Leone*	46	B5
Pemuco, *Chile*	31	C11
Penas, G. de, *Chile*	31	B13
Pend d'Oreille. *Alberta*	14	F6
Pend Oreille, and L., *Ida.*	24	C1
Penedo, *Brazil*	30	K6
Penetanguishene, *Ont.*	16	E3
Penhold, *Alberta*	14	D4
Penhurst, *Ont.*	18	F4
Penicuik, *Scotland*	36	D4
Peninsula B., *Ont.*	18	E4
Pennant, *Sask.*	14	G5
Pennant Pt., *N.S.*	21	D3
Pennfield, *N.B.*	22	D4
Pennine Chain, *Eng.*	37	D4
Pennsylvania, state, *U.S.A.*	25	L2
Penny, *B.C.*	13	K6
Penny Str., *Franklin, N.W.T.*	10	O2
Penobscot B., and R., *Me.*	22	C4
Penobsquis, *N.B.*	21	B2
Penong, *S. Aust.*	49	E6
Penrith, *Eng.*	37	D4
Penrith, *N.S.W.*	50	H6
Pensacola, *Fla.*	25	J4
Pense, *Sask.*	14	J5
Pentecote R., *Que.*	22	D1
Penticton, *B.C.*	13	L8
Pentland Firth, *Scotland*	36	D2
Penyghent, *Eng.*	37	D4
Penzance, *Eng.*	37	C6
Peoria, *Ill.*	25	H2
Percé, *Que.*	22	E2
Pereiro, *Brazil*	30	K5
Pergamino, *Argentina*	31	E10
Peribonca L., *Que.*	22	B1
Peribonca R., *Que.*	22	B2
Perico, *Argentina*	31	E8
Périgueux, *France*	38	E4
Perim I., *Red Sea*	46	H4
Perkins, *Que.*	20	B3
Perlas I., *Pan.*	29	J6
Perow, *B.C.*	13	G5
Perpignan, *France*	38	E5
Perry River, *Mackenzie, N.W.T.*	10	O4
Persian Gulf. See Gulf, The		
Perth, *N.B.*	22	D3
Perth, *Ont.*	17	J3
Perth, co., *Ont.*	16	D4
Perth, *Scotland*	36	D3
Perth, *W. Aust.*	49	B6
Perth, co., *Scotland*	36	C3
Peru, rep., *S. America*	30	B6
Perugia, *Italy*	38	H5
Pervomaysk, *Ukraine*	39	M4
Peshawar, *W. Pak.*	40	D2
Pesqueira, *Brazil*	30	K5
Petacalco B., *Mexico*	28	D4
Petawaga L., *Que.*	20	B2
Petawawa, and R., *Ont.*	17	H2
Peterbell, *Ont.*	18	G4
Peterborough, *Eng.*	37	E5
Peterborough, *Ont.*	17	G3
Peterborough, *S. Aust.*	50	B6
Peterhead, *Scotland*	36	E3
Peterlee, *Eng.*	37	E4
Petermann Peak, *Greenland*	1	O2
Peter Pond L., *Sask.*	14	G3
Petersburg, *Alaska*	12	D4
Petersburg, *Va.*	25	L3
Petit Cap, *Que.*	22	E2
Petitcodiac, *N.B.*	21	B2
Petite Nation R., *Que.*	20	B3
Petite Rivière Bridge, *N.S.*	21	C3
Petit Etang, *N.S.*	21	G1
Petit Nord Penin., *Nfld.*	23	J1
Petitot R., *B.C.*	12	K3
Petitsikapau L., *Lab.*	11	V7
Petone, *N.Z.*	51	E4
Petrolândia, *Brazil*	30	K5
Petrolia, *Ont.*	16	C5
Petrolina, *Brazil*	30	J5
Petropavlovsk, *U.S.S.R.*	43	P3
Petropolis, *Brazil*	31	J8
Petrozavodsk, *U.S.S.R.*	35	N3
Phan Rang, *S. Vietnam*	44	C5
Philadelphia, *N.Y.*	17	K3
Philadelphia. *Pa.*	25	M3
Philip I., *Victoria*	50	E9
Philip Edward I., *Ont.*	18	H5
Philippines, rep., *Pacific Oc.*	44	E5
Philippolis, *Orange F.S.*	47	D3
Philipsburg, *Que.*	20	C3
Philipstown, *Cape Prov., Rep. of S. Africa*	47	C3
Phillips, *Me.*	22	B4
Philomena, *Alberta*	14	F3
Philpots I., *Franklin, N.W.T.*	11	T3
Phnom Penh, *Khmer Rep.*	44	C5
Phœnix, *Ariz.*	24	D4
Phœnix Is., *Pacific Oc.*	2	E5
Phu Kok, *Siam*	40	K6
Piagochiwi R., *Que.*	18	J1
Pianco, *Brazil*	30	K5
Piaui R., and Serre do, *Brazil*	30	J5
Pic I., and R., *Ont.*	18	E4
Pica, *Chile*	30	D8
Pichilemu, *Chile*	31	C10
Pickerel. *Ont.*	16	E2
Pickerel L., *Ont.*	18	C4
Pickerel River, *Ont.*	16	E1
Pickle L., *Ont.*	18	C3
Pickle Crow, *Ont.*	18	C3
Pickle Lake, *Ont.*	18	C3
Pickwick L., *Ala., etc.*	25	J4
Pice Duarte, *Dominican Rep.*	29	K4
Picton, *N.S.W.*	50	H7
Picton, *N.Z.*	51	D4
Picton, *Ont.*	17	H4
Pictou, and I., *N.S.*	21	E2
Pidurutalagalla Mt., *Sri Lanka*	40	F7
Piedras Negras, *Mexico*	28	D2
Pierce L., *Man.-Ont.*	18	B1
Pierce L., *Sask.*	14	G3
Pierre, *S. Dak.*	24	F2
Pierre L., *Ont.*	18	H4
Pierreville, *Que.*	20	C2
Pietarsaari (Jakobstad), *Finland*	35	L3
Pietermaritzburg, *Natal*	47	E2
Pietersburg, *Transvaal*	47	D1
Piet Retief, *Transvaal*	47	E2
Pigeon L., *Alberta*	14	D4
Pigeon L., *Ont.*	17	G3
Pigeon R., *Man.*	15	N4
Pigeon Bay, *Ont.*	16	C5
Pigeon River, *Ont.*	18	D4
Piguari, *Brazil*	30	F7
Pikangikum L., *Ont.*	18	A3
Pikes Peak. *Colo.*	24	E3
Piketberg, *Cape Prov., Rep. of S. Africa*	47	B3
Pikwitonei, *Man.*	15	N3
Pilar, *Paraguay*	31	F9
Pilbara, *W. Aust.*	49	B4
Pilcomayo, R., *Paraguay, etc.*	31	E8
Piles Junc., *Que.*	20	C2
Pilgrim Is., *Que.*	20	E2
Pilgrims Rest, *Transvaal*	47	E1
Pililipu, *Fr. Guiana*	30	G3
Pillinger, *Tasmania*	50	K12
Pilos, *Greece*	39	K6
Pilot Mound, *Man.*	15	M6
Pinang, *Malaya*	44	C6
Pinang I., *Malaysia*	44	C6
Pinar del Rio, *Cuba*	29	H3
Pinawa, *Man.*	15	O5
Pincher Creek, *Alberta*	14	D6
Pinchi, *B.C.*	13	H5
Pinchincha, *Ecuador*	30	A4
Pindus Mts., *Greece*	39	K6
Pine. *Ont.*	18	B4
Pine L., *Nfld.*	23	L3
Pine L., *Cochrane, Ont.*	18	E4
Pine L., *Kenora, Ont.*	18	C4
Pine R., *B.C.*	12	K5
Pine Bluff, *Ark.*	25	H4
Pine Creek, *N. Ter., Aust.*	49	E2
Pine Falls, *Man.*	15	N5
Pinega, and R., *U.S.S.R.*	35	P3
Pine Pass, *B.C.*	12	J5
Pine Pt., *Mackenzie, N.W.T.*	12	N2
Pine Portage, *Ont.*	18	D4
Pine River, *Man.*	15	L5
Pinehouse L., *Sask.*	14	H3
Pinery Provincial Park, *Ont.*	16	C4
Pinewood, *Ont.*	18	A4
Pingo Mt., *Greenland*	11	Y4
Pinkiang (Harbin), *China*	44	E2
Pink Mountain, *B.C.*	12	J4
Pinnaroo, *S. Aust.*	50	C7
Pinos, *Mexico*	28	D3
Pinos, I. de, *W. Indies*	29	H3
Pinos Mt., *Cal.*	24	C4
Pinsk, *Poland*	39	L2
Pinta I., *Pacific Oc.*	31	N6
Pinto Cr., *Sask.*	14	H6
Pioche, *Nev.*	24	D3
Pioneer Mine, *B.C.*	13	J7
Pipeclay Plain, *Victoria*	50	C7
Pipestone L., *Man.*	15	N3
Pipestone L., *Ont.*	18	B4
Pipestone R., *Ont.*	18	C2
Pipestone R., *Sask.*	14	H1
Pipestone R., *Sask.*	15	K5
Pipmuacan, and Res., *Que.*	22	B2
Piquiri R., *Brazil*	31	G8
Piquiry R., *Mato Grosso, Brazil*	30	F7
Piraeus, *Greece*	39	K6
Piranhas R., *Brazil*	30	K4
Pirapora, *Brazil*	30	H7
Pirenopolis, *Brazil*	30	H7
Pires, *Brazil*	30	H7
Piripiri, *Brazil*	30	J5
Pisa, *Italy*	38	G5
Pisagua, *Chile*	30	C7
Piscatosine, L., *Que.*	20	B2

Pisco, Peru 30 B6
Pistolet B., Nfld. 23 K1
Pitcairn I., Pacific Oc. 2 F6
Piteå, Sweden 35 L2
Pitesti, Romania 39 L4
Pitlochry, Scotland 36 D3
Pitrufquen, Chile 31 C11
Pitt I., B.C. 13 F6
Pittsburgh, Pa. 25 K2
Pittsfield, Me. 22 C4
Pittsworth, Queensland 50 H3
Piura, Peru 30 A5
Placentia, and B., Nfld. 23 K3
Placilla, Chile 31 C8
Plantagenet, Ont. 17 K2
Plassey, India 40 G4
Plaster Rock, N.B. 22 D3
Plate R., Argentina-Uruguay 31 F11
Platipi L., Que. 19 C3
Platoa, Queensland 50 J2
Platon Pt., Que. 20 D2
Platte R., Neb., etc. 24 F2
Playgreen, Man. 15 M4
Pleasant B., Me. 22 D4
Pleasant Bay, N.S. 21 G1
Plenty, B. of, N.Z. 51 F2
Plessisville, Que. 20 D2
Pletipi L., Que. 22 C1
Plettenburg B., Cape Prov., Rep. of S. Africa 47 C3
Pleven, Bulgaria 39 L5
Ploiesti, Romania 39 L4
Plonge, Lac la, Sask. 14 H3
Plovdiv (Phillippopolis), Bulgaria 39 L5
Plumas, Man. 15 M5
Plum Coulee, Man. 15 N6
Plymouth, and Sd., Eng. 37 C6
Plzen, Czechoslovakia 38 H3
Po R., Italy 38 G4
Pocahontas, Alberta 14 C4
Pocatello, Ida. 24 D2
Pocos de Caldas, Brazil 31 H8
Podolski, Ukraine 39 L3
Pofadder, Cape Prov., Rep. of S. Africa 47 B2
Pogamasing, Ont. 18 G5
Po Hai, G. of, China 44 D3
Pohenegamook L., Que. 20 E2
Poigan L., Que. 20 A2
Point L., Mackenzie, N.W.T. 10 M4
Point Aux Barques, Mich. 16 C3
Point aux Trembles, Que. 20 D2
Point Caribou, Que. 22 D2
Point Danger, N.S.W. 50 J4
Point de Ca Mau, S. Vietnam 44 C6
Point des Monts, Que. 22 D2
Point-du-bois, Man. 15 O5
Point du Chene, N.B. 22 E3
Pointe à Maurier, Que. 23 H1
Pointe au Baril Sta.. Ont. 16 E2
Pointe au Bouliau, Que. 20 E1
Pointe aux Pins. Ont. 16 D5
Pointe aux Trembles, Que. 20 C3
Pointe Bleue, Que. 20 C1
Pointe des Monts, Que. 22 D2
Pointe du Chene, N.B. 21 C1
Point Edward, Ont. 16 C5
Pointe Louis XIV, Que. 19 A3
Pointe Noir, Que. 20 E1
Pointe Noire, Congo 46 E6
Point Farms Prov. Park, Ont. 16 D4
Point Hope, Alaska 10 A4
Point la Boule, Que. 20 E1
Point Leamington, Nfld. 23 K2
Point Pelee, Ont. 16 C5
Point Pelee National Park, Ont. 16 C5
Point Petre, Ont. 17 H4
Poisson Blanc L. (Whitefish L.). Que. 20 B2
Poitiers, France 38 E4
Pokataroo, N.S.W. 50 G4
Poland, rep., Europe 39 J3
Polaris L., Que. 19 C3
Pollux, mt., N.Z. 51 B6
Polotsk, U.S.S.R. 39 M2
Poltava, Ukraine 39 N3
Poltimore, Que. 17 K2
Polwarth, Sask. 14 H4
Polyarny, U.S.S.R. 35 N2
Pombal, Brazil 30 K5
Pomquet, N.S. 21 E2
Ponask L., Man. 15 P3
Ponca City, Okla. 24 G3
Ponce, Puerto Rico 29 L4
Pondicherry, India 40 F6
Pond Inlet, Baffin I., N.W.T. 11 T3
Ponds, I. of, Lab. 19 F3
Pongola R., Natal, etc. 47 E2
Ponhook Ls., N.S. 21 C3
Ponichratrain L.. La. 25 H4
Ponoi R., U.S.S.R. 35 O2
Ponoka, Alberta 14 E4
Ponta Grossa, Brazil 31 G8
Ponta Pora, Brazil 31 G8
Ponte Nova. Brazil 30 J8
Pontiac, Mich. 16 B5
Pontianak, Borneo 44 C6
Ponton R., Alberta 14 C1
Pontotoc, Miss. 25 J4
Pontypool, Ont. 17 G3

Poolanna L., S. Aust. 50 B3
Poole, Eng. 37 D6
Poona, India 40 D5
Pooncarie, N.S.W. 50 D6
Poopelloe L., N.S.W. 50 E5
Poopo L., Bolivia 30 D7
Popayan, Colombia 30 B3
Poplar Pt., and R., Man. 15 N4
Poplar Grove, Orange F.S. 47 D2
Popocatepetl, Mexico 28 E4
Porcher I., B.C. 13 E6
Porcupine C., Lab. 19 F3
Porcupine Mts., Man.-Sask. 15 L4
Porcupine Plain, Sask. 15 K4
Porcupine R., Alaska-Yukon 10 F4
Pori, Finland 35 L3
Porkkala, Finland 35 L3
Poronaisk, Sakhalin Is. 44 G2
Porquis Junc., Ont. 18 H4
Porsanger Fd., Norway 35 M1
Port Adelaide, S. Aust. 50 B4
Portadown, N. Ire. 37 B7
Portage, P.E.I. 21 C1
Portage du Fort, Que. 20 A3
Portage la Prairie, Man. 15 M6
Portage River I., N.B. 22 E3
Portal, N. Dak. 24 F1
Port Alberni, Vancouver I., B.C. 13 H8
Port Albert, Ont. 16 C4
Port Albert, Victoria 50 F9
Portalegre, Portugal 38 C6
Port Alexander. Alaska 13 C4
Port Alfred, Cape Prov., Rep. of S. Africa 47 D3
Port Alfred, Que. 22 B2
Port Alice. Vancouver I., B.C. 13 G7
Port Alma, Queensland 50 H1
Port Antonio, Jamaica 29 J4
Port Arthur, Tex. 25 H5
Port Augusta, S. Aust. 50 A6
Port au Port, Nfld. 23 H2
Port au Port B., and Penin., Nfld. 23 H2
Port au Prince, Haiti 29 K4
Port Austin, Mich. 16 B3
Port Beaufort, Cape Prov., Rep. of S. Africa 47 C3
Port Blair, Andaman Is. 40 H6
Port Blandford, Nfld. 23 K2
Port Broughton, S. Aust. 50 B6
Port Bruce, Ont. 16 D5
Port Burwell, Ont. 16 E5
Port Burwell, Que. 19 D1
Port Carling, Ont. 16 F2
Port Cartier, Que. 22 D1
Port Chalmers, N.Z. 51 C6
Port Clements, B.C. 13 D6
Port Clyde, N.S. 22 E5
Port Colborne, Ont. 17 F5
Port Coquitlam, B.C. 13 J8
Port Credit, Ont. 16 F4
Port Curtis, Queensland 50 H1
Port Dalhousie, Ont. 17 F4
Port Daniel Park, Que. 22 E2
Port Davey, Tasmania 50 K12
Port de Paix, Haiti 29 K4
Port Dover, Ont. 16 E5
Port Dufferin, N.S. 21 E3
Port Edward, B.C. 13 E5
Port Elgin, Ont. 21 C1
Port Elizabeth, Cape Prov., Rep. of S. Africa 47 D3
Port Ellen, Scotland 36 B4
Porter Landing, B.C. 12 E3
Porterville, Cape Prov., Rep. of S. Africa 47 B3
Port Essington, B.C. 13 F5
Port Essington, N. Ter., Aust. 49 E2
Port Fairy, Victoria 50 D9
Port Felix, N.S. 21 F2
Port Fortune, Ont. 20 B3
Port Gentil, Gabon, Equat. Africa 46 D6
Port George, N.S. 21 B3
Port Greville, N.S. 21 C2
Port Harcourt, Nigeria 46 D5
Port Hardy, Vancouver I., B.C. 13 G7
Port Hastings, N.S. 21 F2
Port Hawkesbury, N.S. 21 F2
Port Hedland, W. Aust. 49 B3
Porthill, Ida. 13 M8
Port Hood, N.S. 21 F2
Port Hope, Lab. 19 F3
Port Hope, Ont. 17 G4
Port Huron, Mich. 16 C5
Port Isabel, Tex. 24 G5
Port Jackson, N.S.W. 50 H6
Port Kembla, N.S.W. 50 H7
Portland, Me. 25 N2
Portland, Ont. 17 J3
Portland, Ore. 24 B1
Portland, Victoria 50 C9
Portland B., Victoria 50 C9
Portland C., Tasmania 50 L11
Portland Can., Alaska 12 E5
Portland Bill, Eng. 35 D6
Portland Creek, Nfld. 23 H1
Portland Inlet, B.C. 12 F5
Portland Promontory. Que. 19 B2

Port Laois, Eire 37 B5
Port Lincoln .S. Aust. 49 F6
Port Lonsdale, Victoria 50 E9
Port Loring, Ont. 16 E2
Port McNicoll, Ont. 16 F3
Port Macquarie, N.S.W. 50 J5
Port Madryn, Argentina 31 D12
Port Maitland, N.S. 21 A3
Port Maitland, Ont. 16 F5
Port Manvers, Lab. 19 E2
Port Medway, N.S. 21 C3
Port Menier ,Anticosti I. 22 E2
Port Moody, B.C. 13 J8
Port Moresby, Papua-New Guinea 49 G1
Port Morien, N.S. 21 G1
Port Mouton, N.S. 21 B4
Port Natal, Natal 47 E2
Port Nelson, Man. 15 P2
Portneuf, Que. 20 D2
Portneuf sur Mer, Que. 20 E1
Port Nicholson, N.Z. 51 E4
Port Nolloth, Cape Prov., Rep. of S. Africa 47 B2
Port Nouveau-Québec, Que. 19 D2
Porto Acre, Brazil 30 D5
Porto Algre, Brazil 31 G9
Porto Arroio, Mozambique 46 G4
Portobelo, Pan. 29 J6
Porto Cortés, Costa Rica, 29 H6
Porto de Moz, Brazil 30 G4
Porto Esperança, Brazil 29 F7
Port of Spain, Trinidad 30 E1
Porto Okha, India 40 C4
Porto Murtinho, Brazil 31 F8
Porto Nacional, Brazil 30 H6
Porto Novo, Dahomey, Africa 46 D5
Pôrto Santana, Brazil 30 G4
Porto Seguro, Brazil 30 K7
Pôrto Velho, Brazil 30 E5
Portoviejo, Ecuador 30 A4
Port Patrick, Scotland 37 C4
Port Pegasus, Stewart I., N.Z. 51 A7
Port Perry, Ont. 17 G3
Port Phillip B., Victoria 50 E8
Port Pirie, S. Aust. 50 A6
Port Radium, Mackenzie, N.W.T. 10 L4
Portree, Skye I., Scotland 36 B3
Port Renfrew, Vancouver I., B.C. 13 H8
Port Rowan, Ont. 16 E5
Port Royal, Ga. 25 K4
Port Royal Natural History Park, Ont. 21 A3
Portrush, N. Ire. 37 B4
Port Said, Egypt 46 G2
Port St. Johns, Cape Prov., Rep. of S. Africa 47 D3
Port Sanilac, Mich. 16 C4
Port Saunders, Nfld. 23 J1
Port Shepstone, Natal 47 E3
Port Simpson, B.C. 12 E5
Portsmouth, Eng. 37 E6
Portsmouth, N.H. 25 M2
Portsmouth, O. 25 K3
Portsmouth, Ont. 17 J3
Portsmouth, Va. 25 L3
Port Stanley, Ont. 16 D5
Port Stephens, N.S.W. 50 J6
Port Sudan, Sudan 46 G4
Port Talbot, Wales 37 D6
Portugal, rep., Europe 38 B6
Portuguesa R., Venezuela 30 D2
Portuguese Guinea, W. Africa 46 B4
Port Union, Nfld. 23 L2
Port Union, Ont. 17 F4
Port Victoria, S. Aust. 50 A7
Port Wakefield, S. Aust. 50 B7
Port Williams, N.S. 21 C2
Posadas, Argentina 31 F9
Posen, Mich. 16 B2
Poso, Celebes 44 E7
Possession I., S.W. Africa 47 B2
Post R., Que. 20 C2
Poste -de-la-Baleine (Great Whale R.), Que. 19 B2
Poste-de-Mistassini, Que. 20 C3
Postmasburg, Cape Prov. 47 B2
Postville, Coast of Lab. 19 F3
Potchefstroom, Transvaal 47 D2
Potgietersrus, Transvaal 47 D1
Potholes Res., Wash. 13 L9
Potosi, Bolivia 30 D7
Potro, Co del, Mt., Chile 31 D9
Potsdam, Ger. 38 H2
Poty R., Brazil 30 J5
Pouce Coupe, B.C. 12 K5
Pouch Cove, Nfld. 23 L3
Poverty B., N.Z. 51 G3
Povungnituk, and B., Que. 19 B2
Povungnituk R., Que. 19 B1
Povyenets, U.S.S.R. 35 N3
Powassan, Ont. 16 F1
Powder R., Mont., etc. 24 E1
Powell L., B.C. 13 H7
Powell L., Ut. 24 D2
Powell River, B.C. 13 H8
Poznan, Poland 39 J2
Prague. Czechoslovakia 39 H3
Prairie R., E. and W.. Alberta 14 C3

Pratt, Kan. 24 G3
Preeceville, Sask. 15 K5
Premier, Alaska 10 H6
Premier, B.C. 12 F4
Premio, Que. 22 E1
Preolenna, Tasmania 50 K11
Prescott, Ariz. 24 D4
Prescott, Ont. 17 K3
Prescott, co., Ont. 17 L2
Pres. Epitacio, Brazil 31 G8
Preservation Inlet, N.Z. 51 A7
Presidio, Tex. 26 F5
Presque Isle, Me. 22 C3
Presqu'ile Provincial Park, Ont. 17 H4
Press, Que. 20 A1
Presteigne, Wales 37 D5
Preston, Eng. 37 D5
Preston, Ont. 16 E4
Prestwick, Scotland 36 C4
Preto R., Brazil 30 J6
Pretoria, Transvaal 47 D2
Price, Que. 22 C2
Price L., B.C. 13 F6
Prieska, Cape Prov., Rep. S. Africa 47 C2
Priest Rapids Res., Wash. 24 C1
Prim Pt., P.E.I. 21 D1
Primrose L., Sask. 14 G3
Prince Albert, Cape Prov., Rep. of S. Africa 47 C3
Prince Albert, Sask. 14 J4
Prince Albert Penin., Victoria I., N.W.T. 10 L3
Prince Albert Sd., Franklin, N.W.T. 10 M3
Prince Albert Park, Sask. 14 H4
Prince Alfred C., Banks I., N.W.T. 10 K3
Prince Charles I., Franklin, N.W.T. 11 T4
Prince Edward, co., Ont. 17 H3
Prince Edward B., Ont. 17 J4
Prince Edward I., Canada 21 D1
Prince Edward I., Indian Oc. 3 M7
Prince Edward Pt., Ont. 17 J4
Prince George, B.C. 13 J6
Prince Gustaf Adolf Sea, Franklin, N.W.T. 10 K2
Prince of Wales C., Alaska 10 A4
Prince of Wales I., Alaska 12 D5
Prince of Wales I., Franklin, N.W.T. 10 O3
Prince of Wales Str., Franklin, N.W.T. 10 L3
Prince Patrick I., Canada 10 K2
Prince Regent Inlet, Franklin, N.W.T. 11 Q3
Prince Rupert. B.C. 13 E5
Princess Charlotte B., Queensland 49 G2
Princess Royal I., B.C. 13 F6
Princeton, B.C. 13 K8
Princeville, Que. 20 D2
Prince William Sd., Alaska 10 E5
Principe I., G. of Guinea 46 D5
Principe de Beira, Brazil 30 E6
Prinzapolea, Nicaragua 29 H5
Pripyat R., U.S.S.R. 39 L3
Pritzler Harb., Baffin I., N.W.T. 19 D1
Privert L., Que. 19 D2
Progreso, Mexico 28 G3
Prokop'yevsk, U.S.S.R. 44 A1
Prome, Burma 40 J5
Prophet R., B.C. 12 J3
Propria, Brazil 30 K6
Prospect, N.S. 21 C3
Pröven, Greenland 11 X3
Providence, R.I. 25 M2
Providence B., Ont. 16 C2
Providence C., N.Z. 51 A7
Providence Point, Alberta 14 E1
Providencia, I. de, Colombia 29 H5
Provincial Cannery, B.C. 13 G7
Provincial Park, Ont. 17 G2
Provo, Ut. 24 D2
Provost, Alberta 14 F4
Prudhoe Bay, Alaska 10 E3
Prudhoe Land, Greenland 11 V2
Prut R., Rumania 39 L4
Przemysl, Polana 39 K3
Pskov, U.S.S.R. 39 M1
Pubnico, N.S. 21 B4
Pubnico Harb., N.S. 21 D5
Pucallpa, Peru 30 C5
Puebla, Mexico 28 E4
Pueblo, Colo. 24 F3
Pueblo Hundido, Chile 31 C9
Puerto Angel, Mexico 28 E4
Puerto Armuelles, Pan. 29 H6
Puerto Ayacucho, Venezuela 30 D4
Puerto Barrios, Guatemala 28 G4
Puerto Cabello, Venezuela 30 D1
Puerto Cabezas, Nicaragua 29 H5
Puerto Carreno, Colombia 30 D2
Puerto Casado, Paraguay 31 F8
Puerto Chandless, Peru 30 C6
Puerto Cortes, Honduras 28 G4
Puerto de Carrizal, Chile 31 C9
Puerto de Chañaral, Chile 31 C9
Puerto de Corral, Chile 31 B12
Puerto de Morelos, Mexico 28 G3

Name	Page	Ref.
Puerto de Sta. Anna, Brazil	30	G7
Puerto La Cruz, Venezuela	30	E1
Puerto Lobos, Argentina	31	D12
Puerto Lomas, Peru	30	B7
Puerto Mexico, Mexico	28	F4
Puerto Montt, Chile	31	C12
Puerto Natales, Chile	31	C14
Puerto Ordaz, Venezuela	30	E2
Puerto Plata, Dominican Rep.	29	K4
Puerto Rico I., W. Indies	29	L4
Puerto Suarez, Bolivia	30	F7
Puerto Sulinas, Argentina	31	D11
Puerto Wilches, Colombia	30	C2
Puget Sd., Wash.	24	B1
Pugwash, N.S.	21	D2
Pugwash Harb., N.S.	21	D2
Pugwash Junc., N.S.	21	D2
Pukaeshun Mt., B.C.	13	L7
Pukaki L., N.Z.	51	C6
Pukaskwa R., Ont.	18	F4
Pukatawagan, Man.	15	L3
Pukekohe, N.Z.	51	E2
Puket I., Siam	40	J7
Pula, Italy	38	H4
Pulog Mt., Philippines	44	E5
Puna I., Ecuador	30	A4
Punakha, India	40	H3
Punchaw, B.C.	13	J6
Punjab, state. India	40	E2
Punjab, The, prov., Pakistan	40	D2
Puno, Peru	30	C7
Punta Alta, Argentina	31	E11
Punta Arenas (Magallanes), Chile	31	C14
Puntarenas, Costa Rica	29	H6
Puntjak Djaja, mt., W. Irian	44	F7
Puntzi L., B.C.	13	H6
Purcell Mts., B.C.	13	M7
Puri, India	40	G5
Purus R., Brazil	30	E5
Pusan, S. Korea	44	E3
Pushthrough, Nfld.	23	J3
Putaruru, N.Z.	51	E3
Putien, China	44	D4
Putumayo R., Colombia,etc.	30	C3
Pwllheli, Wales	37	C5
Pyongyang, N. Korea	44	E3
Pyramid L., Nev.	24	C2
Pyramid Mt., B.C.	12	F3
Pyrenees Mts., France-Spain	38	E5
Pythonga L., Que.	17	J1
Qatar, state, Arabia	42	D6
Qattara Depression, Egypt	46	F3
Quaco Head, N.B.	21	B2
Quang Tri, S. Vietnam	44	C5
Quarryville, N.B.	21	A1
Quatsino,Vancouver I.,B.C.	13	G7
Queanbeyan, N.S.W.	50	G7
Quebec, Que.	20	D2
Quebec, prov., Canada	11	U7
Queen Adelaide Arch., Chile	31	B14
Queen Charlotte, B.C.	13	D6
Queen Charlotte Is., B.C.	13	D6
Queen Charlotte Sd., B.C.	13	E7
Queen Charlotte Str., B.C.	13	F7
Queen Mary Ld., Antarctica	3	O8
Queen Maud G., Mackenzie, N.W.T.	10	O4
Queens Chan., Franklin, N.W.T.	11	P2
Queen's Chan., N. Ter., Aust.	49	D2
Queenscliff, Victoria	50	E9
Queensland, Aust.	49	G4
Queensport, N.S.	21	F2
Queenstown, Cape Prov., Rep. of S. Africa	47	D3
Queenstown (Cobh), Eire	37	A6
Queenstown, N.Z.	51	B6
Queenstown, Tasmania	50	K11
Queimadas, Brazil	30	K6
Quelimane, Mozambique	46	G7
Quelpart I., (Cheju Do), S. Korea	44	E3
Queretaro, Mexico	28	D3
Quesnel, and R., B.C.	13	J6
Quesnel L., B.C.	13	K6
Quetico Park. and L., Ont.	18	C4
Quetta, W. Pak.	40	C2
Quezaltenango, Guatemala	28	F5
Quezon City, Philippines	44	E5
Quibdo, Colombia	30	B2
Quiet L., Yukon	12	D2
Quigley, Alberta	14	F2
Quilan C., Chile	31	B12
Quill Lake, Sask.	15	J4
Quillota, Chile	31	C10
Quilpie, Queensland	50	E3
Quincy, Ill.	25	H3
Quines, Argentina	31	D10
Quintette Mt., B.C.	12	K5
Quinze, L. des, Que.	18	J5
Quirke L., Ont.	16	C1
Quitaro R., Guyana	30	F3
Quito, Ecuador	30	B4
Qumbu, Cape Prov., Rep. of S. Africa	47	D3
Quorn, Ont.	18	C4
Quorn, S. Aust.	50	B6
Quro Preto, Brazil	30	J8
Quthing, Lesotho	47	D3
Quyon, Que.	17	J2
Raasay, Sd. of, Skye I., Scotland	36	B3
Rabast, Cap de, Anti-costi I., Que.	22	F2
Rabat, Morocco	46	C2
Rabaul I., Pacific Oc.	2	D5
Rabbit R., B.C.	12	G3
Raber, Mich.	16	A1
Race C., Nfld.	23	L3
Race I., Que.	20	D2
Racine, Wis.	25	J2
Radisson, Sask.	14	H4
Radnor, co., Wales	37	D5
Radom, Poland	39	K3
Radville, Sask.	15	J6
Rae, Mackenzie, N.W.T.	12	N1
Rae Mt., Alberta	14	D5
Rae Bareli, India	40	F3
Rae Isthmus, Keewatin, N.W.T.	11	R4
Raetihi, N.Z.	51	E3
Rafaela, Argentina	31	E10
Ragueneau, Que.	22	C2
Rahab, Alberta	14	B3
Raigarh, India	40	F4
Rainbow, Victoria	50	F7
Rainier Mt., Wash.	24	B1
Rainy L., Ont.-Minn.	18	B4
Rainy River, Ont.	18	A4
Raipur, India	40	F4
Raith, Ont.	18	D4
Rajasthan, state, India	40	D3
Rakahanga I., Pacific Oc.	2	E5
Rakaio R., N.Z.	51	C5
Raleigh, N.C.	25	L3
Raleigh, Ont.	18	B4
Raleigh B., N.C.	25	L4
Ralph, Sask.	15	K6
Ramah, Lab.	11	W6
Ramah B., Lab.	19	E2
Ramea, Nfld.	23	J3
Ramea Is., Nfld.	23	J3
Ram Head, Victoria	50	G8
Ramore, Ont.	18	H4
Ramoutsa, Botswana	47	D1
Ramree I., Burma	40	H5
Ramsey, Isle of Man	37	C4
Ramsey, Ont.	18	G5
Ramsgate, Eng.	37	F6
Rancagua, Chile	31	C10
Rancheria, Yukon	12	E2
Ranco, L. de, Chile	31	C12
Random I., Nfld.	23	L2
Ranfurly, N.Z.	51	C6
Rangaunu B., N.Z.	51	D1
Rangeley, and L., Me.	22	B4
Rangiora, N.Z.	51	D5
Rangitaiki R., N.Z.	51	F3
Rangitata R., N.Z.	51	C5
Rangoon, Burma	40	J5
Rankin Inlet, Keewatin, N.W.T.	11	Q5
Rankin Springs, N.S.W.	50	E6
Rannes, Queensland	50	H2
Rannoch L., Scotland	36	C3
Ranoke, Ont.	18	H3
Rantekombola, Mt., Celebes	44	D7
Rapid City, Man.	15	M5
Rapid City, S. Dak.	24	F2
Rapide Blanc, Que.	20	C2
Rapides des Joachims, Que.	17	H1
Raquette L., N.Y.	17	L4
Ras al Had, Oman, Arabia	42	E6
Ras Dashan, Mt., Ethiopia	46	G4
Raso C., Brazil	30	H3
Rat R., Que.	20	C2
Rathdrum, Eire	37	B5
Rathkeale, Eire	37	A5
Rathlin I., N. Ire.	37	B4
Rathwell, Man.	15	M6
Rattray Hd., Scotland	36	E3
Ratz Mt., B.C.	12	D4
Raukumara Ra., N.Z.	51	F3
Rauma, Finland	35	L3
Ravenglass, Eng.	37	D4
Ravenna, Italy	38	H4
Ravensworth, Ont.	17	F2
Rawalpindi, W. Pak.	40	D2
Rawdon, Que.	20	C2
Rawene, N.Z.	51	D1
Rawlins, Wyo.	24	E2
Rawson, Argentina	31	E12
Ray C., Nfld.	23	H3
Raymond, Alberta	14	E6
Reading, Eng.	37	E6
Reading, Pa.	25	L2
Readlyn, Sask.	14	J6
Recherche Arch., W. Aust.	49	C6
Recife, Brazil	30	K5
Reconquista, Argentina	31	E9
Recreo, Argentina	30	D9
Red B., Ont.	16	D3
Red C., N.S.	23	G3
Red I., Nfld.	23	K3
Red I., Nfld.	23	H2
Red I., Que.	20	E1
Red L., Minn.	25	H1
Red L., Ont.	18	A3
Red Lake, etc.	25	H4
Red R., N. Dak., etc.	24	G1
Red R., Tex.	24	G4
Red Bay, Lab.	23	J1
Red Cedar R., Ia.	25	H2
Redcliffe, Alberta	14	F5
Red Cliffs, Victoria	50	D7
Red Deer, Alberta	14	E4
Red Deer L., Man.	15	L4
Red Deer R., Alberta	14	E5
Red Deer R., Sask.	15	K4
Redditch, Eng.	37	D5
Redditt Canyon, Ont.	18	A3
Redfield, S. Dak.	24	G2
Red Indian L., Nfld.	23	J2
Redknife R., Mackenzie, N.W.T.	12	L2
Red Lake, Ont.	18	C3
Redonda Bay, B.C.	13	H7
Redondo, Pico, Brazil	30	E3
Red Pass Junction, B.C.-Alberta	14	B4
Red Pine, N.B.	22	E3
Red Rock, B.C.	13	J6
Red Sea, Africa-Arabia	46	G3
Redstone R., Mackenzie, N.W.T.	12	H1
Red Sucker, and L., Man.	15	P3
Ree L., Eire	37	B5
Reed L., Man.	15	L3
Reeder L., Man.	15	L4
Reefton, N.Z.	51	C5
Reese, Mich.	16	B4
Regan, Ont.	18	F4
Regensburg, Ger.	38	G3
Regent, Man.	15	L6
Reggio, N. Italy	38	G4
Reggio, S. Italy	39	H6
Regina, Sask.	14	J5
Rehoboth, S.W. Africa	47	B1
Reigate, Eng.	37	E6
Reims, France	38	F3
Reindeer I., Man.	15	M4
Reindeer L., Man.	15	L2
Reindeer R., Sask.	15	K3
Reindeer Depot, Mac-kenzie, N.W.T.	10	H4
Ren Ld., Greenland	11	Z3
Rencontre, East, Nfld.	23	K3
Renews, Nfld.	23	L3
Renfrew, Ont.	17	J2
Renfrew, co., Scotland	36	C4
Renison, Ont.	18	H3
Renmark, S. Aust.	50	C7
Rennes, France	38	D3
Reno, Nev.	24	C3
Renous, N.B.	21	B1
Republican R., Neb.	24	F2
Rep. of South Africa, Africa	47	C2
Repulse B., Keewatin, N.W.T.	11	R4
Resistencia, Argentina	31	E9
Resolution, Mackenzie, N.W.T.	10	M5
Resolution I., Franklin, N.W.T.	19	E1
Resolution I., N.Z.	51	A6
Resolution L., Que.	19	E2
Resthaven Mt., Alberta	14	B4
Restigouche, Que.	22	D2
Restigouche R., N.B.	22	D3
Reston, Man.	15	L6
Restoule, Ont.	16	F1
Retlaw, Alberta	14	E5
Réunion I., Indian Oc.	3	M6
Revelstoke, B.C.	13	L7
Revillagigedo I., Alaska	12	E5
Revilla Gigedo Is., Mexico	28	B4
Rexton, N.B.	21	B1
Reykiavik, Iceland	35	B3
Rezekne, Latvia	39	L1
Rhein, Sask.	15	K5
Rhine R., Ger.	38	F3
Rhode Island, state, U.S.A.	25	M2
Rhodes, and I., Ægean Sea	37	M6
Rhodesia, Africa	46	F7
Rhodope Mts., Bulgaria	39	K5
Rhondda, Wales	37	D6
Rhône R., France	38	F4
Rhyl, Wales	37	D5
Ribble R., Eng.	37	D5
Ribbon R., Que.	20	B2
Ribeira R., Brazil	31	H8
Ribeirão Preto, Brazil	31	H8
Riberalta, Bolivia	30	D6
Ribstone Cr., Alberta	14	F4
Rice L., Ont.	17	G3
Richan, Ont.	18	B3
Richard, Sask.	14	H4
Richards B., Natal	47	E2
Richards L., Sask.	14	H1
Richards Landing, Ont.	16	A1
Richardson L., and R., Alberta	14	F1
Riche Pt., Nfld.	23	J1
Richelieu R., Que.	20	C3
Richibucto, N.B.	21	C1
Richland, Wash.	24	C1
Richmond, Cape Prov., Rep. of S. Africa	47	C3
Richmond, Me.	22	C4
Richmond, Natal	47	E2
Richmond, N.S.W.	50	H6
Richmond, N.Z.	51	D4
Richmond, Ont.	17	J2
Richmond, P.E.I.	21	C1
Richmond, Que.	20	C3
Richmond, Surrey, Eng.	37	E6
Richmond, Va.	25	L3
Richmond, Yorks., Eng.	37	E4
Richmond G., Que.	19	B2
Richmond R., N.S.W.	50	J4
Richmond Hill, Ont.	16	F4
Rideau Can., Ont.	17	K3
Rideau L., Ont.	17	J3
Rideau R., Ont.	17	K2
Rider, B.C.	13	K6
Ridgetown, Ont.	16	D5
Riding Mt., Man.	15	L5
Riding Mt. National Park, Man.	15	L5
Ridout, Ont.	18	G5
Riet R., Cape Prov., Rep. of S. Africa	47	C3
Riet R., Orange F.S.	47	D2
Rietbron, Cape Prov., Rep. of S. Africa	47	C3
Rietfontein, S.W. Africa	47	C2
Riga, Latvia	39	L1
Riga, G. of, Latvia	39	K1
Rigaud, Que.	20	B3
Rigny Mt., Greenland	11	Z4
Rigolet, Lab.	19	F3
Rijeka (Fiume), Yugoslavia	39	H4
Rimbey, Alberta	14	D4
Rimouski, Que.	22	C2
Rimouski Park, Que.	22	C2
Ringköbing, Denmark	35	H4
Riobamba, Ecuador	30	B4
Rio Branco, Brazil	30	D5
Rio Bravo del Norte, Mexico-U.S.A.	24	F5
Rio Claro, Brazil	31	H8
Rio Cuarto, Argentina	31	E10
Rio de Janeiro, Brazil	31	J8
Rio Gallegos, Argentina	31	D14
Rio Grande, Brazil	31	G10
Rio Grande, U.S.A.-Mexico	28	D2
Rio Grande do Sul, Brazil	31	G9
Rio Hacha, Colombia	30	C1
Rio Muni, Equat. Guinea	46	E5
Rio Negro, Brazil	30	D4
Rio Negro Res., Uruguay	31	F10
Rio Pardo, Brazil	31	G10
Rio Pecos, N. Mex.	24	F4
Riou L., Sask.	14	H1
Rio Verde, Mexico	28	D3
Ripley, Ont.	16	D3
Ripon, Eng.	37	E4
Ripon, Que.	17	K2
Riske Cr., B.C.	13	J7
Rivadavia, Argentina	31	E8
Rivas, Nicaragua	29	G5
Rivera, Uruguay	31	F10
River Denys, N.S.	21	F2
River Herbert, N.S.	21	C2
Riverhurst, Sask.	14	H5
Riverina, N.S.W.	50	E7
River John, N.S.	21	D2
River Lake, Ont.	18	G1
River of Ponds, N.S.	23	J1
Riverport, N.S.	21	C3
Rivers, Man.	15	L5
Rivers, L. of the, Sask.	14	J6
Riversdale, Cape Prov.	47	C3
Rivers Inlet, B.C.	13	G7
Riverton, Man.	15	N5
Riverton, N.Z.	51	B7
Riviere Pte., Que.	20	D2
Rivière-a-la-Loutre, Que.	22	F2
Rivière à Pierre, Que.	20	C2
Rivière au Rat, Que.	20	C2
Rivière aux Graines, Que.	22	E1
Rivière Bleue, Que.	22	C3
Rivière de la Chaloupe, Que.	22	F2
Rivière du Loup, Que.	20	E2
Rivière Ouelle, Que.	20	E2
Rivière Pentecôte, Que.	22	D2
Rivière St. Jean, Que.	22	E1
Riyadh, Saudi Arabia	42	C6
Rizaiyeh L., Persia	42	C5
Roanoke, Va.	25	L3
Roanoke R., N.C., etc.	25	L3
Robbins I., Tasmania	50	K11
Robe, S. Aust.	50	B8
Roberts Bank, B.C.	13	J8
Robertson, Que.	20	D2
Roberval, Que.	20	C1
Robinson, Baffin Island, Yukon	12	C2
Robinson Crusoe I. (Más á Tierra, I.), S. Pacific Oc.	31	B10
Robinson's, Nfld.	23	H2
Robinson Sd., N.W.T.	19	E1
Roblin, Man.	15	L5
Robore, Bolivia	30	E7
Robson, B.C.	13	M8
Robson Mt., B.C.	13	L6
Rocafeurte, Peru	30	B4
Rocanville, Sask.	15	L5
Roca Partida, Mexico	28	B4
Rocha, Uruguay	31	G10
Rochefort, France	38	D4
Rocher River, Mackenzie, N.W.T.	10	M5
Rochester, Eng.	37	F6
Rochester, Minn.	25	H2
Rochester, N.H.	22	B5
Rochester, N.Y.	25	L2
Rock R., Yukon	12	G2
Rock Bay, Vancouver I., B.C.	13	H7
Rockford, Ill.	25	J2
Rockglen, Sask.	14	H6
Rockhampton, Queensland	50	H1
Rock Island, Ill.	25	H2

Rockland, *Me.* 22 C4
Rockland, *Ont.* 17 K2
Rockport, *Tex.* 24 G5
Rock Springs, *Wyo.* 24 E2
Rockwood, *Ont.* 16 E4
Rocky Mts., *N. America* 1 D3
Rocky Mountain House, *Alberta* 14 D4
Roddickton, *Nfld.* 23 J1
Rodney, *Ont.* 16 D5
Rodriguez I., *Indian Oc.* 3 N5
Roebourne, *W. Aust.* 49 B4
Roebuck B., *W. Aust.* 49 C3
Roes Welcome, *Mackenzie, N.W.T.* 11 R5
Rogagua L., *Bolivia* 30 D6
Rogers, *B.C.* 13 M7
Rogers City, *Mich.* 16 B2
Rogersville, *N.B.* 21 B1
Roggan R., *Que.* 19 B3
Roggeveld Mts., *Cape Prov., Rep. of S. Africa* 47 C3
Rogoaguado L., *Bolivia* 30 D6
Rolla, *B.C.* 12 K5
Rolla, *Mo.* 25 H3
Rolleston, *Queensland* 50 G2
Rolphton, *Ont.* 17 H1
Roma, *Queensland* 50 G3
Romaine R., *Que.* 22 F1
Romania, rep., *Europe* 39 K4
Romanzof C., *Alaska* 10 A5
Rome, *Ga.* 25 J4
Rome, *Italy* 38 H5
Romeo, *Mich.* 16 B5
Ronaldsay, S., *Orkney Is., Scotland* 36 D2
Roncador, Serra do. *Brazil* 30 G6
Rond L., *Que.* 20 A2
Rondeau, and Park, *Ont.* 16 D5
Ronge, Lac la, *Sask.* 14 J3
Roosevelt, F. D., L. *Wash.* 24 C1
Roosevelt Mt., *B.C.* 12 H3
Root R., *Mackenzie, N.W.T.* 12 H1
Root R., *Ont.* 15 Q5
Roper R., *N. Ter., Aust.* 49 E2
Roques, Los, *Venezuela* 30 D1
Roraima, Sa., *Venezuela* 30 E2
Rorkes Drift, *Natal* 47 E2
Rorketon, *Man.* 15 M5
Röros, *Norway* 35 J3
Rosa, Monte, *Italy* 38 F4
Rosario, *Entre Rois, Argentina* 31 E10
Rosario, *Lower Cal.* 28 A2
Rosario, *Mexico* 28 C3
Rosario, *Paraguay* 31 F8
Rosario, *Salta, Argentina* 31 E9
Roscoe, *Sask.* 15 L4
Roscommon, and co., *Eire* 37 A5
Roscrea, *Eire* 37 B5
Rose Pt., *B.C.* 13 E5
Roseau, *Dominica, W. Indies* 29 M4
Rose Blanche, *Nfld.* 23 H3
Rosebud R., *Alberta* 14 E5
Roseburg, *Ore.* 24 B2
Rosee L., *Que.* 19 C3
Roseneath, *Ont.* 17 G3
Rosenfeld, *Man.* 15 N6
Rosenheim, *Ger.* 38 G4
Rosetown, *Sask.* 14 H5
Rosiers C., *Que.* 22 E2
Roslavi, *U.S.S.R.* 39 N2
Rosmead, *Cape Prov., Rep. of S. Africa* 47 D3
Ross, *N.Z.* 51 C5
Ross and Cromarty, co., *Scotland* 36 C3
Ross I., *Man.* 15 N3
Ross R., *Yukon* 12 E1
Rossburn, *Man.* 15 L5
Rosseau, *Ont.* 16 F2
Rossignol L., *Que.* 19 C3
Rossignol Lake, *N.S.* 21 A3
Rossland, *B.C.* 13 M8
Rosslare Harb., *Eire* 37 B5
Rossport, *Ont.* 18 E4
Ross River, *Yukon* 12 D1
Rossway, *N.S.* 21 A3
Rosthern, *Sask.* 14 H4
Rostock, *Ger.* 38 H2
Rostov, *U.S.S.R.* 35 O4
Rostov-on-Don, *U.S.S.R.* 39 O4
Roswell, *N. Mex.* 24 F4
Rotherham, *Eng.* 37 E5
Rothesay, *N.B.* 21 B2
Rothesay, *Scotland* 36 C4
Rotorua, and L., *N.Z.* 51 F3
Rotosi, C. de, *Bolivia* 30 D7
Rotterdam, *Netherlands* 38 E3
Rotumah I., *Pacific Oc.* 2 D5
Roubaix, *Belgium* 38 E3
Rouen, *France* 38 E3
Rouge C., *Que.* 20 D2
Rouge R., *Que.* 20 B2
Rouleau, *Sask.* 14 J5
Round Mt., *N.S.W.* 51 J5
Round Pond, *Nfld.* 23 J2
Rousay I., *Orkney Is., Scotland* 36 D2
Routhierville, *Que.* 22 D3
Rouvray L., *Que.* 22 B2
Rouxville, *Orange F.S.* 47 D3
Rouyn, *Que.* 19 B4
Rovno, *Ukraine* 39 L3

Rowan L., *Ont.* 18 B4
Roxburgh, *N.Z.* 51 B6
Roxburgh, co., *Scotland* 37 D4
Roxton, *Que.* 20 D3
Roxton Falls, *Que.* 20 C3
Royal B., *S. Georgia I., S. Atlantic Oc.* 31 K14
Royal Natal National Park, *S. Africa* 47 D2
Ruahine Ra., *N.Z.* 51 E4
Ruapehu Mt., *N.Z.* 51 E3
Ruapuke I., *N.Z.* 51 B7
Rub al Khali, *Saudi Arabia* 42 C7
Ruby, *Alaska* 10 D5
Rudolf L., *Kenya* 46 G5
Ruel, *Ont.* 18 H5
Rufino, *Argentina* 31 E10
Rugby, *Eng.* 37 E5
Rügen (I.), *Ger.* 39 H2
Rum I., *Scotland* 36 B3
Rum Cay, *Bahamas* 29 K3
Rumford, *Me.* 22 B4
Runanga, *N.Z.* 51 C5
Runaway C., *N.Z.* 51 F2
Rupert L., *Que.* 19 B3
Rupununi R., *Guyana* 30 F3
Rurrenabaque, *Bolivia* 30 D6
Ruse, *Bulgaria* 39 L5
Rush Lake, *Sask.* 14 H5
Russell, *Man.* 15 L5
Russell, *N.Z.* 51 E1
Russell, *Ont.* 17 K2
Russell, co., *Ont.* 17 K2
Russell L., *Franklin, N.W.T.* 10 O3
Russell L., *Alberta* 14 D2
Russell L., *Mackenzie, N.W.T.* 12 N1
Russell L., *Man.* 15 L2
Russell Mt., *Yukon* 12 D1
Rustenburg, *Transvaal* 47 D2
Rutan, *Sask.* 14 J4
Ruthergien, *Ont.* 17 H3
Rutland, *Vt.* 25 M2
Rutland, co., *Eng.* 37 E5
Rutter, *Ont.* 16 E1
Ruvuma R., *E. Africa* 46 G7
Ruwenzori Mt., *Uganda* 46 F5
Rwanda, *Cent. Africa* 46 C6
Ryan L., *Scotland* 37 C4
Ryazan, *U.S.S.R.* 39 O2
Ryazhsk, *U.S.S.R.* 39 O2
Rybinsk, *U.S.S.R.* 35 O4
Rybinsk Res., *U.S.S.R.* 35 O4
Rydal Bank, *Ont.* 16 B1
Ryukyu Arch., *Japan* 44 E4
Rzhev, *U.S.S.R.* 39 N1

Saarbrücken, *France* 38 F3
Saaremaa, *Estonia* 35 L4
Sabadell, *Spain* 38 E5
Sabah, *Malaysia* 44 D6
Sabara, *Brazil* 30 J7
Sabine Penin., *Melville I., N.W.T.* 10 N2
Sabine R., *La.-Tex.* 25 H4
Sable C., *Fla.* 25 K5
Sable C., *N.S.* 22 E5
Sable I., *N.S.* 23 G5
Sable R., *Ont.* 18 G5
Sable River, *N.S.* 21 C3
Sables, L. aux, *Que.* 20 C2
Sabtaneh R., *B.C.* 12 K3
Sabzewar, *Iran* 40 A1
Sachigo L., *Ont.* 18 B2
Sachigo R., *Ont.* 15 Q3
Sachs Harb., *Franklin, N.W.T.* 10 K3
Sackets Harb., *N.Y.* 17 J4
Sackville, *N.B.* 21 C2
Saco, *Me.* 22 B5
Sacramento, and R., *Cal.* 24 B3
Sacre Coeur de Marie, *Que.* 20 D2
Saddle I., *Lab.* 19 D2
Saddle Mt., *Que.* 20 D3
Saddleback Mt., *Me.* 22 B4
Sadiya, *India* 40 J3
Safala, *Mozambique* 46 G8
Sagaing, *Burma* 40 J4
Saganaga L., *Ont.* 18 C4
Sagawitchewan, *Man.* 15 P4
Saginaw, *Mich.* 16 A4
Saginaw Bay, *Mich.* 16 B4
Saglek B., *Lab.* 19 E2
Saglouc, *Que.* 19 B1
Sagua la Grande, *Cuba* 29 H3
Saguenay R., *Que.* 22 B2
Sahara, *N. Africa* 46 C3
Saharan Atlas (Mts.), *Algeria* 46 D2
Saharanpur, *India* 40 E3
Sahuaripa, *Mexico* 28 C2
Saigon, *S. Vietnam* 44 C5
Saimaa, L., *Finland* 35 M3
St. Adolphe, *Que.* 20 D2
St. Agapit, *Que.* 20 D2
St. Agatha, *Me.* 22 C3
St. Agathe, *Man.* 15 N6
Ste. Agathe des Monts, *Que.* 20 B2
St. Aime, *Que.* 20 C3
St. Albans, *Eng.* 37 E6
St. Albans, *Nfld.* 23 J3
St. Albans Hd., *Eng.* 37 E6
St. Albert, *Alberta* 14 E4
St. Alexandre, *Que.* 20 E2
St. Alexis, *Que.* 20 C3
Ste. Anastasie, *Que.* 20 D2

St. André, *Avellin, Que.* 20 B3
St. André, *Kamouraska, Que.* 20 E2
St. André, *L. St. John, W. Que.* 20 C1
St. Andrews, *N.B.* 22 D4
St. Andrews, *Scotland* 36 D3
St. Andrews Chan., *N.S.* 21 G1
Ste. Angele, *Que.* 20 C3
St. Anicet, *Que.* 20 B3
St. Ann, and L., *Alberta* 14 D4
Ste. Anne L., *Que.* 20 D2
Ste. Anne R., *Que.* 20 D2
Ste. Anne-de-Beaupré, *Que.* 20 D2
Ste. Anne de la Perade, *Que.* 20 C2
Ste. Anne des Chênes, *Man.* 15 N6
Ste. Anne des Monts, *Que.* 22 D2
Ste. Anne du Lac, *Que.* 20 B2
St. Anns, *N.S.* 21 G1
St. Ann's Bay, *N.S.* 23 G1
St. Anselme, *Que.* 20 D2
St. Anthony, *Nfld.* 23 J1
St. Anthony C., *Nfld.* 23 K1
St. Antoine, *Que.* 20 B3
St. Antonio de los Cobres, *Argentina* 31 D8
St. Arsène. *Que.* 20 E2
St. Augustin, *Que.* 20 B3
St. Augustin R., *N.W., Que.* 23 H1
St. Augustin Saguenay, and R., *Que.* 23 H1
St. Augustine, *Fla.* 25 K5
St. Barbe Is., *Nfld.* 23 K1
St. Basile de Portneuf, *Que.* 20 D2
Ste. Beatrix, *Que.* 20 C2
St. Bees Hd., *Eng.* 37 D4
St. Benjamin, *Que.* 20 D2
St. Benoit Labre, *Que.* 20 D2
St. Bernard, *Que.* 20 D2
St. Bonaventure, *Que.* 20 C2
St. Boniface, *Man.* 15 N6
St. Brendans, *Nfld.* 23 L2
St. Bride's B., *Wales* 37 C6
St. Brieuc, *France* 38 D3
St. Brieux, *Sask.* 14 J4
St. Camille, *Que.* 20 D3
St. Casimir, *Que.* 20 C2
Ste. Catherine, *Que.* 20 D2
St. Catherines, *Ont.* 17 F4
Ste. Cécile, *Que.* 20 D3
St. Celestin, *Que.* 20 C2
St. Cesaire, *Que.* 20 C3
St. Charles, *Que.* 20 D2
St. Charles C., *Lab.* 19 F3
St. Christopher I., *W. Indies* 29 M4
St. Clair, *Mich.* 16 C5
St. Clair L., and R., *Mich.-Ont.* 16 C5
Ste. Claire, *Que.* 20 D2
St. Claud, *Minn.* 25 H1
St. Clement, *Que.* 20 E2
Ste. Clothilde, *Que.* 20 C3
St. Croix, *W. Indies* 29 M4
St. Croix L., *N.S.* 21 E2
St. Cyprien, *Que.* 20 C3
St. Cyr, *Que.* 20 D1
St. Cyriac, *Que.* 20 D1
St. Cyrille, *Drummond, Que.* 20 C3
St. Cyrille, *L'Islet, Que.* 20 D2
St. Damase, *Que.* 20 D2
St. David's Hd., *Wales* 37 C6
St. Denis, *Kamouraska, Que.* 20 E2
St. Denis, *St. Hyacinthe, Que.* 20 C3
St. Didace, *Que.* 20 C2
St. Elias Mts., *B.C., etc.* 13 A3
St. Elic, *Que.* 20 C2
St. Eloi, *Que.* 20 E1
St. Emilien, *Que.* 20 C1
St. Émilien(Desbiens), *Que.* 20 D1
St. Ephrem, *Que.* 20 D2
St. Etienne, *France* 38 E4
St. Etienne, *Que.* 22 B2
St. Eustache, *Que.* 20 C3
St. Evariste, *Que.* 20 D3
St. Fabien, *Que.* 22 C2
Ste. Famille d'Aumond, *Que.* 17 J1
St. Felicien, *Que.* 20 C1
Ste. Félicité, *Que.* 22 D2
St. Felix, *Que.* 20 C2
St. Ferdinand, *Que.* 20 D2
St. Feréol, *Que.* 20 D2
St. Fidele, *Que.* 20 D2
St. Francis, *Me.* 22 C3
St. Francis, and L., *Que.* 20 E2
St. Francis B., *Cape Prov., Rep. of S. Africa* 47 D3
St. Francis C., *Cape Prov., Rep. of S. Africa* 47 C3
St. Francis, C., *Nfld.* 23 L3
St. Francis L., *Que.* 20 B3
St. Francis R., *Que.* 20 D3
St. Francis R., *Que.* 20 E2
St. Francois, I. of Orleans, *Que.* 20 D2
St. Francois, *Yamaska, Que.* 20 C2
Ste. Francois L., *Que.* 20 D3
Ste. Francoise, *Que.* 20 E1
St. Fulgence, *Que.* 20 D1
St. Gabriel, *Que.* 20 C2
St. Gédéon, *Que.* 20 D1
St. George, *N.B.* 22 D4
St. George, *Queensland* 50 G3

St. George, *Ut.* 24 D3
St. George L., *Man.* 15 N5
St. George Head, *N.S.W.* 50 H7
St. George's, *Grenada, W. Indies* 29 M5
St. Georges, *Nfld.* 23 H2
St. Georges, *Que.* 20 D2
St. George's B., and C., *Nfld.* 23 H2
St. George's Chan., *Wales-Eire* 37 B6
Ste. Gertrude, *Que.* 20 C2
St. Gervais, *Que.* 20 D2
St. Gotthard Pass, *Switzerland* 38 G4
St. Gregory C., *Nfld.* 23 H2
St. Guillaume, *Que.* 20 C3
St. Helen, *Mich.* 16 A3
St. Helena B., *Cape Prov., Rep. of S. Africa* 47 B3
St. Helena I., *S. Atlantic Oc.* 46 C7
St. Hélène, *Que.* 20 E2
Ste. Henodine, *Que.* 20 D2
St. Henri, *Que.* 20 D1
St. Henri L., *Que.* 20 D2
St. Henry Junc., *Que.* 20 E2
St. Honore, *Que.* 20 D1
St. Honore, *Que.* 20 D3
St. Hughes, *Que.* 20 C3
St. Hyacinthe, *Que.* 20 C3
St. Ignace I., *L. Superior, Ont.* 18 E4
St. Ignacio, *Bolivia* 30 E7
Ste. Irénée, *Que.* 20 D2
St. Ives, *Eng.* 37 C6
St. Jacques, *Que.* 22 C3
St. James, *Man.* 15 N6
St. James C., *B.C.* 13 E7
St. Jean, *L'Islet, Que.* 20 D2
St. Jean, *Que.* 20 C3
St. Jean L., *Que.* 20 D1
St. Jean R., *Que.* 22 E1
St. Jean de Dieu, *Que.* 22 C2
St. Jean de Matha, *Que.* 20 C2
St. Jean Port Joli, *Que.* 20 D2
St. Jean River Park, *Que.* 22 E2
St. Jerome, *St. John E., Que.* 20 D1
St. Jérôme, *Terrebonne, Que.* 20 B3
St. Joachim, *Que.* 20 D2
St. João Is., *Brazil* 30 J4
St. John, *N.B.* 21 B2
St. John B., *Nfld.* 23 J1
St. John C., *Nfld.* 23 K1
St. John I., *Lab.* 20 F3
St. John L., *Que.* 20 B2
St. John R., *Me.* 22 C3
St. John's, *Nfld.* 23 L3
St. Joseph, *Dorchester, Que.* 20 D2
St. Joseph, *Mo.* 25 H3
St. Joseph, *Richelieu, Que.* 20 C2
St. Joseph I., *Ont.* 16 B1
St. Joseph L., *Ont.* 18 C3
St. Joseph's, *Nfld.* 23 L3
St. Jovite, *Que.* 17 L1
St. Jude, *Que.* 20 C3
St. Julie, *Que.* 20 D2
Ste. Julienne, *Que.* 20 C3
Ste. Justine, *Que.* 20 D2
St. Kilda I., *Scotland* 36 A3
St. Kitts I., *W. Indies* 29 M4
St. Laurent, *Man.* 15 N5
St. Laurent du Maroni, *Fr. Guiana* 30 G3
St. Lawrence, *Nfld.* 23 K3
St. Lawrence, G. of, *Canada* 22 F2
St. Lawrence I., *Bering Sea* 10 A5
St. Lawrence R., *Canada-U.S.A.* 25 N1
St. Lawrence Seaway, *Can.-U.S.A.* 17 K3
St. Lawrence Islands National Park, *Ont.* 17 J3
St. Leonard, *N.B.* 22 D3
St. Lewis Sd., *Lab* 19 F3
St. Lin, *Que.* 20 C3
St. Louis, *Mo.* 25 J3
St. Louis, *P.E.I.* 21 C1
St. Louis, *Senegal, W. Africa* 46 B4
St. Louis L., *Que.* 20 B2
St. Louis de Ha Ha, *Que.* 20 E2
St. Louis de Kent, *N.B.* 21 C1
St. Louis de Nord, *Haiti* 29 K4
St. Lucia I., *W. Indies* 29 M5
St. Lucia L., and B., *Natal* 47 E2
Ste. Lucie de Doncaster, *Que.* 20 B2
St. Luiz I., *Brazil* 30 J4
St. Magnus B., *Shetland Is., Scotland* 36 E1
St. Malo, *Que.* 20 D3
St. Marc, *Que.* 20 C3
St. Marcel, *Que.* 20 C3
St. Margaret's B., *N.S.* 22 F4
Ste. Marguerite, *Que.* 20 E1
Ste. Marguerite R., *Que.* 20 D2
Ste. Marie C., *Madagascar* 46 H8
Ste. Marie I., *Madagascar* 46 J7
Ste. Marie Beauce, *Que.* 20 D2
St. Martin C., *Cape Prov., Rep. of S. Africa* 47 B3
St. Martin I., *W. Indies* 29 M4
St. Martin L., *Man.* 15 M5
Ste. Martine, *Que.* 20 C3
St. Martin's, *N.B.* 21 B2
St. Mary C., *Nfld.* 23 K3
St. Mary's, *Nfld.* 23 L3

Name	Pl.	Ref.
St. Mary's, *Ont.*	16	A1
St. Marys, *Ont.*	16	D4
St. Mary's, *Tasmania*	50	M11
St. Mary's B., *Nfld.*	23	L3
St. Mary's R., *N.S.*	21	A3
St. Mary's R., *N.S.*	21	E2
St. Mathieu, *Que.*	20	E1
St. Maurice, *Que.*	20	C2
St. Maurice R., *Que.*	20	B1
St. Mothode, *Que.*	20	C1
St. Michael, *Alaska*	10	B5
St. Michael B., *Lab.*	19	F3
St. Michel, *Que.*	20	D2
St. Michel des Saints, *Que.*	20	C2
St. Nazaire, *France*	38	D4
St. Nicholas, *Que.*	20	D2
St. Nicholas C., *Que.*	22	D2
St. Onesime, *Que.*	20	E2
St. Ours, *Que.*	20	C3
St. Pamphile, *Que.*	20	E2
St. Pascal, *Que.*	20	E3
St. Patrice, L., *Quebec*	17	H1
St. Paul, *Alberta*	14	F4
St. Paul, *Minn.*	23	H1
St. Paul, *Que.*	20	D2
St. Paul I., *Indian Oc.*	2	A6
St. Paul I., *N.S.*	23	G3
St. Paul R., *Que.*	23	J1
St. Paul du Nord, *Que.*	22	C2
St. Paulin, *Que.*	20	C2
St. Paul Rocks, *Atlantic Oc.*	3	K5
St. Paul's B., *Nfld.*	23	H2
St. Peters, *N.S.*	21	G2
St. Peters Bay, *P.E.I.*	21	E1
St. Petersburg. *Fla.*	25	K5
St. Philemon, *Que.*	20	D2
St. Pie, *Que.*	20	C3
St. Pierre, *Man.*	15	N6
St. Pierre, *Martinique, W. Indies*	29	M5
St. Pierre, *Que.*	20	D2
St. Pierre and Miquelon Is., *Atlantic Oc.*	23	J3
St. Pierre L., *Que.*	20	C2
St. Pierre les Becquets, *Que.*	20	C2
St. Pölten, *Austria*	39	H3
St. Prime, *L. St. John W., Que.*	20	C1
St. Prime, *Yamaska, Que.*	20	C3
St. Quentin, *N.B.*	22	D3
St. Raymond, *Que.*	20	D2
St. Remi, *Que.*	20	C3
St. Rémi d'Amherst, *Que.*	17	K1
St. Roch, *Que.*	20	D2
St. Rosalie, *Que*	20	C3
Sto. Rose, *Dorchester, Que.*	22	C3
Ste. Rose, *Terrebonne, Que.*	20	C3
Sto. Rose du Lac, *Man.*	15	M5
Sto. Rufino, *Que.*	20	D3
St. Sabine, *Que.*	20	D2
St. Scholastique, *Que.*	20	B3
St. Sebastian B., *Cape Prov., Rep. of S. Africa*	47	C3
St. Sebastien, *Que.*	20	D2
St. Simeon, *Que.*	20	E1
St. Simon, *Bagot, Que.*	20	C3
St. Simon, *Rimouski, Que.*	22	C2
Ste. Sophie, *Que.*	20	C2
St. Stanislas, *Que.*	20	C2
St. Stephen, *N.B.*	22	D4
St. Stephens, *Ala.*	25	J4
St. Sylvestre, *Que.*	20	D2
Ste. Thècle, *Que.*	20	C2
Ste. Thérèse, *Que.*	20	C3
St. Thomas, *Ont.*	16	D5
St. Thomas I., *W. Indies*	3	H4
St. Tite, *Que.*	20	C2
St. Tite des Caps, *Que.*	20	D2
St. Ubald, *Que.*	20	C2
St. Urbain de Charlevoix, *Que.*	20	D2
St. Valerien, *Que.*	20	C3
St. Vallier, *Que.*	20	D2
St. Victor, *Que.*	20	D2
St. Vincent, *Que.*	20	C3
St. Vincent C., *Portugal*	38	B6
St. Vincent G., *S. Aust.*	50	B7
St. Vincent I., *W. Indies*	29	M5
St. Walburg, *Sask.*	14	G4
St. Williams, *Ont.*	16	E5
St. Zacharie, *Que.*	20	D2
Sakami L., and R., *Que.*	19	B3
Sakaria R., *Turkey*	39	M6
Sakhalin I., *U.S.S.R.*	44	G1
Sakishima Gunto, *Japan*	44	E4
Saladillo R., *Argentina*	31	E9
Salado R., *Argentina*	31	F11
Salama, *Guatemala*	28	F4
Salamanca, *Spain*	38	C5
Salavina, *Argentina*	31	E9
Sala-y-Gomez I, *Pacific Oc.*	2	G6
Saldanha, *Cape Prov., Rep. of S. Africa*	47	B3
Saldanha B., *Cape Prov., Rep. of S. Africa*	47	B3
Sal de Uyuni, *Bolivia*	30	D8
Sale, *Victoria*	50	F9
Salekhard, *U.S.S.R.*	42	C7
Salem, *India*	40	E6
Salem, *Ore.*	24	B2
Salem, *S.W. Africa*	47	B1
Salerno, and G. of, *Italy*	39	H5
Salford, *Eng.*	37	D5
Salgueiro, *Brazil*	30	K5
Salina, *Kan.*	24	G3
Salina Cruz, *Mexico*	28	E4
Salinas Grandes, *Argentina*	31	D10
Salinópolis, *Brazil*	30	H4
Salisbury, *Eng.*	37	E6
Salisbury, *N.B.*	21	B1
Salisbury, *Rhodesia*	46	G7
Salisbury I., *Keewatin, N.W.T.*	11	T5
Salisbury Plain, *Eng.*	37	D6
Sally's Cove, *N.S.*	23	J2
Salmo, *B.C.*	13	M8
Salmon, and R., *Ida.*	24	D1
Salmon R., *B.C.*	13	J5
Salmon R., *N.B.*	21	B1
Salmon R., *Que.*	22	F2
Salmon Arm, *B.C.*	13	L7
Salmon Cove, *Nfld.*	23	L3
Salmon River, *N.S.*	22	D4
Salonica (Thessaloniki), *Greece*	39	K5
Salta, *Argentina*	31	D8
Salt Desert, *Persia*	42	D5
Saltillo, *Mexico*	28	D2
Salt Lake City, *Ut.*	24	D2
Salto, *Uruguay*	30	F10
Salton, and L., *Cal.*	24	C3
Saltrou, *Haiti*	29	K4
Salvador (Bahai), *Brazil*	30	K6
Salvador, *Cent. America*	28	G5
Salvage, *Nfld.*	23	L2
Salween R., *Burma*	40	J5
Salzburg, *Austria*	38	H4
Sama R., *Peru*	30	C7
Samaná, *Dominican Rep.*	29	L4
Samar I., *Philippine Is.*	44	E5
Samarinda, *Borneo*	44	D7
Samarkand, *U.S.S.R.*	42	E4
Sambre R., *France-Belgium*	38	F3
Sambro C., *N.S.*	22	F4
Samoan Is., *Pacific Oc.*	2	E5
Samos I., *Greece*	39	L6
Samsun, *Turkey*	39	O5
Samut Prakan, *Siam*	40	K6
San'a, *Arabia*	42	C7
San Amaro, *Brazil*	30	K6
San Ambrosio I., *Chile*	31	B9
San Ana, *Salvador*	28	G5
San Andreas Tuxtla, *Mexico*	28	E4
San Andrés, I. de, *Colombia*	29	H5
San Angelo, *Brazil*	31	F9
San Angelo, *Tex.*	24	F4
San Antonio, *Chile*	31	C10
San Antonio, *Tex.*	24	G5
San Antonio C., *Argentina*	31	F11
San Antonio C., *Cuba*	29	H3
San Antonio Oeste, *Argentina*	31	D12
San Barbara, *Honduras*	28	G5
San Benedicto I., *Mexico*	28	B4
San Bernardino, *Cal.*	24	C4
San Blas, *Mexico*	28	C3
San Borja, *Brazil*	31	F9
Sanborn, *Que.*	20	D3
San Carlos, *Argentina*	31	D9
San Carlos, *Venezuela*	30	D2
San Carlos L., *Ariz.*	24	D4
San Carlos de Bariloche, *Argentina*	32	B7
Sanchez, *Dominican Rep.*	29	L4
San Christobal, *Colombia*	30	C2
San Cristobal, *Argentina*	31	E9
San Cristobal I., *Pacific Oc.*	31	O17
San Cristobal de las Casas, *Mexico*	28	F4
Sancti Spiritus, *Cuba*	29	J3
Sand L., *Ont.*	18	A3
Sand R., *Alberta*	14	F3
Sand R., *Transvaal, etc.*	47	D1
Sandakan, *Sabah*	44	D6
Sanday, *Orkney Is., Scotland*	36	D2
San Diego, *Cal.*	24	C4
San Diego C., *Argentina*	31	E14
Sand Lake, *Ont.*	18	F5
Sand Point, *Que.*	20	A3
Sandstone, *W. Aust.*	49	B5
Sandwich B., *Lab.*	19	F3
Sandwich Harb., *S.W. Africa*	47	A1
Sandwich Is., *S. Atlantic Oc.*	31	M15
Sandy B., *Nfld.*	23	J1
Sandy C., *Queensland*	50	J2
Sandy Cr., *Que.*	17	J1
Sandy L., *Nfld.*	23	J2
Sandy L., *Ont.*	18	B2
Sandy Creek, *N.Y.*	17	J4
Sandy Lake, *Sask.*	14	H2
Sandy Narrows, *Sask.*	15	K3
San Felipe, *Chile*	31	C10
San Felipe, *Venezuela*	30	D1
San Felix I., *S. Pacific Oc.*	31	B9
San Fernando, *Chile*	31	C10
San Fernando, *Luzon*	44	E5
San Fernando de Apure *Venezuela*	30	D2
San Fernando de Atabapo *Venezuela*	30	D3
San Fidelis, *Brazil*	31	J8
Sanford, *N.H.*	22	B5
Sanford Mt., *Alaska*	10	F5
San Francisco, *Argentina*	31	E10
San Francisco, *Cal.*	24	B3
San Francisco I., *Brazil*	31	H9
San Francisco Mt., *Ariz.*	24	D3
San Francisco R., *Brazil*	30	H7
Sangihe Is., *Philippine Is.*	44	E6
Sangre de Cristo Mts., *Colo., etc.*	24	E3
Sangudo, *Alberta*	14	D4
Sangue R., *Brazil*	30	F6
San Ignacio, *Mexico*	28	C3
San Joaquin R., *Cal.*	24	B3
San Jorge, G. de, *Argentina*	31	D13
San José, *Bolivia*	30	E7
San José *Costa Rica*	29	H6
San José, *Guatemala*	28	F5
San Jose, *Uruguay*	31	F10
San José I., *Mexico*	28	B2
San Jose do Norte, *Brazil*	31	H9
San Juan, *Argentina*	31	D10
San Juan, *Puerto Rico*	29	L4
San Juan Mts., *Colo.-N. Mex.*	24	E3
San Juan R., *Costa Rica-Nicaragua*	29	H5
San Juan R., *Utah-New Mexico*	24	E3
San Juan de Guadalupe, *Mexico*	28	D3
San Juan del Norte, *Nicaragua*	29	H5
San Juan del Sur, *Nicaragua*	29	G5
San Julian, *Argentina*	31	D13
San Lazaro C., *Mexico*	28	B3
San Lorenzo, *Ecuador*	30	B3
San Lorenzo, *Venezuela*	30	C2
San Louis Obispo, *Cal.*	24	B3
San Lucas C., *Mexico*	28	B3
San Luis, *Argentina*	31	D10
San Luis, *Mexico*	28	C2
San Luis Potosi, *Mexico*	28	D3
San Maria del Rio, *Mexico*	28	D3
San Marino, *Italy*	38	H5
San Martin L., *Argentina-Chile*	31	C13
San Matias, G., *Argentina*	31	E12
Sanmaur, *Que.*	20	C2
San Miguel, *Salvador*	28	G5
San Miguel R., *Bolivia*	30	E7
San Miguel de Tucumán, *Argentina*	31	D9
Sannas Post, *Orange F.S.*	47	D2
San Nicolas, *Argentina*	31	E10
San Pedro, *Bolivia*	30	E6
San Pedro, *Paraguay*	31	F8
San Pedro Pt., *Costa Rica*	29	H6
San Pedro Sula, *Honduras*	28	G4
Sanquhar, *Scotland*	37	D4
San Quintin, *Mexico*	28	A1
San Rafael, *Argentina*	31	D10
San Ramon, *Peru*	30	B6
San Salvador, *Salvador*	28	G5
San Salvador I., *Pacific Oc.*	31	N17
San Salvador I. (Watling I.), *Bahamas*	25	M6
San Sebastian, *Spain*	38	D5
San Sebastian B., *Argentina*	31	D14
San Sebastian Vizcaino B., *Mexico*	28	B2
São Sebastião I., *Brazil*	31	J8
Santa R., *Peru*	30	B5
Santa Barbara, *Mexico*	28	C2
Santa Barbara, and Chan., *Cal.*	24	C4
Santa Catalina, *Cal.*	24	C4
Santa Catalina Mt., *Mexico*	28	A1
Santa Catarina I., *Brazil*	31	H9
Santa Clara, *Cuba*	29	J3
Santa Clara I., *S. Atlantic Oc.*	31	B10
Santa Clemente, *Cal.*	24	C4
Santa Cruz, *Argentina*	31	D14
Santa Cruz, *Bolivia*	30	E7
Santa Cruz, *Cal.*	24	B3
Santa Cruz, *Cal.*	24	B3
Santa Cruz I., *Pacific Oc.*	31	N17
Santa Cruz Is., *Pacific Oc.*	2	D5
Santa Cruz R., *Argentina*	31	C14
Santa Cruz del Quiche, *Guatemala*	28	F4
Santa Cruz del Sur, *Cuba*	29	J3
Santa Elena C., *Costa Rica*	28	G3
Santa Fé, *Argentina*	31	E10
Santa Fé, *N. Mex.*	24	E3
Santa Fé I., *Pacific Oc.*	31	N17
Santa Ines I., *Chile*	31	C14
Santa Inez C., *Argentina*	31	D11
Santa Isabel, *Fernando Po I.*	46	D5
Santa Lucia I., *W. Indies*	29	M5
Santa Maria, *Brazil*	31	G9
Santa Maria I., *Pacific Oc.*	31	N17
Santa Maria di Leuca C., *Italy*	39	J6
Santa Marta, *Colombia*	30	C1
Santander, *Spain*	38	C5
Santander Jimenez, *Mexico*	28	E3
Santarem, *Brazil*	30	G4
Santa Rita, *Peru*	30	C5
Santa Rosa, *Cal.*	24	B3
Santa Rosa, *Cordoba, Argentina*	31	E10
Santa Rosa, *Mendoza, Argentina*	31	D10
Santa Rosa, *Uruguay*	31	F10
Santa Rosa I., *Cal.*	24	B4
Santa Rosa de Toay, *Argentina*	31	D11
Santa Rosalia, *Mexico*	28	B2
San Telmo, Pta., *Mexico*	28	D4
Santiago, *Chile*	31	C10
Santiago, *Pan.*	29	H6
Santiago, *Dominican Rep.*	29	K4
Santiago, *Spain*	38	B5
Santiago de Cuba, *Cuba*	29	J4
Santiago del Estero, *Argentina*	31	E9
Santo Corazon, *Bolivia*	30	F7
Santo Domingo, *Dominican Rep.*	29	L4
San Tomé de Guayana, *Venezuela*	30	E2
Santos, *Brazil*	31	H8
San Valentin, Mt., *Chile*	31	D8
São Amaro, *Brazil*	30	K6
São Angelo, *Brazil*	31	F9
São Borja, *Brazil*	31	F9
São Fidelis, *Brazil*	31	J8
São Francisco I., *Brazil*	31	H9
São Francisco R., *Brazil*	30	H7
São Francisco do Sul, *Brazil*	31	H9
São João I., *Brazil*	30	J4
São João da Barra, *Brazil*	31	J8
São João do Araguaya, *Brazil*	30	H5
São Leopoldo, *Brazil*	31	G9
São Luis, *Brazil*	30	J4
São Marco, G. of, *Brazil*	30	J4
São Mateus, *Brazil*	30	K7
Saona I., *Dominican Rep.*	29	L4
Saône R., *France*	38	F4
São Paulo, *Brazil*	31	H8
São Paulo de Olivenca, *Brazil*	30	D4
São Raimundo, *Brazil*	30	J5
São Romão, *Brazil*	30	H7
São Roque C., *Brazil*	30	K5
São Simão, *Brazil*	31	H8
São Tomé I., *G. of Guinea*	46	D5
Saposoa, *Peru*	30	B5
Sapporo, *Japan*	44	G2
Saragossa, *Spain*	38	D5
Sarajevo, *Yugoslavia*	39	J5
Saratov, *U.S.S.R.*	42	C3
Sarawak, *Malaysia*	44	D6
Sardinia (I.), *Italy*	38	G5
Sarmiento, *Argentina*	31	D13
Sarnia, *Ont.*	16	C5
Saronic G., *Greece*	39	K6
Saskatchewan, prov., *Canada*	10	N7
Saskatchewan Mt., *Alberta*	14	C4
Saskatchewan R., *Sask.-Man.*	15	J4
Saskatchewan R., N., *Alberta-Sask.*	14	F4
Saskatchewan R., S., *Alberta-Sask.*	14	F5
Saskatoon, *Sask.*	14	H4
Saskeram L., *Man.*	15	L4
Sasovo, *U.S.S.R.*	39	P2
Sassari, *Sardinia*	38	G5
Sassnitz, *Ger.*	38	H2
Satpura Ra., *India*	40	E4
Satu-Mare *Romania*	39	K4
Sauces, *Bolivia*	30	E7
Saudi Arabia *S.W. Asia*	42	C6
Saugeen R., *Ont.*	16	D3
Saulnierville, *N.S.*	21	A3
Sault au Mouton, *Que.*	20	E1
Sault Ste. Marie, *Mich.*	16	A1
Sault Ste. Marie, *Ont.*	16	A1
Saunders C., *N.Z.*	51	C6
Sava R., *Yugoslavia*	39	J4
Savane R., *Que.*	22	B1
Savannah, and R., *Ga.*	25	K4
Savanna la Mar, *Jamaica*	29	J4
Savanne, *Ont.*	18	C4
Savant Lake, *Ont.*	18	C3
Savona, *Italy*	38	G4
Savu Sea, *Indonesia*	44	E7
Sawbill, *Coast of Lab.-Nfld.*	19	D3
Sawbill, *Man.*	15	L2
Sawyerville, *Que.*	20	D3
Sayabec, *Que.*	22	D2
Sayan Mts., *U.S.S.R.*	44	A1
Sayula, *Mexico*	28	D4
Scalloway, *Shetland Is., Scotland*	36	E1
Scandia, *Alberta*	14	F5
Scapa, *Alberta*	14	E5
Scapa Flow, *Orkney Is. Scotland*	36	D2
Scarboro, *Me.*	22	B5
Scarborough, *Eng.*	37	E4
Scatarie I., *N.S.*	23	H3
Scavaig L., *Skye I., Scotland*	36	B3
Sceptre, *Sask.*	14	G5
Schaffhausen, *Switzerland*	38	G4
Schanck C., *Victoria*	50	E9
Schefferville (Knob Lake), *Que.*	19	D3
Schenectady, *N.Y.*	25	L2
Schiehallion, Mt., *Scotland*	36	D3
Schleswig, *Ger.*	38	G2
Schreiber, *Ont.*	18	E4
Schumacher, *Ont.*	18	H4

Schwaner Mts., *Borneo* 44 D7
Schweizer Reneke, *Transvaal* 47 D2
Scilly Is., *Eng.* 37 B6
Scone, *N.S.W.* 50 H6
Scotia Bay, *B.C.* 12 D3
Scotland, *Brit. Isles* 36 C3
Scotsburn, *N.S.* 21 D2
Scotstown, *Que.* 20 D3
Scotsville, *N.S.* 21 F1
Scott, *Sask.* 14 G4
Scott C., *Vancouver I., B.C.* 13 F7
Scott Inlet, *Baffin I., N.W.T.* 11 U3
Scott Is., *Vancouver I., B.C.* 13 F7
Scott Junc., *Que.* 20 D2
Scott L., *Que.* 20 C2
Scottburgh, *Natal* 48 E3
Scotts Bay, *N.S.* 21 C2
Scottsdale, *Tasmania* 50 L11
Scovil, *Ont.* 18 A4
Scranton, *Pa.* 25 L2
Scugog L., *Ont.* 17 F3
Scunthorpe, *Eng.* 37 E5
Seaforth, *Ont.* 16 D4
Seal C., *Cape Prov., Rep. of S. Africa* 47 C3
Seal Is., *N.S.* 22 D5
Seal L., *Lab.* 19 E3
Seal L., Lower, *Que.* 11 T6
Seal L., Upper, *Que.* 11 U6
Seal R., *Man.* 15 O1
Seal R., S., *Man.* 15 M1
Sea Lake, *Victoria* 50 D7
Seanio, *Man.* 15 M5
Searchmont, *Ont.* 18 F5
Seaton, *B.C.* 12 G5
Seattle, *Wash.* 24 B1
Sebago L., *Me.* 22 B5
Sechelt, *B.C.* 13 J8
Sechura, and B., *Peru* 30 A5
Secretan, *Sask.* 14 H5
Secretary L., *N.Z.* 51 A6
Secunderabad, *India* 40 E5
Sedalia, *Mo.* 25 H3
Seddon C., *Greenland* 11 X2
Seddonville, *N.Z.* 51 C4
Sedgewick, *Alberta* 14 F4
Seeheim, *S.W. Africa* 47 B2
Seeleys Bay, *Ont* 17 J3
Seg L., *U.S.S.R.* 35 N3
Séguin, L., *Que.* 20 A2
Seine R., *France* 38 E3
Seine R., *Ont.* 18 C4
Selawik L., *Alaska* 10 B4
Selenga R., *Mongolia* 44 C1
Selkirk, *Man.* 15 N5
Selkirk, *Ont.* 16 F5
Selkirk, *Yukon* 10 G5
Selkirk, and co., *Scotland* 36 D4
Selkirk, E., *Man.* 15 N5
Selkirk I., *Man.* 15 M4
Selkirk Mts., *B.C.* 13 M7
Selma, *Ala.* 25 J4
Solsey Bill, *Eng.* 37 E6
Selvas. *Brazil* 30 D4
Selwyn L., *Mackenzie, N.W.T.* 10 N5
Selwyn Mts., *Yukon* 12 E1
Selwyn Ra., *Queensland* 49 F4
Semarang, *Java* 44 D7
Semuru, Mt., *Java* 44 D7
Semidi Is., *Alaska* 10 C6
Semipalatinsk, *U.S.S.R.* 42 F3
Semmering Pass, *Austria* 39 H4
Sendai, *Japan* 44 G3
Senegal, rep., and R., *W. Africa* 46 B4
Senekal, *Orange F.S.* 47 D2
Senja, *Norway* 35 K2
Sennar Dam, *Sudan* 46 G4
Senneterre, *Que.* 19 B4
Seoul (Soul), *S. Korea* 44 E3
Separation Pt., *Mackenzie, N.W.T.* 10 H4
Sept Îles (Seven Islands), *Que.* 22 D1
Seram I., and Sea, *Indonesia* 44 E7
Seret R., *Ukraine* 39 L3
Serowe, *Botswana* 47 D1
Serpent Mounds Park, *Ont.* 17 G3
Serpentine R., *N.B.* 22 D3
Serpentine Park, *Newfoundland* 23 H2
Serpukhov, *U.S.S.R.* 39 O2
Serra do Navio, *Brazil* 30 G3
Serrai, *Greece* 39 K5
Serviceton, *Victoria* 50 C8
Seseganaga L., *Ont.* 18 C3
Sète, *France* 38 E5
Sete Quedas. I. das, *Brazil* 31 G8
Seton Lake. *B.C.* 13 J7
Setting L., *Man.* 15 M3
Seul, Lac, *Ont.* 18 B3
Sevastopol, *U.S.S.R.* 39 N4
Seven Islands, and B., *Que.* 22 D1
Seventy Mile House, *B.C.* 13 K7
Severn L., *Ont.* 18 C2
Severn R., *Eng.* 37 D5
Severn R., *Ont.* 15 Q3
Severodvinsk, *U.S.S.R.* 35 O3
Sevier L., *Ut.* 24 D3
Seville, *Spain* 38 C6
Seward, *Alaska* 10 E5
Seward Penin., *Alaska* 10 A4

Sexsmith, *Alberta* 12 L5
Seychelles (Is.), *Indian Oc.* 3 M5
Seydisdjordur, *Iceland* 35 D2
Seymour, *Victoria* 50 E8
Seymour Inlet, *B.C.* 13 G7
Shabumeni L., *Ont.* 18 B3
Shahjahanpur, *India* 40 F3
Shakespeare I., *Ont.* 18 D4
Shalatth, *B.C.* 13 J7
Shallow Lake, *Ont.* 16 D3
Shamattawa, *Ont.* 15 Q3
Shamo (Gobi), *China-Mongolia* 43 J4
Shanghai, *China* 44 E3
Shannon R., *Eire* 37 A5
Shantung Penin., *China* 44 E3
Shapio L., *Lab.* 19 E2
Sharbot L. *Ont.* 17 H3
Sharpe, L., *S. Dak.* 26 F2
Shark B. *W. Aust.* 49 A5
Shark I., *James B.* 18 J3
Shasta Mt., *Cal.* 24 B2
Shatt-al-Arab, *Iraq/Iran* 42 C5
Shaunavon, *Sask.* 14 G6
Shawanaga. *Ont.* 16 E2
Shawinigan, *Que.* 20 C2
Shawnee, *Okla.* 24 G3
Shawville, *Que.* 17 J2
Shearer Dale, *B.C.* 12 L4
Shebandowan, *Ont.* 18 C4
Sheboygan, *Wis.* 25 J2
Shedden, *Ont.* 16 D5
Shediac, *N.B.* 21 C1
Sheenboro, *Que.* 17 H1
Sheenjek R., *Alaska* 10 F4
Sheep Haven, *Eire* 37 A4
Sheerness, *Eng.* 37 F6
Sheet Harbour, *N.S.* 21 E3
Sheffield, *Eng.* 37 E5
Sheguindah, *Ont.* 16 D2
Sheho. *Sask.* 15 K5
Shekak, and R.. *Ont.* 18 F4
Shekak L., *Ont.* 18 C3
Shekatika B., *Que.* 23 H1
Shekatika Bay, *Que.* 23 H1
Shelagskoi C., *U.S.S.R.* 43 P1
Shelburne, *N.S.* 22 E5
Shelburne, *Ont.* 16 E3
Shelby, *Mont.* 24 D1
Sheldrake, and R., *Que.* 22 E1
Shelikof Str., *Alaska* 10 C6
Shellbrook, *Sask.* 14 H4
Shelldon L., *Yukon* 12 E1
Shell Harbour, *N.S.W.* 50 H7
Shenkursk, *U.S.S.R.* 35 P3
Shenyang (Mukden), *China* 44 E2
Shepparton, *Victoria* 50 E8
Sheppey, I. of, *Eng.* 37 F6
Sherbrooke, *N.S* 21 E2
Sherbrooke, and Park, *Que.* 20 D3
Sherbrooke L., *N.S.* 21 C3
Shere, *B.C.* 13 L6
Sheridan, *Wyo.* 24 E2
Sherridon, *Man.* 15 L3
Sherwood, *Tex.* 24 F4
Shesheeb B., *Ont.* 18 D4
Shesley, *B.C.* 12 E3
Shethanei L., *Man.* 15 N1
Shetland Is. (Zetland), *Scotland* 36 D1
Shetter Bay, *Que.* 22 D1
Shiawassee R., *Mich.* 16 A4
Shibogama L., *Ont.* 18 D2
Shickshock Mts., *Que.* 22 D2
Shiel L., *Scotland* 36 C3
Shikarpur, *W. Pak.* 40 C3
Shikoku (I.), *Japan* 44 F3
Shillelagh, *Eire* 37 B5
Shillong, *India* 40 H3
Shimanovsk, *U.S.S.R.* 40 E1
Shimonoseki, *Japan* 40 F3
Shin L., *Scotland* 36 C2
Shiningtree L.. W.. *Ont.* 18 H5
Ship Harbour, *N.S.* 22 F4
Shippegan, and I., *N.B.* 22 E3
Shipshaw R., *Que.* 22 B2
Shitka R., *U.S.S.R.* 44 D1
Shiukwan .*China* 44 D4
Shkoder (Scutari), *Albania* 39 J5
Shoal L.. *Man.* 15 N5
Shoal L., *Ont.* 22 E3
Shoal Harbour, *Nfld.* 23 K2
Shoalhaven R., *N.S.W.* 50 H7
Shoal Lake, *Man.* 15 L5
Shoals Park, *Ont.* 18 G5
Sholapur, *India* 40 E5
Shoshone, *Ida.* 24 D2
Shreveport, *La.* 25 H4
Shrewsbury *Eng.* 37 D5
Shropshire, co., *Eng.* 37 D5
Shubenacadie, *N.S.* 21 D2
Shubenacadie L., *N.S.* 21 C3
Shuswap L., *B.C.* 13 L7
Sialkot. *W. Pak.* 40 D2
Siam, G. of, *Siam* 44 C5
Sian (Hsi-an), *China* 44 C3
Siangtan, *China* 44 D4
Siaulai, *Lithuania* 39 K2
Sibbald, *Alberta* 14 F5
Sibbald Point Park, *Ont.* 17 F3
Sibenik, *Yugoslavia* 39 H5
Siberian Pl., W., *U.S.S.R.* 42 F2
Siberian Plat., Cent., *U.S.S.R.* 42 H2
Sibiu, *Romania* 39 L4
Sibley Park, *Ont.* 18 D4

Sibolga, *Sumatra* 44 B6
Sicamous, *B.C.* 13 L7
Sicily (I.), *Italy* 38 H6
Sicuani, *Peru* 30 C6
Sidney, *Neb.* 24 F3
Sidney, *Vancouver I., B.C.* 13 J8
Sidra, G. of, *Libya* 46 E2
Siedlce, *Poland* 39 K2
Sierra de la Ventana, *Argentina* 31 E11
Sierra Leone, *W. Africa* 46 B5
Sierra Madre, *Mexico* 28 C2
Sierra Madre del Sur, *Mexico* 28 D4
Sierra Madre Plat., *N. Mex.* 24 E4
Sierra Moestra, *Cuba* 29 J3
Sierra Mojada, *Mexico* 28 D2
Sierra Morena, *Spain* 38 C6
Sierra Nevada, *Cal.* 24 B2
Sierra Nevada, *Spain* 38 D6
Sierra Nevada de Santa Marta, *Colombia* 30 C1
Sierra Pacaraima, *Ven.* 30 E3
Sierra Tarahumare, *Mexico* 28 C2
Sifton, *Man.* 15 L5
Sifton Pass, *B.C.* 12 G4
Siglufjördur, *Iceland* 35 C2
Sigutlat L., *B.C* 13 G6
Sikanni Chief, and R.. *B.C.* 12 J4
Sikhote Alin, *U.S.S.R.* 44 F2
Si Kiang R., *China* 44 C4
Sikkim, state, *N. India* 40 G3
Silchar, *India* 40 H4
Silcot, *Man.* 15 O2
Sillery, *Que.* 20 D2
Silloth. *Eng.* 37 D4
Silver L. Park, *Ont.* 17 J3
Silver Mt., *Ont.* 18 C4
Silver R., *N.S.* 21 A3
Silver Star Park, *B.C.* 13 L7
Silverton, *Colo.* 24 E3
Silverton. *N.S.W.* 50 C5
Simão Dias, *Brazil* 30 K6
Simcoe, *Ont.* 16 E5
Simcoe, co., *Ont.* 16 E3
Simcoe L., *Ont.* 17 F3
Simferopol, *U.S.S.R.* 39 N4
Simla, *India* 40 E2
Simmie, *Sask.* 14 G6
Simojovel de Allende, *Mexico* 28 F4
Simon L., *Que.* 17 K2
Simonette R., *Alberta* 14 B3
Simonhouse L., *Man.* 15 J3
Simonstown, *Cape Prov., Rep. of S. Africa* 47 B3
Simoom Sd., *B.C.* 13 G7
Simplon Pass, *Switzerland* 38 G4
Simpson, *Lab.* 19 F3
Simpson, *Sask.* 14 J5
Simpson I., *L. Superior, Ont.* 18 E4
Simpson Is., *Mackenzie, N.W.T.* 12 O2
Sinai Mt., *Egypt* 42 B6
Sinaloa, *Mexico* 28 C2
Sinclair Mills, *B.C.* 13 K6
Sind, prov., *Pak.* 40 C3
Singapore, rep., *S.E. Asia* 44 C6
Singleton, *N.S.W* 50 H6
Sinkiang, *China* 42 G4
Sinnamary, *Fr. Guiana* 30 G2
Sinop, *Turkey* 39 N5
Sintaluta, *Sask.* 15 K5
Sinu R., *Colombia* 30 C2
Sioux City, *Ia.* 24 G2
Sioux Falls, *S. Dak.* 24 G2
Sioux Lookout. *Ont.* 18 C3
Sipiwesk, *Man.* 15 N3
Sir Alexander Mt., *B.C.* 13 K5
Sirdar, *B.C.* 13 M8
Sir Darya R., *Cent. Asia* 43 E4
Sir Douglas Mt., *Alberta* 14 D5
Siret R., *Romania* 39 L4
Sir James McBrien Mt., *Mackenzie, N.W.T.* 12 F1
Sir R. Squires Mem. Park, *Nfld.* 23 J2
Sir Sanford Mt.. *B.C.* 13 M7
Sishen, *Cape Prov.* 47 C2
Sisipuk L., *Man.* 15 L3
Sistan, *Persia-Afghanistan* 40 B2
Sisters, The, *Tasmania* 50 G9
Sitka, *Alaska* 13 C4
Sivas, *Turkey* 39 O6
Siwa, *Egypt* 46 F3
Siwalik Range, *India-Nepal* 40 E2
Sixteen Island L., *Que.* 20 B3
Skagerrak, *Denmark, etc.* 38 F1
Skagway, *Alaska* 12 C3
Skaw, The, *Denmark* 38 G1
Skeena, *B.C.* 13 F5
Skeena Mts., *B.C.* 12 F4
Skeena R., *B.C.* 12 G4
Skegness, *Eng.* 37 F5
Skerryvore I.. *Scotland* 36 B3
Skibbereen. *Eire* 37 A6
Skiddaw, Mt., *Eng.* 37 D4
Skidegate, *B.C.* 13 E6
Skien, *Norway* 35 H4
Skihist Mt., *B.C.* 13 K7
Skikda (Philippeville), *Algeria* 38 F6
Skipton, *Eng.* 37 D5
Skiros I., *Greece* 39 L6
Skootumchuck, *B.C.* 13 N8
Skopje, *Yugoslavia* 39 K5

Skovorodino, *U.S.S.R.* 44 E1
Skowhegan. *Me.* 22 C4
Skownan, *Man.* 15 M5
Skuyak I., *Alaska* 10 D6
Skye I., *Scotland* 36 B3
Slate Is., *L. Superior. Ont.* 18 E4
Slave Falls, *Man.* 15 O5
Slave L., Gt., *Mackenzie. N.W.T.* 10 M5
Slave L., Lesser, *Alberta* 14 D3
Slave Point, *Mackenzie, N.W.T.* 12 N2
Slave R., *Alberta* 14 F1
Slave R., *N.W.T., etc.* 10 M5
Slave Lake, *Alberta* 14 D3
Sleaford, *Eng.* 37 E5
Sleat, Sd. of, *Scotland* 36 C3
Sled L., *Sask.* 14 H3
Sleeper Is., *Hudson B.* 11 S6
Slieve Aughty Mts., *Eire* 37 A5
Sligo, and co., *Eire* 37 A4
Sligo B., *Eire* 37 A4
Slocan, and L., *B.C.* 13 M8
Smith, *Alberta* 12 N5
Smith B., *Alaska* 10 D3
Smith B., *Mackenzie, N.W.T.* 10 K4
Smith I., *Que.* 19 B1
Smith Sd., *B.C.* 13 G5
Smith Sd., *Greenland* 11 T2
Smith Arm, *Mackenzie, N.W.T.* 10 K4
Smithers, *B.C.* 12 G5
Smithfield. *Orange F.S.* 47 D3
Smith Point, *N.S.* 21 D2
Smith River, *B.C.* 12 G3
Smith's Falls. *Ont.* 17 J3
Smithton, *Tasmania* 50 K11
Smoky Cape, *N.S.* 21 G1
Smoky Falls, *Ont.* 18 G3
Smoky R., *Alberta* 14 B3
Smoky R., Lit., *Alberta* 14 C3
Smoky Hill R., *Kan.* 24 F3
Smolensk, *U.S.S.R.* 39 N2
Smooth Rock L., *Ont.* 18 D3
Smooth Rock Falls, *Ont.* 18 H4
Smoothstone L., *Sask.* 14 H3
Snaefell, *Isle of Man* 37 C4
Snake I., *Victoria* 50 F9
Snake R., *Ida., etc.* 24 D2
Snare River, *Mackenzie. N.W.T.* 12 N1
Snaring, *Alberta* 14 B4
Snipe L., *Alberta* 14 C3
Snizort L., *Skye I., Scotland* 36 B3
Snow L., *Man.* 15 L3
Snow Mts., *N.S.W.* 50 G8
Snowdon. Mt., *Wales* 37 C5
Snowdrift, *Mackenzie, N.W.T.* 10 M5
Snow Road, *Ont.* 17 J3
Snowy R., *Victoria* 50 G8
Snug Harb., *Lab.* 19 F3
Sobral, *Brazil* 30 J4
Society Is., *Pacific Oc.* 2 E5
Socorro, *Colombia* 30 C2
Socorro, *N. Mex.* 24 E4
Socorro I., *Mexico* 28 B4
Socotra I., *Indian Oc.* 46 J4
Soda Cr., *B.C.* 13 J6
Söderhamn, *Sweden* 35 K3
Sodus, *N.Y.* 17 H4
Sofia, *Bulgaria* 39 K5
Sogamoso, *Colombia* 30 C2
Sogn Fjord, *Norway* 35 G3
Sokoto, *Nigeria* 46 D4
Soledad, *Argentina* 31 E10
Solent, The, *Eng.* 37 E6
Solimões R., *Brazil* 30 E4
Solomon Is., *Pacific Oc.* 2 D5
Solomon's Temples, *James B.* 18 J2
Solvay. *N.Y.* 17 J4
Solway Firth, *Scotland-Eng.* 37 D4
Somali Rep., *N.E. Africa* 46 H5
Sombra, *Ont.* 16 C5
Sombrerete, *Mexico* 28 D3
Somerset .*Man.* 15 M6
Somerset .*Queensland* 49 G2
Somerset, co., *Eng.* 37 D6
Somerset I. *Franklin, N.W.T.* 11 P3
Somerset East, *Cape Prov., Rep. of S. Africa* 47 D3
Somerset West, *Cape Prov., Rep. of S. Africa* 47 B3
Somersworth, *N.H.* 22 B5
Somkele, *Zululand, Natal* 47 E2
Söndre Strömfjord, *Greenland* 11 Y4
Sonequera Mt., *Chile* 31 D8
Songkhla, *Thailand* 44 C6
Sonora, *N.S.* 22 G4
Sonora R., *Mexico* 28 B2
Sonsonate, *Salvador* 28 G5
Soo Canals, *Ont.* 25 J1
Soochow, *China* 44 E3
Sooke, *Vancouver I., B.C.* 13 J8
Sopron, *Hungary* 39 J4
Sops I., *Nfld.* 23 J2
Sops Arm, *N.S.* 23 J2
Sorcier L., *Que.* 20 C2
Sorel, *Que.* 20 C2
Sorell, *Tasmania* 50 L12
Sorell C., *Tasmania* 50 K12
Sorocaba, *Brazil* 31 H8

Name	Map	Grid
Soul (Seoul), S. Korea	44	E3
Soulanges Canal, Que.	20	B3
Sound, The, Sweden-Denmark	38	H1
Sounding Cr., Alberta	14	F5
Sources, Mt. aux, Orange F.S.	47	D2
Souris, P.E.I.	21	E1
Souris, and R., Man.	15	L6
Souris R., Man., etc.	15	L6
South C., New Guinea	49	H2
South C., Spitsbergen	3	L1
South C., Tasmania	49	H8
South I., N.Z.	51	B5
South Pt., Anticosti I., Que.	22	F2
South Africa, Rep. of, Africa	46	F9
Southampton, Eng.	37	E6
Southampton, N.S.	21	C2
Southampton, Ont.	16	D3
Southampton C., Coats I. N.W.T.	11	S5
Southampton I., Keewatin, N.W.T.	11	R5
South Auckland, Bay of Plenty, N.Z.	51	E2
South Australia, state, Aust.	49	E5
Southbank, B.C.	13	H5
South Bay, Ont.	16	C2
South Baymouth, Ont.	16	C2
South Bend, Ind.	25	J2
South Branch, Nfld.	23	H3
Southbridge, N.Z.	51	D5
South Carolina, state, U.S.A.	25	K4
South China Sea, China	44	D5
South Dakota, state, U.S.A.	24	F2
South Downs, Eng.	37	E6
South Durham, Que.	20	C3
Southend, Eng.	37	F6
Southend, Sask.	15	K2
Southern Hd., Nfld.	23	H2
Southern Alps, N.Z.	51	B6
Southern Cross, W. Aust.	49	B6
Southern Indian L., Man.	15	M2
Southern Rhodesia, See Rhodesia		
South Falk R., Alaska	10	D5
South Georgia Is., S. Atlantic Oc.	31	J14
South Harbour, N.S.	21	G1
South Island, N.Z.	51	B5
South Kootenay Pass, Alberta, B.C.	14	E6
South Lochaber, N.S.	21	E2
South Macmillan R., Yukon	12	D1
South Magnetawan, Ont.	16	E2
South Nahanni, Mackenzie, N.W.T.	12	J2
South Nelson, N.B.	22	E3
South Orkneys, Antarctica	3	J8
South Porcupine, Ont.	18	H4
Southport, Eng.	37	D5
Southport, P.E.I.	22	F3
Southport, Queensland	50	J3
South River, Ont.	17	F2
South Sandwich Group Is., S. Atlantic Oc.	3	K7
South Shetlands, Antarctica	3	H8
South Shields, Eng.	37	E4
South Twin, James B.	18	H2
Southwest Pt., Anticosti I., Que.	22	E2
South-West Africa, (Namibia), Africa	46	E8
Soutpans Berg, Transvaal	47	D1
Sovereign, Sask.	14	H5
Sovetsk, U.S.S.R.	35	L4
Sovetskaya Gavan, U.S.S.R.	44	F2
Soya Str. (La Perouse Str.), Japan	44	G2
Spain, rep., Europe	38	B5
Spalding, Eng.	37	E5
Spanish, Ont.	16	C1
Spanish R., Ont.	16	D1
Spanish Sahara, Africa	46	B3
Spanish Town, Jamaica	29	J4
Sparta, Greece	39	K6
Spartivento C., Italy	39	J6
Spartivento C., Sardinia	38	G6
Spatsizi R., B.C.	12	F4
Spednik L., N.B.	22	D4
Spencer C., Alaska	13	B3
Spencer G., S. Aust.	49	E7
Spencer I., James B.	18	J2
Spence's Bridge, B.C.	13	K7
Sperrin Mts., N. Ire.	37	B4
Spey R., Scotland	36	D3
Spezia, Italy	38	G4
Spicer I., Hudson Str.	19	C1
Spioen Berg II., Cape Prov., Rep. of S. Africa	47	B3
Spionkop, Cape Prov., Rep. of S. Africa	47	C3
Spion Kop, Natal	47	D2
Spirit River, Alberta	14	B3
Spitsbergen, Arctic Oc.	1	P2
Split (Spalato), Yugoslavia	39	J5
Split C., N.S.	21	C2
Split L., Man.	15	N2
Spokane, Wash.	24	C1
Spondin, Alberta	14	F5
Sporades Is., Aegean Sea	39	L6
Spotted Island, Lab.	19	F3
Spragge, Ont.	16	C1
Spranger Mt., B.C.	13	K6
Spree R., Ger.	39	H3
Springbok, Cape Prov., Rep. of S. Africa	47	B2
Springdale, Nfld.	23	J2
Springfield, Ill.	25	J3
Springfield, Mo.	25	H3
Springfield, N.B.	21	A2
Springfield, N.S.	21	B3
Springfield, O.	25	K2
Springfield, Ont.	16	D5
Springfontein, Orange F.S.	47	D3
Springhill, N.S.	21	C2
Springhill, Que.	20	D3
Springs, Transvaal	47	D2
Springsure, Queensland	50	G1
Springville, N.Y.	17	G5
Springwater Prov. Park, Ont.	16	F3
Spruce R., Sask.	14	J4
Spruce Brook, Nfld.	23	H2
Sprucedale, Ont.	16	F2
Spruce Woods Park, Man.	15	M6
Spurn Hd., Eng.	37	F5
Squamish, B.C.	13	J8
Sri Lanka, Asia	40	F7
Srinagar, Kashmir	40	E2
Staaten R., Queensland	49	G3
Stacpool, Ont.	18	H5
Stack Skerry, Scotland	36	C2
Stadacona, Que.	20	D3
Staffa I., Scotland	36	B3
Stafford, and co., Eng.	37	D5
Stalin Mt., B.C.	12	H3
Stanbridge, Que.	20	C3
Standard, Alberta	14	E5
Standerton, Transvaal	47	D2
Standish, Ont.	16	A4
Stanger, Natal	47	E2
Stanley, Falkland Is.	31	F14
Stanley, Ont.	18	D4
Stanley, Sask.	15	J3
Stanley, Tasmania	50	K11
Stanley Falls, Zaire	46	F6
Stanovoy Mts., U.S.S.R.	43	L3
Stanstead, Que.	20	C3
Stanthorpe, Queensland	50	H4
Stanton, Mackenzie, N.W.T.	10	J4
Starbuck I., Line Is., Pacific Oc.	2	E5
Stargard, Poland	39	H2
Start Pt., Eng.	37	D6
Staten I., Argentina	31	E14
Staunton, Va.	25	L3
Stavanger, Norway	38	F1
Staveley, Alberta	14	E5
Stawell, Victoria	50	D8
Stayner, Ont.	16	E3
Steam Boat, B.C.	12	J3
Steckstroom, Cape Prov., Rep. of S. Africa	47	D3
Steel L., and R., Ont.	18	E4
Steelport, Transvaal	47	E1
Steen R., Alberta	12	M3
Steenkamps Berg, Transvaal	47	D2
Steep Pt., W. Aust.	49	A5
Steep Rock, Man.	15	M5
Steep Rock Lake, Ont.	18	C4
Stefansson I., Franklin, N.W.T.	10	N3
Steinbach, Man.	15	N6
Steinkopf, Cape Prov., Rep. of S. Africa	47	B2
Stellarton, N.S.	21	E2
Stellenbosch, Cape Prov., Rep. of S. Africa	47	B3
Stensele, Sweden	35	K2
Stephens Passage, Alaska	12	D4
Stephenville, Nfld.	23	H2
Stettin. See Szczecin		
Stettler, Alberta	14	E4
Stevenage, Eng.	37	E5
Stevens, Ont.	18	F4
Stevenson L., Man.	15	N3
Steveston, B.C.	13	J8
Stewart, B.C.	12	F5
Stewart I., N.Z.	51	A7
Stewart R., Yukon	10	G5
Stewart River, Yukon	10	G5
Stewart Valley, Sask.	14	H5
Stewiacke, N.S.	21	D2
Stikine Ranges, B.C.	12	F3
Stikine R., B.C.	12	E4
Stirling, Alberta	14	E6
Stirling, Ont.	17	H3
Stirling, Que.	20	C2
Stirling, and co., Scotland	36	C3
Stittsville, Ont.	17	K2
Stockholm, Sweden	35	K4
Stockport, Eng.	37	D5
Stockton, Cal.	24	B3
Stockwell L., Sask.	14	H5
Stokes B., Ont.	16	D2
Stokes Pt., King I.	50	D10
Stoke-upon-Trent, Eng.	37	D5
Stolzenfels, S.W. Africa	47	B2
Stonecliffe, Ont.	17	H1
Stonehaven, Scotland	36	D3
Stone Mt. Park, B.C.	12	H3
Stonewall, Man.	15	N5
Stoney Creek, Ont.	16	F4
Stony L., Man.	15	M1
Stony L., Ont.	17	G3
Stony Pt., N.Y.	17	J4
Stony Pt., Victoria	50	E9
Stonyplain, Alberta	14	D4
Stony Rapids, Sask.	14	J1
Stooping R., Ont.	18	G3
Stor L., Sweden	35	J3
Storm B., Tasmania	50	L12
Stormberg, and Ra., Cape Prov., Rep. of S. Africa	47	D3
Stormont, co., Ont.	17	K2
Stornoway, Hebrides, Scotland	36	B2
Stornoway, Que.	20	D3
Stouffville, Ont.	17	F3
Stoughton, Sask.	15	K6
Stour R., Dorset, Eng.	37	D6
Stour R., Kent, Eng.	37	F6
Stout L., Ont.	18	A2
Surabaja, Java	44	D7
Strachan, Que.	20	B1
Strahan, Tasmania	50	K12
Stralsund, Ger.	38	H2
Strangford L., N. Ire.	37	C4
Stranraer, Scotland	37	C4
Strasbourg, France	38	F3
Strasbourg, Sask.	14	J5
Stratford, N.Z.	51	E3
Stratford, Ont.	16	D4
Stratford-on-Avon, Eng.	37	E5
Strathcona Is., Baffin I.	19	C1
Strathcona Park, B.C.	13	H8
Strathlorne, N.S.	21	F1
Strathmore, Alberta	14	E5
Strathnaver, B.C.	13	J6
Strathroy, Ont.	16	D5
Stratton, Me.	20	D3
Streaky B., S. Aust.	49	E6
Strezelecki Cr., S. Aust.	50	C4
Strickland, Ont.	18	H4
Stroedur, Argentina	31	E12
Stromboli, Lipari Is., Italy	39	H6
Stromness, Orkney Is., Scotland	36	D2
Stronsay, Orkney Is., Scotland	36	D2
Struma R., Bulgaria-Greece	39	K5
Strumble Hd., Wales	37	C5
Strutton I., James B.	18	J2
Struys B., Cape Prov., Rep. of S. Africa	47	C3
Stuart Cr., W. Aust.	49	D3
Stuart L., B.C.	13	H5
Stuart R., B.C.	13	J5
Stuart Highway, N. Ter., Aust.	47	E3
Stull L., Man.-Ont.	18	B1
Stump L., B.C.	13	K7
Sturgeon B., Man.	15	M4
Sturgeon L., Alberta	14	C3
Sturgeon L., Ont.	17	G3
Sturgeon R., Ont.	18	H5
Sturgeon Falls, Ont.	16	F1
Sturgeon Landing, Man.	15	L3
Sturgis, Sask.	15	K5
Sturt Desert, N.S.W.-Queensland	50	C4
Stutterheim, Cape Prov., Rep. of S. Africa	47	D3
Stuttgart, Ger.	38	G3
Suakin Sudan	46	G4
Suata R., Venezuela	30	D2
Subotica, Yugoslavia	39	J4
Suck R., Eire	37	A5
Suckling C., Alaska	10	F6
Sucre, Bolivia	30	E7
Sud, R. du. Que.	20	D2
Sudan, E. Africa	46	F4
Sudbury, Ont.	16	D1
Sudbury, dist., Ont.	18	G5
Sudd, Sudan	46	F5
Sudety (Mts.), Czechoslovakia	39	H3
Suez, Egypt	46	G3
Suez, G. of, Egypt	42	B6
Suez. Isthmus of, Egypt	42	B5
Suffolk, co., Eng.	37	F5
Sugarloaf Pt., N.S.W.	50	J6
Suggi L., Sask.	15	K3
Suir R., Eire	37	B5
Sukkertoppen, Greenland	11	Y4
Sukunka R., B.C.	12	K5
Sula Arch., Philippines	43	L8
Sula Is., Moluccas. Indonesia	44	E7
Sula Sgeir I., Scotland	36	B2
Sulaiman Mts., W. Pak.	36	C2
Sule Skerry. Scotland	40	C3
Sullana. Peru	30	A4
Sullivan B., B.C.	13	G7
Sullivan L., Alberta	14	F5
Sultan, Ont.	18	G5
Sulu Arch., Philippine Is.	44	E6
Sulu Sea, Borneo-Philippine Is.	44	D6
Sumatra I., Indonesia	44	B6
Sumba I., Indonesia	44	D7
Sumbawa I., Indonesia	44	D7
Sumburgh Hd., Shetland Is., Scotland	36	E2
Summerford, Nfld.	23	K2
Summerland, B.C.	13	L8
Summerside, P.E.I.	21	C1
Summit, Que.	20	C2
Summit L., B.C.	12	H3
Summit Lake, B.C.	13	J5
Sumner Str., Alaska	12	D4
Sumy, Ukraine	39	N3
Sunda Str., Indonesia	44	C7
Sundarbans, India-Bangladesh	40	G4
Sundays R., Cape Prov., Rep. of S. Africa	47	D3
Sunderland, Eng.	37	E4
Sunderland, Ont.	17	F3
Sundridge, Ont.	16	F2
Sundsvall, Sweden	35	K3
Sungari R. and Res., China	44	E2
Sunnybank, Queensland	50	Q3
Sunnybrae, N.S.	21	C1
Sunny Brae, N.S.	21	E2
Superb, Sask.	14	G5
Superior, Wis.	25	H1
Superior Junc., Ont.	18	C3
Superior L., Canada-U.S.A.	18	C3
Strabane, N. Ire.	37	B4
Suramacca R., Surinam	30	F2
Surat, India	40	D4
Surat, Queensland	50	G3
Surdance, Wyo.	24	F2
Surf Inlet, B.C.	13	F6
Surinam, S. America	30	F3
Suriname R., Surinam	30	F2
Suripa R., Venezuela	30	C2
Surprise, B.C.	12	D3
Surrey, co., Eng.	37	E6
Susitna R., Alaska	10	D5
Sussex, N.B.	21	B2
Sussex, co., Eng.	37	E6
Sustut Peak, B.C.	12	G4
Sutherland, Cape Prov., Rep. of S. Africa	14	H4
Sutherland, Sask.	14	H4
Sutherland. co... Scotland	36	C2
Sutlej R., W. Pak.	40	D3
Sutton, Ont.	17	F3
Sutton, Que.	20	C3
Sutton L., Ont.	18	F1
Suva, Fiji Is.	2	D5
Suvorov I., Pacific Oc.	2	E5
Suwalki, Poland	39	K2
Svalbard, Arctic Oc.	3	L1
Svartenhuk Penin., Greenland	11	X3
Sverdlovsk, U.S.S.R.	42	E3
Sverdrup Is., Franklin, N.W.T.	11	P2
Svir R., U.S.S.R.	35	N3
Svishtov, Bulgaria	39	L5
Svoboda, U.S.S.R.	39	O3
Swakop R., S.W. Africa	47	B1
Swakopmund, S.W. Africa	47	A1
Swale R., Eng.	37	E4
Swampy L., Man.	15	O3
Swan I., Me.	22	C4
Swan L., Man.	15	L4
Swan R., Sask.	15	L5
Swan R., W. Aust.	49	B6
Swan R., Lit., Sask.	15	K4
Swan Hill, Victoria	50	D7
Swan River, Man.	15	L4
Swansea, Wales	37	C6
Swansea B., Wales	37	C6
Swanson Bay, B.C.	13	F6
Swarberg, C. of Good Hope	47	C3
Swart Berg, C. of Good Hope	47	D3
Swastika, Ont.	18	H4
Swatow, China	44	D4
Swaziland, S.E. Africa	47	E2
Sweden, kingdom, Europe	35	J4
Sweetsburg, Que.	20	C3
Swellendam, Cape Prov.	47	C3
Swift Current, Sask.	14	H5
Swift Current Cr., Sask.	14	G6
Swift River, Yukon	12	E2
Swilly L., Eire	37	B4
Swindon, Eng.	37	E6
Swinoujscie (Swinemünde), Poland	39	H2
Switzerland, rep., Europe	38	F4
Sydenham, Ont.	17	J3
Sydney, N.S.W.	50	H6
Sydney, N.S.	21	G1
Sydney L., Ont.	18	A3
Sydney Mines, N.S.	21	G1
Sydproven, Greenland	11	Z5
Sykes Mt., Nfld.	23	J2
Syktyvkar, U.S.S.R.	42	D2
Sylhet, Bangladesh	40	H4
Sylvan Lake, Alberta	14	D4
Syracuse, N.Y.	17	J4
Syracuse, Sicily	39	H6
Syria, state, W. Asia	42	B5
Syrian Desert, Syria, etc.	42	B5
Szczecin (Stettin), Poland	39	H2
Szeged, Hungary	39	J4
Tabatinga, Brazil	30	D4
Tabatinga, Serra da, Brazil	30	H5
Taber, Alberta	14	E6
Table B., Lab.	19	F3
Table B., and Mt., Cape Prov., Rep. of S. Africa	47	B3
Tabora, Tanzania	46	G6
Tache, Ont.	18	B4
Tacna, Peru	30	C7
Taco, Argentina	31	E9
Tacoma, Wash.	24	B1
Tacora Peak, Peru	30	D7
Tacu, B.C.	12	D3
Tacuarembo, Uruguay	31	F10
Tadoule L., Man.	15	M1

Tadoussac, Que.	22	C2
Tadzhik, U.S.S.R.	40	C1
Taff R., Wales	37	D6
Taganrog, U.S.S.R.	39	O4
Taggart, Ont.	18	B3
Tagish, Yukon	12	C2
Tagish L., B.C.	12	C3
Tagus R., Spain-Portugal	38	C6
Tahiti, Pacific Oc.	2	F5
Tahlequah, Okla.	24	G4
Tahltan, B.C.	12	E3
Tahoe L., Cal.	24	B3
Ta Hsingan Shan, China	44	D2
Tahsis, Vancouver I., B.C.	13	G8
Tahtsa R., and L., B.C.	13	G6
Taihape, N.Z.	51	E3
Taillon, Que.	20	D1
Tain, Scotland	36	C3
Taipei, Taiwan	44	E4
Taitao Penin., Chile	31	B13
Taiwan (Formosa) I., E. Asia	44	E4
Taiwan Str., E. Asia	44	D4
T'ai-yüan, China	44	D3
Takapuna, N.Z.	51	E2
Takipy, Man.	15	L3
Takla L., B.C.	12	G5
Takla Landing, B.C.	12	H5
Takla Makan Desert, U.S.S.R.	42	G5
Takoradi, Ghana	46	C5
Taku R., B.C., etc.	12	D3
Talana Hill, Natal	47	E2
Talar Ra., W. Pak.	40	C3
Talara, Peru	30	A4
Talaud Is., Philippine Is.	44	E6
Talbot, Que.	20	C2
Talca, Chile	31	C11
Talcahuano, Chile	31	C11
Tallahassee, Fla.	25	K4
Tallangatta, Victoria	50	E8
Tallinn, Estonia	35	L4
Taltal, Chile	31	C9
Tamale, Ghana	46	C5
Tamar R., Eng.	37	C6
Tamar R., Tasmania	50	L11
Tamarac Is., Man.	15	N5
Tamatave, Madagascar	46	J7
Tamazunchale, Mexico	28	E3
Tambo, Queensland	50	F2
Tambo R., Victoria	50	F8
Tambov, U.S.S.R.	39	P2
Tamil Nadu, state, India	40	E6
Tamizhagam (Madras) state, India	40	E6
Tampa, and B., Fla.	25	K5
Tampere, Finland	35	L3
Tampico, Mexico	28	E3
Tamworth, N.S.W.	50	H5
Tamworth, Ont.	17	H3
Tana Elv, Finland-Norway	35	M2
Tana L., Ethiopia	46	G4
Tanana, Alaska	10	D4
Tananarive (Antananarivo), Madagascar	46	H7
Tandil, Argentina	31	F11
Tandjungselor, Borneo	44	D6
Tandou L., N.S.W.	50	C6
Taneatua, N.Z.	51	F3
Tanganyika L., Cent. Africa	46	F6
Tangier, Morocco	46	C2
Tangier, N.S.	21	E3
Tangier Grand Lake, N.S.	21	E3
Tanglia Ra., Tibet	40	H2
Tanimbar, Indonesia	44	F7
Tannu Ola Mts., U.S.S.R.	44	B1
Tanzania, rep. E. Africa	46	G6
Tanzilla R., B.C.	12	E3
Tapachula, Mexico	28	F5
Tapajós R., Brazil	30	F5
Tapalque, Argentina	31	E11
Tapanahuni R., Surinam	30	F3
Tapanui, N.Z.	51	B6
Tapauá, Brazil	30	E5
Tapauá R., Brazil	30	D5
Tapti R., India	40	D4
Tapuaenuku, N.Z.	51	D4
Taquanalsinho, Brazil	30	E5
Taquari R., Brazil	30	F7
Tara, Eire	37	B5
Tara, Ont.	16	D3
Tara, Queensland	50	H3
Taradale, N.Z.	51	E3
Tarakan, Borneo	44	D6
Taranaki Bight, N., and S., N.Z.	51	E3
Taranto, and G. of, Italy	39	J5
Tararua Ra., N.Z.	51	E4
Tarawera, N.Z.	51	F3
Tarbagatay Mts., U.S.S.R.	44	A2
Tarbat Ness, Scotland	36	D3
Tarcoola, S. Aust.	49	E6
Taree, N.S.W.	50	J5
Tarija, Bolivia	31	E8
Tarim R., Sinkiang	42	G4
Tarkastad, Cape Prov., Rep. of S. Africa	47	D3
Tarn R., France	38	E5
Tarong, Queensland	50	H3
Taroom, Queensland	50	G2
Tarragona, Spain	38	E5
Tartu, Estonia	39	L1
Taseko R., and Ls., B.C.	13	J7
Tashkent, U.S.S.R.	42	E4
Tasman B., and Mts., N.Z.	51	D4
Tasman Mt., N.Z.	51	C5
Tasman Penin., Tasmania	50	M12
Tasman Sea, Australasia	2	D6
Tasmania (I.), Aust.	50	H12
Tassialuk L., Que.	19	B2
Tatamagouche, N.S.	21	D2
Tatarsk Str., U.S.S.R.	44	F2
Tathlina L., Mackenzie, N.W.T.	12	M2
Tatla, and L., B.C.	13	H6
Tatlatui L., B.C.	12	G4
Tatlayoko L., B.C.	13	H7
Tatlow Mt., B.C.	13	J7
Tatnam C., Man.	15	Q2
Tatra Mts., Czechoslovakia-Poland	39	J3
Tatshenshini R., B.C.	13	B3
Taua, Brazil	30	J5
Tauiri Grande Cataract, Brazil	30	H4
Taumarunui, N.Z.	51	E3
Taung, Cape Prov., Rep. of S. Africa	47	C2
Taunton, Eng.	37	D6
Taupo, N.Z.	51	F3
Taupo L., N.Z.	51	E3
Taupse, U.S.S.R.	39	O4
Tauranga, and Harb., N.Z.	51	F2
Taureau, L., Que.	20	C2
Tauroa Pt., N.Z.	51	D1
Taurus Mts., Turkey	39	M6
Tavani, Keewatin, N.W.T.	11	Q5
Tavistock, Eng.	37	C6
Tavistock, Ont.	16	E4
Tavoy, Burma	40	J6
Tawas City, Mich.	16	B3
Tawatinaw, Alberta	14	E3
Tay, Firth of, Scotland	36	D3
Tay L., Scotland	36	C3
Tay R., Scotland	36	D3
Tay R., Yukon	12	D1
Taylor, B.C.	12	K4
Taylor Hd., N.S.	22	F4
Taylor Mt., N. Mex.	24	E3
Taymyr Penin., U.S.S.R.	43	H1
Tazin L., Sask.	14	G1
Tchentlo L., B.C.	12	H5
Team Valley, Eng.	37	E4
Te Anau L., N.Z.	51	B6
Teapa, Mexico	28	F4
Te Aroha, N.Z.	51	E2
Te Awamutu, N.Z.	51	E3
Tecumseh, Ont.	16	C5
Tees R., Eng.	37	D4
Teesside, Eng.	37	E4
Teeswater, Ont.	16	D3
Tefé, and R., Brazil	30	D4
Tegucigalpa, Honduras	29	G5
Tehama, Saudi Arabia	42	C7
Tehran, Iran	42	D5
Tehuacan, Mexico	28	E4
Tehuantepec, and G., Mexico	28	E4
Tehuantepec, Isthmus of, Mexico	28	F4
Teignmouth, Eng.	37	D6
Tekapo L., N.Z.	51	C5
Tekirdag, Turkey	39	L5
Te Kuiti, N.Z.	51	E3
Telegraph Ra., B.C.	13	J6
Telegraph Creek, B.C.	12	E4
Teles Pires R. (S. Manuel R.), Brazil	30	F5
Telkwa, B.C.	12	G5
Teller, Alaska	10	A4
Tel-pos-iz, U.S.S.R.	42	D2
Telukbetung, Sumatra	44	C7
Temax, Mexico	28	G3
Temblador, Venezuela	30	E2
Temiscamie R., Que.	22	A1
Temiscouata L., Que.	20	F2
Temora, N.S.W.	50	F7
Temple, Tex.	24	G4
Temuco, Chile	31	C11
Temuka, N.Z.	51	C6
Tenby Bay, Ont.	16	B1
Ten Mile Lake, Nfld.	23	J1
Tennant Creek, N. Ter., Aust.	49	E4
Tennessee, state, U.S.A.	25	J3
Tennessee R., Tenn., etc.	25	J4
Tenosique de Pino Suárez, Mexico	28	F4
Tenterfield, N.S.W.	50	J4
Ten Thousand Is., Fla.	25	K5
Tent Peak, Yukon	12	F2
Teófilo Otoni, Brazil	30	J7
Tepehuanes, Mexico	28	C2
Tepic, Mexico	28	D3
Te Puke, N.Z.	51	F2
Terence Bay, N.S.	21	D3
Teresina, Brazil	30	J5
Termez, U.S.S.R.	40	C1
Terminos Lagoon, Mexico	28	F4
Ternate I., Indonesia	44	E6
Terni, Italy	38	H5
Ternopol, U.S.S.R.	39	L3
Terowie, S. Aust.	50	B6
Terrace, B.C.	12	F5
Terra Nova, Nfld.	23	K2
Terrebonne, Que.	20	C3
Terre Haute, Ind.	25	J3
Terrenceville, Nfld.	23	K3
Teruel, Spain	38	D5
Teshekpuk L., Alaska	10	D3
Teslin, and L., Yukon	12	D2
Teslin Mt., B.C.	12	E3
Teslin R., Yukon	12	C2
Tetachuck L., B.C.	13	G6
Tete Jaune Cache, B.C.	13	L6
Teulon, Man.	15	N5
Te Waewae B., N.Z.	51	A7
Texada I., B.C.	13	H8
Texarkana, Tex.	25	H4
Texas, state, U.S.A.	24	F4
Texoma L., Okla.	24	G4
Teziutlan, Mexico	28	E4
Tezzeron L., B.C.	13	H5
Thaba Nchu, Orange F.S.	47	D2
Thabazimbi, Transvaal	47	D1
Thailand, E. Asia	44	C5
Thallon, Queensland	50	G4
Thames, and R., N.Z.	51	E2
Thames R., Eng.	37	E6
Thames R., Ont.	16	C5
Thamesford, Ont.	16	D4
Thamesville, Ont.	16	C5
Thanh Hoa, N. Vietnam	44	C4
Thar Desert, India	40	D3
Thásos I., Greece	39	L5
Thedford, Ont.	16	C4
Thelon R., Mackenzie, N.W.T.	10	O5
Theodore, Queensland	50	H2
Theodore Roosevelt R., Brazil	30	E5
Thérmai, G. of, Greece	39	K5
Thessalon, Ont.	16	B1
Thetford, Eng.	37	F5
Thetford Mines, Que.	20	D2
Thicket Portage, Man.	15	N3
Thimbu, Bhutan	40	H3
Thinahtea L., B.C.	12	K3
Thirty-one Mile L., Que.	20	B2
Thirty Thousand Is., co., Ont.	16	E2
Thisted, Denmark	38	G1
Thjorsa R., Iceland	35	C3
Thlewiaza R., Keewatin, N.W.T.	11	P5
Thomasville, Ga.	25	K4
Thom Bay, Franklin, N.W.T.	11	Q3
Thompson, Man.	15	N3
Thompson L., Mackenzie, N.W.T.	12	O1
Thompson R., B.C.	13	K7
Thomson R., Queensland	50	D2
Thorburn, N.S.	21	E2
Thorhild, Alberta	14	E3
Thornbury, Ont.	16	E3
Thornhill, Ont.	17	F4
Thorold, Ont.	16	F4
Thorshavn, Faeroe Is.	35	E3
Thousand Is., N.Y.	17	J3
Three Hills, Alberta	14	E5
Three Hummock I., Tasmania	50	E10
Three Kings Is., N.Z.	51	D1
Three Rivers, Que.	20	C2
Thule, Greenland	11	V2
Thunder B., Ont.	18	D4
Thunder Bay, Ont.	18	D4
Thunder Bay, Mich.	16	B3
Thunder Bay, dist., Ont.	18	D3
Thurles, Eire	37	B5
Thursday I., Queensland	49	G2
Thurso, Que.	17	K2
Thurso, Scotland	36	D2
Thutade L., B.C.	12	G4
Tibagi R., Brazil	31	G8
Tiber R., Italy	38	H5
Tibesti, Chad, W. Africa	46	E4
Tibet, China	40	F2
Tibooburra, N.S.W.	50	D4
Tiburon I., Mexico	28	B2
Tichborne, Ont.	17	J3
Tichfield, Sask.	14	H5
Tidal, Man.	15	O1
Tide L., Alberta	14	F5
Tidnish, N.S.	21	C2
Tien Shan Mts., Sinkiang	42	F4
Tientsin, China	44	D3
Tierra del Fuego, Argentina-Chile	31	D14
Tiete R., Brazil	31	G8
Tiflis, U.S.S.R.	42	C4
Tignish, P.E.I.	21	D1
Tigris R., Iraq	42	C5
Tijoca, Brazil	30	H4
Tijuana, Mexico	28	A1
Tika, Que.	19	D3
Tikchik L., Alaska	10	C5
Tikhvin, U.S.S.R.	35	N4
Tiksi, U.S.S.R.	43	L1
Tilbury, Ont.	16	C5
Tilcara, Argentina	31	D8
Tillei L., Yukon	12	F2
Tilley, Alberta	14	F5
Tillsonburg, Ont.	16	D5
Tilly L., Que.	19	C3
Timagami and L., Ont.	18	J5
Timan Ridge, U.S.S.R.	35	Q2
Timaru, N.Z.	51	C6
Timbo, Brazil	30	K6
Timboon, Victoria	50	D9
Timbuktu, Mali, W. Africa	46	C4
Timimoun, Algeria	46	D3
Timiskaming, dist., Ont.	18	J5
Timiskaming L., Que.-Ont.	18	J5
Timiskaming Sta., Que.	18	J5
Timisoara, Romania	39	K4
Timmins, Ont.	18	H4
Timor I., E. Indies	44	F7
Timor Sea, Australasia	49	C2
Timote, Argentina	31	E11
Tina Mt., Dominican Rep.	29	K4
Tingo Maria, Peru	30	B5
Tingwick, Que.	20	D3
Tinogasta, Argentina	31	D9
Tinos I., Greece	39	L6
Tintagel, B.C.	13	H5
Tintagel Hd., Eng.	37	C6
Tintina, Argentina	31	E9
Tinto, Scotland	36	D4
Tionega, Ont.	18	G4
Tipperary, and co., Eire	37	A5
Tipton, Eng.	37	D5
Tirana, Albania	39	J5
Tiraspol, Moldavia	39	M4
Tiree I., Scotland	36	B3
Tirgu Mures, Romania	39	L4
Tirol, Austria	38	G4
Tirua Pt., N.Z.	51	E3
Tiruchchirappalli (Trichinopoly), India	40	E6
Tisa R., Hungary	39	K4
Tisdale, Sask.	15	J4
Tishinakamau L., Lab.	19	E3
Titicaca L., Peru-Bolivia	30	C7
Titograd, Yugoslavia	39	J5
Titusville, Fla.	25	K5
Tiuba, Serra Da, Brazil	30	J6
Tiverton, Eng.	37	D6
Tiverton, N.S.	21	A3
Tiverton, Ont.	16	D3
Tizimin, Mexico	28	G3
Tjirebon, Java	44	C7
Tlacotalpan, Mexico	28	E4
Tlaxcala, Mexico	28	E4
Tlaxiaco, Mexico	28	E4
Tlell, B.C.	13	E6
Toad R., B.C.	12	H3
Toad Hotsprings, B.C.	12	H3
Tobago I., W. Indies	29	M5
Toba Inlet, B.C.	13	H7
Tobermory, Mull, Scotland	36	C3
Tobermory, Ont.	16	D2
Tobique R., N.B.	22	D3
Tobol R., U.S.S.R.	42	E3
Tobolsk, U.S.S.R.	42	F3
Tobruk, Libya	46	F2
Tocantinopolis, Brazil	30	H5
Tocantins R., Brazil	30	H5
Tochcha L., B.C.	12	H5
Tocopilla, Chile	31	C8
Tocorpuri Mt., Chile	31	D8
Tocuyo R., Venezuela	30	D1
Todos os Santos, B. of, Brazil	30	K6
Tofield, Alberta	14	E4
Tofin, Vancouver I., B.C.	13	H8
Togo, Sask.	15	L5
Togumwal, N.S.W.	50	E7
Tokara Gunto, Japan	44	F4
Tokat, Turkey	39	O5
Tokelau Is., Pacific Oc.	2	E5
Tokyo, Japan	44	G3
Tolaga B., N.Z.	51	G3
Tolbukhin, Bulgaria	39	L5
Toledo, O.	25	K2
Toledo, Spain	38	C6
Toledo Bend Res., Texas-Louisiana	28	F1
Tolima, vol., Colombia	30	B3
Tolo, G. of, Celebes	44	E7
Toluca, Mexico	28	E4
Tomar, Brazil	30	E4
Tomasine R., Que.	20	A2
Tome-Acu, Brazil	30	H4
Tomiko, Ont.	17	F1
Tomini, G. of, Celebes	44	E7
Tom Price, Mt., W. Aust.	49	B4
Tomsk, U.S.S.R.	43	G3
Tonacross, Alaska	10	F5
Tonala, Mexico	28	F4
Tonawanda, N.Y.	17	G4
Tondern, Ont.	18	F4
Tonga Is., Pacific Oc.	2	E5
Tongareva I., Pacific Oc.	2	E5
Tongking, G. of, China-Vietnam	44	C4
Tongoy, Chile	31	C10
Tongue, Scotland	36	C4
Tonle Sap, Khmer Rep.	44	C5
Tonopah, Nev.	24	C2
Toowoomba, Queensland	50	H5
Top L., U.S.S.R.	35	N3
Topeka, Kan.	24	G3
Topolobampo, Mexico	28	C2
Torbay, Nfld.	23	L3
Tor Bay, N.S.	21	F2
Torbay (Torquay), Eng.	37	D4
Torch R., Sask.	15	K3
Tormentine C., N.B.	21	C2
Torne Alv, Sweden-Finland	35	L4
Torne Träsk, Sweden	35	L1
Tornio, Finland	35	L2
Toro, L. del, Argentina	31	C12
Toronto, Ont.	17	F2
Toronto L., Mexico	28	C4
Torrance, Ont.	16	F2
Torre Str., Queensland	49	G6
Torrens L., S. Aust.	49	F3
Torreon, Mexico	28	D2
Tôrres, Brazil	31	H6
Torres Vedras, Portugal	38	B2
Torrowangee, N.S.W.	50	C9
Tortoral, Chile	31	C6
Tortosa, Spain	38	E5

Name	Page	Ref
Tortuga I., *Venezuela*	30	D1
Tortuga I. (Tortue I.), *W. Indies*	29	K3
Torun, *Poland*	39	J2
Tory Hill, *Ont.*	17	G3
Totma, *U.S.S.R.*	35	P4
Tottenham, *N.S.W.*	50	F6
Tottenham, *Ont.*	16	E3
Touggourt, *Algeria*	46	D2
Toulnustouc R., *Que.*	22	D1
Toulon, *France*	38	F5
Toulouse, *France*	38	E5
Tourbis L., *Que.*	20	B2
Tourmente C., *Que.*	20	D2
Tours, *France*	38	E4
Tousside, *Chad, W. Africa*	46	E3
Touwsrivier, *Cape Prov. Rep. of S. Africa*	47	C3
Towcester, *Eng.*	37	E5
Tower, *Minn.*	18	B5
Townsville, *Queensland*	49	H3
Tracadie, *N.B.*	22	E3
Tracadie, *N.S.*	21	C6
Trafalgar C., *Spain*	38	F2
Traiguen, *Chile*	31	C11
Trail, *B.C.*	13	M8
Trairi, *Brazil*	30	K4
Tralee, *Eire*	37	A5
Tramore, *Eire*	37	B5
Tramping L., *Sask.*	14	G4
Transcona, *Man.*	15	N6
Transvaal, *S. Africa*	47	D1
Transylvanian Alps, *Romania*	39	K4
Trapani, *Sicily*	38	H6
Traralgon, *Victoria*	50	F9
Travancore, *India*	40	E7
Traverse I., *S. Atlantic Oc.*	31	L15
Traverse L., *Ont.*	17	G2
Travesia del Norte, *Argentina*	31	E11
Travesia del Puntana, *Argentina*	31	D10
Treinta-y-Tres, *Uruguay*	31	G10
Trelleborg, *Sweden*	35	J4
Tremadoc B., *Wales*	37	C5
Trembleur L., *B.C.*	12	H5
Trembling L., *Que.*	20	B2
Tremont, *Me.*	22	C4
Trenche R., *Que.*	20	C1
Trent, *Italy*	38	G4
Trent R., *Eng.*	37	E5
Trent Canal, *Ont.*	17	H3
Trente-et-un-Milles, L., *Que.*	20	B2
Trenton, *Mo.*	25	H2
Trenton, *N.J.*	25	M2
Trenton, *N.S.*	21	E2
Trenton, *Ont.*	17	H3
Trepassey, and B., *Nfld.*	23	L3
Tres Arroyos, *Argentina*	31	E11
Tres Marias, Las, *Mexico*	28	C3
Trial B., *N.S.W.*	50	J5
Triangles, The, *Mexico*	28	F3
Trida, *N.S.W.*	50	E6
Trier, *Ger.*	38	F3
Trieste, *Italy*	39	H4
Trim, *Eire*	37	B5
Trincomalee, *Ceylon*	40	F7
Tring, *Que.*	20	D2
Trinidad, *Bolivia*	30	E6
Trinidad, *Colo.*	24	F3
Trinidad, *Cuba*	29	J3
Trinidad, *Uruguay*	31	F10
Trinidad I., *W. Indies*	30	E1
Trinidad and Tobago, *W. Indies*	30	E1
Trinity, and B., *Nfld.*	23	L2
Trinity R., *Tex.*	24	G4
Trinity Bay, *Que.*	20	D1
Tripoli, *Lebanon*	42	B5
Tripoli, *Libya*	46	E2
Tripura, ter., *India*	40	H4
Tristan da Cunha, *S. Atlantic Oc.*	3	K6
Triton Club, *Que.*	20	C2
Triunfo, *Brazil*	30	K5
Trivandrum, *India*	40	E7
Trois Pistoles, *Que.*	22	C2
Trois Rivières, *Ont.*	20	C2
Trombetas R., *Brazil*	30	F4
Trompsburg, *Orange F.S., Rep. of S. Africa*	47	D2
Tromsø, *Norway*	35	K2
Trondheim, *Norway*	35	J3
Trondheim Fd., *Norway*	35	H3
Trout L., *Kenora, Ont.*	18	B3
Trout L., *Que.*	22	D1
Trout L., and R., *Mackenzie, N.W.T.*	12	K2
Trout Creek, *Ont.*	17	F2
Trout Lake, *Alberta*	14	D2
Trout Lake, *B.C.*	13	M7
Trout River, *N.S.*	23	H2
Trowutta, *Tasmania*	50	K11
Troy, *Turkey*	39	L6
Troyes, *France*	38	F3
Trucial States, *Arabia*	42	D6
Trujillo, *Honduras*	29	G4
Trujillo, *Peru*	30	B5
Trujillo, *Venezuela*	30	C2
Truk I., *Pacific Oc.*	2	D4
Truro, *Eng.*	37	C6
Truro, *N.S*	21	D2
Trutch, *B.C.*	12	J4
Tsabong, *Botswana*	47	C2
Tsacha L., *B.C.*	13	H6
Tsaidam Swamp, *China*	44	B3
Tsangpo (R.), *Tibet*	40	G3
Tsayta L., *B.C.*	12	H5
Tsinan, *China*	44	D3
Tsing Hai, *China*	43	H5
Tsingtao, *China*	44	E3
Tsin-ling-shan, *China*	43	J5
Tsitsihar (Ch'i-ch'i-ha-erh) *China*	44	E3
Tsugaru Str., *Japan*	44	F2
Tsumeb, *S.W. Africa*	46	E7
Tsushima Str., *Japan*	44	E3
Tuam, *Eire*	37	A5
Tuamotu Arch., *Pacific Oc.*	2	F5
Tubarão, *Brazil*	31	H9
Tubuai Is. (Austral Is.), *Pacific Oc.*	2	F6
Tucacas, *Venezuela*	30	D1
Tucson, *Ariz.*	24	D4
Tucurui, *Brazil*	30	H4
Tudor L., *Que.*	19	D2
Tugaske, *Sask.*	14	H5
Tugela R., *Natal*	47	E2
Tugtokortok, *Greenland*	11	X3
Tukanui, *N.Z.*	51	B6
Tukarak I., *Hudson B.*	19	B2
Tula, *Mexico*	28	E3
Tula, *U.S.S.R.*	39	O2
Tulameen, *B.C.*	13	K8
Tulancingo, *Mexico*	28	E3
Tulare L., *Cal.*	24	C3
Tulbagh, *Cape Prov., Rep. of S. Africa*	47	B3
Tuli, *Rhodesia*	47	D1
Tullamore, *Eire*	37	B5
Tullamore, *N.S.W.*	50	F6
Tullet Pt., *Prince Patrick I., N.W.T.*	10	K2
Tully, *Queensland*	49	H3
Tulsa, *Okla.*	24	G3
Tulsequah, *B.C.*	12	D3
Tumac Humac Mts., *Brazil, etc.*	30	F3
Tumaco, *Colombia*	30	B3
Tumana R., *Alaska*	10	E5
Tumbarumba, *N.S.W.*	50	F7
Tumbes, *Peru*	30	A4
Tummo, *Libya*	46	E3
Tumut, *N.S.W.*	50	G7
Tunbridge Wells, *Eng.*	37	F6
Tungsten, *Mackenzie, N.W.T.*	12	F2
Tung Ting L., *China*	44	D4
Tunguska R., Lower, *U.S.S.R.*	43	H2
Tunguska R., Middle, *U.S.S.R.*	43	H2
Tunguska R., Upper, *U.S.S.R.*	43	H3
Tunis, *Tunisia*	46	E2
Tunisia, *N. Africa*	46	D2
Tunja, *Colombia*	30	C2
Tunnel Dam, *Ont.*	16	B1
Tunungayualok I., *Lab.*	19	E2
Tunuyan R., *Argentina*	31	D10
Tupiza, *Bolivia*	31	D8
Tupper, *B.C.*	12	L5
Turfan, *Sinkiang*	44	A2
Turin, *Alberta*	14	E6
Turin, *Italy*	38	F4
Turkey, rep., *Europe-Asia*	39	M6
Turkey Point Prov. Park, *Ont.*	16	E5
Turkistan, E., *Sinkiang*	42	F5
Turkistan, W., Plain of, *U.S.S.R.*	42	E4
Turks Is., *W. Indies*	29	K3
Turku, *Finland*	35	L3
Turnagain C., *N.Z.*	51	F4
Turnagain R., *B.C.*	12	F3
Turnberry, *Man.*	15	L4
Turneffe I., *Brit. Honduras*	28	G4
Turner Valley, *Alberta*	14	D5
Turnor L., *Sask.*	14	G2
Turnovo, *Bulgaria*	39	L5
Tuross R., *N.S.W.*	50	H8
Turtle L., *Sask.*	14	G4
Turtle Mts., *Man.*	15	L6
Turtle R., *Ont.*	18	B4
Turtle Creek, *N.B.*	21	C1
Turtleford, *Sask.*	14	G4
Turvo R., *Brazil*	31	H8
Tuscaloosa, *Ala.*	25	J4
Tusket, *N.S.*	21	B4
Tusket I., *N.S.*	22	D5
Tutoia, *Brazil*	30	J4
Tutoyaktuk (Port Brabant), *Mackenzie, N.W.T.*	10	H4
Tutuila I., *Pacific Oc.*	2	E5
Tutuko Mt., *N.Z.*	51	B6
Tuxpan, *Mexico E.*	28	E3
Tuxpan, *Mexico W.*	28	C3
Tuxtla Gutierrez, *Mexico*	28	F4
Tuya L., and R., *B.C.*	12	E3
Tuz Gol, *Turkey*	39	N6
Tweed, *Ont.*	17	H3
Tweed R., *Scotland*	36	D4
Tweedsmuir Is., *Franklin, N.W.T.*	11	T4
Tweedsmuir Park, *B.C.*	13	G6
Twelve Mile L., *Sask.*	14	H6
Twillingate, *Nfld.*	23	K2
Twin Brothers (Is.), *Hudson B.*	19	A1
Twins, N. and S. (Is.), *Ont.*	19	A2
Twofold B., *N.S.W.*	50	H2
Two Mountains, Park, and L. of, *Que.*	20	B3
Two Rivers, *Sask.*	15	K3
Tyler, *Tex.*	24	G3
Tyne R., *Eng.*	37	D4
Tynemouth, *Eng.*	37	E4
Tyne Valley, *P.E.I.*	21	D1
Tyrone, co., *N. Ire.*	37	B3
Tyrrell L., *Victoria*	50	D4
Tyrrhenian Sea, *Italy*	38	G7
Tywyn, *Wales*	37	C5
Tzaneen, *Transvaal*	47	E1
Uatuma R., *Brazil*	30	F4
Uaupés, and R., *Brazil*	30	D3
Ubangi R., *Africa*	46	E5
Uberaba, *Brazil*	30	H7
Uberlandia, *Brazil*	30	H7
Ubombo, *Natal*	47	E2
Ubon. See Muang Ubon		
Ucayali R., *Peru*	30	C6
Ucluelet, *B.C.*	13	H8
Udaipur, *India*	40	D4
Udine, *Italy*	38	H4
Uele R., *Zaire*	46	F5
Uganda, *E. Africa*	46	G5
Uist, N., *Hebrides, Scotland*	36	B3
Uist, S., *Hebrides, Scotland*	36	B3
Uitenhage, *Cape Prov., Rep. of S. Africa*	47	D3
Ujiji, *Tanzania*	46	G6
Ujjain, *India*	40	E4
Ukasiksalik, *Lab.*	19	E2
Ukraine, rep., *U.S.S.R.*	39	M3
Ulaanbaator (Ulan Bator), *Mongolia*	43	J4
Ulan Ude, *U.S.S.R.*	44	C1
Ulith Is., *Pacific Oc.*	44	F5
Ulkatcho, *B.C.*	13	H6
Ullapool, *Scotland*	36	C3
Ulm, *Ger.*	38	G3
Ulverston, *Eng.*	37	D4
Ulverstone, *Tasmania*	50	L11
Umab Desert, *S.W. Africa*	47	B1
Umeå, *Sweden*	35	L3
Ume Älv, *Sweden*	35	K3
Umkomaas, *Natal*	47	E3
Umtata, *Cape Prov., Rep. of S. Africa*	47	D3
Unalakleet, *Alaska*	10	B5
Unalaska, *Aleutian Is.*	2	B4
Unapool, *Scotland*	36	C2
Underberg, *Natal*	47	D2
Ungava B., *Que.*	19	D2
Union B., *Argentina*	31	E12
Union Bay. *Vancouver I., B.C.*	13	H8
Uniondale, *Cape Prov., Rep. of S. Africa*	47	C3
Union of Soviet Socialist Republics (U.S.S.R.) *Europe-Asia*	3	M1
Unionville, *Mich.*	16	B4
United Arab Emirates, *Arabia*	42	D6
United Kingdom of Gt. Britain and N. Ireland, *Europe*	35	E4
Unity, *Sask.*	14	G4
Unknown L., *Sask.*	15	J1
Unst I., *Shetland Is., Scotland*	36	E1
Unuk R., *Alaska*	12	E4
Upernavik, *Greenland*	11	X3
Upington, *Cape Prov., Rep. of S. Africa*	47	C2
Uplands, *Ont.*	17	K2
Upper Blackville, *N.B.*	21	A1
Upper Hutt, *N.Z.*	51	E4
Upper Laberge, *Yukon*	12	C2
Upper Musquodoboit, *N.S.*	21	E2
Upper Ohio, *N.S.*	22	E5
Upper Stewiacke, *N.S.*	21	D2
Upper Vaughan, *N.S.*	21	C3
Upper Volta, *W. Africa*	46	C4
Uppsala, *Sweden*	35	K3
Upsala, *Ont.*	18	C4
Upsalquitch, *N.B.*	22	D3
Ural R., and Mts., *U.S.S.R.*	42	D3
Uralla, *N.S.W.*	50	H5
Uranium City, *Sask.*	14	G1
Uraricoera R., *Brazil*	30	E3
Ure R., *Eng.*	37	E4
Uren, *Sask.*	14	H5
Ures, *Mexico*	28	B2
UrreLauquenL., *Argentina*	31	D11
Uruapan del Progreso, *Mexico*	28	D4
Urubamba R., *Peru*	30	C6
Urubicha, *Bolivia*	30	E7
Uruguaiana, *Brazil*	31	F9
Uruguay, rep., *S. America*	31	F10
Uruguay R., *Argentina-Uruguay, etc.*	31	F10
Urumchi, *Sinkiang*	44	A2
Urville, C. d', *W. Irian*	44	F7
Ushant I., *France*	38	C3
Ushuaia, *Argentina*	31	D14
Usk, *B.C.*	12	F5
Usk R., *Eng.*	37	D6
Üsküdar (Skutari), *Turkey*	39	M5
Uspallata Pt., *Argentina*	31	D10
Ussuri R., *U.S.S.R.*	44	F2
Ussuriysk, *U.S.S.R.*	44	F2
Ust Izhma, *U.S.S.R.*	35	R2
Ust' Kut, *U.S.S.R.*	43	J3
Ust Port, *U.S.S.R.*	42	G2
Ust Tzilma, *U.S.S.R.*	35	R2
Ust-Urt Plat., *U.S.S.R.*	42	D4
Utah, state, *U.S.A.*	24	D3
Utah L., *Ut.*	24	D2
Utica, *N.Y.*	25	M2
Utik L., *Man.*	15	O3
Utikama L., *Alberta*	14	D3
Utrecht, *Netherlands*	38	F2
Utrecht, *Natal*	47	E2
Uttar Pradesh, state, *India*	40	F3
Utterson, *Ont.*	17	F2
Uva L., *Colombia*	30	C3
Uxbridge, *Ont.*	17	F3
Uzh R., *Ukraine*	39	M3
Uzhgorod, *Ukraine*	39	K3
Vaal R., *S. Africa*	47	D2
Vaal Dam, *Transvaal*	47	D2
Vaasa, *Finland*	35	L3
Vacaria, *Brazil*	31	G9
Vadsö, *Norway*	35	M1
Váh R., *Czechoslovakia, etc.*	39	J3
Val Barrette, *Que.*	17	K1
Val Brillant, *Que.*	22	C2
Valcartier, *Que.*	20	D2
Valcourt, *Que.*	20	C3
Valdai, and Hills, *U.S.S.R.*	39	N1
Valdes Penin., *Argentina*	31	E12
Val des Bois, *Que.*	17	K2
Valdesia, *Transvaal*	47	E1
Valdez, *Alaska*	10	E5
Valdivia, *Chile*	31	C11
Val d'Or, *Que.*	19	B4
Valença, *Brazil*	30	K6
Valencia, *Spain*	38	D6
Valencia, *Venezuela*	30	D1
Valentine, *Neb.*	24	F2
Valets L., *Que.*	20	A1
Valga, *Estonia*	39	L1
Valladolid, *Mexico*	28	G3
Valladolid, *Spain*	38	C5
Valledupar, *Colombia*	30	C1
Vallée Junc., *Que.*	20	D2
Valle Grande, *Bolivia*	30	E7
Vallejo, *Cal.*	24	B3
Vallenar, *Chile*	31	C9
Valley, *N.S.*	21	D2
Valley N., *Man.*	15	L5
Valleyfield, *Que.*	20	B3
Valley Marie, *Sask.*	14	H6
Valleyview, *Alberta*	14	C3
Val Marie, *Sask.*	14	H6
Valora, *Ont.*	18	C4
Valparaiso, *Chile*	31	C10
Vals, C., *W. Irian*	44	F7
Valuiki, *U.S.S.R.*	39	O3
Van L., *Turkey*	42	C5
Van Bruyssells, *Que.*	20	C2
Van Buren, *Me.*	22	D3
Vanceboro', *Me.*	22	D4
Vancouver, *B.C.*	13	J8
Vancouver I., *B.C.*	13	H8
Vancouver Mt., *Yukon*	13	A2
Vanderbijl Park, *Transvaal*	47	D2
Vanderhoof, *B.C.*	13	J5
Van Diemen G., *N. Ter., Aust.*	49	E2
Vandry, *Que.*	20	C2
Vänerna, *Sweden*	35	J4
Vänersborg, *Sweden*	38	H1
Vanguard, *Sask.*	14	H6
Vankleek Hill, *Ont.*	17	L2
Van Rhynsdorp, *Cape Prov., Rep. of S. Africa*	47	B3
Vansittart I., *Keewatin, N.W.T.*	11	S4
Van Wyks Vlei, *Cape Prov., Rep. of S. Africa*	47	C3
Varanasi (Benares), *India*	40	F3
Varanger Fd., *Norway*	35	N1
Varaka, *Queensland*	49	G5
Vardar R., *Yugoslavia*	39	K5
Vardö, *Norway*	35	N1
Varennes, *Que.*	20	C3
Varna, *Bulgaria*	39	L5
Vasa Barris R., *Brazil*	30	K5
Vassar, *Mich.*	16	B4
Västeras, *Sweden*	35	K4
Västervik, *Sweden*	39	J1
Vatna Jökull, *Iceland*	35	C3
Vättern, *Sweden*	39	H1
Vaudreuil, *Que.*	20	B3
Vavenby, *B.C.*	13	L7
Växjö, *Sweden*	39	H1
Vegreville, *Alberta*	14	F4
Vela, C. de la, *Colombia*	30	C1
Velas S., *Costa Rica*	29	G5
Velddriff, *Cape Prov., Rep. of S. Africa*	47	B3
Velikaya R., *U.S.S.R.*	39	M1
Veliki Ustyug, *U.S.S.R.*	35	Q3
Velikiye Luki, *U.S.S.R.*	39	M1
Velsk, *U.S.S.R.*	35	P3
Venado, *Mexico*	28	D3
Venezuela, rep., *S. America*	30	D2
Venezuela, G. of, *Venezuela*	30	C1
Venice, and B. of, *Italy*	38	H4
Venosta, *Que.*	17	J2
Ventersburg, *Orange F.S.*	47	D2
Ventnor, *Eng.*	37	E6
Ventspils, *Latvia*	39	K1
Ventuari R., *Venezuela*	30	D2
Venus B., *Victoria*	50	E9

Name	Page	Grid
Vera, B. de, *Argentina*	31	E12
Veracruz, *Mexico*	28	E4
Vercheres, *Que.*	20	C3
Verde C., *Senegal, Africa*	46	B4
Verde R., *Brazil*	30	J7
Verdun, *Que.*	20	C3
Vereeniging, *Transvaal*	47	D2
Verendrye Park, La, *Que.*	20	A2
Verkhoyansk, and Mts., *U.S.S.R.*	43	L2
Verlo, *Sask.*	14	G5
Vermilion Bay, *Ont.*	18	B4
Vermilion Chutes, *Alberta*	14	D1
Vermillion, *Alberta*	14	F4
Vermillion R., *Que.*	20	C2
Vermont, state, *U.S.A.*	25	M2
Verner, *Ont.*	16	E1
Verneuk Pan, *Cape Prov., Rep. of S. Africa*	47	C2
Vernon, *B.C.*	13	L7
Vernon, *P.E.I.*	21	E1
Verona, *Italy*	38	G4
Verona, *Ont.*	17	J3
Versailles, *France*	38	E3
Verte B., *Nfld.*	23	K1
Verte R., *Que.*	20	E2
Verulam, *Natal*	47	E2
Verviers, *Belgium*	38	F3
Vest Fd. *Norway*	35	J2
Vestmannaeyjar, *Iceland*	35	B3
Vecuvius Mt., *Italy*	39	H5
Vet R., *Orange F.S.*	47	D2
Viana, *Brazil*	30	H4
Vichada R., *Colombia*	30	D2
Vichegda R., *U.S.S.R.*	35	Q3
Vicksburg, *Miss.*	25	H4
Victor Harb., *S. Aust.*	50	B7
Victoria, *Aust.*	50	D8
Victoria, *Hong Kong, China*	44	F4
Victoria, *Nfld.*	23	L3
Victoria, *Vancouver I., B.C.*	13	J8
Victoria, co., *Ont.*	17	J3
Victoria Desert, *W. Aust.*	49	D5
Victoria Falls, *Zambesi R.*	46	F7
Victoria Harb., *Ont.*	16	F3
Victoria I., *Franklin, N.W.T.*	10	M3
Victoria L., *E. Africa*	46	G6
Victoria L., *Nfld.*	23	J2
Victoria L., *N.S.W.*	50	C6
Victoria L., *Que.*	19	B4
Victoria L., *Victoria*	50	F8
Victoria Mt., *Alberta*	14	D6
Victoria Peak, *Vancouver I., B.C.*	13	G7
Victoria Pt., *Burma*	40	J7
Victoria R., *N. Ter., Aust.*	49	E3
Victoria Beach, *Man.*	15	N5
Victoria Beach, *N.S.*	22	E4
Victoria de Durango, *Mexico*	28	D3
Victoria Land, *Victoria I.*	10	N4
Victoria Mine, *Ont.*	16	D1
Victoriaville, *Que.*	20	D2
Victoria West, *Cape Prov., Rep. of S. Africa*	47	C3
Vicuna, *Chile*	31	C10
Vidin, *Bulgaria*	39	K4
Viedma, *Argentina*	31	E12
Viedma L., *Argentina*	31	C12
Viejas Is., *Peru*	30	B6
Vienna, *Austria*	39	J3
Vientiane, *Laos*	44	C5
Vieques, I. de, *W. Indies*	29	L4
Vierfontein, *Orange F.S.*	47	D2
Viesca, *Mexico*	28	D2
Vietnam, N. & S., *S.E. Asia*	44	C5
View, L., *Ore.*	24	B2
Vigia Chico, *Mexico*	28	G4
Vigo, *Spain*	38	B5
Vik, *Norway*	35	H3
Viking, *Alberta*	14	F4
Vikna Is., *Norway*	35	J2
Vilhelmina, *Sweden*	35	K3
Villa Bella, *Bolivia*	30	D6
Villa Bella, *Brazil*	31	J8
Villach, *Austria*	38	H4
Villa Cisneros. *Span. Sahara*	46	B3
Villa de Cura, *Venezuela*	30	D1
Villa de Mercedes, *Argentina*	31	D10
Villa Dolores, *Cordoba, Argentina*	31	D10
Villa General Roca, *Argentina*	31	D11
Villahermosa, *Mexico*	28	F4
Villaldama, *Mexico*	28	D2
Villa Maria, *Argentina*	31	E10
Villa Montes, *Bolivia*	31	E8
Villa Nueva, *Argentina*	31	E10
Villa Rica, *Brazil*	31	G8
Villarrica, *Chile*	31	C11
Villarrica, *Paraguay*	31	F9
Villa Valeria, *Argentina*	31	E10
Villavicencio, *Colombia*	30	C3
Ville Marie, *Que.*	18	J5
Villeroy, *Que.*	20	C2
Vilnius (Vilna), *Lithuania*	39	L2
Vilyuysk, *U.S.S.R.*	43	K2
Vina del Mar, *Chile*	31	C10
Vinal Haven I., *Me.*	22	C5
Vincennes, *Ind.*	25	J3
Vincent C., *N.Y.*	17	J3
Vindhya Ra., *India*	40	E4
Vinh, *N. Vietnam*	44	C4
Vinita, *Okla.*	24	G3
Vinnitsa, *Ukraine*	39	M3
Vinton, *Que.*	20	A3
Virden, *Man.*	15	L6
Virgin Falls, *Ont.*	18	D4
Virgin Is., *W. Indies*	29	M4
Virginia, state, *U.S.A.*	25	L3
Virginia City, *Nev.*	24	C3
Virginia Falls, *Mackenzie, N.W.T.*	12	H2
Virjenes C., *Chile-Argentina*	31	D14
Visby, *Gotland I., Sweden*	39	J1
Viscount Melville Sd., *N.W.T.*	10	N3
Vishakhapatnam, *India*	40	F5
Vishniy Volochok, *U.S.S.R.*	39	N1
Viso, Monte, *Italy*	38	F4
Vistula R., *Poland*	39	J2
Vitebsk, *U.S.S.R.*	39	M2
Vitim, *U.S.S.R.*	43	J3
Vitim R., and Plat., *U.S.S.R.*	43	K3
Vitoria, *Brazil*	30	K8
Vitoria, *Spain*	38	D5
Vitória de Conquista. *Brazil*	30	J6
Vitória de Sto. Antão, *Brazil*	30	K5
Vittoria, *Ont.*	16	E5
Vivonne B., *Kangaroo I., Aust.*	50	A8
Vladimir, *U.S.S.R.*	39	P1
Vladivostok, *U.S.S.R.*	44	F2
Vltava R., *Czechoslovakia*	39	H3
Volga R., *U.S.S.R.*	39	O1
Volgograd, *U.S.S.R.*	42	C4
Volkhov R., *U.S.S.R.*	35	N4
Volksrust, *Transvaal*	47	D2
Vologda, *U.S.S.R.*	35	P4
Vonda, *Sask.*	14	H4
Vontersdorp, *Transvaal*	47	D2
Voronezh, *U.S.S.R.*	39	O3
Voroshilovgrad, *Ukraine*	39	O3
Vosges Mts., *France*	38	F3
Vrede, *Orange F.S.*	47	D2
Vredenburg. *Cape Prov., Rep. of S. Africa*	47	B3
Vryburg, *Cape Prov., Rep. of S. Africa*	47	C2
Vryhoid, *Natal*	47	E2
Vulcan, *Alberta*	14	E5
Vyazma, *U.S.S.R.*	39	N2
Vyborg, *U.S.S.R.*	35	M3
Vyma R., *U.S.S.R.*	35	R3
Vytegra, *U.S.S.R.*	35	O3
Wabakimi L., *Ont.*	18	C3
Wabana, *Nfld.*	23	L3
Wabasca, *Alberta*	14	E3
Wabasca Ls., *Alberta*	14	E2
Wabasca R., *Alberta*	12	N4
Wabash R., *Ind.*	25	J3
Wabigoon R., *Ont.*	18	B3
Wabowden, *Man.*	15	M3
Wabush, *Lab.*	19	D3
Wabush L., *Lab.*	19	D3
Waco, *Que.*	19	D3
Waco, *Tex.*	24	G4
Waddamana, *Tasmania*	50	L12
Waddington, *Ont.*	17	K3
Waddington Mt., *B.C.*	13	H7
Wadena, *Sask.*	15	K4
Wadham Is., *Nfld.*	23	L2
Wadhams, *B.C.*	13	G7
Wadhope, *Man.*	15	O5
Wadi Halfa, *Sudan*	46	F3
Wagga Wagga, *N.S.W.*	50	F7
Wagner, *Alberta*	14	D3
Wagner B., *Keewatin, N.W.T.*	11	R4
Waiau, *N.Z.*	51	D5
Waiau R., *Canterbury, N.Z.*	51	D5
Waiau R., *Southland, N.Z.*	51	A7
Waihi, *N.Z.*	51	E2
Waikaia. *N.Z.*	51	B6
Waikaremoana L., *N.Z.*	51	F3
Waikato R., *N.Z.*	51	E3
Waikerie. *S. Aust.*	50	B7
Waimate, *N.Z.*	51	C6
Wainwright, *Alaska*	10	B3
Wainwright, *Alberta*	14	F4
Waiotira, *N.Z.*	51	E1
Waipapa Point, *N.Z.*	51	B7
Waipara, *N.Z.*	51	D5
Waipukurau, *N.Z.*	51	F3
Wairau R., *N.Z.*	51	D4
Wairoa, *N.Z.*	51	F3
Waitaki R.. *N.Z.*	51	C6
Waitara, *N.Z.*	51	E3
Waitomo, *N.Z.*	51	E3
Wakatipu L., *N.Z.*	51	B6
Wakaw, *Sask.*	14	J4
Wake I., *Pacific Oc.*	2	D4
Wakefield, *Que.*	17	J2
Wakkanai, *Japan*	44	G2
Wakkerstroom, *Transvaal, Rep. of S. Africa*	47	E2
Wakuach L., *Que.*	19	D2
Walcott, *B.C.*	13	G5
Waldeck, *Sask.*	14	H5
Waldo, *B.C.*	13	N8
Waldoboro, *Me.*	22	C5
Wales, *Brit. Isles*	37	D6
Wales C., *Que.*	19	C1
Wales I., *Hudson Str.*	19	C1
Walgett, *N.S.W.*	50	G5
Walhalla, *Victoria*	50	F9
Walker, *Que.*	20	C2
Walker B., *Cape Prov., Rep. of S. Africa*	47	B3
Walker C., *Greenland*	11	W2
Walker L., *Man.*	15	N3
Walker L., *Nev.*	24	C3
Walkerton, *Ont.*	16	D3
Wallace, *Ida.*	24	C1
Wallace, *N.S.*	21	D2
Wallace, *Ont.*	17	G2
Wallaceburg, *Ont.*	16	C5
Wallacetown, *Ont.*	16	D5
Wallaroo, *S. Aust.*	50	A6
Walla Walla, *Wash.*	24	C1
Walsall. *Eng.*	37	E5
Walsh, *Alberta*	14	G6
Walsingham C., *Baffin I., N.W.T.*	11	W4
Walter I., *James B.*	18	J2
Waltham, *Que.*	17	J2
Walton, *N.S.*	21	D2
Walton, *Ont.*	16	D4
Walvis B.y, *S.W. Africa*	47	A1
Wanaaring, *N.S.W.*	50	E4
Wanaka, and L., *N.Z.*	51	B6
Wanapitei L., *Ont.*	18	H5
Wandoan, *Queensland*	50	G3
Wanganui, *N.Z.*	51	E4
Wanganui R., *N.Z.*	51	E3
Wangaratta, *Victoria*	50	F8
Wanless, *Man.*	15	L3
Wanop, *Ont.*	16	E1
Wapapewekka L., *Sask.*	14	J3
Wapella, *Sask.*	15	L5
Wapikopa L., *Ont.*	18	D2
Wapiti R., *Alberta*	14	B3
Waratah, *Tasmania*	50	K11
Waratah B., *Victoria*	50	F9
Wardlow, *Alberta*	14	F5
Warialda, *N.S.W.*	50	H4
Warkworth, *N.Z.*	51	E2
Warkworth, *Ont.*	17	H3
Warman, *Sask.*	14	H4
Warmbad, *S.W. Africa*	47	B2
Warmbad, *Transvaal*	47	D1
Warm Bay Hotsprings, *B.C.*	12	D3
Warner, *Alberta*	14	E6
Warner C., *Ore.*	24	C2
Warracknabeal, *Victoria*	50	D8
Warragul, *Victoria*	50	E9
Warrego Ra., *Queensland*	50	E2
Warrego R., *N.S.W., and Queensland*	50	E4
Warren, *Ida.*	24	C1
Warren, *N.S.W.*	50	F5
Warren, *Ont.*	16	E1
Warren Landing, *Man.*	15	N4
Warrenpoint, *N. Ire.*	37	B4
Warrenton, *Cape Prov., Rep. of S. Africa*	47	C2
Warrington, *Eng.*	37	D5
Warrnambool, *Victoria*	50	D9
Warsaw, *Poland*	39	K2
Warta R., *Poland*	39	J2
Warwick, *Que.*	20	D3
Warwick, *Queensland*	50	A4
Warwick, and co., *Eng.*	37	E5
Wasaga Beach, *Ont.*	16	E3
Wasatch Mts., *Ut.*	24	D3
Wasekamio L., *Sask.*	14	G2
Wash, The, *Eng.*	37	F5
Washago, *Ont.*	17	F3
Washington, state, *U.S.A.*	24	B1
Washington, City of, *D.C.*	25	L3
Washington I., *Pacific Oc.*	2	E4
Washow B., *Man.*	15	N5
Waskada, *Man.*	15	L6
Waskaiowaka L., *Man.*	15	N2
Waskesiu L., *Sask.*	14	H4
Waswanipi, and L., *Que.*	19	B4
Waterberge, *Transvaal*	47	D1
Waterdown, *Ont.*	16	F4
Waterford, *N.B.*	22	E4
Waterford, *Ont.*	16	E5
Waterford, and co., *Eire*	37	B5
Waterford Harb., *Eire*	37	B5
Waterhen L., *Man.*	15	M4
Waterhen L., *Sask.*	14	G3
Waterloo, *Ida.*	25	H2
Waterloo, *Ont.*	16	E4
Waterloo, *Que.*	20	C3
Waterloo, co., *Ont.*	16	E4
Waterton L., *Alberta*	14	E6
Waterton Lakes National Park, *Alberta*	14	E6
Watertown, *N.Y.*	17	K4
Watertown, *S. Dak.*	24	G2
Waterville, *Me.*	22	B4
Waterville, *N.S.*	21	C2
Waterville, *Que.*	20	D3
Waterways, *Alberta*	14	F2
Wathaman L., *Sask.*	15	K2
Wathaman R., *Sask.*	15	J2
Watino, *Alberta*	12	M5
Watling I., (S. Salvador I.), *Bahamas*	29	K3
Watoussi I., *Que.*	20	C2
Watrous, *Sask.*	14	J5
Watson, *Sask.*	15	J4
Watson Lake, *Yukon*	12	F2
Watt, *N.B.*	22	D4
Watt Mt., *B.C.*	13	K6
Waubamik, *Ont.*	16	F2
Waubaushene, *Ont.*	16	F3
Waubra, *Victoria*	50	D8
Wauchope, *Sask.*	15	L6
Waugh, *Man.*	18	A4
Wausau, *Wis.*	25	J1
Waveney R., *Eng.*	37	F5
Waverley, *N.S.*	21	D3
Wawa, *Ont.*	18	F4
Wawansea, *Man.*	15	M6
Wayagamack, and L., *Que.*	20	C2
Waycross, *Ga.*	25	K4
Wayne, *Neb.*	24	G2
Wazirabad, *Afghanistan*	40	C1
Weagamow L., *Ont.*	18	C2
Weald, *Alberta*	14	C4
Weald, The, *Eng.*	37	F6
Wear R., *Eng.*	37	D4
Webbwood, *Ont.*	16	C1
Wecho R., *Mackenzie, N.W.T.*	12	N1
Wedge Mt., *B.C.*	13	J7
Wedgeport, *N.S.*	21	A4
Wednesbury, *Eng.*	37	E5
Weedon, *Que.*	20	D3
Wee Waa, *N.S.W.*	50	G5
Weir, *Que.*	17	L2
Weir River, *Man.*	15	O2
Weiser, *Ida.*	24	C2
Wekusko, and L., *Man.*	15	M3
Weldon, *Sask.*	14	J4
Welford, *Queensland*	50	D2
Welkom, *Orange F.S.*	47	D2
Welland, and R., *Ont.*	17	F5
Welland, co., *Ont.*	17	F4
Welland Can., *Ont.*	16	F5
Welland R., *Eng.*	37	E5
Wellesley Is., *Queensland*	49	F3
Wellington, *Cape Prov., Rep. of S. Africa*	47	B3
Wellington, *N.S.W.*	50	G6
Wellington, *N.Z.*	51	E4
Wellington, *N.S.*	21	D3
Wellington, *Ont.*	17	H4
Wellington, *P.E.I.*	21	C1
Wellington, *Victoria*	50	F9
Wellington, co., *Ont.*	16	E4
Wellington Chan., *Franklin, N.W.T.*	11	Q2
Wellington I., *Chile*	31	B13
Wellington Bay, *Ont.*	17	H4
Wells, *B.C.*	13	K6
Wells, *Norfolk. Eng.*	37	F5
Wellsford, *N.Z.*	51	E2
Wells Gray Park, *B.C.*	13	K6
Welsford, *N.B.*	22	D4
Welshpool, *Wales*	37	D5
Welspoort, *Cape Prov., Rep. of S. Africa*	47	C3
Welwood, *Man.*	15	M5
Wembley, *Alberta*	14	B3
Wemyss Bay, *Scotland*	36	C4
Wentworth. *N.S.W.*	50	D7
Wentworth, co., *Ont.*	16	E4
Wentworth Centre, *N.S.*	21	D2
Wepener, *Orange F.S.*	47	D2
Werris Creek, *N.S.W.*	50	H5
Wesel, *Ger.*	38	F3
Weser R., *Ger.*	38	G2
Wesiemkoon L., *Ont.*	17	H3
Wesleyville, *Nfld.*	23	K2
Wessel C., *N. Ter., Aust.*	49	F2
West C., *N.Z.*	51	A6
West Pt., *Anticosti I.*	22	E2
West Pt., *P.E.I.*	21	C1
West Pt., *Sable I., N.S.*	23	G5
West Pt., *Tasmania*	50	E10
West Bengal, state, *India*	40	G4
West Branch, *Mich.*	16	A3
West Bromwich, *Eng.*	37	E5
Westbrook, *Me.*	22	B5
Westbury, *Que.*	20	D3
West Duck I., *Ont.*	16	B2
Western Is., *Ont.*	16	E2
Western Australia, state, *Aust.*	49	B4
Western Ghats, *India*	40	D5
Western Head, *N.S.*	21	C4
Western Port, *Victoria*	50	E9
Westfield, *N.B.*	22	D4
Westfield, *N.Y.*	16	F5
Westgate, *Queensland*	50	F3
West Ham. *Eng.*	37	F6
West Hill, *Ont.*	17	F4
West Indies Is., *Atlantic Oc.*	29	K3
West Irian, *Indonesia*	44	F7
Westlock, *Alberta*	14	E3
West Lorne, *Ont.*	16	D5
Westmeath, *Ont.*	17	J2
Westmeath, co., *Eire*	37	B5
Westmorland, co., *Eng.*	37	D4
Weston, *Ont.*	16	F4
Weston-super-Mare, *Eng.*	37	D6
Westport, *Eire*	37	A5
Westport, *N.Z.*	51	C4
Westport, *Ont.*	17	J3
West Pubnico, *N.S.*	21	A4
Westray, *Orkney Is., Scotland*	36	D7
Westree, *Ont.*	18	H4
West Road R., *B.C.*	13	J5
West St. John, *N.B.*	22	D2
Westville, *Fla.*	25	J5
Westville, *N.S.*	21	D2
West Virginia, state, *U.S.A.*	25	K4
Westwold, *B.C.*	13	L4
Wetaskiwin, *Alberta*	14	E2
Wexford, and co., *Eire*	37	B3

Name	Page	Grid
Wexford Harb., *Eire*	37	B5
Wey R., *Eng.*	37	E6
Weyakwin L., *Sask.*	14	H3
Weyburn. *Sask.*	15	K6
Weyburn L., *Mackenzie, N.W.T.*	12	M1
Weymont, *Que.*	20	C2
Weymouth, *Eng.*	37	D6
Weymouth, *N.S.*	22	E4
Whakatane, *N.Z.*	51	F2
Whaleback, Mt., *W. Aust.*	49	B4
Whale R., Gt., *Que.*	11	T6
Whale River, *Que.*	19	D2
Whalsay, *Shetland Is., Scotland*	36	E1
Whangarei, *N.Z.*	51	E1
Wharfe R., *Eng.*	37	E5
Wheatley, *Ont.*	16	C5
Wheeler R., *Sask.*	14	J2
Wheeler Peak, *Nev.*	24	D3
Wheeling, *W. Va.*	25	K2
Whernside, Mt., *Eng.*	37	D4
Whipple Pt., *N.S.*	21	A3
Whiskey Gap, *Alberta*	14	E6
Whiskey Jock L., *Man.*	15	L1
Whitbourne, *Nfld.*	23	L3
Whitby, *Eng.*	37	E4
Whitby, *Ont.*	17	F4
White B., *Nfld.*	23	J1
White I., *Que.*	20	E2
White L., *Ont.*	17	J2
White Mts.. *N.H.*	22	B4
White R., *Ont.*	18	B3
White R., *Ont.*	18	G5
White R., *Yukon*	10	F5
White Bear, *Sask.*	14	G5
White Bear B., *Baffin I., N.W.T.*	19	C1
White Bear R., *Nfld.*	23	J3
Whiteclay L., *Ont.*	18	D3
White Cliffs, *N.S.W.*	50	D5
Whitecourt, *Alberta*	14	C3
Whitefish, *Ont.*	16	D1
Whitefish B., *Ont.-Mich.*	18	F5
Whitefish L., *Que.*	20	B3
Whitefish Falls. *Ont.*	16	D1
White Fox R., *Sask.*	14	J4
Whitegull L., *Que.*	19	E2
Whitehorse, *Yukon*	12	C2
White Lake, *Ont.*	17	J2
Whitemud R., *Alberta*	14	C2
Whitemud Fall, *Man.*	15	P3
White Otter L., *Ont.*	18	C4
White River, *Ont.*	18	F4
White Russia, rep., *U.S.S.R.*	39	L2
Whitesail L., *B.C.*	13	G6
Whitesand R., *Sask.*	15	K5
White Sea, *U.S.S.R.*	35	O2
Whiteshell Park, *Man.*	15	N5
Whitestone L., *Man.*	15	N2
Whitestone L., *Ont.*	18	C3
Whitewater, *B.C.*	12	H4
Whitewater L., *Ont.*	18	D3
Whiteway Pt., *Man.*	15	N5
Whitewood, *Sask.*	15	K5
Whitney, *Ont.*	17	G2
Whitney Mt., *Cal.*	24	C3
Whittle C., *Que.*	23	H1
Whittlesea, *Victoria*	50	E8
Wholdaia L., *Mackenzie, N.W.T.*	10	N5
Whyalla, *S. Aust.*	49	F6
Whycocomagh, *N.S.*	21	F2
Wiarton, *Ont.*	16	D3
Wichita, *Kan.*	24	G3
Wichita Falls, *Tex.*	24	G4
Wick, *Scotland*	36	D2
Wicked Pt., *Man.*	15	M4
Wickham C., *King I., Tasmania*	50	D9
Wicklow, and co., *Eire*	37	B5
Wicklow Mts., *Eire*	37	B5
Widdifield, *Ont.*	17	F1
Wide B., *Queensland*	50	J2
Wiener Neustadt, *Austria*	39	J4
Wigan, *Eng.*	37	D5
Wight, I. of, *Eng.*	37	E6
Wigtown, and co., *Scotland*	37	C4
Wigtown B., *Scotland*	37	C4
Wikwemikong, *Ont.*	16	D2
Wilberforce, *Ont.*	17	G2
Wilcannia, *N.S.W.*	50	D5
Wilcox, *Sask.*	14	J5
Wildhay R., *Alberta*	14	C4
Wilhelmshaven, *W. Ger.*	38	F2
Wilkes Barre, *Pa.*	25	L2
Wilkie, *Sask.*	14	G4
Willara L., *S. Aust.*	50	C3
Willemstad, *Curaçao I., Dutch W. Indies*	30	D1
Willet, *Ont.*	18	D3
William L., *Que.*	20	D2
William Mt.. *W. Aust.*	49	B6
William R., *Sask.*	14	G1
Williams L., *Ont.*	18	C3
Williamsford. *Ont.*	16	E3
Williams Lake. *B.C.*	13	J6
Williamsport, *Nfld.*	23	J1
Williamsport, *Pa.*	25	L2
Williamston, *Mich.*	16	A5
Williamstown, *Ont.*	20	B3
Williamstown. *Victoria*	50	E8
Willingdon, *Alberta*	14	F4
Willingdon Mt., *Alberta*	14	C5
Williston, *Cape Prov., Rep. of S. Africa*	47	C3
Williston, *N. Dak.*	24	F1
Willmore Wilderness Park, *Alberta*	13	L6
Willow Cr., *Alberta*	14	D5
Willow L., *Mackenzie, N.W.T.*	12	L1
Willow R., *B.C.*	13	J6
Willow Bunch, and L., *Sask.*	14	J6
Willowmore, *Cape Prov., Rep. of S. Africa*	47	C3
Willow River, *B.C.*	13	J5
Willow Run, *Mich.*	16	B5
Wilmer, *B.C.*	13	M7
Wilmington, *Del.*	25	L3
Wilmington, *N.C.*	25	L4
Wilno, *Ont.*	17	H2
Wilson's Promontory, *Victoria*	50	F9
Wiltshire, co., *Eng.*	37	E6
Wiluna, *W. Aust.*	49	C5
Wimborne, *Alberta*	14	E5
Winagami L., *Alberta*	14	C3
Winburg, *Orange F.S.*	47	D2
Winchester, *Eng.*	37	E6
Winchester, *Ont.*	17	K2
Windera, *Queensland*	50	H3
Windermere L., *B.C.*	13	M7
Windermere L., *Eng.*	37	D4
Windermere L., *Ont.*	18	G5
Windhoek, *S.W. Africa*	47	B1
Windigo, *Que.*	20	C2
Windigo L., *Ont.*	18	C2
Windigo R., *Que.*	20	C1
Windigo Lake, *Ont.*	18	C2
Windorah, *Queensland*	50	D2
Wind River Ra., *Wyo.*	24	E2
Windscale, *Eng.*	37	D4
Windsor, *Eng.*	37	E6
Windsor, *Nfld.*	23	K2
Windsor, *N.S.*	21	C3
Windsor, *Ont.*	16	C5
Windsor, *Que.*	22	B4
Windward Is., *W. Indies*	29	M5
Windward Passage, *W. Indies*	29	K4
Windygates, *Man.*	15	M6
Winefred R., and L., *Alberta*	14	F3
Winfield, *Alberta*	14	D4
Winfield, *Kan.*	24	G3
Wingamow L., *Ont.*	15	Q4
Wingham, *N.S.W.*	50	J5
Wingham, *Ont.*	16	D4
Winikapau L., *Lab.*	19	E3
Winisk L. and R., *Ont.*	18	E2
Winkler, *Man.*	15	N6
Winlaw, *B.C.*	13	M8
Winnemucca *Nev.*	24	C2
Winnifred, *Alberta*	14	F6
Winnipeg, *Man.*	15	N5
Winnipeg L., *Man.*	15	M4
Winnipeg R., *Man.*	15	O5
Winnipeg Beach, *Man.*	15	N5
Winnipegosis, *Man.*	15	L5
Winnipegosis L., *Man.*	15	L4
Winnipesaukee L., *N.H.*	22	B5
Winona, *Minn.*	25	H2
Winslow, *Ariz.*	24	D3
Winston Salem, *N.C.*	25	K3
Winter I., *Keewatin, N.W.T.*	11	S4
Winterberg, *C. of Good Hope*	47	D3
Wintering L., *Man.*	15	N3
Winterport, *Me.*	22	C4
Winthrop, *N.Y.*	17	L3
Winton, *N.Z.*	51	B7
Winton, *Queensland*	49	G4
Wisbech, *Eng.*	37	F5
Wisconsin, state, *U.S.A.*	25	H2
Wisconsin R., *Wis.*	25	H2
Wiseton, *Sask.*	14	H5
Wishart, *Sask.*	15	K5
Witbank, *Transvaal*	47	D2
Witchican L., *Sask.*	14	H4
Witham R., *Eng.*	37	E5
Withernsea, *Eng.*	37	F5
Witney, *Eng.*	37	E6
Witte Berg, *Cape Prov., Rep. of S. Africa*	47	C3
Wittenoom, *W. Aust.*	49	B4
Witwatersrand, *Transvaal*	47	D2
Wiwa Cr., *Sask.*	14	H5
Woburn, *Que.*	20	D3
Wodonga, *Victoria*	50	F8
Woito, *Ont.*	17	H2
Wolcott, *N.Y.*	17	J4
Woking, *Alberta*	14	B3
Wolf L., *Yukon*	12	E2
Wolf R., *Ont.*	15	R2
Wolf Bay, *Que.*	23	G1
Wolfe I., *Ont.*	17	J3
Wolfeboro, *N.H.*	22	B5
Wolfenden, *B.C.*	13	L7
Wolfestown, *Que.*	20	D3
Wolf Rock, *Eng.*	37	C7
Wolfville, *N.S.*	21	C2
Wollandilly R., *N.S.W.*	50	H6
Wollaston Is., *Chile*	31	D15
Wollaston L., *Sask.*	15	K1
Wollaston Penin., *Victoria I., N.W.T.*	10	M4
Wollaston Lake, *Sask.*	15	K1
Wollongong, *N.S.W.*	50	H7
Wolseley. *Sask.*	15	K5
Wolseley, *S. Aust.*	50	C8
Wolstenholme, and C., *Que.*	19	B1
Wolverhampton, *Eng.*	37	D5
Wolverine Cr., *Sask.*	14	J5
Wolverine R., *Alberta*	14	C2
Wolwehoek, *Orange F.S.*	47	D2
Woman L., *Ont.*	18	B3
Woman River, *Ont.*	18	G5
Wonsan, *N. Korea*	44	E3
Wonthaggi, *Victoria*	50	E9
Wood L., *Sask.*	15	K3
Wood R., *Sask.*	14	H6
Woodbridge, *Ont.*	16	F4
Wood Buffalo National Park. *Alberta*	14	E1
Woodlark I., *New Guinea*	49	J1
Wood Mountain, *Sask.*	14	H6
Woodpecker, *B.C.*	13	J6
Woodroffe Mt.. *S. Aust.*	49	E5
Woods, L. of the, *Ont.-Minn.*	18	A4
Woodstock, *N.B.*	22	D3
Woodstock, *Ont.*	16	E4
Woodville, *N.Z.*	51	E4
Woodville, *Ont.*	17	G3
Woodward, *Okla.*	24	G3
Woollet L., *Que.*	19	C3
Woolwich, *Eng.*	37	F6
Woomera, *S. Aust.*	49	F6
Worcester, *Cape Prov., Rep. of S. Africa*	47	B3
Worcester, *Mass.*	25	M2
Worcester, and co., *Eng.*	37	D5
Workington, *Eng.*	37	D4
Worms Hd.. *Wales*	37	C6
Worthing, *Eng.*	37	E6
Worthington, *Ont.*	18	G5
Wotton, *Que.*	20	C3
Wrangel I., *U.S.S.R.*	43	Q1
Wrangell, and I., *Alaska*	10	D4
Wrangell Mts., *Alaska*	10	F5
Wrath C., *Scotland*	36	C2
Wrexham, *Wales*	37	D5
Wrigley, *Mackenzie,N.W.T.*	12	L1
Wrocław (Breslau), *Poland*	39	J3
Wroxton, *Sask.*	15	L5
Wuchang, *China*	44	D3
Wuhan (Hankow), *China*	44	D3
Wunnummin L., *Ont.*	18	D2
Wurasoord, *Orange F.S.*	47	D2
Würzburg, *Ger.*	38	G3
Wuskwatim L., *Man.*	15	M3
Wyalong, *N.S.W.*	50	F6
Wyandra, *Queensland*	50	F3
Wye R., *Eng.*	37	D6
Wykes, *Que.*	20	B2
Wymark, *Sask.*	14	H5
Wyndham, *N.Z.*	51	B7
Wyndham, *W. Aust.*	49	D3
Wynndel, *B.C.*	13	M8
Wynyard, *Sask.*	15	J5
Wyoming, *Ont.*	16	C5
Wyoming, state, *U.S.A.*	24	E2
Xarayes, Swamp of, *Brazil, etc.*	30	F7
Xingu R., *Brazil*	30	G5
Yablonovy Mts., *U.S.S.R.*	43	K3
Yacuiba, *Bolivia*	31	E8
Yahk, *B.C.*	13	M8
Yakima, *Wash.*	24	B1
Yakutat, *Alaska*	10	G6
Yakutat, *Alaska*	13	A3
Yakutat B., *Alaska*	10	G6
Yakutsk, *U.S.S.R.*	43	L2
Yale, *B.C.*	13	K8
Yallourn, *Victoria*	50	F9
Yalta, *Crimea, U.S.S.R.*	39	N4
Yalu, *China*	44	E2
Yamachiche, *Que.*	20	C2
Yambol, *Bulgaria*	39	L5
Yamal Penin., *U.S.S.R.*	42	E1
Yamaska, *Que.*	20	C3
Yamdrok Tso, *Tibet*	40	H3
Yamma Yamma L., *Queensland*	50	C3
Yana R., *U.S.S.R.*	43	M2
Yanac. *Victoria*	50	C8
Yanam, *India*	40	F5
Yangtze-Kiang (R.), *China*	44	C4
Yankton, *S. Dak.*	24	G2
Yantara L., *N.S.W.*	50	D4
Yaounde, *Cameroun*	46	E5
Yap I., *Pacific Oc.*	44	F4
Yaque R., *Dominican Rep.*	29	K4
Yaqui R., *Mexico*	28	C2
Yaraka, *Queensland*	50	E2
Yare R., *Eng.*	37	F5
Yarensk, *U.S.S.R.*	35	Q3
Yari R., *Colombia*	30	C3
Yarkand, *Sinkiang*	40	E1
Yarmouth, *Me.*	22	B5
Yarmouth, *N.S.*	21	A4
Yaroslavl, *U.S.S.R.*	35	P4
Yarraman, *Queensland*	50	H3
Yarrawonga, *Victoria*	50	E8
Yarra Yarra R., *Victoria*	50	E8
Yass, *N.S.W.*	50	G7
Yates R., *Alberta*	12	M3
Yathkyed L., *Keewatin, N.W.T.*	11	P5
Yautepec, *Mexico*	28	E4
Yavi, *Argentina*	31	D8
Ycliff, *Ont.*	18	C3
Ye. *Burma*	40	J5
Yelgava, *Latvia*	39	K1
Yelizavety C. *Sakhalin I.*	44	G1
Yell, *Shetland Is., Scotland*	36	E1
Yellow Grass, *Sask.*	15	J6
Yellowhead Pass, *Alberta-B.C.*	14	B4
Yellowknife, and R., *Mackenzie, N.W.T.*	12	N1
Yellow Sea, *China*	44	E3
Yellowstone R., *Mont.*	24	E1
Yellowstone National Park, and L., *Wyo.*	24	D2
Yellowtail Res.. *Mont.*	24	E1
Yelsho R., *Chile-Argentina*	31	C12
Yemen, *S.W. Asia*	42	C7
Yenisei R., *U.S.S.R.*	42	G2
Yentai, *China*	44	E3
Yeovil, *Eng.*	37	C6
Yes Tor, *Eng.*	37	C6
Ymir, *B.C.*	13	M8
Yoho Park, *B.C.*	13	M7
Yokohama, *Japan*	44	F3
York, *Eng.*	37	E5
York, *Pa.*	25	L2
York, *W. Aust.*	49	B6
York, co., *Eng.*	37	E4
York, co., *Ont.*	16	F4
York C., *Greenland*	11	V2
York C., *Queensland*	49	G2
York Pt., *Que.*	23	K1
Yorke Penin., *S. Aust.*	50	A7
York Factory, *Man.*	15	P2
Yorkshire Moors, *Eng.*	37	E4
Yorkton, *Sask.*	15	K5
Youbou,*Vancouver I.,B.C.*	13	H8
Youghal, *Eire*	37	B6
Youghal B.. *Eire*	37	B6
Young, *N.S.W.*	50	G7
Young, *Sask.*	14	J5
Youngstown, *Alberta*	14	F5
Yozgat, *Turkey*	39	N6
Ypsilanti, *Mich.*	16	B5
Yreka, *Cal.*	24	B2
Yucatan Chan., *Mexico*	28	G3
Yugoslavia, rep., *Europe*	39	J4
Yukon, ter., *Canada*	10	G5
Yukon R., *Alaska-Yukon*	10	B5
Yukon Crossing, *Yukon*	12	B1
Yuma, *Ariz.*	24	D4
Yumen, *China*	44	B2
Yungas, *Bolivia*	30	D7
Yungki (Kirin), *China*	44	E2
Yungkia (Wenchow), *China*	44	E4
Yunta, *S. Aust.*	50	B6
Yu Shan, *Taiwan, China*	44	E4
Yütien, *Sinkiang*	40	F1
Yuzhno Sakhalinsk, *U.S.S.R.*	44	G2
Zabul, *Iran*	40	B2
Zacapa, *Guatemala*	28	G5
Zacatecas. *Mexico*	28	D3
Zadar (Zara), *Yugoslavia*	39	H4
Zagreb, *Yugoslavia*	39	J4
Zagros Mts.. *Iran*	42	C5
Zāhedān, *Iran*	40	A3
Zaire, *Africa*	46	F6
Zaire, R. *Africa*	46	F5
Zaisan L., *Cent. Asia*	42	G4
Zak River, *Cape Prov., Rep. of S. Africa*	47	C3
Zama L., *Alberta*	14	B1
Zambezi R., *Africa*	46	F7
Zambia (N. Rhodesia), rep., *E. Africa*	46	F7
Zamboanga, *Philippine Is.*	44	E6
Zamora, *Mexico*	28	D4
Zanesville, *O.*	25	K2
Zante I., *Greece*	39	K6
Zanzibar I., *Tanzania, E. Africa*	46	H6
Zaporozhye, *Ukraine*	39	N4
Zapotlanejo, *Mexico*	28	D3
Zaraza, *Venezuela*	30	D2
Zarembo I., *Alaska*	12	D4
Zaruma, *Ecuador*	30	B4
Zastron, *Orange F.S.*	47	D3
Zealand, *N.B.*	22	D3
Zealand I., *Denmark*	38	G2
Zealandia, *Sask.*	14	G5
Zeballos, *Vancouver I., B.C.*	13	G8
Zeehan, *Tasmania*	50	K9
Zeerust, *Transvaal*	47	D2
Zemun, *Yugoslavia*	39	K4
Zetland (Shetland Is.), *Scotland*	36	D1
Zhdanov (Mariupol), *Ukraine*	39	O4
Zhitomir, *Ukraine*	39	M3
Zhlobin, *U.S.S.R.*	39	M2
Zillong Tso, *Tibet*	40	G2
Zimatlan, *Mexico*	28	E4
Ziraquira, *Colombia*	30	C2
Zoar, *Lab.*	11	W6
Zomba, *Nyasaland*	46	G7
Zonguldak, *Turkey*	39	M5
Zuara, *Libya*	46	E2
Zuider Zee. *See* IJsselmeer		
Zulu Land, *Natal*	47	E2
Zumpango, *Mexico*	28	E4
Zurich, *Ont.*	16	D4
Zürich, *Switzerland*	38	G4